grzimek's
Student Animal Life Resource

• • • •

grzimek's
Student Animal Life Resource

• • • •

Birds
volume 3

Sandgrouse to Woodpeckers

THOMSON

GALE

Detroit • New York • San Francisco • San Diego • New Haven, Conn. • Waterville, Maine • London • Munich

Grzimek's Student Animal Life Resource
Birds

Project Editor
Melissa C. McDade

Editorial
Julie L. Carnagie, Madeline Harris,
Heather Price

Indexing Services
Synapse, the Knowledge Link
Corporation

Rights and Acquisitions
Sheila Spencer, Mari Masalin-Cooper

Imaging and Multimedia
Randy Bassett, Michael Logusz, Dan
Newell, Chris O'Bryan, Robyn Young

Product Design
Tracey Rowens, Jennifer Wahi

Composition
Evi Seoud, Mary Beth Trimper

Manufacturing
Wendy Blurton, Dorothy Maki

LIBRARY OF CONGRESS CATALOGING-IN-PUBLICATION DATA

Grzimek's student animal life resource. Birds / Melissa C. McDade, project editor.
    p. cm.
  Includes bibliographical references and index.
  ISBN 0-7876-9235-2 (set hardcover : alk. paper) — ISBN 0-7876-9236-0
  (volume 1) — ISBN 0-7876-9237-9 (volume 2) — ISBN 0-7876-9238-7 (volume 3)
  — ISBN 0-7876-9239-5 (volume 4) — ISBN 0-7876-9240-9 (volume 5)
  1. Birds—Juvenile literature. I. Grzimek, Bernhard. II. McDade, Melissa C.
  QL673.G79 2005
  598—dc22   2004015729

ISBN 0-7876-9402-9 (21-vol set), ISBN 0-7876-9235-2 (Birds set),
ISBN 0-7876-9236-0 (v.1), ISBN 0-7876-9237-9 (v.2), ISBN 0-7876-9238-7 (v.3),
ISBN 0-7876-9239-5 (v.4), ISBN 0-7876-9240-9 (v.5)

This title is also available as an e-book
Contact your Thomson Gale sales representative for ordering information.

Printed in Canada
10 9 8 7 6 5 4 3 2 1

Contents

BIRDS: VOLUME 3

BIRDS: VOLUME 4

BIRDS: VOLUME 5

Reader's Guide

Grzimek's Student Animal Life Resource: Birds offers readers comprehensive and easy-to-use information on Earth's birds. Entries are arranged by taxonomy, the science through which living things are classified into related groups. Order entries provide an overview of a group of families, and family entries provide an overview of a particular family. Each entry includes sections on physical characteristics; geographic range; habitat; diet; behavior and reproduction; animals and people; and conservation status. Family entries are followed by one or more species accounts with the same information as well as a range map and photo or illustration for each species. Entries conclude with a list of books, periodicals, and Web sites that may be used for further research.

ADDITIONAL FEATURES

Each volume of *Grzimek's Student Animal Life Resource: Birds* includes a pronunciation guide for scientific names, a glossary, an overview of birds, a list of species in the set by biome, a list of species by geographic location, and an index. The set has 640 full-color maps, photos, and illustrations to enliven the text, and sidebars provide additional facts and related information.

NOTES

The classification of animals into orders, families, and even species is not a completed exercise. As researchers learn more about animals and their relationships, classifications may change. In some cases, researchers do not agree on how or whether to make a change. For this reason, the heading "Number of species" in the introduction of an entry may read "About 36 species" or "34 to 37 species." It is not a question of whether some animals exist or not, but a question of how they are classified. Some researchers are more likely to "lump" animals into the same species classification, while others may "split" animals into separate species.

Grzimek's Student Animal Life Resource: Birds has standardized information in the Conservation Status section. The IUCN Red List provides the world's most comprehensive inventory of the global conservation status of plants and animals. Using a set of criteria to evaluate extinction risk, the IUCN recognizes the following categories: Extinct, Extinct in the Wild, Critically Endangered, Endangered, Vulnerable, Conservation Dependent, Near Threatened, Least Concern, and Data Deficient. These terms are defined where they are used in the text, but for a complete explanation of each category, visit the IUCN web page at http://www.iucn.org/themes/ssc/redlists/RLcats2001booklet.html.

ACKNOWLEDGEMENTS

Special thanks are due for the invaluable comments and suggestions provided by the *Grzimek's Student Animal Life Resource: Birds* advisors:

- Mary Alice Anderson, Media Specialist, Winona Middle School, Winona, Minnesota
- Thane Johnson, Librarian, Oklahoma City Zoo, Oklahoma City, Oklahoma
- Debra Kachel, Media Specialist, Ephrata Senior High School, Ephrata, Pennsylvania
- Nina Levine, Media Specialist, Blue Mountain Middle School, Courtlandt Manor, New York
- Ruth Mormon, Media Specialist, The Meadows School, Las Vegas, Nevada

COMMENTS AND SUGGESTIONS

We welcome your comments on *Grzimek's Student Animal Life Resource: Birds* and suggestions for future editions of this work. Please write: Editors, *Grzimek's Student Animal Life Resource: Birds*, U•X•L, 27500 Drake Rd., Farmington Hills, Michigan 48331-3535; call toll free: 1-800-877-4253; fax: 248-699-8097; or send e-mail via www.gale.com.

Pronunciation Guide for Scientific Names

Acanthisitta chloris uh-kan-thuh-SIT-tuh KLOR-is

Acanthisittidae uh-kan-thuh-SIT-tuh-dee

Acanthiza chrysorrhoa uh-KAN-thih-zuh KRIH-soh-ROH-uh

Acanthizidae uh-kan-THIZ-uh-dee

Accipitridae ak-sip-IT-ruh-dee

Aceros cassidix AH-ser-uhs KAS-sid-iks

Acridotheres tristis AK-rid-uh-THER-eez TRIS-tis

Actenoides concretus ak-TEN-oi-deez con-CREE-tuhs

Actinodura sodangorum AK-tin-uh-DYOOR-uh soh-dan-GOH-rum

Actophilornis africanus ak-tuh-FIL-or-nis AF-rih-kan-uhs

Aechmophorus occidentalis ek-MOH-for-uhs OK-sih-DEN-tal-is

Aegithalidae ee-jih-THAL-uh-dee

Aegithina tiphia ee-JIH-thin-uh TIF-ee-uh

Aegotheles insignis ee-GO-thel-eez IN-sig-nis

Aegothelidae ee-go-THEL-uh-dee

Agelaioides badius ah-jeh-LAY-oid-eez BAD-ee-uhs

Agelaius phoeniceus ah-jeh-LAY-ee-uhs fee-nih-SEE-uhs

Aix sponsa AKS SPON-suh

Ajaia ajaja ah-JAH-ee-uh AH-jah-juh

Alaemon alaudipes al-EE-mon ah-LAUD-ih-peez

Alaudidae ah-LAUD-uh-dee

Alcedinidae al-sed-IN-uh-dee

Alcidae AL-suh-dee

Amytornis striatus am-IT-or-nis stry-AH-tuhs

Anas platyrhynchos AH-nuhs PLA-tee-RIN-koz

Anatidae ah-NA-tuh-dee

Andigena hypoglauca an-DIH-jin-uh HI-poh-GLO-kuh

Anhima cornuta AN-him-uh KOR-nyoo-tuh

Anhimidae an-HIM-uh-dee

Anhinga anhinga AN-hin-guh AN-hin-guh

Anseriformes an-ser-uh-FORM-eez

Anthus spragueii AN-thuhs SPRAG-ee-eye

Aphelocoma californica uh-fel-uh-KOH-muh kal-uh-FORN-ik-uh

Apodidae a-POD-uh-dee

Apodiformes a-pod-uh-FORM-eez

Aptenodytes forsteri ap-ten-uh-DIE-teez FOS-ter-eye

Apterygidae ap-ter-IJ-uh-dee

Apteryx australis AP-ter-iks au-STRA-lis

Ara macao AR-uh MUH-kow

Aramidae ar-UH-muh-dee

Aramus guarauna AR-uh-muhs GWAR-aw-nuh

Ardea herodias AR-dee-uh hir-OH-dee-uhs

Ardeidae ar-DEE-uh-dee

Arenaria interpres ar-en-AIR-ee-uh IN-ter-preez

Artamidae ar-TAM-uh-dee

Artamus cyanopterus AR-tam-uhs SIGH-an-OP-ter-uhs

Astrapia mayeri as-truh-PEE-uh MAY-er-eye

Atrichornis rufescens a-TRIK-or-nis ROO-fehs-sens

Atrichornithidae a-trik-or-NITH-uh-dee

Attagis gayi AT-uh-jis GAY-eye

Auriparus flaviceps aw-RIP-ar-uhs FLAV-uh-seps

Balaeniceps rex bal-EEN-uh-seps REX

Balaenicipitidae BAL-een-uh-sip-IH-tuh-dee

Balearica regulorum BAL-ih-AR-ik-uh reg-YOO-lor-um

Batis capensis BAT-is KAP-en-sis

Bombycilla cedrorum bom-bih-SILL-uh SEED-roh-rum

Bombycillidae bom-bih-SILL-uh-dee

Botaurus stellaris BOH-tor-uhs STEL-lar-is

Branta canadensis BRAN-tuh kan-uh-DEN-sis

Bubo sumatranus BYOO-boh SOO-mah-TRAN-uhs

Bucconidae buck-ON-uh-dee

Bucerotidae byoo-ser-UH-tuh-dee

Bucorvus leadbeateri BYOO-kor-vuhs LED-bet-er-eye

Buphagus erythrorhynchus BYOO-fag-uhs eh-RITH-roh-RIN-
   kuhs
Burhinidae bur-HIN-uh-dee
Callaeas cinerea cal-LEE-uhs sin-EAR-ee-uh
Callaeidae cal-LEE-uh-dee
Calypte anna kuh-LIP-tee AN-nuh
Campephagidae kam-pee-FAJ-uh-dee
Campephilus principalis KAM-pee-FIL-uhs PRIN-sih-PAL-is
Campylorhamphus trochilirostris KAM-pie-luh-RAM-fuhs
   TRO-kil-ih-ROS-tris
Campylorhynchus brunneicapillus KAM-pie-luh-RIN-kuhs
   BROO-nee-kap-ILL-uhs
Capitonidae kap-ih-TON-uh-dee
Caprimulgidae kap-rih-MUL-juh-dee
Caprimulgiformes kal-rih-mul-juh-FORM-eez
Caprimulgus indicus KAP-rih-MUL-juhs IN-dih-kuhs
Caprimulgus vociferus KAP-rih-MUL-juhs voh-SIF-er-uhs
Carduelis tristis KAR-doo-lis TRIS-tis
Cariama cristata KAR-ee-ah-muh KRIS-tah-tuh
Cariamidae kar-ee-AH-muh-dee
Casuariidae kas-oo-ar-EYE-uh-dee
Casuarius casuarius kas-oo-AR-ee-uhs kas-oo-AR-ee-uhs
Cathartidae kath-ART-uh-dee
Cephalopterus ornatus SEFF-uhl-OP-ter-uhs AWR-nah-tuhs
Cercomacra cinerascens SIR-koh-MAK-ruh si-NEAR-ass-enz
Certhia americana SIR-thee-uh uh-mer-uh-kAN-uh
Certhiidae sirth-EYE-uh-dee
Chaetura pelagica KEE-tur-uh peh-LAJ-ik-uh
Chalcoparia singalensis kal-kuh-PAIR-ee-uh sin-GAHL-en-sis
Chamaea fasciata kam-EE-uh fah-she-AH-tuh
Chamaepetes unicolor kam-ee-PEET-eez YOO-nih-KUH-luhr
Charadriidae kar-ad-RYE-uh-dee
Charadriiformes kar-ad-rye-uh-FORM-eez
Charadrius vociferus kar-ad-REE-uhs voh-SIF-er-uhs
Chionidae ky-ON-uh-dee
Chionis minor KY-on-is MY-ner
Chiroxiphia linearis ky-roh-ZIF-ee-uh lin-EE-air-is
Chlamydera maculata klam-EE-der-uh mak-yoo-LAH-tuh
Chlidonias niger klih-DON-ee-uhs NY-jer
Cicinnurus regius sih-SIN-yoor-uhs RAY-jee-uhs

Ciconia ciconia SIK-uh-nee-uh SIK-uh-nee-uh
Ciconiidae sik-uh-NYE-uh-dee
Ciconiiformes sik-uh-nee-uh-FORM-eez
Cinclidae SIN-kluh-dee
Cinclosoma punctatum sin-cluh-SOH-muh PUNK-tah-tum
Cinclus cinclus SIN-kluhs SIN-kluhs
Cinclus mexicanus SIN-kluhs MEK-sih-KAN-uhs
Cinnyris asiaticus SIN-ny-ris AY-zhi-AT-ik-uhs
Cissa chinensis SIS-suh CHIN-en-sis
Cisticola juncidis sis-tuh-KOH-luh JUNK-id-is
Climacteridae kly-mak-TER-uh-dee
Climacteris rufa kly-MAK-ter-is ROO-fuh
Colibri coruscans KOH-lee-bree KOR-us-kans
Coliidae kol-EYE-uh-dee
Coliiformes kol-eye-uh-FORM-eez
Colinus virginianus KOL-eye-nuhs ver-JIN-ee-an-nuhs
Colius striatus KOL-ee-uhs stry-AH-tuhs
Columba livia KUH-lum-buh LIV-ee-uh
Columbidae kuh-LUM-buh-dee
Columbiformes kuh-lum-buh-FORM-eez
Coracias garrulus kor-UH-see-uhs GAR-oo-luhs
Coraciidae kor-uh-SIGH-uh-dee
Coraciiformes kor-uh-sigh-uh-FORM-eez
Coracina typica kor-uh-SEE-nuh TIP-ik-uh
Corvidae KOR-vuh-dee
Corvus corax KOR-vuhs KOR-aks
Corythaeola cristata kor-ih-thee-OH-luh KRIS-tah-tuh
Corythaixoides concolor kor-ih-THAKS-oi-deez CON-kuh-luhr
Cotinga cayana KOH-ting-guh KAY-ah-nuh
Cotingidae koh-TING-guh-dee
Cracidae KRA-suh-dee
Cracticidae krak-TIK-uh-dee
Cracticus torquatus KRAK-tik-uhs TOR-kwah-tuhs
Crax globulosa KRAKS glob-yoo-LOH-suh
Crex crex CREKS CREKS
Cuculidae kyoo-KYOO-luh-dee
Cuculiformes kyoo-kyoo-luh-FORM-eez
Cuculus canorus KYOO-kyoo-luhs KAN-or-uhs
Cyanocitta cristata SIGH-an-uh-SIT-tuh KRIS-tah-tuh
Cyclarhis gujanensis SIGH-klar-is GOO-jan-en-sis

Cygnus olor   SIG-nuhs OH-lor

Cymbirhynchus macrorhynchos SIM-bih-RIN-kuhs ma-crow-RIN-kuhs

Cypsiurus parvus sip-SIH-yoor-uhs PAR-vuhs

Dacelo novaeguineae   DAY-sel-oh NOH-vee-GIN-ee-ee

Dendrocolaptidae den-droh-koh-LAP-tuh-dee

Dendroica kirtlandii DEN-droy-kuh KIRT-land-ee-eye

Dendropicos goertae   den-droh-PEE-kuhs GER-tee

Dicaeidae die-SEE-uh-dee

Dicaeum ignipectus   DIE-see-um IG-nih-PEK-tuhs

Dicruridae die-KRU-ruh-dee

Dicrurus ludwigii DIE-kru-ruhs LOOT-vig-ee-eye

Dicrurus paradiseus DIE-kru-ruhs par-uh-DIE-see-uhs

Diomedea cauta eremite DIE-uh-MED-ee-uh CAW-tuh ER-ih-mite

Diomedea immutabilis DIE-uh-MED-ee-uh im-myoo-TUH-bil-is

Diomedeidae die-uh-med-EYE-dee

Donacobius atricapillus don-uh-KOH-bee-uhs ay-trih-kap-ILL-uhs

Drepanididae dre-pan-ID-uh-dee

Drepanorhynchus reichenowi   DRE-pan-uh-RIN-kuhs RYE-keh-now-eye

Dromadidae droh-MAD-uh-dee

Dromaiidae droh-MAY-uh-dee

Dromaius novaehollandiae DROH-may-uhs NO-vee-hol-LAND-ee-ee

Dromas ardeola DROH-muhs ar-dee-OH-luh

Drymodes brunneopygia dry-MOH-deez BROO-nee-oh-PIJ-ee-uh

Dulidae DYOO-luh-dee

Dulus dominicus DYOO-luhs duh-MIN-ih-kuhs

Dumetella carolinensis   dum-uh-TELL-uh kar-uh-LINE-en-sis

Eclectus roratus EK-lek-tuhs ROH-rat-uhs

Egretta ibis EE-gret-uh EYE-bis

Emberizidae em-ber-IZ-uh-dee

Epthianuridae ep-thy-an-YOOR-uh-dee

Epthianura tricolor ep-thy-an-YOOR-uh TRY-kuh-luhr

Eremophila alpestris ER-em-uh-FIL-uh al-PES-tris

Esacus magnirostris EH-sak-uhs MAG-nuh-ROS-tris

Estrilda astrild   ES-tril-duh AS-trild
Estrildidae es-TRIL-duh-dee
Eudyptes chrysolophus   YOO-dip-teez krih-soh-LOH-fuhs
Eupetidae yoo-PET-uh-dee
Euplectes orix YOO-plek-teez OR-iks
Eupodotis caerulescens yoo-pod-OH-tis see-ROO-less-sens
Eurylaimidae yoo-rih-lay-IM-uh-dee
Eurypyga helias yoo-RIH-pij-uh HEE-lee-uhs
Eurypygidae yoo-rih-PIJ-uh-dee
Eurystomus orientalis yoo-rih-STOH-muhs or-ih-EN-tal-is
Falco peregrinus FAL-koh PEHR-eh-GRIN-uhs
Falco rusticolis   FAL-koh rus-TIH-kol-is
Falconidae fal-KON-uh-dee
Falconiformes   fal-kon-uh-FORM-eez
Ficedula basilanica fih-SEH-duh-luh bas-ill-AN-ik-uh
Formicariidae for-mih-kar-EYE-uh-dee
Fratercula arctica   frah-TER-kuh-luh ARK-tik-uh
Fregata magnificens FREH-gah-tuh mag-NIH-fih-sens
Fregatidae freh-GAH-tuh-dee
Fringilla coelebs   frin-JILL-uh SEE-lebz
Fringillidae frin-JILL-uh-dee
Fulmarus glacialis FULL-mar-uhs glay-SHE-al-is
Furnariidae fur-nar-EYE-uh-dee
Furnarius rufus   fur-NAR-ee-uhs ROO-fuhs
Galbula pastazae GAL-bull-uh PAS-tah-zee
Galbula ruficauda   GAL-bull-uh roo-fee-KAW-duh
Galbulidae gal-BULL-uh-dee
Gallicolumba luzonica gal-ih-KUH-lum-buh loo-ZON-ik-uh
Galliformes gal-uh-FORM-eez
Gallinago nigripennis gal-uh-NAY-go NY-gruh-PEN-is
Gavia immer GAV-ee-uh IM-mer
Gavia stellata   GAV-ee-uh STEL-lah-tuh
Gaviidae gav-EYE-uh-dee
Gaviiformes gav-eye-uh-FORM-eez
Geococcyx californiana GEE-oh-COCK-siks kal-uh-FORN-uh-kuh
Glareola pratincola   glar-ee-OH-luh prat-in-KOH-luh
Glareolidae glar-ee-OH-luh-dee
Glaucis hirsuta   GLO-kis her-SOO-tuh
Grallina cyanoleuca GRAL-line-uh SIGH-an-uh-LYOO-kuh

Grallinidae gral-LINE-uh-dee

Gruidae GROO-uh-dee

Gruiformes groo-uh-FORM-eez

Grus canadensis GROOS kan-uh-DEN-sis

Grus japonensis GROOS jap-ON-en-sis

Gymnogyps californianus JIM-nuh-jips kal-uh-FORN-uh-kuhs

Haematopodidae hee-muh-toh-POD-uh-dee

Haematopus unicolor hee-muh-TOH-puhs YOO-nih-KUH-luhr

Harpactes oreskios hahr-PAK-teez or-es-KEE-uhs

Heliornis fulica hee-LEE-or-nis FUL-ik-uh

Heliornithidae hee-lee-or-NITH-uh-dee

Hemiprocne coronata HEMI-prok-nee koh-roh-NAH-tuh

Hemiprocnidae hemi-PROK-nuh-dee

Himantopus himantopus hih-MAN-tuh-puhs hih-MAN-tuh-puhs

Himatione sanguinea hih-MAY-shun-ee san-GWIN-ee-uh

Hirundinidae hir-un-DIN-uh-dee

Hirundo pyrrhonota HIR-un-doh pir-uh-NOH-tuh

Hirundo rustica HIR-un-doh RUS-tik-uh

Hydrobatidae hi-droh-BAT-uh-dee

Hydrophasianus chirurgus hi-droh-fay-SEE-an-uhs KY-ruhr-guhs

Hypocolius ampelinus hi-poh-KOL-ee-uhs am-peh-LINE-uhs

Hypothymis azurea hi-poh-THY-mis az-YOOR-ee-uh

Hypsipetes madagascariensis hip-sih-PEET-eez mad-uh-GAS-kar-EE-en-sis

Icteria virens ik-TER-ee-uh VY-renz

Icteridae ik-TER-uh-dee

Icterus galbula IK-ter-uhs GAL-bull-uh

Indicator archipelagicus in-dih-KAY-ter AR-kih-peh-LAJ-ik-uhs

Indicatoridae in-dih-kay-TER-uh-dee

Irena puella eye-REEN-uh poo-ELL-uh

Irenidae eye-REEN-uh-dee

Jacanidae juh-KAN-uh-dee

Jynx torquilla JINKS tor-KWILL-uh

Lagopus lagopus LAG-uh-puhs LAG-uh-puhs

Laniidae lan-EYE-uh-dee

Lanius ludovicianus lan-ee-uhs LOO-doh-vih-SHE-an-uhs

Laridae LAR-uh-dee

Larus saundersi LAR-uhs SON-ders-eye
Laterallus jamaicensis lat-er-ALL-uhs ja-MAY-sen-sis
Leipoa ocellata LYE-poh-uh os-ELL-ah-tuh
Liosceles thoracicus lye-OS-sel-eez tho-RAS-ik-uhs
Lonchura punctulata LON-chur-uh punk-TOO-lah-tuh
Loxia curvirostra LOK-see-uh KUR-vih-ROS-truh
Macrocephalon maleo ma-crow-SEFF-uh-lon MAL-ee-oh
Macronyx ameliae MA-cron-iks am-EEL-ee-ee
Maluridae mal-YOOR-uh-dee
Malurus splendens MAL-yoor-uhs SPLEN-denz
Megaceryle alcyon MEG-uh-ser-EYE-lee al-SIGH-on
Megapodiidae meg-uh-pod-EYE-uh-dee
Megalaima haemacephala meg-uh-LAY-muh hee-muh-SEFF-ah-luh
Melanocharis versteri mel-uh-NOH-kar-is VER-ster-eye
Meleagris gallopavo mel-ee-AY-gris gal-uh-PAY-voh
Melichneutes robustus mel-ik-NOO-teez ro-BUHS-tuhs
Meliphagidae mel-ih-FAJ-uh-dee
Melospiza melodia mel-uh-SPY-zuh meh-LOH-dee-uh
Menura alberti MEN-yoor-uh AL-bert-eye
Menuridae men-YOOR-uh-dee
Meropidae mer-OP-uh-dee
Meropogon forsteni mer-uh-POH-gon FOR-sten-eye
Merops apiaster MER-ops ay-PEE-as-ter
Mesitornis variegata meh-SIT-or-nis VAIR-ree-uh-GAH-tuh
Mesitornithidae meh-sit-or-NITH-uh-dee
Microeca fascinans my-CROW-ek-uh FAS-sin-ans
Mimidae MIH-muh-dee
Mirafra javanica MIR-af-ruh jah-VAH-nik-uh
Mniotilta varia ny-OH-til-tuh VAIR-ee-uh
Moho bishopi MOH-hoh BISH-up-eye
Mohua ochrocephala MOH-hyoo-uh OH-kruh-SEFF-ah-luh
Momotidae moh-MOH-tuh-dee
Momotus momota MOH-moh-tuhs MOH-moh-tuh
Monarchidae mon-ARK-uh-dee
Montifringilla nivalis mon-tih-frin-JILL-uh NYE-val-is
Morus bassanus MOR-uhs BASS-an-uhs
Motacilla cinerea moh-tuh-SILL-uh sin-EAR-ee-uh
Motacillidae moh-tuh-SILL-uh-dee
Muscicapidae mus-kih-KAP-uh-dee

Muscicaps striata   MUS-kih-kaps stry-AH-tuh

Musophagidae mus-oh-FAJ-uh-dee

Musophagiformes   mus-oh-faj-uh-FORM-eez

Mycteria americana   mik-TER-ee-uh uh-mer-uh-KAN-uh

Nectariniidae nek-tar-in-EYE-uh-dee

Neodrepanis coruscans nee-oh-DREH-pan-is KOR-us-kans

Neophron percnopterus NEE-oh-fron perk-NOP-ter-uhs

Nesomimus macdonaldi NEZ-oh-MIH-muhs mak-DON-uld-eye

Nonnula ruficapilla NON-nuh-luh roo-fih-kap-ILL-uh

Notharchus macrorhynchos   NOTH-ark-uhs ma-crow-RIN-kuhs

Nothocercus bonapartei NOTH-uh-SER-kuhs BOH-nuh-PART-eye

Nucifraga caryocatactes   NYOO-sih-FRAG-uh KAR-ee-oh-KAT-ak-teez

Numenius americanus   nyoo-MEN-ee-uhs uh-mer-uh-KAN-uhs

Numida meleagris NYOO-mid-uh mel-ee-AY-gris

Numididae nyoo-MID-uh-dee

Nyctea scandiaca NIK-tee-uh skan-DEE-uh-kuh

Nyctibiidae nik-tih-BYE-uh-dee

Nyctibius griseus nik-TIB-ee-uhs GRIS-ee-uhs

Oceanites oceanicus OH-shih-NYE-teez OH-shih-AN-uh-kuhs

Odontophoridae OH-don-tuh-FOR-uh-dee

Opisthocomidae op-is-thuh-KOM-eh-dee

Opisthocomiformes op-is-thuh-kom-eh-FORM-eez

Opisthocomus hoazin op-is-thuh-KOM-uhs HOH-ah-sin

Oriolidae or-ih-OH-lu-dee

Oriolus oriolus or-ih-OH-luhs or-ih-OH-luhs

Ortalis vetula   OR-tal-is VET-uh-luh

Orthonychidae or-thuh-NIK-uh-dee

Orthonyx temminckii OR-thon-iks TEM-ink-ee-eye

Otididae oh-TID-uh-dee

Otis tarda   OH-tis TAR-duh

Otus asio   OH-tuhs AS-ee-oh

Oxyruncidae ok-sih-RUN-kuh-dee

Oxyruncus cristatus OK-sih-RUN-kuhs KRIS-tah-tuhs

Pachycephala pectoralis   pak-ih-SEFF-ah-luh pek-TOR-al-is

Pachycephalidae pak-ih-seff-AL-uh-dee

Pachyramphus aglaiae PAK-ih-RAM-fuhs ag-LAY-ee-ee

Pandion haliaetus PAN-die-on HAL-ee-ee-tuhs

Parabuteo unicinctus par-uh-BYOO-tee-oh YOO-nih-SINK-tuhs

Paradisaeidae par-uh-die-SEE-uh-dee

Pardalotidae par-duh-LOT-uh-dee

Pardalotus striatus par-duh-LOT-uhs stry-AH-tuhs

Paridae PAR-uh-dee

Parulidae par-YOOL-uh-dee

Parus major PAR-uhs MAY-jur

Passer domesticus PASS-er doh-MES-tuh-kuhs

Passerculus sandwichensis pass-ER-kyoo-luhs SAND-wich-en-sis

Passeridae pass-ER-uh-dee

Passeriformes pass-er-uh-FORM-eez

Pelecanidae pel-uh-KAN-uh-dee

Pelecaniformes pel-uh-kan-uh-FORM-eez

Pelecanoides urinatrix pel-uh-KAN-oi-deez yoor-in-AY-triks

Pelecanoididae pel-uh-kan-OI-duh-dee

Pelecanus erythrorhynchos pel-uh-KAN-uhs eh-RITH-roh-RIN-kuhs

Pelecanus occidentalis pel-uh-KAN-uhs ok-sih-DEN-tal-is

Pericrocotus igneus per-ih-CROW-kot-uhs IG-nee-uhs

Petroicidae pet-ROY-kuh-dee

Phacellodomus ruber fay-sell-uh-DOH-muhs ROO-ber

Phaethon lepturus FEE-thon LEPT-yoor-uhs

Phaethontidae fee-THON-tuh-dee

Phalacrocoracidae fal-uh-crow-kor-AY-suh-dee

Phalacrocorax carbo fal-uh-crow-cor-aks KAR-boh

Pharomachrus mocinno far-uh-MAK-ruhs MOH-sin-noh

Phasianidae fay-see-AN-uh-dee

Philepittidae fil-uh-PIT-tuh-dee

Phoenicopteridae FEE-nih-kop-TER-uh-dee

Phoenicopteriformes FEE-nih-KOP-ter-uh-FORM-eez

Phoenicopterus ruber FEE-nih-KOP-ter-uhs ROO-ber

Phoeniculidae FEE-nih-KYOO-luh-dee

Phoeniculus purpureus fee-NIH-kyoo-luhs purh-PURH-ee-uhs

Phyllastrephus scandens FIL-uh-STRE-fuhs SKAN-denz

Phylloscopus borealis FIL-uh-SKOH-puhs BOHR-ee-al-is

Phytotoma raimondii fye-toh-TOH-muh RAY-mund-ee-eye

Phytotomidae fye-toh-TOH-muh-dee

Picathartes oreas PIK-uh-THAR-teez OR-ee-uhs

Picoides borealis PIK-oy-deez BOHR-ee-al-is

Picidae PIS-uh-dee

Piciformes pis-uh-FORM-eez

Pinguinus impennis PIN-gwin-uhs IM-pen-is

Pipra filicauda PIP-ruh fil-eh-KAW-duh

Pipridae PIP-ruh-dee

Pitangus sulphuratus PIT-an-guhs sul-FUR-ah-tuhs

Pitohui kirhocephalus PIT-oo-eey kir-uh-SEFF-ah-luhs

Pitta angolensis PIT-tuh an-GOH-len-sis

Pitta sordida PIT-tuh SOR-dih-duh

Pittidae PIT-tuh-dee

Pityriasis gymnocephala pit-ih-RYE-uh-sis jim-nuh-SEFF-ah-luh

Plectoryncha lanceolata PLEK-tuh-RIN-kuh LAN-see-oh-LAH-tuh

Plectrophenax nivalis PLEK-troh-FEN-aks NYE-val-is

Ploceidae ploh-SEE-uh-dee

Ploceus cucullatus PLOH-see-uhs kyoo-KYOO-lah-tuhs

Ploceus philippinus PLOH-see-uhs fil-ih-PINE-uhs

Podargidae pod-AR-juh-dee

Podargus strigoides POD-ar-guhs STRI-goy-deez

Podiceps cristatus POD-ih-seps KRIS-tah-tuhs

Podicipedidae pod-ih-sih-PED-uh-dee

Podicipediformes pod-ih-sih-ped-uh-FORM-eez

Poecile atricapilla PEE-suh-lee ay-trih-kap-ILL-uh

Pogoniulus chrysoconus po-go-NYE-uh-luhs KRIS-oh-KON-uhs

Polioptila caerulea poh-lih-OP-til-uh see-ROO-lee-uh

Polyborus plancus pol-ih-BOHR-uhs PLAN-kuhs

Pomatostomidae poh-may-tuh-STOH-muh-dee

Pomatostomus temporalis poh-may-tuh-STOH-muhs tem-PER-al-is

Prionops plumatus PRY-on-ops PLOO-mah-tuhs

Procellariidae pro-sell-ar-EYE-uh-dee

Procellariiformes pro-sell-ar-eye-uh-FORM-eez

Promerops cafer PRO-mer-ops KAF-er

Prunella modularis proo-NELL-uh mod-YOO-lar-is

Prunellidae proo-NELL-uh-dee

Psaltriparus minimus sol-TRI-par-uhs MIN-ih-muhs

Psittacidae sit-UH-suh-dee

Psittaciformes sit-uh-suh-FORM-eez

Psittacula krameri sit-UH-kuh-luh KRAY-mer-eye

Psittacus erithacus SIT-uh-kuhs eh-RITH-uh-kuhs

Psittirostra cantans SIT-uh-ROS-truh KAN-tanz

Psophia crepitans SOH-fee-uh KREP-ih-tanz

Psophiidae soh-FYE-uh-dee

Pterocles namaqua TER-oh-kleez nah-MAH-kwuh

Pteroclididae ter-oh-KLID-uh-dee

Pterocliformes ter-oh-cluh-FORM-eez

Pterocnemia pennata ter-ok-NEE-mee-uh PEN-ah-tuh

Ptilonorhynchidae TIL-on-oh-RIN-kuh-dee

Ptilonorhynchus violaceus TIL-on-oh-RIN-kuhs vee-o-LAY-see-uhs

Ptiloris victoriae TIL-or-is vik-TOR-ee-ee

Ptyonoprogne rupestris TY-on-oh-PROG-nee ROO-pes-tris

Puffinus puffinus PUFF-in-uhs PUFF-in-uhs

Pycnonotidae pik-noh-NOH-tuh-dee

Pycnonotus barbatus pik-noh-NOH-tuhs BAR-bat-uhs

Rallidae RALL-uh-dee

Ramphastidae ram-FAS-tuh-dee

Ramphastos toco RAM-fas-tuhs TOH-coh

Raphidae RAF-uh-dee

Raphus cucullatus RAF-uhs kyoo-KYOO-lah-tuhs

Recurvirostra americana re-CURV-ih-ROS-truh uh-mer-uh-KAN-uh

Recurvirostridae re-CURV-ih-ROS-truh-dee

Remizidae rem-IZ-uh-dee

Rhabdornis mysticalis RAB-dor-nis mis-TIH-kal-is

Rhabdornithidae rab-dor-NITH-uh-dee

Rheidae REE-uh-dee

Rhinocryptidae RYE-noh-KRIP-tuh-dee

Rhinoplax vigil RYE-noh-plaks VIH-jil

Rhipidura albicollis rip-ih-DYOOR-uh ahl-bih-KOLL-is

Rhipidura leucophrys rip-ih-DYOOR-uh LYOO-kuh-frees

Rhipiduridae rip-ih-DYOOR-uh-dee

Rhynochetidae rye-noh-KEE-tuh-dee

Rhynochetos jubatus rye-noh-KEE-tuhs JOO-bat-uhs

Rostratula benghalensis ros-TRAT-uh-luh ben-GOL-en-sis

Rostratulidae ros-trat-UH-luh-dee

Rupicola rupicola roo-pih-KOH-luh roo-pih-KOH-luh

Sagittariidae saj-ih-tar-EYE-uh-dee

Sagittarius serpentarius saj-ih-TAR-ee-uhs ser-pen-TAR-ee-uhs

Sarcoramphus papa sar-KOH-ram-fuhs PAH-pah

Sarothrura elegans sar-oh-THROO-ruh EL-eh-ganz

Saxicola torquata sax-ih-KOH-luh TOR-kwah-tuh

Sayornis phoebe SAY-ro-nis FEE-bee

Schetba rufa SKET-buh ROO-fuh

Scolopacidae skoh-loh-PAY-suh-dee

Scopidae SKOH-puh-dee

Scopus umbretta SKOH-puhs UM-bret-tuh

Semnornis ramphastinus SEM-nor-nis ram-FAS-tin-uhs

Sialia sialis sigh-AL-ee-uh SIGH-al-is

Sitta canadensis SIT-tuh kan-uh-DEN-sis

Sitta europaea SIT-tuh yoor-uh-PEE-uh

Sittidae SIT-tuh-dee

Smithornis capensis SMITH-or-nis KAP-en-sis

Somateria spectabilis soh-muh-TER-ee-uh spek-TAB-ih-lis

Sphecotheres vieilloti sfek-UH-ther-eez VYE-ill-oh-eye

Spheniscidae sfen-IS-kuh-dee

Sphenisciformes sfen-is-kuh-FORM-eez

Spheniscus magellanicus SFEN-is-kuhs maj-eh-LAN-ik-uhs

Sphyrapicus varius sfir-AP-ik-uhs VAIR-ee-uhs

Steatornis caripensis stee-AT-or-nis kar-IH-pen-sis

Steatornithidae stee-at-or-NITH-uh-dee

Stercorarius parasiticus ster-koh-RARE-ee-uhs par-uh-SIT-ik-uhs

Stiltia isabella STILT-ee-uh IZ-uh-BELL-uh

Strigidae STRIJ-uh-dee

Strigiformes strij-uh-FORM-eez

Struthio camelus STROO-thee-oh KAM-el-uhs

Struthionidae stroo-thee-ON-uh-dee

Struthioniformes stroo-thee-on-uh-FORM-eez

Sturnidae STURN-uh-dee

Sturnus vulgaris STURN-uhs VUL-gar-is

Sula nebouxii SUL-uh NEB-oo-ee-eye

Sulidae SUL-uh-dee

Sylviidae sil-VYE-uh-dee

Syrrhaptes paradoxus SIR-rap-teez PAR-uh-DOKS-uhs

Taeniopygia guttata tee-nee-uh-PIJ-ee-uh GUT-tah-tuh

Terpsiphone viridis terp-SIF-oh-nee VIR-id-is

Thamnophilus doliatus THAM-nuh-FIL-uhs dol-EE-ah-tuhs

Thinocoridae thin-uh-KOR-uh-dee

Threskiornis aethiopicus THRES-kih-OR-nis EE-thi-OH-pi-kuhs

Threskiornithidae thres-kih-or-NITH-uh-dee

Timaliidae tim-al-EYE-uh-dee

Tinamidae tin-AM-uh-dee

Todidae TOH-duh-dee

Todus multicolor TOH-duhs MULL-tee-KUH-luhr

Tragopan satyra TRAG-uh-pan SAT-eye-ruh

Trichoglossus haematodus TRIK-uh-GLOS-uhs HEE-muh-TOH-duhs

Trochilidae trok-ILL-uh-dee

Troglodytes aedon trog-luh-DIE-teez EE-don

Troglodytes troglodytes trog-luh-DIE-teez trog-luh-DIE-teez

Troglodytidae trog-luh-DIE-tuh-dee

Trogonidae troh-GON-uh-dee

Trogoniformes troh-gon-uh-FORM-eez

Turdidae TUR-duh-dee

Turdus migratorius TUR-duhs my-gruh-TOR-ee-uhs

Turnicidae tur-NIS-uh-dee

Turnix sylvatica TUR-niks sil-VAT-ik-uh

Turnix varia TUR-niks VAIR-ee-uh

Tyrannidae tie-RAN-uh-dee

Tyto alba TIE-toh AHL-buh

Tytonidae tie-TON-uh-dee

Upupa epops UP-up-uh EE-pops

Upupidae up-UP-uh-dee

Uria aalge YOOR-ee-uh AHL-jee

Vanellus vanellus vah-NELL-uhs vah-NELL-uhs

Vangidae VAN-juh-dee

Vireo atricapillus VIR-e-oh ay-trih-kap-ILL-uhs

Vireonidae vir-e-ON-uh-dee

Volatinia jacarina vol-uh-TIN-ee-uh jak-uh-REE-nuh

Zenaida macroura ZEN-ay-duh ma-crow-YOOR-uh

Zosteropidae zos-ter-OP-uh-dee

Zosterops japonicus ZOS-ter-ops jap-ON-ik-uhs

Words to Know

A

Acacia: A thorny tree, or any of several trees, shrubs, or other plants of the legume family that tend to be ornamental.

Adaptation: Any structural, physiological, or behavioral trait that aids an organism's survival and ability to reproduce in its existing environment.

Adaptive evolution: Changes in organisms over time that allow them to cope more efficiently with their biomes.

Adaptive shift: An evolutionary process by which the descendants of an organism adapt, over time, to ecological niches, or natural lifestyles, that are new to that organism and usually filled in other places by much different organisms.

Aftershaft: The secondary feather that branches from the base of the main feather.

Algae: Tiny plants or plantlike organisms that grow in water and in damp places.

Alpine: Used to refer to the mountainous region of the Alps, or to describe other areas related to mountains.

Altitude: The height of something in relation to the earth's surface or sea level.

Altricial: Chicks that hatch at an early developmental stage, often blind and without feathers.

Anisodactyl: Toe arrangement with three toes pointing forward and one toe facing backward.

Anting: A behavior birds use to interact with ants, either by rolling in an ant hill or placing ants into their feathers.

Aphrodisiac: Anything that intensifies or arouses sexual desires.

Aquatic: Related to water.

Arachnid: Eight-legged animals, including spiders, scorpions, and mites.

Arboreal: Living primarily or entirely in trees and bushes.

Arthropod: A member of the largest single animal phylum, consisting of organisms with segmented bodies, jointed legs or wings, and exoskeletons.

Asynchronous hatching: A situation in which the eggs in a nest hatch at different times, so that some chicks (the older ones) are larger and stronger than others.

Australasia: Region consisting of Australia, New Zealand, New Guinea, and the neighboring islands of the South Pacific.

Avian: Relating to birds.

Aviary: Large enclosure or cage for birds.

B

Barb: Stiff filament that forms the framework of a feather.

Bib: Area under the bill of a bird, just above the breast.

Biodiversity: Abundance of species in a particular biome or geographical area.

Biparental: Both male and female of the species incubate, feed, and fledge their young.

Bower: Shady, leafy shelter or recess.

Brackish: Water that is a mix of freshwater and saltwater.

Bromeliads: A family of tropical plants. Many bromeliads grow high on the branches and trunks of trees rather than in the soil.

Brood: Young birds that are born and raised together.

Brood parasite: An animal species, most often a bird, in which the female lays its own eggs in the nests of other bird species. The host mother raises the chick as if it were her own. This behavior has also been observed in fish.

Brushland: Habitat characterized by a cover of bushes or shrubs.

Burrow: Tunnel or hole that an animal digs in the ground to use as a home.

C

Cache: A hidden supply area.

Camouflage: Device used by an animal, such as coloration, allowing it to blend in with the surroundings to avoid being seen by prey and predators.

Canopy: The uppermost layer of a forest formed naturally by the leaves and branches of trees and plants.

Cap: Patch on top of bird's head.

Carcass: The dead body of an animal. Vultures gather around a carcass to eat it.

Carnivore: Meat-eating organism.

Carrion: Dead and decaying animal flesh.

Caruncle: A genetically controlled outgrowth of skin on an animal, usually for dominance or mating displays.

Casque: A horny growth on the head of a bird resembling a helmet.

Cavity: Hollow area within a body.

Churring: Referring to a low, trilled, or whirring sound that some birds make.

Circumpolar: Able to live at the North and South Pole.

Clutch: Group of eggs hatched together.

Collagen: A type of protein formed within an animal body that is assembled into various structures, most notably tendons.

Colony: A group of animals of the same type living together.

Comb: Fleshy red crest on top of the head.

Coniferous: Refers to evergreen trees, such as pines and firs, that bear cones and have needle-like leaves that are not shed all at once.

Coniferous forest: An evergreen forest where plants stay green all year.

Continental margin: A gently sloping ledge of a continent that is submerged in the ocean.

Convergence: In adaptive evolution, a process by which unrelated or only distantly related living things come to resemble one another in adapting to similar environments.

Cooperative breeding: A social organization of breeding where several birds (not just the parents) feed a group of hatchlings.

Courtship: Behaviors related to attracting a mate and preparing to breed.

Courtship display: Actions of a male and female animal that demonstrate their interest in becoming or remaining a pair for breeding.

Covert: Term derived from the word for something that is concealed, and used to describe the small feathers that cover the bases of the larger feathers on a bird's wing and tail.

Crèche: A group of young of the same species, which gather together in order to better avoid predators.

Crepuscular: Most active at dawn and dusk.

Crest: A group of feathers on the top or back of a bird's head.

Critically Endangered: A term used by the IUCN in reference to a species that is at an extremely high risk of extinction in the wild.

Crop: A pouch-like organ in the throat where crop milk is produced.

Crop milk: A cheesy, nutritious substance produced by adult pigeons and doves and fed to chicks.

Crown: Top of a bird's head.

Cryptic: To be colored so as to blend into the environment.

D

Deciduous: Shedding leaves at the end of the growing season.

Deciduous forest: A forest with four seasons in which trees drop their leaves in the fall.

Decurved: Down-curved; slightly bent.

Defensive posture: A position adopted to frighten away potential predators.

Deforestation: Those practices or processes that result in the change of forested lands to non-forest uses, such as human settlement or farming. This is often cited as one of the major causes of the enhanced greenhouse effect.

Distal: Away from the point of attachment.

Distraction display: Behaviors intended to distract potential predators from the nest site.

Diurnal: Refers to animals that are active during the day.

Domesticated: Tamed.

Dominant: The top male or female of a social group, sometimes called the alpha male or alpha female.

Dormant: Not active.

Dorsal: Located in the back.

Dung: Feces, or solid waste from an animal.

E

Ecological niche: The role a living creature, plant or animal, plays in its community.

Ecotourist: A person who visits a place in order to observe the plants and animals in the area while making minimal human impact on the natural environment.

Elevation: The height of land when measured from sea level.

Endangered: A term used by the U.S. Endangered Species Act of 1973 and by the IUCN in reference to a species that is facing a very high risk of extinction from all or a significant portion of its natural home.

Endemic: Native to or occuring only in a particular place.

Epiphyte: Plant such as mosses that grows on another plant but does not depend on that host plant for nutrition.

Estuary: Lower end of a river where ocean tides meet the river's current.

Eucalyptus: Tall, aromatic trees.

Evolve: To change slowly over time.

Extinct: A species without living members.

Extinction: The total disappearance of a species or the disappearance of a species from a given area.

Eyespot: Colored feathers on the body that resemble the eyes of a large animal, which function in helping to frighten away potential predators.

F

Family: A grouping of genera that share certain characteristics and appear to have evolved from the same ancestors.

Feather tract: Spacing of feathers in a pattern.

Feces: Solid body waste.

Fermentation: Chemical reaction in which enzymes break down complex organic compounds into simpler ones. This can make digestion easier.

Fledgling: Bird that has recently grown the feathers necessary to fly.

Flightless: Species that have lost the ability to fly.

Flock: A large group of birds of the same species.

Forage: To search for food.

Frugivore: Animal that primarily eats fruit. Many bats and birds are frugivores.

G

Gape: The width of the open mouth.

Genera: Plural of genus.

Generalist feeder: A species that eats a wide variety of foods.

Genus (pl. genera): A category of classification made up of species sharing similar characteristics.

Granivore: Animal that primarily eats seeds and grains.

Grassland: Region in which the climate is dry for long periods of the summer, and freezes in the winter. Grasslands are characterized by grasses and other erect herbs, usually without trees or shrubs, and occur in the dry temperate interiors of continents.

Gregarious: Used to describe birds that tend to live in flocks, and are very sociable with other birds. The word has come to be used to describe people who are very outgoing and sociable, as well.

H

Habitat: The area or region where a particular type of plant or animal lives and grows.

Hallux: The big toe, or first digit, on the part of the foot facing inwards.

Hatchling: Birds that have just hatched, or broken out of the egg.

Hawking: Hunting for food by sitting on a perch, flying out and capturing the food, and returning to the perch to eat.

Heath: Grassy and shrubby uncultivated land.

Herbivore: Plant eating organism.

Heterodactyl: With toes pointed in opposite directions; usually with first and second inner front toes turned backward and the third and fourth toes turned forward.

Homeotherm: Organism with stable independent body temperature.

Host: A living plant or animal from which a parasite takes nutrition

I

Igapó: Black waters of the Amazon river area.

Incubation: Process of sitting on and warming eggs in order for them to hatch.

Indicator species: A bird or animal whose presence reveals a specific environmental characteristic

Indigenous: Originating in a region or country.

Insectivore: An animal that eats primarily insects.

Introduced: Not native to the area; brought in by humans.

Invertebrate: Animal lacking a spinal column (backbone).

Iridescent: Having a lustrous or brilliant appearance or quality.

IUCN: Abbreviation for the International Union for Conservation of Nature and Natural Resources, now the World Conservation Union. A conservation organization of government agencies and nongovernmental organizations best known for its Red Lists of threatened an

K

Keel: A projection from a bone.

Keratin: Protein found in hair, nails, and skin.

Kleptoparasite: An individual that steals food or other resources from another individual.

L

Lamellae: Plural of lamella; comb-like bristles inside a flamingos bill.

Larva (pl. larvae): Immature form (wormlike in insects; fishlike in amphibians) of an organism capable of surviving on its own. A larva does not resemble the parent and must go through metamorphosis, or change, to reach its adult stage.

Lek: An area where birds come to display courtship behaviors to attract a mate (noun); to sing, flutter, hop and perform other courtship behaviors at a lek (verb).

Lerp: Sugary lumps of secretions of psillid insects, small plant-sucking insects living on Eucalyptus trees.

Lichen: A complex of algae and fungi found growing on trees, rocks, or other solid surfaces.

Litter: A layer of dead vegetation and other material covering the ground.

M

Mandible: Upper or lower part of a bird's bill; jaw.

Mangrove: Tropical coastal trees or shrubs that produce many supporting roots and that provide dense vegetation.

Mantle: Back, inner-wing, and shoulder area.

Mesic: Referring to any area that is known to be wet or moist.

Midstory: The level of tropical forests between ground level (understory) and treetops (overstory).

Migrate: To move from one area or climate to another as the seasons change, usually to find food or to mate..

Mixed-species flock: A flock of birds that includes multiple species.

Mobbing: A group of birds gathering together to defend themselves from another large bird by calling loudly and flying at the intruder.

Molt: The process by which an organism sheds its outermost layer of feathers, fur, skin, or exoskeleton.

Monogamous: Refers to a breeding system in which a male and a female mate only with each other during a breeding season or lifetime.

Montane forest: Forest found in mountainous areas.

Mutualism: A relationship between two species where both gain something and neither is harmed.

N

Nape: Back part of the neck.

Near Threatened: A category defined by the IUCN suggesting that a species could become threatened with extinction in the future.

Nectar: Sweet liquid secreted by the flowers of various plants to attract pollinators (animals that pollinate, or fertilize, the flowers).

Neotropical: Relating to a geographic area of plant and animal life east, south, and west of Mexico's central plateau that includes Central and South America and the West Indies.

Nest box: A small, human-made shelter intended as a nest site for birds. Usually a rectangular wooden box with a round entrance hole.

Nestling: Young bird unable to leave the nest.

New World: Made up of North America, Central America, and South America; the western half of the world.

Niche: A habitat with everything an animal needs.

Nictating membranes: Clear coverings under the eyelids that can be moved over the eye.

Nocturnal: Occuring or active at night.

O

Omnivore: A plant- and meat- eating animal.

Opportunistic feeder: One that is able to take advantage of whatever food resources become available.

Overstory: The level of tropical forests nearest treetops.

P

Palearctic: The area or subregion of Europe, Africa, and the Middle East, that is north of the Tropic of Cancer, and the area north of the Himalayas mountain range.

Pampas: Open grasslands of South America.

Parasite: An organism that lives in or on a host organism and that gets its nourishment from that host.

Pelagic: To live on the open ocean.

Permafrost: Permanently frozen lands.

Plain: Large expanse of land that is fairly dry and with few trees.

Plumage: Feathers of a bird.

Pneumatic: Air-filled cavities in the bones of birds.

Poisonous: Containing or producing toxic materials.

Pollen: Dust-like grains or particles produced by a plant that contain male sex cells.

Pollinate: To transfer pollen from the male organ to the female organ of a flower.

Polyandry: A mating system in which a single female mates with multiple males.

Polygamy: A mating system in which males and females mate with multiple partners.

Polygynous lek: A mating system in which several males display together for the attention of females. A female, after watching the displaying males, may mate with one or more males in the lek.

Polygyny: A mating system in which a single male mates with multiple females.

Precocial: Young that hatch at an advanced stage of development, with feathers and able to move.

Predator: An animal that eats other animals.

Preen: To clean and smooth feathers using the bill.

Preen gland: A gland on the rear of most birds which secretes an oil the birds use in grooming.

Prey: Organism hunted and eaten by a predator.

Primary forest: A forest characterized by a full-ceiling canopy formed by the branches of tall trees and several layers of smaller trees. This type of forest lacks ground vegetation because sunlight cannot penetrate through the canopy.

Promiscuity: Mating in which individuals mate with as many other individuals as they can or want to.

Pupae: Plural of pupa; developing insects inside cocoon.

Q

Quill: Hollow feather shaft.

R

Rainforest: An evergreen woodland of the tropics distinguished by a continuous leaf canopy and an average rainfall of about 100 inches (250 centimeters) per year.

Raptor: A bird of prey.

Regurgitate: Eject the contents of the stomach through the mouth; to vomit.

Resident: Bird species that do not migrate.

Retrices: Plural of retrix; paired flight feathers of the tail, which extend from the margins of a bird's tail.

Rictal bristles: Modified feathers composed mainly of the vertical shaft.

Riparian: Having to do with the edges of streams or rivers.

Riverine: Located near a river.

Roe: Fish eggs.

Roost: A place where animals, such as bats, sit or rest on a perch, branch, etc.

S

Savanna: A biome characterized by an extensive cover of grasses with scattered trees, usually transitioning between areas dominated by forests and those dominated by grasses and having alternating seasonal climates of precipitation and drought.

Scavenger: An animal that eats carrion.

Scrub forest: A forest with short trees and shrubs.

Secondary forest: A forest characterized by a less-developed canopy, smaller trees, and a dense ground vegetation found on the edges of fores

Sedentary: Living in a fixed location, as with most plants, tunicates, sponges, etc. Contrast with motile.

Semi-precocial: To be born in a state between altricial and precocial. Semi-precocial chicks can usually leave the nest after a few days.

Sequential polyandry: A mating system in which a female mates with one male, leaves him a clutch of eggs to tend, and then mates with another male, repeating the process throughout the breeding season.

Serial monogamy: Mating for a single nesting then finding another mate or mates for other nestings.

Serrated: Having notches like a saw blade.

Sexual dichromatism: Difference in coloration between the sexes of a species.

Sexual dimorphism: Differences in size and in shapes of body or body parts between sexes of a species.

Sexually mature: Capable of reproducing.

Sheath: Tubular-shaped covering used to protect a body part.

Snag: A dead tree, still standing, with the top broken off.

Social: Species in which individuals are found with other individuals of the same species.

Solitary: Living alone or avoiding the company of others.

Specialist feeder: A species that eats only one or a few food items.

Species: A group of living things that share certain distinctive characteristics and can breed together in the wild.

Squab: Young pigeons and doves.

Steppe: Wide expanse of semiarid relatively level plains, found in cool climates and characterized by shrubs, grasses, and few trees.

Sternum: The breastbone.

Subalpine forest: Forest found at elevations between 9,190 and 10,500 feet (2,800 and 3,200 meters).

Sub-canopy: Below the treetops.

Subordinate: An individual that has lower rank than other, dominant, members of the group.

Subspecies: Divisions within a species based on significant differences and on genetics. Subspecies within a species look different from one another but are still genetically close to be considered separate species. In most cases, subspecies can interbreed and produc

Subtropical: Referring to large areas near the tropics that are not quite as warm as tropical areas.

Syndactyly: A condition in which two bones (or digits) fuse together to become a single bone.

Syrinx (pl. syringes): Vocal organ of birds.

T

Taiga: Subarctic wet evergreen forests.

Tail coverts: The short feathers bordering the quills of the long tail feathers of a bird. They may be over-tail or under-tail (i.e., top or bottom).

Tail streamer: A central part of a bird's tail that is longer than other parts.

Talon: A sharp hooked claw.

Taxonomy: The science dealing with the identification, naming, and classification of plants and animals.

Temperate: Areas with moderate temperatures in which the climate undergoes seasonal change in temperature and moisture. Temperate regions of the earth lie primarily between 30 and 60° latitude in both hemispheres.

Terrestrial: Relating to the land or living primarily on land.

Territorial: A pattern of behavior that causes an animal to stay in a limited area and/or to keep certain other animals of the same species (other than its mate, herd, or family group) out of the

Tetrapod: Any vertebrate having four legs or limbs, including mammals, birds, reptiles, and others.

Thermal: Rising bubble of warm air.

Thicket: An area represented by a thick, or dense, growth of shrubs, underbrush, or small trees.

Threat display: A set of characteristic motions used to communicate aggression and warning to other individuals of the same species.

Threatened: Describes a species that is threatened with extinction.

Torpor: A short period of inactivity characterized by an energy-saving, deep sleep-like state in which heart rate, respiratory rate and body temperature drop.

Tropical: The area between 23.5° north and south of the equator. This region has small daily and seasonal changes in temperature, but great seasonal changes in precipitation. Generally, a hot and humid climate that is completely or almost free of frost.

Tundra: A type of ecosystem dominated by lichens, mosses, grasses, and woody plants. It is found at high latitudes (arctic tundra) and high altitudes (alpine tundra). Arctic tundra is underlain by permafrost and usually very wet.

U

Understory: The trees and shrubs between the forest canopy and the ground cover.

V

Vertebra (pl. vertebrae): A component of the vertebral column, or backbone, found in vertebrates.

Vertebrate: An animal having a spinal column (backbone).

Vocalization: Sound made by vibration of the vocal tract.

Vulnerable: An IUCN category referring to a species that faces a high risk of extinction.

W

Wattle: A fold of skin, often brightly colored, that hangs from the throat area.

Wetlands: Areas that are wet or covered with water for at least part of the year and support aquatic plants, such as marshes, swamps, and bogs.

Wingbars: Stripes of coloration on the wing.

Wingspan: The distance from wingtip to wingtip when the wings are extended in flight.

X

Xeric forest: Forest adapted to very dry conditions.

Z

Zygodactyl: Two pairs of toes, with two toes pointing forward and two toes facing backward.

Getting to Know Birds

FEATHERS

It is easy to tell that an animal is a bird. If it has feathers, it is one of the more than 8,600 kinds of birds in the world. Birds can also be recognized by their bills, wings, and two legs, but feathers are what make them different from every other animal.

First feathers

Scientists are not sure when feathers first appeared on animals. They might have begun as feather-like scales on some of the dinosaurs. In 1861, fossils of a feathered animal, *Archaeopteryx* (ar-key-OP-tuh-rix), were found in Germany. These are the first animals known to scientists that were covered with feathers. These crow-sized animals with heads like lizards lived on the Earth about 150 million years ago.

How birds use different types of feathers

Feathers in most birds' wings and tail help them fly. Each of these flight feathers has a stiff shaft that goes from one end to the other. Flight feathers are light, but they are surprisingly strong. Birds that can fly can escape enemies and get to food sources and nesting places they wouldn't be able to walk to.

Feathers have many other uses in addition to flight. The outer feathers on a bird's body give it color and shape and help to waterproof the bird. Outer feathers with patterns are useful for camouflaging some birds, and colorful feathers send messages. For example, male birds show off their bright feathers to impress females or wave them as warnings to others. Downy inner feathers trap air to keep the bird warm.

Archaeopteryx is the first animal known to be covered with feathers. (© François Gohier/Photo Researchers, Inc. Reproduced by permission.)

Scientists have names for different types of feathers and also for groups of feathers according to where they grow on a bird's body.

Flight

Most birds' bodies are built for flight. Air sacs in their chests and hollow bones keep them light. They have powerful chest muscles that move their wings. The wing and tail feathers are tough, and birds can turn some of them for steering. A bird usually shuts its wing feathers to trap the air as its wings go down. This lifts the bird into the air and pushes it forward. Then, as it raises the wings, it fans the feathers open to let the air through.

How birds fly depends somewhat on the shape of their wings. Vultures and seabirds have long, narrow wings that are great for soaring high on air currents or gliding over the ocean. Songbirds have short, broad wings that are made for flapping as the birds fly among trees. Falcons have narrow, pointed wings that curve backward. These wings help them fly fast and steer well. But all birds flap their wings at times and glide at other times, depending on what they are doing and how the wind is blowing.

Some birds use their wings in unusual ways. Hummingbirds can flap their wings about fifty times every second. This allows them to hover at one spot as they lap nectar from flowers. Flipper-like wings help penguins to "fly" through the water, and even ostriches use their wings to keep their balance as they run.

The wing of a bird is rounded on top and flat on the bottom, similar to the wing of an airplane. This shape is what gives the bird the lift it needs to stay up in the air.

Birds take off and land facing the wind. Small birds (up to the size of pigeons) can jump up from the ground and fly right off into the air. Larger birds have to jump off something high or run along the ground or the water to get going.

BIRDS' BODIES

Different, but the same

A 400-pound (181-kilogram) ostrich may seem very different from a tiny bee hummingbird that weighs less than an ounce (about 2 grams). But all birds have many things in common besides having feathers. They have bills, two legs, a backbone, they are warm-blooded (keep an even body temperature), and they lay hard-shelled eggs.

Body shapes

Birds have many different shapes. Wading birds such as flamingos have long necks and long legs. Eagles have short necks and legs. But both kinds of birds are able to find their food in the water. Falcons and penguins have sleek, torpedo-shaped bodies that are perfect for catching speedy prey. Turkeys' heavier bodies are just right for their quiet lives in the forest searching for acorns and insects.

Bill shapes

Bird bills come in a wide variety of shapes. They use their bills to gather food, build nests, fix their feathers, feed their young, attract mates, and attack their enemies. The type of food a bird eats depends on its bills' shape. For example, the sturdy bills of sparrows are good for cracking seeds, and hawks' hooked beaks are perfect for tearing up prey.

Legs and feet

Bird legs and feet fit their many different lifestyles. For example, hawks have sharp talons for hunting and ducks have webbed feet to help them swim. Some of the birds that spend most of their lives in the air or on the water are not good at walking. Most birds have four toes, but some have three, and ostriches have only two.

BIRDS' SENSES

Sight

For most birds, sight is their best sense. They can see much better than humans, and they can see in color, unlike many mammals.

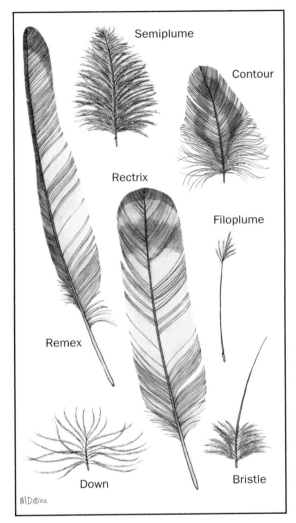

A bird's stiffest feathers are the remex feathers of the wing and the retrix feathers of the tail. The outside of a bird's body is covered with contour feathers that give the body shape and waterproof the bird. Underneath the contour feathers are the semiplume and down feathers that help keep the bird warm. Filoplumes lie alongside the contour feathers and help the bird tell if its feathers are in place. Some birds have bristles around their beaks that allow them to feel insects in the air. (Illustration by Marguette Dongvillo. Reproduced by permission.)

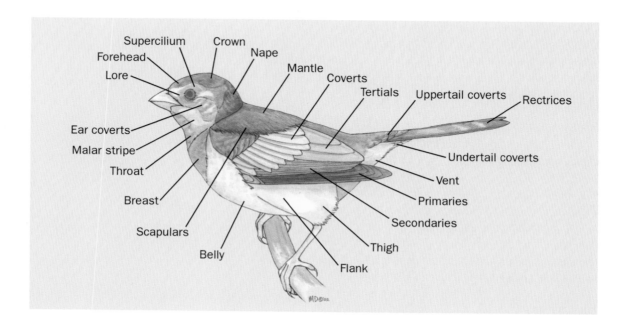

Labels on illustration:
Supercilium, Crown, Nape, Forehead, Mantle, Lore, Coverts, Tertials, Uppertail coverts, Rectrices, Ear coverts, Malar stripe, Undertail coverts, Throat, Vent, Breast, Primaries, Secondaries, Scapulars, Thigh, Belly, Flank

Scientists have names for groups of feathers according to where they grow on a bird's body. (Illustration by Marguette Dongvillo. Reproduced by permission.)

A bird's eyes are big and are usually set on the sides of its head. The eyes focus independently, so that the bird sees two different things at the same time. This gives the bird a very wide view and helps it to watch for predators in most directions. Most birds cannot roll their eyes, but they can turn their heads farther around than mammals can. Owls and other birds of prey have forward-facing eyes that usually work together. This helps them judge distance as they swoop down on prey.

Hearing

Birds have a good sense of hearing—they can hear about as well as mammals. The sound goes in through a little opening near each eye. The holes are usually covered with feathers. They lead to the bird's middle and inner ear, which are very sensitive to sounds. Because owls hunt at night, hearing is especially important to them. Some owls have a disc of stiff feathers on the face. The disc catches sounds, such as the squeaks of a mouse, and leads them to the ears.

Touch

Birds have many nerve endings, which shows that they have a good sense of touch. They can also feel pain, hot, and cold.

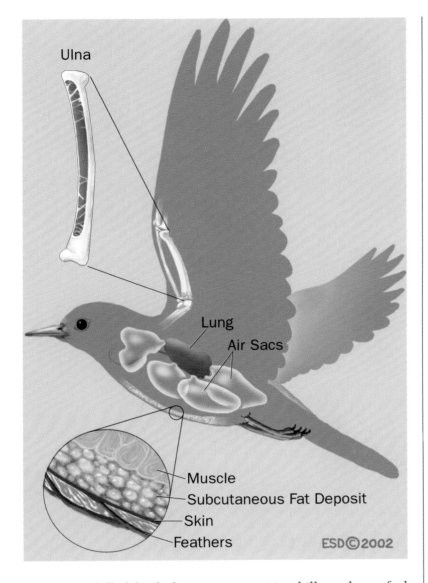

Ulna

Lung

Air Sacs

Muscle
Subcutaneous Fat Deposit
Skin
Feathers

ESD©2002

Birds' bodies have adaptations for flight, including air sacs in the chest and hollow bones to keep them light, and strong chest muscles. (Illustration by Emily Damstra. Reproduced by permission.)

Some long-billed birds have very sensitive bills and can feel their prey in muddy water.

Smell and taste

Most birds' sense of smell seems to be poorly developed. But kiwis, turkey vultures, and several other birds are able to find food by sniffing it. Although birds do not have many taste buds on their tongues, they can often taste well enough to avoid eating harmful foods.

Bills are different shapes and sizes for different eating methods: 1. The greater flamingo filters microorganisms from water; 2. A peregrine falcon tears its prey; 3. Roseate spoonbills sift water for fish; 4. The Dalmation pelican scoops fish in its pouch; 5. Anna's hummingbird sips nectar; 6. The brown kiwi probes the soil for invertebrates; 7. The green woodhoopoe probes bark for insects; 8. Rufous flycatchers catch insects; 9. Java sparrows eat seeds; 10. Papuan frogmouths catch insects; 11. The bicornis hornbill eats fruit; 12. American anhingas spear fish; 13. Rainbow lorikeets crack nuts. (Illustration by Jacqueline Mahannah. Reproduced by permission.)

WHAT'S INSIDE?

Organs and muscles

Birds have many of the same organs that humans have, but they have special features that help with flight and keep them light. Their biggest, strongest muscles control their wings. Birds

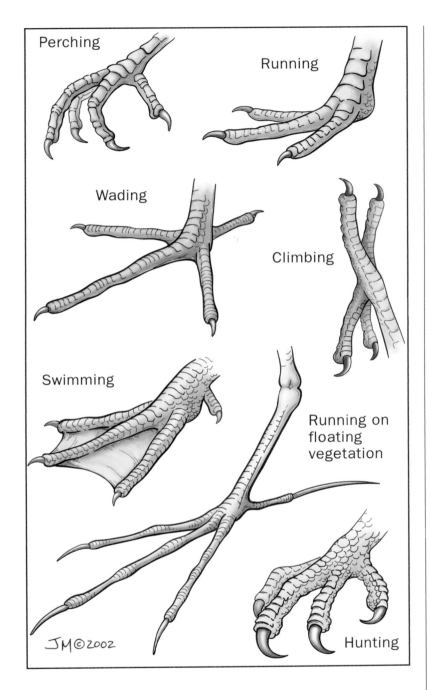

Perching

Running

Wading

Climbing

Swimming

Running on floating vegetation

Hunting

JM©2002

The number of toes, and the arrangement of their toes and feet fit birds' different lifestyles. (Illustration by Jacqueline Mahannah. Reproduced by permission.)

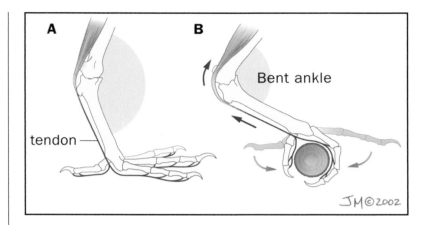

do not have a heavy jaw with teeth to grind their food. Instead, it is ground up in a muscular stomach called a gizzard, and they swallow gravel to help with the grinding. To get the energy they need for flight, birds digest their food quickly. Their fast digestion also keeps them from being weighed down for long by the food they have eaten.

Skeleton

A birds' skeleton is strong, even though it light. Many of the bones are hollow, and some of them are joined together to give the skeleton extra strength. (Loons and other diving birds have some solid bones to help the birds sink in the water.) The breastbone, or sternum, of a flying bird has a part called the keel. The bird's big flight muscles are attached to the keel. What looks like a backward-bending knee on a bird is really its ankle. The bird's knee is hidden high up inside its body feathers.

Body temperature

Birds are warm-blooded, which means their bodies stay at an even temperature no matter how warm or cold it is outside. They make their own heat from the food that they eat. Some birds cope with cold weather by growing extra feathers or a layer of fat, fluffing their feathers to trap more air, and huddling together with other birds. When birds can't find enough food to keep warm, they fly to warmer places. In hot weather, they cool down by panting, swimming in cool water, sitting in the shade, and raising their wings to catch a breeze.

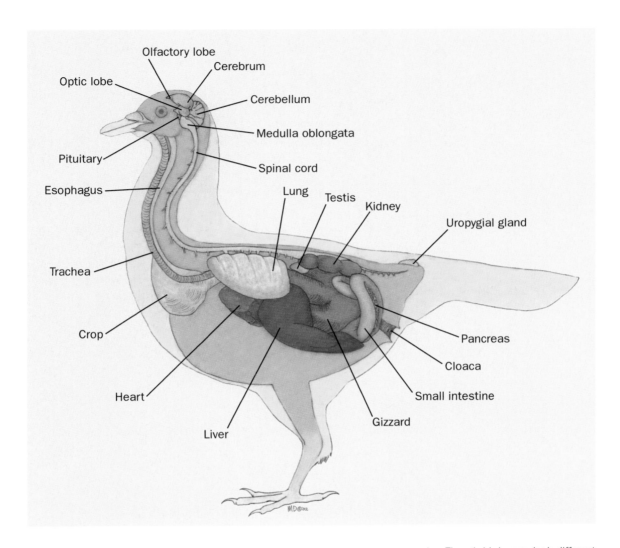

Labels on illustration:
Olfactory lobe, Cerebrum, Optic lobe, Cerebellum, Medulla oblongata, Pituitary, Spinal cord, Esophagus, Lung, Testis, Kidney, Uropygial gland, Trachea, Crop, Heart, Liver, Gizzard, Small intestine, Cloaca, Pancreas

FAMILY LIFE

Singing

Singing is one of the most important ways that songbirds communicate. Birds do not sing just because they are happy. Instead, a male songbird sings to say that he "owns" a certain territory, and he warns birds of the same species to stay away. Songbirds do not have to see each other to know who is nearby. Birds can recognize the songs of their neighbors, because each bird of the same species sounds a little different. Male birds show off to females by singing the most complicated songs they can. Often the best singers are the strongest, healthiest males.

Though birds may look different on the outside, they have the same organs on the inside. (Illustration by Marguette Dongvillo. Reproduced by permission.)

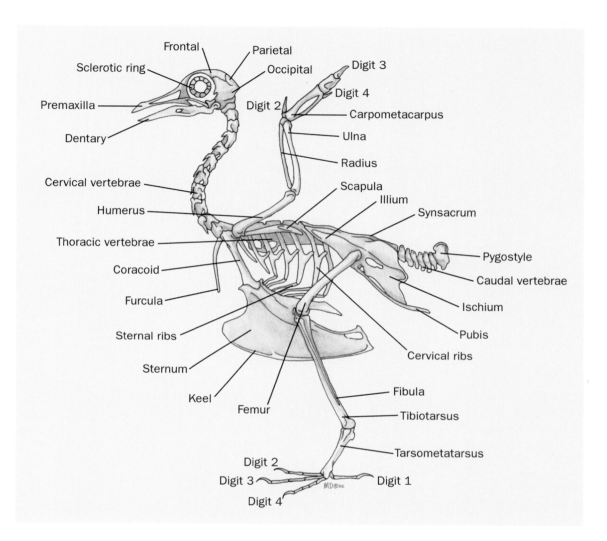

Frontal
Parietal
Sclerotic ring
Occipital
Digit 3
Digit 4
Premaxilla
Digit 2
Carpometacarpus
Dentary
Ulna
Radius
Cervical vertebrae
Scapula
Illium
Synsacrum
Humerus
Pygostyle
Thoracic vertebrae
Caudal vertebrae
Coracoid
Furcula
Ischium
Pubis
Sternal ribs
Cervical ribs
Sternum
Keel
Fibula
Femur
Tibiotarsus
Tarsometatarsus
Digit 2
Digit 3
Digit 1
Digit 4

Birds have a strong, light skeleton. (Illustration by Marguette Dongvillo. Reproduced by permission.)

When a female songbird hears her mate singing, her brain tells her body to make hormones (special chemicals). These hormones make eggs start to grow inside her body.

Other ways birds communicate

Singing is just one of the many ways that birds communicate with each other. They have warning calls that tell other birds that a predator is nearby. They chirp to say, "I am here, where are you?" And young birds sometimes beg noisily to be fed. At breeding time, birds have a variety of courtships displays that ask, "Will you be mine?" and state, "We belong together." These include bowing, flight displays, and calling together. Male birds

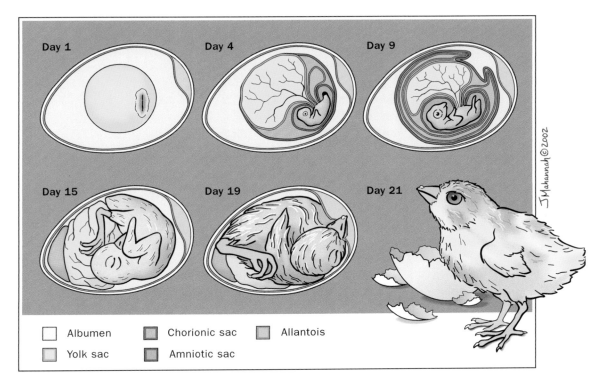

Day 1   Day 4   Day 9

Day 15   Day 19   Day 21

J.Mahannah © 2002

| ☐ | Albumen | ☐ | Chorionic sac | ☐ | Allantois |
| ☐ | Yolk sac | ☐ | Amniotic sac | | |

parade and show off bright feathers or blow up colorful throat sacs to impress females.

Nests

When a bird has found a mate, it is nest-building time. Birds lay their hard-shelled eggs where they can be protected from predators and rain. There are many different kinds of nests. Some birds lay their eggs right on the ground or on the sides of cliffs, some use tree holes or burrows, and some weave complicated stick nests. A few kinds of birds even bury their eggs in mounds of soil and leaves.

Eggs and hatching

Eggs come in many different sizes and colors. Those laid on the ground usually have camouflage colors, and eggs laid in hidden places are often white. The female bird usually incubates the eggs (keeps them warm), especially if she has duller, harder-to-see feathers than the male. Sometimes males and females take turns, and occasionally the males incubate by themselves. Some birds, such as cowbirds, lay their eggs in the nests of other bird species and let the other birds incubate them.

An egg is a perfect package for the chick developing inside it. The albumen (egg white) and yolk provide all the food and water it needs, and are used up as the bird develops. Air moves in and out through hundreds of tiny holes in the shell. Waste from the developing chick is stored in a sac called the allantois (uh-LAN-tuh-wus). The chorionic (kor-ee-AHN-ik) sac lines the inside of the shell, and the amniotic sac surrounds the chick. Time spent in the egg is different for each species, but for this chick, feathers have started to grow by Day 15, and the chick begins making noises by Day 19. There is a little egg tooth on the tip of the chick's bill that it uses to break out of the shell on Day 21. (Illustration by Jacqueline Mahannah. Reproduced by permission.)

Growth of young birds

There are two main types of newly hatched birds. Young chickens, ducks, geese, turkeys, and ostriches are precocial (pre-KOH-shul). Precocial chicks are covered with down feathers and can run or swim after their parents soon after hatching. Before long, they learn to find their own food, but the parents usually protect them for a while longer. Altricial (al-TRISH-ul) birds are helpless when they hatch. Songbirds, seabirds, owls, parrots, and woodpeckers are some of the altricial birds. They are naked, blind, and weak, and they need to be fed by adults at least until they leave the nest.

HABITATS, HABITS, AND PEOPLE

Surviving in a habitat

In order to live in a habitat, birds need food, water, and shelter (such as a hedge to hide in). At breeding time, they also need a place to raise their young. Many different kinds of birds can live in the same habitat because they eat different foods and nest in different places. Some birds, such as crows, can often adapt to changes in their habitat, but other birds are very particular and have to leave if something changes.

Staying alive and keeping fit

Birds have to have their feathers in flying shape at all times so that they can escape predators. Well-cared-for feathers are also necessary for keeping the birds warm and waterproof. Birds often have to stop what they are doing and take time out to fix their messed-up feathers. Sometimes they start with a bath. But they always finish by preening. To preen, the birds nibble along each feather to remove dirt and tiny pests. Most birds also get oil on their beaks from a gland near their tails. They spread the oil on each feather and straighten it by zipping it through their beaks. The oil keeps the feathers from drying out and waterproofs them. When a feather gets too worn, it either falls out or gets pushed out by a new feather growing in its place.

Migration

Migration is one way birds cope with natural changes in their habitats. When the weather gets cold and insects get scarce in fall, for example, insect-eating birds fly to warmer places where

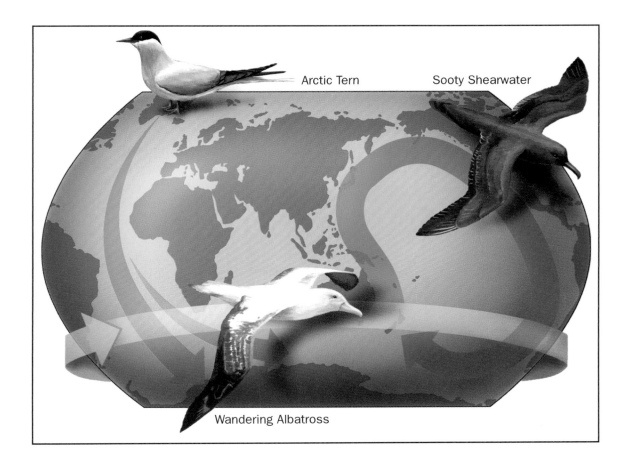

Arctic Tern

Sooty Shearwater

Wandering Albatross

they will be able to find the food they need. Their bodies are programmed to tell them that when the days start getting shorter, they have to eat more so they will have enough fuel for the journey. They follow the same migration routes year after year, and they know the general direction they should go and where to stop. The migrating birds are guided by the stars and by the direction the sun moves across the sky. Birds have a built-in compass and are able to follow magnetic fields in the earth. Some birds also rely on landmarks such as rivers and mountains to follow, and some may use sounds and smells to help them find their way.

Birds and people

Birds are some of the most visible wild animals on Earth, and they play an important part in people's lives. Humans

Seabirds have some of the longest migrations. The arctic tern migrates about 25,000 miles (40,000 kilometers) round-trip each year. The sooty shearwater breeds around New Zealand and the southern tip of South America and migrates in the spring to the northern Pacific and Atlantic Oceans. The wandering albatross moves around the Earth from west to east over the oceans south of the tips of the southern continents. (Illustration by Emily Damstra. Reproduced by permission.)

learned about flight from birds, they eat birds and their eggs, and they keep birds as pets. They appreciate the way birds eat insect pests and weed seeds, and they enjoy watching and listening to birds. Sometimes people kill the birds that eat fish or destroy their crops. People have also harmed birds unintentionally by polluting their habitats or turning them into farms and cities.

Humans now take the disappearance of birds from an area as a warning—there may be harmful poisons in the air or water. Many people are working hard to preserve natural places for birds and all wild animals. They are also having some success with fixing habitats that have been destroyed, but fixing them is much harder than preserving them in the first place.

FOR MORE INFORMATION

Books

Johnson, Jinny. *Children's Guide to Birds.* New York: Simon & Schuster, 1996.

MacKay, Barry Kent. *Bird Sounds.* Mechanicsburg, PA: Stackpole Books, 2001.

Markle, Sandra. *Outside and Inside Birds.* New York: Bradbury Press, 1994.

Perrins, Christopher M. *The Illustrated Encyclopedia of Birds.* New York: Prentice Hall Press, 1990.

Proctor, Noble S., and Patrick J. Lynch. *Manual of Ornithology, Avian Structure and Function.* New Haven, CT: Yale University Press, 1993.

Reid, Struan. *Bird World.* Brookfield, CT: The Millbrook Press, 1991.

Rupp, Rebecca. *Everything You Never Learned About Birds.* Pownal, VT: Storey Communications, Inc., 1995.

Sibley, David Allen, Chris Elphick, and John B. Dunning, Jr., eds. *National Audubon Society: The Sibley Guide to Bird Life & Behavior.* New York: Alfred A. Knopf, 2001.

Taylor, Kim. *Flight.* New York: John Wiley & sons, Inc., 1992.

Periodicals

Able, Kenneth P. "The Concepts and Terminology of Bird Navigation." *Journal of Aviation Biology* 32 (2000): 174–182.

Berger, Cynthia. "Fluffy, Fancy, Fantastic Feathers." *Ranger Rick* (January 2001): 2–10.

Greij, Eldon. "Happy Returns: Landing Safely Is Every Bit as Tricky as Flying." *Birders World* (February 2003): 58–60.

Kerlinger, Paul. "How High? How High a Bird Flies Depends on the Weather, the Time of Day, Whether Land or Water Lies Below—and the Bird." *Birder's World* (February 2003): 62–65.

Miller, Claire. "Guess Where They Nest." *Ranger Rick* (March 1996): 19–27.

Pennisi, Elizabeth. "Colorful Males Flaunt Their Health." *Science* (April 4, 2003): 29–30.

Web sites

"Act for the Environment." National Wildlife Federation. http://www.nwf.org/action/ (accessed on May 3, 2004).

"All About Birds." Cornell Lab of Ornithology. http://www.birds.cornell.edu/programs/AllAboutBirds/ (accessed on May 3, 2004).

American Bird Conservancy. http://www.abcbirds.org (accessed on May 3, 2004).

American Ornithologists' Union. http://www.aou.org (accessed on May 3, 2004).

"Bird and Wildlife Information Center." National Audubon Society. http://www.audubon.org/educate/expert/index.html (accessed on May 3, 2004).

BirdLife International. http://www.birdlife.net (accessed on May 3, 2004).

"Birdlife Worldwide." Birdlife International. http://www.birdlife.net/worldwide/index.html (accessed on May 3, 2004).

National Audubon Society. http://www.Audubon.org (accessed on May 3, 2004).

National Wildlife Federation. http://www.nwf.org (accessed on May 3, 2004).

The Nature Conservancy. http://nature.org (accessed on May 3, 2004).

Class: Aves
Order: Pterocliformes
One family: Pteroclididae
Number of species: 16 species

monotypic order
CHAPTER

PHYSICAL CHARACTERISTICS

Sandgrouse vary in size from 9.8 to 19 inches (25 to 48 centimeters) in length and 4.6 to 19.4 ounces (130 to 550 grams) in weight. Sandgrouse are generally colored to blend into their environments. Females and males have different coloration in most species, with females being colored more similarly to their environments. Sandgrouse are also characterized by extremely dense down that is well suited to their sometimes cold habitats. Some sandgrouse have partially feathered legs, while other species have feathers covering all of their legs and toes. Sandgrouse have short legs and long, pointed wings. They are good runners and extremely good fliers.

GEOGRAPHIC RANGE

Sandgrouse are found exclusively in the Old World, including portions of Africa, Europe, the Middle East, India, China, and Mongolia.

HABITAT

Sandgrouse are found in desert and semi-desert areas as well as in various grassland habitats.

DIET

Sandgrouse eat seeds almost exclusively. They pick seeds off the surface of the ground, and may also look for buried seeds by flicking away the surface layer of sand with their bills. Sandgrouse also drink water frequently, often daily. They drink by

phylum

class

subclass

order

● **monotypic order**

suborder

family

WATERING CHICKS

Sandgrouse, which generally occupy extremely dry habitats, have an unusual way of providing water to chicks that is not seen in any other group of birds. The male parent flies to the watering hole and dips his belly feathers in water. He then flies back to the nest, where the chicks take water from his feathers. The male continues to do this regularly for several weeks, until the chicks are able to fly to the watering hole themselves.

dipping their bills in water and sucking, and then raising their heads to swallow.

BEHAVIOR AND REPRODUCTION

Sandgrouse feed, rest, and nest on the ground. They fly to water every day, a trip that, depending on the population, can be as far as 75 miles (120 kilometers) round-trip. Sandgrouse are generally found in large flocks that can include several hundreds or even thousands of individuals. Because sandgrouse occupy desert habitats, they generally forage, or search for food, during the cooler hours of the day.

During the breeding season, sandgrouse are monogamous (muh-NAH-guh-mus), a single male mates with a single female. Nests are made by scraping the ground, often in the shade of a small plant. Nests may be lined with stones or with bits of vegetation. The female lays three eggs at a time. Sandgrouse eggs are long and spotted. The female incubates, sits on, the eggs during the day, while the male incubates during the night hours. Chicks hatch after twenty-one to thirty-one days. Parents do not feed the chicks. However, the male does provide water to the young by soaking his belly feathers with water and flying back to the nest. Chicks are able to fly after four or five weeks.

SANDGROUSE AND PEOPLE

Sandgrouse are sometimes hunted for food, usually at their watering holes.

CONSERVATION STATUS

No sandgrouse species are considered threatened at this time. However, hunting has affected some populations.

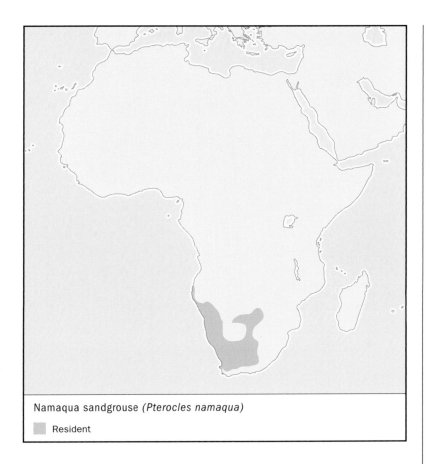

Namaqua sandgrouse (*Pterocles namaqua*)

■ Resident

NAMAQUA SANDGROUSE
Pterocles namaqua

Physical characteristics: Namaqua sandgrouse are medium-sized sandgrouse that vary between 9.4 and 11 inches (24 to 28 centimeters) in length and 5 and 8.5 ounces (143 to 240 grams) in weight. The male has a yellow-olive head and breast, a maroon and white band across the breast, a brown belly, and a brown back spotted with pearl-gray. The female has brown and cream bars on most of its body, with streaks on the head and neck.

Geographic range: Namaqua sandgrouse are found in southern Africa, including southwestern Angola, Namibia, Botswana, and western South Africa.

Namaqua sandgrouse usually drink water in the first few hours after sunrise. Some individuals drink only once every three to five days. (© M.P. Kahl/Photo Researchers, Inc. Reproduced by permission.)

Habitat: Namaqua sandgrouse occupy stony desert regions marked by low shrubs, as well as sandy deserts with scattered bits of grass.

Diet: Namaqua sandgrouse eat small seeds from the ground. They also drink water, usually in the first few hours after sunrise. Some individuals drink only once every three to five days.

Behavior and reproduction: Namaqua sandgrouse form large flocks of hundreds or thousands of birds. They call to each other while flying, and can reach speeds of up to 45 miles per hour (70 kilometers per hour). Namaqua sandgrouse build their nests on open ground by scraping in the soil and lining the shallow depression with pebbles and dry vegetation. Three eggs are laid by the female. The female incubates the eggs during the day. The male incubates at night. Eggs hatch after about three weeks, and chicks are able to leave the nest after twenty-four hours. However, they are dependent on the male parent for water for two to three weeks, until they are able to fly to the watering hole themselves.

Namaqua sandgrouse and people: Namaqua sandgrouse are hunted for both food and sport.

Conservation status: Namaqua sandgrouse are not considered threatened at this time. ■

Pallas's sandgrouse *(Syrrhaptes paradoxus)*

 ▪ Resident ▪ Breeding ▪ Nonbreeding

PALLAS'S SANDGROUSE
Syrrhaptes paradoxus

Physical characteristics: Pallas's sandgrouse are medium-sized sandgrouse that range from 15 to 16 inches (38 to 40.6 centimeters) in length and from 7.1 to 10.6 ounces (200 to 300 grams) in weight. Males are slightly larger than females. Males have orange backs barred with black, tawny necks, gray breasts, and black bellies. Females have barred backs and black bellies. The legs and the feet are feathered.

Geographic range: Pallas's sandgrouse are found in southern Russia, Tibet, Mongolia, and China. Some populations occasionally appear in Europe.

Habitat: Pallas's sandgrouse occupy steppe, a semiarid grass-covered plain, and sandy desert habitats, often with a scrub covering. They are generally found between 4,300 and 10,500 feet (1,300 to 3,200 meters) during the summer, but may occupy lower elevations during the winter.

Diet: Pallas's sandgrouse eat primarily legume seeds. Sometimes individuals also eat the green shoots of plants.

Behavior and reproduction: Pallas's sandgrouse are found in large flocks during the nonbreeding season. Most populations stay in the same place throughout the year, or move short distances, but some populations migrate large distances from breeding to wintering grounds. The wings of Pallas's sandgrouse whistle during flight. Individuals generally fly to water sometime during the morning hours. The breeding season is usually between April and June. Nests are scraped in the ground either near vegetation or out in the open. Eggs hatch after twenty-two to twenty-six days. The reproductive behavior of this species has not been studied in the wild. In captivity, only the female incubates while the male remains close by.

Pallas's sandgrouse and people: This species may occasionally be hunted for food.

Conservation status: Pallas's sandgrouse are not considered threatened at this time. ■

FOR MORE INFORMATION

Books:

del Hoyo, J., A. Elliott, and J. Sargatal, eds. *Handbook of the Birds of the World.* Vol. 4, *Sandgrouse to Cuckoos.* Barcelona: Lynx Edicions, 1997.

Johnsgard, P. A. *Bustards, Hemipodes and Sandgrouse: Birds of Dry Places.* Oxford, U.K.: Oxford University Press, 1991.

Perrins, Christopher, ed. *Firefly Encyclopedia of Birds.* Buffalo, NY: Firefly Books, 2003.

Web sites:

"Pteroclidae (Sandgrouse)." The Internet Bird Collection. http://www.hbw.com/ibc/phtml/familia.phtml?idFamilia=70 (accessed on June 11, 2004).

Class: Aves

Order: Columbiformes

Number of families: 2 families

order

CHAPTER

PHYSICAL CHARACTERISTICS

Species of the order Columbiformes include the pigeons and doves, which are compact birds with broad, rounded, powerful wings; short bills; short legs; and short necks. They range in size from the tiny 1.1-ounce (30-gram) Australian diamond dove to the large Victoria-crowned pigeon, which can weigh as much as 6.6 pounds (3 kilograms). Males tend to be slightly larger than females in size. In most species, males and females are similarly colored, although there are a few tropical species where males are much more colorful than females. Many pigeon and dove species are gray, brown, or cream in color. However, some tropical species may be green, red, purple, pink, blue, or orange. One particularly colorful species is the golden dove of Fiji, which can be brilliant orange or a metallic green and gold.

The extinct dodos were large, flightless species weighing as much as 62 pounds (28 kilograms). They had large bellies; short, strong legs; and large bills. They had tiny wings and short tails. They were probably blue or brownish gray in color.

GEOGRAPHIC RANGE

Pigeons and doves are found worldwide, except in the Arctic and Antarctic regions and at high elevations. Particularly large numbers of species are found in tropical areas, especially those near the Indian Ocean and Pacific Ocean. About 60 percent of pigeons and doves are found on small islands far from continental land masses. Dodos were previously found on several small islands in the Indian Ocean.

HABITAT

Pigeons and doves occupy many habitat types, although most species live in forests. Most pigeons and doves are arboreal, they live in trees. A few tropical pigeons and doves are terrestrial, ground-dwelling, and some occupy cliff faces. Dodos inhabited forests as well.

DIET

Most species of pigeons and doves eat primarily seeds, fruits, and leaves. Some also eat invertebrates, animals without backbones, such as insects, though they generally do not form a large part of the diet. One exception is the atoll fruit-dove, which eats large numbers of insects as well as small vertebrates, animals with backbones, such as lizards. Pigeons are also able to drink water by sucking it up directly. Dodos ate fruit, seeds, and other vegetable matter.

ESCAPING PREDATORS

Birds of the order Columbiformes have an unusual strategy for escaping predators. Their feathers are only loosely attached to the skin and fall out very easily. When a predator grabs a pigeon or dove, a large number of feathers are shed at once, leaving the predator with a mouthful of feathers while the bird quickly escapes.

BEHAVIOR AND REPRODUCTION

Some pigeons and doves are solitary, with individuals living alone. The majority of species, however, form small or large flocks, and many even breed together in large colonies. Pigeons and doves often gather near food sources. For example, as many as 100,000 wood pigeons have been observed in a grain field in Germany. During the breeding season, the South American eared dove regularly gathers in flocks of as many as five million individuals. The North America passenger pigeon, which is now extinct, may once have been the most abundant bird on earth. Flocks of passenger pigeons could include as many as billions of individuals.

Most pigeons and doves make noises that sound like "coos" and "oohs." Other species can make whistles, grunts, or clicks. A number of species are almost completely silent.

Courtship in pigeons and doves involves bowing, stretching, and flying. Pigeons and doves are monogamous, a single male mates with a single female during the breeding season. However, the same mate is not necessarily kept from one breeding season to the next. Arboreal species build a simple nest of twigs, while terrestrial species scrape a small depression on the ground. The female lays one or two eggs at a time in most species,

CROP MILK

Pigeons and doves are unique among birds in that adults produce a special "crop milk" to feed their young. Crop milk is named after the crop, a pouch-like organ in the adult throat where the milk is produced. Crop milk is a soft, nutritious, cheesy substance. Because of crop milk, pigeon and dove parents are able to feed their young even when there is little food available, as long as they themselves are fat and healthy. Crop milk is produced by both parents.

although some species may lay as many as four. Species that breed in large colonies, or large pigeons and doves in rainforest habitats, tend to produce only one egg during the breeding season. The eggs are usually white in color, though some species have cream or brownish eggs. Pigeon chicks, which are sometimes called "squabs," are helpless at birth, and have only a few feathers. Both parents help feed and take care of the young. Pigeons and doves are unique among birds in that adults produce a cheesy secretion in their crops known as "crop milk" which they feed to their young. This means that even when food is scarce, parents are able to feed the young. Chicks grow very quickly, and are able to leave the nest between seven and twenty-eight days after hatching. Some leave the nest before their wing feathers are fully grown. Chicks tend to have brown feathers, and only gradually take on the adult coloration.

PIGEONS, DOVES, DODOS, AND PEOPLE

Pigeons have long been raised and bred by human beings for food or as pets. Some species have also been trained to transport written messages. Dodos were hunted for food and sport until they became extinct. The passenger pigeon also went extinct due to human hunting.

CONSERVATION STATUS

About one-third of the 316 existing pigeons and doves are believed to be threatened. Many of these species occupy small islands and have very small ranges. Some species have already been driven to extinction by human activity, including the passenger pigeon and the dodo.

FOR MORE INFORMATION

Books:

del Hoyo, J., A. Elliott, and J. Sargatal, eds. *Handbook of the Birds of the World.* Vol. 4, *Sandgrouse to Cuckoos.* Barcelona: Lynx Edicions, 1997.

Perrins, Christopher, ed. *Firefly Encyclopedia of Birds.* Buffalo, NY: Firefly Books, 2003.

Web sites:

"Columbidae (Pigeons and Doves)." The Internet Bird Collection. http://www.hbw.com/ibc/phtml/familia.phtml?idFamilia=71 (accessed on June 12, 2004).

"Order Columbiformes (Doves and Pigeons)." The University of Michigan Museum of Zoology Animal Diversity Web. http://animaldiversity. ummz.umich.edu/site/accounts/classification/Columbiformes.html# Columbiformes (accessed on June 12, 2004).

PIGEONS AND DOVES
Columbidae

Class: Aves
Order: Columbiformes
Family: Columbidae
Number of species: 316 species

family
CHAPTER

phylum
class
subclass
order
monotypic order
suborder
▲ **family**

PHYSICAL CHARACTERISTICS

Pigeons and doves vary in size from 5.9 to 31.5 inches (15 to 120 centimeters) in length and from 1.1 to 4.4 pounds (0.5 to 2 kilograms) in weight. They have compact bodies, short necks, and small heads. The wings are long and broad and the tail is long and either broad or pointed. The bill is short. The eyes are surrounded by an area of bare skin. Males and females are usually similarly colored, although males are often somewhat larger in size. Many species are gray, brown, or cream in color although some tropical species are much brighter.

GEOGRAPHIC RANGE

Pigeons and doves are found worldwide except in the Arctic and Antarctica. There are particularly large numbers of species in Asia, especially Southeast Asia, including on the many islands in that part of the world.

HABITAT

Pigeons and doves occupy a wide variety of habitat types, including desert, grassland, and forest. The largest number of species is found in forested areas, particularly rainforest. Most pigeons and doves are arboreal, which means they live in trees. This includes most species that occupy grassland areas. Rainforest species may be arboreal or terrestrial, ground-dwelling. Some European and Asian pigeons nest in mountainous cliffs at high altitudes. Desert species are found in California and Australia.

DIET

Some pigeons and doves, including tropical fruit doves, are exclusively frugivorous, fruit-eating. Most species swallow fruit whole. After the flesh of the fruit is digested in the stomach, the pit is regurgitated, vomited from the stomach. Other pigeons and doves are granivorous, eating primarily grains and seeds. Seeds are typically picked from the surface of the ground or stripped from the stems of grasses. One species, the Galápagos dove, is known to use its curved bill to dig for hard seeds in the ground. Granivorous doves and pigeons may also eat leaves, stems, buds, and flowers when seeds are unavailable. A few pigeon and dove species eat primarily animal matter. This includes the atoll fruit dove of the Toamotu archipelago in the Pacific Ocean, which eats insects and small vertebrates, animals with backbones, such as lizards, and the Wonga pigeon of Australia, which eats insects and other invertebrates, animals without backbones. Pigeons and doves are also able to drink water by putting their bills underwater and sucking, an ability that is unusual in birds.

CONSEQUENCES OF AN ALL-FRUIT DIET

Fruit doves eat only fruit. This is an unusual diet among pigeons and doves, and among birds in general, because fruit contains very little protein compared to seeds and insects. Because of their low-protein diet, fruit doves lay only one egg at a time, rather than two like most other pigeons and doves. Also, fruit doves feed their chicks crop milk throughout the nestling period. In other pigeons and doves, adults feed young crop milk for a few days and then gradually replace it with other foods.

BEHAVIOR AND REPRODUCTION

Many species of pigeons and doves form large or small flocks for feeding and other activities. Within flocks, there are dominant and subordinate individuals. The dominant birds, which tend to be larger in size, are usually found in the center of flocks. The smaller, subordinate birds are closer to the edge.

Most species of pigeons and doves are monogamous (muh-NAH-guh-mus), a single male breeds with a single female during the breeding season. Courtship, behaviors that lead to mating, in many species involve flight displays. For example, male wood pigeons fly several feet upwards, clap their wings nine times, and then glide. Flight displays are not found in forest or terrestrial species, however. In most pigeons and doves, males perform a "bow-coo" display involving cooing and bowing just before mating. Each pigeon and dove species has a unique "bow-coo" display.

Pigeons build a simple nest of sticks, straw, and other material. The male collects nesting material and passes it to the female, who tucks it around her body. Pairs are territorial and defend their nesting areas from other members of the species. In fights over territory, individuals peck at each other's heads, particularly at the skin around the eye, and beat their wings. In most species, the female lays two eggs at a time. In a few species, only one egg is laid. In many species, both parents share incubation duties, with males incubating, sitting on the nest, from morning to afternoon, and females incubating from the afternoon to the next morning. Eggs hatch after eleven to thirty days. The young are altricial (al-TRISH-uhl), they hatch at an early developmental stage, blind and with few or no feathers. For the first few days, pigeons and doves feed their young crop milk, a fatty substance produced in the crop organs, located in the throat. Both parents produce crop milk. Chicks are able to leave the nest between seven and twenty-eight days after hatching.

PIGEONS, DOVES, AND PEOPLE

Humans have hunted and raised pigeons for food, as pets, and even to transport written messages.

CONSERVATION STATUS

A third of the 316 existing pigeon and dove species are believed to be Threatened by the World Conservation Union (IUCN). Many of these species occupy small oceanic islands and have very limited ranges. The passenger pigeon, once found in North America in flocks of millions, was driven to extinction by human hunting.

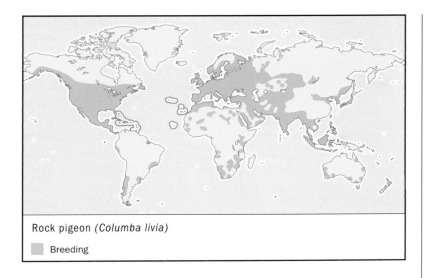

Rock pigeon (*Columba livia*)

Breeding

ROCK PIGEON
Columba livia

Physical characteristics: Rock pigeons are blue-gray in color, with short tails and long, strong wings.

Geographic range: Rock pigeons are found worldwide.

Habitat: Rock pigeons breed in cliff areas or on human buildings. They occupy diverse areas including deserts and grasslands, as well as urban settings.

Diet: Rock pigeons eat grains and seeds.

Behavior and reproduction: Rock pigeons are strong fliers. They generally begin to roost before the sun goes down and wake at dawn. Rock pigeons do not sleep in trees but use a wide variety of crevices, including spaces under rooftops. Rock pigeons are extremely curious birds who investigate their surroundings carefully.

Courtship in rock pigeons involves both partners using their bills to preen, or smooth, their back feathers. Females may stick their bills in the male's bill during courtship, the way young pigeons do when they feed. Both partners then preen each other's heads and necks. The female lays two eggs at a time. Chicks hatch after seventeen or

Rock pigeons are well-known to humans. They may breed on buildings and live in urban settings. (© T. Vezo/VIREO. Reproduced by permission.)

eighteen days. Young are fed crop milk and, later, seeds. Chicks are able to fly after four to five weeks.

Rock pigeons and people: The rock pigeon has been domesticated, tamed, several times, in several different places, by humans. The first domestication may have occurred as long as 10,000 years ago. Rock pigeons have been trained to carry messages. In urban settings, they may be a health hazard to humans since many pigeons carry disease and parasites such as mites and ticks.

Conservation status: Interbreeding with domesticated rock pigeons that have returned to the wild threatens the species, because their young then carry genes from the domesticated varieties, which are usually bred by humans. ■

American mourning dove *(Zenaida macroura)*

Resident   Breeding   Nonbreeding

AMERICAN MOURNING DOVE
Zenaida macroura

Physical characteristics: American mourning doves have olive-gray backs and brownish gray bellies. Their necks are an iridescent pink and purple.

Geographic range: American mourning doves are found in North America and Central America.

Habitat: American mourning doves are found in grassland areas, in hot, dry areas, and sometimes on agricultural lands.

Diet: American mourning doves eat primarily seeds.

American mourning doves get their name from the mournful, sad, call that they make.
(C. C. Lockwood/Bruce Coleman Inc. Reproduced by permission.)

Behavior and reproduction: In American mourning doves, males court females by standing behind them and cooing. Males also inflate their crop, showing off the colors of their throat. Males do not bow. At the nest site, males continue to call while spreading their tails in order to show off their white feather tips.

American mourning doves and people: American mourning doves are hunted for sport and food in the United States and Mexico.

Conservation status: American mourning doves are not threatened. ■

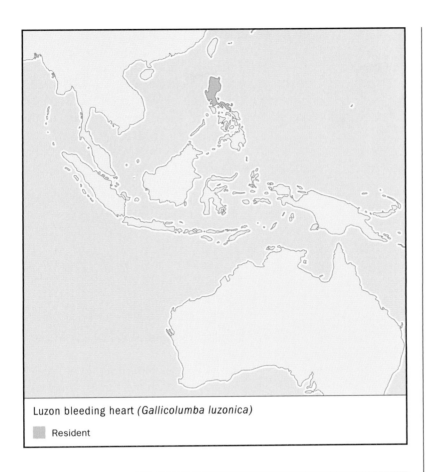

Luzon bleeding heart (*Gallicolumba luzonica*)

Resident

LUZON BLEEDING HEART
Gallicolumba luzonica

Physical characteristics: Luzon bleeding hearts have blue gray backs and white bellies. There is a bright, red-orange spot on the breast which gives this species its name.

Geographic range: Luzon bleeding hearts are found in the Philippines.

Habitat: Luzon bleeding hearts inhabit Philippine rainforest areas.

Diet: Luzon bleeding hearts eat seeds, berries, and invertebrates. This species feeds on the forest floor.

Behavior and reproduction: The Luzon bleeding heart male starts the courtship by chasing the female across the forest floor. Males then stop, raise their tails, puff their feathers, lower their heads, and arch their wings. Then they throw back their heads and stick out their breast to show off the bright red breast spot. Males then bow and coo. Little else is known about Luzon bleeding heart reproductive biology and behavior.

Luzon bleeding heart and people: No significant interaction between Luzon bleeding hearts and humans is known.

Conservation status: Luzon bleeding hearts are not threatened. ■

Luzon bleeding hearts fluff their feathers to conserve body heat. Their name comes from the bright spot on their breast. (© Tom McHugh/Photo Researchers, Inc. Reproduced by permission.)

FOR MORE INFORMATION

Books:

del Hoyo, J., A. Elliott, and J. Sargatal, eds. *Handbook of the Birds of the World.* Vol. 4, *Sandgrouse to Cuckoos.* Barcelona: Lynx Edicions, 1997.

Gibbs, D., E. Barnes, and J. Cox. *Pigeons and Doves. A Guide to the Pigeons and Doves of the World.* Sussex, U.K.: Pica Press, 2001.

Perrins, Christopher, ed. *Firefly Encyclopedia of Birds.* Buffalo, NY: Firefly Books, 2003.

Web sites:

"Columbidae (Pigeons and Doves)." The Internet Bird Collection. http://www.hbw.com/ibc/phtml/familia.phtml?idFamilia=71 (accessed on June 10, 2004).

"Order Columbiformes (Doves and Pigeons)." Animal Diversity Web. http://animaldiversity.ummz.umich.edu/site/accounts/classification/Columbiformes.html#Columbiformes (accessed on June 10, 2004).

Class: Aves
Order: Columbiformes
Family: Raphidae
Number of species: 3 species;
                      all extinct

PHYSICAL CHARACTERISTICS

Dodos and solitaires were about 40 inches (100 centimeters) long and probably weighed between 24 and 40 pounds (10.5 to 17.5 kilograms). However there are some accounts of birds that may have weighed as much as 50 pounds (22.5 kilograms). Dodos were heavily built, with tiny, non-functional wings, strong legs and feet, and a large, strong hooked bill. Dodos had bare faces without feathers. The rest of the body was covered by bluish or brownish gray feathers. Rodrigues solitaires were somewhat taller and more slender than the dodo. Their heads and bills were smaller. They were brownish in color. Males were significantly larger than females. Very little is known of the physical appearance of the third species in the family, the Réunion solitaire. In fact, accounts are so vague that it is not certain they describe a member of this family at all.

GEOGRAPHIC RANGE

Dodos and solitaires are Extinct, no longer existing, but were once found on the Mascarene Islands of Mauritius, Rodrigues, and perhaps Réunion in the Indian Ocean.

HABITAT

Dodos and solitaires inhabited woodland areas.

DIET

Dodos were described as eating fruit primarily. The Rodrigues solitaire was described as eating seeds, fruit, and leaves.

GIGANTISM AND FLIGHTLESSNESS

Dodos and solitaires were close relatives of the pigeons and doves. Unlike existing pigeons and doves, however, they were unable to fly. They were also much larger in size. These features of flightlessness and gigantism (jie-GAN-tiz-um) likely evolved because their island habitats included no predators. In fact, flightlessness and gigantism have evolved in many other island birds. Unfortunately for dodos and solitaires, flightlessness was an extreme disadvantage when humans and other predators reached the Mascarene Islands.

Both dodos and Rodrigues solitaires had an annual fat cycle during which they were fat for several months and thin the rest of the year. In the Rodrigues solitaire, individuals were fat from March to September and then thin. It was reported by one observer that two Rodrigues solitaire chicks had a fat layer 1 inch (2.5 centimeters) thick over the entire body. This fat cycle is common in many bird species of the Mascarene islands.

BEHAVIOR AND REPRODUCTION

Dodos were unable to fly, but could run quickly. They were not afraid of humans. When caught, however, a dodo screamed, causing other dodos to rush to its aid. These dodos were then caught as well. Rodrigues solitaires were territorial, pairs defended territories from other individuals of the species. Rodrigues solitaires had a courtship ritual that involved making noises with the wings. Their wing spurs were used in aggressive encounters between individual birds.

Little is known of the reproductive biology of dodos. It is likely that species built their nests on the ground, and that females laid only one egg at a time. The young were very likely altricial, hatched at an early developmental stage, blind and with few or no feathers. In the Rodrigues solitaire, nests were built from palm leaves. They were generally built on the ground. Both male and female helped incubate, or sit on, the eggs. Chicks were cared for by their parents for some time, then joined crèches, large groups of chicks.

DODOS, SOLITAIRES, AND PEOPLE

Dodos and solitaires were driven to extinction by human hunting. They were frequently killed for food, particularly by sailors visiting the islands they once inhabited. They also suffered from the introduction of non-native species such as pigs, cats, and rats by humans. Some dodos and solitaires were brought to Europe where they were associated with exotic islands. Because dodos were so quickly hunted to extinction, they continue to serve as symbols of extinction.

CONSERVATION STATUS

The dodo and the two species of solitaires are Extinct, due to human hunting and to the introduction of non-native species such as cats, rats, and pigs.

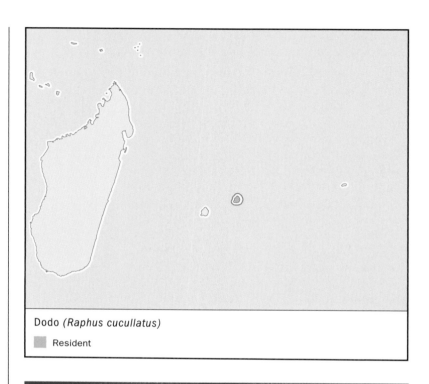

Dodo *(Raphus cucullatus)*

▨ Resident

**SPECIES
ACCOUNT**

DODO
Raphus cucullatus

Physical characteristics: Dodos were large birds about the size of a turkey. They had dark gray feathers on the back and somewhat lighter gray feathers on the belly. The wings were tiny and yellowish white in color. The tail was small and short, made up of five curled feathers. Dodos had large, yellow hooked bills. The face was featherless, with gray skin.

Geographic range: Dodos were found on the island of Mauritius in the Indian Ocean, about 500 miles (800 kilometers) east of Madagascar.

Habitat: The dodo inhabited woodland areas.

Diet: Dodos ate fruit. They also swallowed small stones to help with digesting food in the crop, an organ found near the throat.

Behavior and reproduction: Dodos could not fly, but were able to run quickly. When a dodo was caught, it would scream and other dodos would rush to the site, getting caught themselves. One sailor described dodos as "serene and majestic" and said that they did not run away from humans.

Dodos built nests on the ground. Only one egg was laid at a time. Judging by their size, eggs probably hatched after about thirty-seven days.

Dodos and people: Sailors traveling in the Indian Ocean caught dodos in large numbers for food. The dodo is the first recorded species that was driven to extinction by human activity.

Conservation status: The dodo is Extinct. Not only did sailors eat the dodos, but the pigs, cats, and monkeys brought to Mauritius by sailors ate large numbers of dodo eggs. ■

Because dodos could not fly, they were easy to hunt. When a dodo was caught, it would scream and other dodos would rush to the site, getting caught themselves. (Illustration by Gillian Harris. Reproduced by permission.)

FOR MORE INFORMATION

Books:

del Hoyo, J., A. Elliott, and J. Sargatal, eds. *Handbook of the Birds of the World*. Vol. 4, *Sandgrouse to Cuckoos*. Barcelona: Lynx Edicions, 1997.

Hachisuka, M. *The Dodo and Kindred Birds, or the Extinct Birds of the Mascarene Islands*. London: Witherby, 1953.

Perrins, Christopher, ed. *Firefly Encyclopedia of Birds*. Buffalo, NY: Firefly Books, 2003.

Quammen, D. *The Song of the Dodo: Island Biogeography in an Age of Extinctions*. New York: Scriber, 1996.

Web sites:

"Family Raphidae (Dodo and Solitaires)." Animal Diversity Web. http://animaldiversity.ummz.umich.edu/site/accounts/classification/Raphidae.html#Raphidae (accessed on June 12, 2004).

PARROTS

Psittaciformes

Class: Aves

Order: Psittaciformes

One family: Psittacidae

Number of species: 353 species

monotypic order

C H A P T E R

PHYSICAL CHARACTERISTICS

The family Psittacidae contains more than 300 species of birds. Parrots usually have brightly colored plumage (feathers). Most have green feathers, and many parrots are blue, red, and yellow. The parrots range in length from the 3.5-inch (9-centimeter) red-breasted pygmy parrot to the 3.3-foot (1-meter) hyacinth macaw.

Parrots have large heads, short necks, and curved beaks. They use their hooked beaks to crack nuts and grab branches. Birds use their beaks and feet to pick up food and carry it their mouths. Parrots have zygodactyl (zye-guh-DACK-tuhl) feet; two toes on each foot face forward and two face backward.

GEOGRAPHIC RANGE

Most parrots live in the Southern Hemisphere, the portion of Earth south of the equator. This range includes the continents of South America, Australia, and Africa. Parrots also live in Central American countries including Belize, as well as countries including Mexico, New Zealand, New Guinea, India, and Afghanistan.

HABITAT

Parrots are tree-dwellers that live in various habitats. They live in rainforests where heavy rainfall throughout the year produces an abundance of trees and plants. In deciduous forests, parrots live in trees that shed leaves. Parrots also nest in coniferous forests where evergreen trees don't shed leaves. Some birds also live in grasslands, where there are few trees.

DIET

Parrots eat seeds and fruit. Lorikeets also eat pollen and nectar. The amount eaten varies with the bird's size.

BEHAVIOR AND REPRODUCTION

Parrot behavior varies by species. A group of birds may form a flock. Birds in the flock often pair up. Some parrots are active in the day and sleep in trees at night. Other birds are nocturnal, active at night.

Most parrots are monogamous (muh-NAH-guh-mus) and pair up for life. Birds often breed in cavities, nests located in the hollow part of trees. Usually, only the female broods, staying with the eggs until they hatch. Females of most species lay four to eight white eggs. They hatch in eighteen to twenty days.

Parrots are thought to be intelligent. In the wild, they screech or scream to warn the flock of danger from predators like eagles and falcons.

Cage birds (birds in captivity) often imitate the words of the people they live with, and some tamed parrots live to age of eighty or longer.

PARROTS AND PEOPLE

Parrots have been popular as cage birds since ancient times. While there is still a demand for parrots as pets, birds in the wild are sometimes considered pests because flocks of birds may ruin crops.

CONSERVATION STATUS

About one-third of parrot species face danger of extinction, with species dying out as habitat is lost because of human development. Extinct species include the Carolina parakeet, the only parrot that lived naturally in the United States.

WHY PARROTS TALK

The gray parrot is the most talkative bird in the parrot family. These domesticated parrots are intelligent. They imitate sounds, something that usually doesn't happen in the wild where birds chatter with other parrots. Scientists believe that cage birds repeat human words when kept without other parrots as companions.

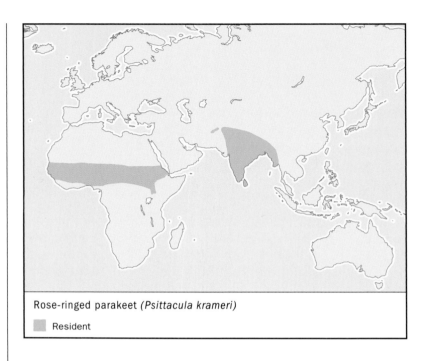

Rose-ringed parakeet (*Psittacula krameri*)

■ Resident

ROSE-RINGED PARAKEET
Psittacula krameri

Physical characteristics: The rose-ringed parakeet has green feathers, black feet, and a red beak with a black band around it. The rose ring is the black-and-red collar around the bird's neck. Birds measure 15.7 inches (40 centimeters) from their heads to their tails. They weigh from 4.1 to 4.9 ounces (116 to 139 grams).

Geographic range: Rose-ringed parakeets live naturally in the African countries of Sudan, Mauritania, Uganda, Eritrea, Ethiopia, and Somalia. In Asia, they range in India, Sri Lanka, Pakistan, Myanmar, and China. Parakeets have been introduced into countries including the United States and England.

Habitat: Rose-ringed parakeets are adaptive, able to adjust to living conditions in a range of countries. They live in deciduous forests, grassland, and rainforests. In addition to their natural habitats, parakeet populations grew in the United States and England after caged birds escaped or were released by people.

Diet: Parakeets eat seeds, grain, flowers, fruit, nectar, and berries.

Behavior and reproduction: Rose-ringed parakeets are semi-nomadic, traveling to find food. They usually travel in a small flock, but some food sources can attract a flock of thousands of birds.

Parakeets are monogamous. The female selects the nest location and lines it with wood chips. The nest may be in a hole in a tree or one in a house wall. The hen lays a clutch of three to four eggs. They hatch in twenty-two days and are cared for by both parents.

Rose-ringed parakeets and people: Rose-ringed parakeets are valued as cage birds. In the wild, they are sometimes considered pests because they destroy crops while trying to feed.

Conservation status: Rose-ringed parakeets are not in danger of extinction. ■

The rose-ringed parakeet gets its name from the black-and-red collar around its neck. (Illustration by Joseph E. Trumpey. Reproduced by permission.)

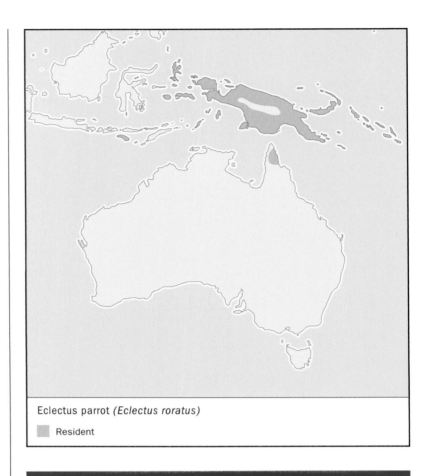

Eclectus parrot (*Eclectus roratus*)

▨ Resident

ECLECTUS PARROT
Eclectus roratus

Physical characteristics: The coloring of male and female eclectus parrots is so different that they were once thought to be two different species. The female bird has red and blue feathers and a black bill. The male has green plumage and a yellow bill. All eclectus parrots have feathers of a smooth texture that have been compared to silk. The birds are 16.5 inches (42 centimeters) in length and weigh 0.9 to 1.2 pounds (440 to 660 grams).

Geographic range: Eclectus parrots live in Indonesia in Moluccas, Sumba Island, the Tanimbar Islands, Aru Islands, Biak Island, and Irian Jaya. They also range in the South Pacific in New Guinea and

nearby islands, the Solomon Islands, Admiralty Islands, Bismarck Archipelago, and the Cape York Peninsula in Australia.

Habitat: In the rainforest, eclectus parrots often live in tall trees with nests located 72 feet (22 meters) or more from the ground. The birds also live in trees in grassland.

Diet: Eclectus parrots eat nuts, seeds, fruits, berries, and nectar.

Behavior and reproduction: Eclectus parrots are monogamous and are believed to breed year-round. However, they are thought to mate mostly between August and January. Birds are group-oriented, and there may be four nests in a tree. The parrots are cooperative breeders, parents are helped by other birds. The assistants are thought to be offspring or adult relatives of the expectant parents. The female has a clutch of two eggs that hatch in twenty-six days.

Eclectus parrots and people: Eclectus parrots are popular cage birds. While people in their native lands sometimes keep them as pets, some people are upset when wild parrots steal their fruit.

Conservation status: Due to concern that populations will decline, a permit is required to remove eclectus parrots from their natural habitat. A CITES (Convention on International Trade in Endangered Species in Wild Fauna and Flora) permit is needed to import the parrots.   ■

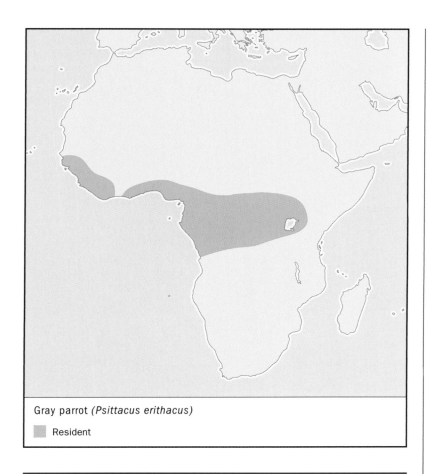

Gray parrot *(Psittacus erithacus)*

■ Resident

GRAY PARROT
Psittacus erithacus

Physical characteristics: The African gray parrot's plumage consists of various shades of gray. Tail feathers are red. Birds are 13 inches (33 centimeters) from head to tail and weigh up to 0.8 pounds (407 grams).

Geographic range: Gray parrots are found in western Africa in coastal countries including Sierra Leone, Ghana, and the Ivory Coast. Birds also range inland in central and east Africa.

Habitat: Parrots make their nests in tree holes, sometimes choosing locations abandoned by birds like woodpeckers. The parrots live in evergreen forests and other wooded areas.

The African gray parrot is a popular pet because it can learn many words. Populations are declining in some areas because smugglers steal birds to sell them, and their habitats are destroyed. (Daniel Zupanc/Bruce Coleman Inc. Reproduced by permission.)

Diet: Parrots eat seeds, fruit, nuts, and berries. Birds usually pick their food from the trees. They sometimes land on the ground and eat dirt or tiny rocks. This helps the parrots digest their food.

Behavior and reproduction: Gray parrots are social birds. They travel during the day in pairs or small groups. At dusk, a large group of birds meets at one spot. This large flock will chatter and then roost, resting for the night. When the sun rises, pairs and groups fly away to eat. Birds often take a midday break and then feed again.

Gray parrots are monogamous. When they breed is based on where the birds are. Parrots in western Africa breed from November to April. The breeding season in eastern Africa is during June and July. In the Congo River basin, birds breed from July through December.

The female lays two to three eggs. Sometimes there is a clutch of four eggs. In the wild, eggs hatch in twenty-one days. The incubation period for cage birds is thirty days.

Gray parrots and people: The gray is an extremely popular cage bird because it can learn many words.

Conservation status: Populations are declining in some areas as smugglers steal birds and habitats are destroyed, but the gray parrot is not currently in danger of extinction.   ■

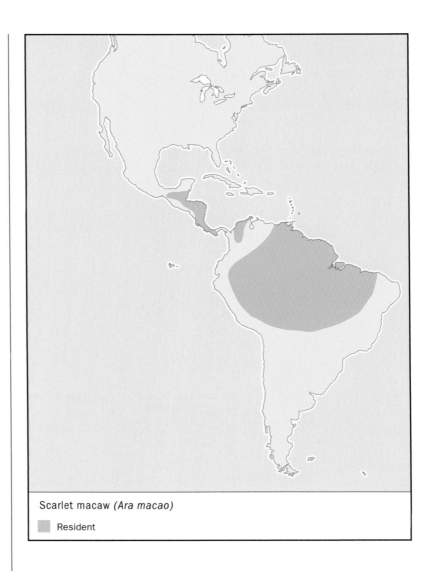

Scarlet macaw (Ara macao)

Resident

SCARLET MACAW
Ara macao

Physical characteristics: Scarlet macaws are colorful birds. The macaw's head, tail, and much of its body is red. Wings are blue, green, and yellow. Birds measure 33 inches (85 centimeters) from head to tail. The tail accounts for most of the length. Macaws weigh from 2.1 to 2.2 pounds (1.06 to 1.12 kilograms).

Geographic range: Scarlet macaws are found in southern Mexico and in Central American countries including Guatemala and Costa Rica. They also range in northwestern South American countries like Colombia, Ecuador, and Peru.

Habitat: Macaws live in evergreen, coniferous forests and other wooded areas like deciduous forests.

Diet: Macaws eat berries, seeds, fruit, nuts, and flowers. After eating, macaws join other birds at riverbanks. There the birds eat mineralized clay. Scientists think that birds do this to stop the effect of being poisoned by unripe fruit and other dangerous plants.

Behavior and reproduction: Macaws travel in pairs and fly close to each other. Pairs may be part of a family group or a flock of up to twenty birds. Birds look for food during the day and roost in trees at night.

Birds in the north nest in March and April. The season lasts from October through March in the south. Females usually lay one or two eggs. Sometimes there is a clutch of four eggs.

Scarlet macaws and people: While macaws screech to keep humans away, people want to own these colorful birds. Macaws are also hunted for food or for their feathers.

Conservation status: Scarlet macaw populations are declining as habitat is destroyed when trees are cut down. Smuggling also reduces the population. In 2003, poachers armed with guns followed biologists in a Guatemala reserve, an area set aside to protect species. The poachers stole macaw eggs, knowing there is a demand for the birds. ∎

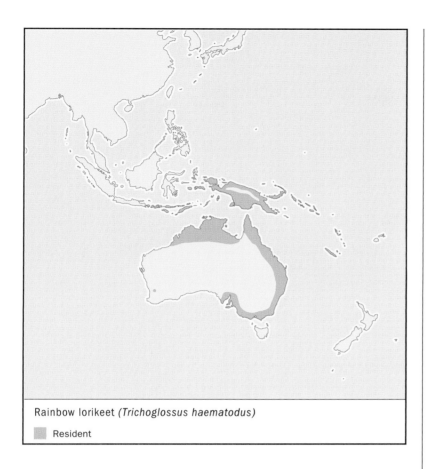

Rainbow lorikeet (*Trichoglossus haematodus*)

Resident

RAINBOW LORIKEET
Trichoglossus haematodus

Physical characteristics: The bird named for the rainbow has an orange beak and red, yellow, green, and blue feathers. Body color varies by location. Some birds have blue and purple heads and green feather collars around their necks. Lorikeets measure 10 inches (26 centimeters) from head to tail. The birds weigh from 3.5 to 5.8 ounces (100 to 167 grams).

Unlike other members of the parrot family, the lorikeet can't open seeds with its beak. The lorikeet has a pointed bill and a "brush-tipped" tongue. The brush is made of tiny hairs on the tongue. This allows the lorikeet to eat pollen and nectar.

Geographic range: Rainbow lorikeets live in Australia, New Guinea, Indonesia, and South Pacific islands including the Papuan Islands.

Habitat: Rainbow lorikeets live in wooded areas where flowers grow. Habitats include rainforests thick with trees, grasslands where there are few trees, and people's gardens.

Diet: Rainbow lorikeets use their brush-tipped tongues to get nectar, the liquid in flowers that bees turn into honey. The birds also eat pollen, which also comes from flowers. Birds also eat fruit, berries, grain, leaf buds, insect larvae (LAR-vee), and some seeds. They feed in the wild and from feeders in people's gardens.

Behavior and reproduction: The lorikeets travel in pairs, family groups, and flocks. Rainbows are monogamous and breed from October to January. The months when birds mate vary by region. Nests are built in a hollow tree limb where the female lays from two to three eggs. Both parents incubate the eggs until they hatch in about twenty-five days.

Rainbow lorikeets and people: Rainbow lorikeets are popular cage birds. However, in the wild they can damage crops because an abundant food source could attract hundreds of birds.

Conservation status: Rainbow lorikeets are not at risk of extinction. ∎

FOR MORE INFORMATION

Books:

Freud, Arthur. *The Complete Parrot.* New York: Howell Book House, 1995.

Rauzon, Mark. *Parrots Around the World.* New York: Franklin Watts, 2001.

Wade, Nicholas, ed. *The New York Times Book of Birds.* New York: The Lyons Press, 2001.

Periodicals:

Greij, Eldon. "Bird Brain: Feats Performed by One African Grey Parrot Raise Questions About How Much All Birds Think." *Birder's World* 17, no. 6 (Dec 2003): 76.

"Maybe What Polly Wants is a New Toy." *Science News* 164, no. 5 (August 2, 2003): 78.

Myers, Jack. "Parrots That Eat Dirt: Why Do They Do It?" *Highlights for Children* 56, no. 12 (Dec 2001): 12.

Smith, Dottie. "Parrot Talk." *Fun For Kidz* 2, no. 2 (March–April 2003): 34.

Web sites:

Brightsmith, Don. "What Eats Parrots?" Duke University. http://www.duke.edu/djb4 (accessed on April 23, 2004).

"Rainbow Lorikeets." San Francisco Zoo. http://www.sfzoo.org/cgi-bin/animals.py?ID=60 (accessed on April 26, 2004).

Triveldi, Brian. "Poachers and Fires Menace Endangered Parrots." NationalGeographic.com. http://www.nationalgeographic.com.news/2003/06/0609_tvmacaw.html (accessed on April 27, 2004).

**TURACOS AND
PLANTAIN EATERS**
Musophagiformes

Class: Aves
Order: Musophagiformes
One family: Musophagidae
Number of species: 23 species

monotypic order
C H A P T E R

PHYSICAL CHARACTERISTICS

These birds have long tails, short bills and short, round wings. They are weak fliers, but they can walk, run, and leap on tree twigs and branches. The birds move so well on their feet because they are able to bend their outer toes forward and backwards.

Seventeen Musophagidae species are very colorful. Turacos (TOOR-ah-koz) living in forests have blue, green, or purple plumage, with red in their wing feathers. The species living in grasslands are mainly gray and brown. The great blue turaco is the largest bird in this family. From head-to-tail, it measures 28 to 30 inches (70 to 76 centimeters). Other birds in the family range in length from 16 to 21 inches (40 to 53 centimeters).

GEOGRAPHIC RANGE

Turacos and plantain eaters are unique to Africa. They live in sub-Saharan Africa, the part of the continent below the Sahara Desert. The birds are found in the countries of Angola, Congo, Democratic Republic of the Congo, Tanzania, Zambia, Malawi, Mozambique, Namibia, Zimbabwe, Botswana, Guinea, Sierra Leone, Ivory Coast, Ghana, Nigeria, Cameroon, Central African Republic, Sudan, Kenya, Gabon, Uganda, Equatorial Guinea, Rwanda, and Burundi.

HABITAT

Members of the Musophagidae family are arboreal, meaning they live in trees. Their habitat ranges from tropical forests thick with trees to grasslands, where there are few trees.

DIET

Although "musophaga" means banana and plantain eater, These birds hardly ever eat bananas or the tropical bananas called plantains. Instead, the birds eat the fruits of trees including the parasol and waterberry. The birds eat fruit that grows wild as well as fruit grown by people. Some species also eat flowers, leaves, caterpillars, moths, snails, slugs, termites, and beetles.

BEHAVIOR AND REPRODUCTION

Birds live in pairs or in small family groups. Most species are thought to be monogamous (muh-NAH-guh-mus), mating for life. The birds build a flat nest of twigs, and both parents incubate (sit on) eggs. The female usually lays two eggs. Hens in the grassland have a clutch of two or three eggs. They hatch in twenty-two to thirty-one days, depending on the species.

Predators that hunt turacos and plantain eaters include eagles and chimpanzees.

MUSOPHAGIFORMES AND PEOPLE

For centuries, people hunted turacos for food and used their feathers for tribal headgear. Some turaco species are popular as cage birds. Hunters don't like the gray go-away-bird because they believe the bird's call warns animals of potential attacks.

CONSERVATION STATUS

Three turaco species are threatened, according to the World Conservation Union (IUCN). One Cameroon species, Bannerman's turaco, is Endangered, facing a very high risk of extinction. Environmental groups are working with local people to save the birds threatened by loss of habitat.

TURACOS RECOGNIZE PREDATORS' CALLS

Great blue turacos can recognize the difference between the calls of other species, according to biologist Klaus Zuberbühler of St. Andrew's University in Scotland. His research showed that the great blue knew the calls of predators like eagles and chimpanzees. The fruit-eating birds also recognized the calls of other fruit-eaters like monkeys and hornbills.

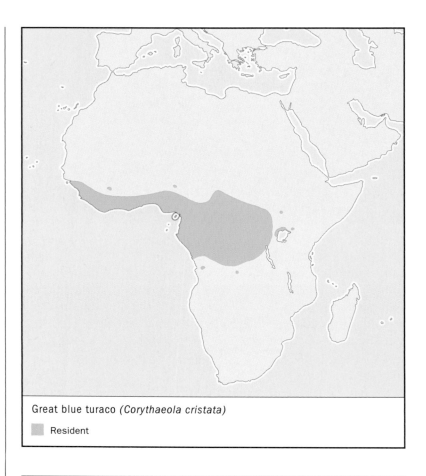

Great blue turaco (*Corythaeola cristata*)

■ Resident

GREAT BLUE TURACO
Corythaeola cristata

Physical characteristics: The great blue turaco is regarded as one of the most beautiful birds in Africa. Its bill is yellow, with a red tip as if it's wearing lipstick. The bird's head is topped by a blue, almost black, crest. Plumage on the head, back, and wings is greenish blue. There is yellow on the chest and other areas including the tail, and red plumage above the feet.

The great blues are the largest members of their family. Males measure from 28 to 30 inches (70 to 76 centimeters) and weigh from 1.9 to 2.1 pounds (0.9 to 1 kilograms). Females weigh from 1.8 to 2.7 pounds (0.8 to 1.2 kilograms).

Geographic range: Great blue turacos live in Guinea, Sierra Leone, Ivory Coast, Ghana, Nigeria, Cameroon, Central African Republic, Sudan, Kenya, Gabon, Uganda, Equatorial Guinea, Rwanda, Democratic Republic of the Congo, and Burundi.

Habitat: Turacos spend most of their days in the canopies or tops of trees in Africa's forests.

Diet: Turacos mostly eat fruit, and they pluck it from trees or shrubs. When there is little fruit around, they eat leaves and flowers. Sometimes great blue turacos eat algae (AL-jee), tiny plants that grow in water.

Behavior and reproduction: Great blue turacos are sociable and form parties, groups of up to eighteen birds. A party stakes out a territory of its own. They communicate with two types of calls. One is a low tone that has been compared to a purr. The other is harsher, and sounds like the word "cow" being repeated.

Birds travel in parties and pairs. After mating, they make a nest resembling a platform out of sticks. The hen lays two blue-green eggs. Both parents incubate the eggs, which hatch in twenty-nine to thirty-one days. In five to six weeks, hatchlings fledge, growing the feathers needed to fly. They will be cared for by their parents for about three months.

Great blue turacos and people: Some people eat turaco meat.

Conservation status: Although the great blue turaco is not threatened, people fear that the destruction of forests, along with trapping and hunting, will cause a drop in the bird population. ■

Great blue turacos are sociable and form parties, groups of up to eighteen birds, that stake out a territory as their own. (Illustration by Joseph E. Trumpey. Reproduced by permission.)

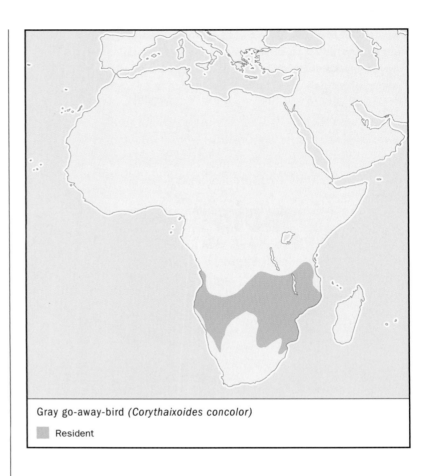

Gray go-away-bird *(Corythaixoides concolor)*

Resident

GRAY GO-AWAY-BIRD
Corythaixoides concolor

Physical characteristics: Go-away birds are dark gray and with lighter coloring around the eyes. Plumage is darkest on the tail, chin, chest, throat, and on small feathers called coverts. The crest on the bird's head consists of feathers of different lengths. The bird can raise or lower its crest.

The gray go-away bird is 18 to 20 inches (46 to 51 centimeters) in length and weighs from 7.1 to 12 ounces (202 to 340 grams). While not as colorful as turacos, go-away-birds have more wing strength and are better fliers.

Geographic range: Go-away birds live in Angola, the Congo, Democratic Republic of the Congo, Tanzania, Zambia, Malawi, Mozambique, Namibia, Zimbabwe, and Botswana.

Habitat: Go-away-birds live in savannas, grassland areas with some trees. The birds generally roost, or stay, in acacia (uh-KAY-shah) trees.

Diet: Go-away-birds eat fruit, leaves, seeds, flowers, and termites. The birds sometimes eat clay, and are the only members of the Musophagidae family to do so. Birds may raid gardens, and their feeding can cause the destruction of crops such as lettuce.

Behavior and reproduction: The go-away-bird is named for its call. People think the call sounds like the words, "Go away." Since the bird calls when people approach, hunters think that the birds are giving a warning to animals.

When gray go-away-birds breed, the female has a clutch of one to four gray eggs. Both parents incubate the eggs, which hatch in twenty-six to twenty-eight days. Both parents care for the hatchlings. Parents may be assisted by helpers, birds thought to be offspring from an earlier mating.

The go-away-birds often pair up and are part of small family groups. They also form parties of up to twenty birds. They climb and hop in trees and appear to be curious about the world around them. They are less shy around humans than other birds in the Musophagidae family. And just as in human families, not all relatives get along. Go-away birds may chase turacos away from water and food sources like fruit trees. However, the go-away-birds will not object if they are joined by birds such as parrots or pigeons.

Gray go-away-birds and people: Gray go-away-birds annoy hunters because the birds' call sounds an alarm that warns animals that hunters are approaching.

Conservation status: Go-away-birds are not considered at risk of extinction.   ■

FOR MORE INFORMATION

Books:

del Hoyo, Josep, et al, eds. *Handbook of the Birds of the World.* Barcelona: Lynx Edicions, 1992.

Forshaw, Joseph, ed. *Encyclopedia of Birds,* 2nd ed. San Diego, CA: Academic Press, 1998.

Sibley, David. *The Sibley Guide to Birds.* New York: Alfred A. Knopf, 2000.

Stuart, Chris and Tilde. *Birds of Africa From Seabirds to Seed Eaters.* Cambridge, MA: The MIT Press, 1999.

Web sites:

BirdLife International. http://www.birdlife.org/news/features/2003/08/kilum.html (accessed on April 25, 2004).

Pickrell, John. "African Birds Understand Monkey Communication, Study Says." NationalGeographic.com.   http://www.nationalgeographic.com/news/2004/03/18_040313_hornbills.html (accessed on April 25, 2004).

**CUCKOOS, ANIS, AND
ROADRUNNERS**
Cuculiformes

Class: Aves
Order: Cuculiformes
One family: Cuculidae
Number of species: 129 species

monotypic order
CHAPTER

PHYSICAL CHARACTERISTICS

The Cuculidae family is also called the cuckoo family. It is a large family, with more than 128 species. Species in this family include common cuckoos, anis, and roadrunners. Birds range in length from the 5.1-inch (13-centimeter) pheasant cuckoo to the greater roadrunner, which is 22.1 inches (56 centimeters) long. Anis (ah-NEEZ) are also known as black cuckoos because of their dark plumage. The birds' heavy bill is either smooth or ridged. The greater ani is about 18.1 inches (46 centimeters) long.

Most Cuculidae are not colorful; their feathers are gray, black, or brown. They are slender and have narrow bills, long tails, and zygodactyl (zye-guh-DACK-tuhl) feet. Two toes on each foot face forward, and two face backward. Members of this family are terrestrial, meaning that some species live on land. However, they are able to fly.

GEOGRAPHIC RANGE

Cuckoos are located on every continent except Antarctica. The great spotted cuckoo is found in countries including France, Iraq, and Egypt. The common cuckoo spends summers in Europe and Asia, then winters in Africa. The greater anis range in Central and South America. Greater roadrunners live in the United States and Mexico.

HABITAT

Members of this large family live in a variety of habitats. Some cuckoos range in rainforests, where heavy rainfall

phylum

class

subclass

order

● **monotypic order**

suborder

family

produces an abundance of trees. Greater anis live in tropical coniferous forests, where trees don't shed leaves. They also range in grasslands where there are few trees. Roadrunners live in the desert.

DIET

Cuculidae eat insects like caterpillars and grasshoppers. Some species eat lizards, seeds, fruit, berries, and bird eggs.

BEHAVIOR AND REPRODUCTION

Most cuckoos are solitary, staying alone until they pair up to breed. Many species are monogamous (muh-NAH-guh-mus), mating with the same bird for life. About fifty cuckoo species are brood parasites. The female lays eggs in the nests of other birds. She leaves one egg in the nest, expecting the other bird to care for her hatchling. Some cuckoos leave their eggs in a particular species' nest, but other cuckoos may use many hosts, birds that care for the cuckoo's eggs and young.

Anis live in groups and build nests after breeding. They are helped by cooperative breeders. Helpers, usually older offspring, help the parents care for the hatched birds. Roadrunners also nest and care for their young.

CUCULIFORMES AND PEOPLE

People who have never seen a cuckoo may recognize its call. They've heard an imitation of it when a cuckoo clock chimes the hours. Some people think that the actual cuckoo's call means that rain is on the way. In some places, cuckoos are called rainbirds.

CONSERVATION STATUS

Most species aren't at risk of becoming extinct, dying out. However, populations may decline if the amount of rainforest is reduced.

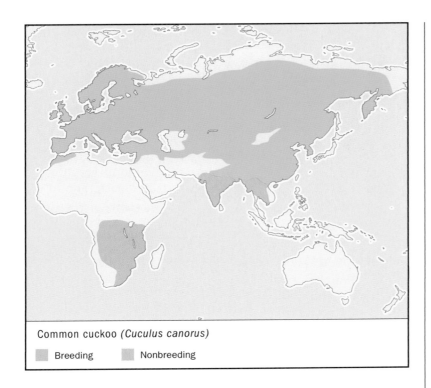

Common cuckoo (*Cuculus canorus*)

■ Breeding   ■ Nonbreeding

COMMON CUCKOO
Cuculus canorus

Physical characteristics: Both males and females have dark gray feathers on the top of their bodies. On the lower body are gray and white feathers. Females of some species have brownish red feathers on their upper breasts. The cuckoo's long tail is black.

Cuckoos have black bills and weigh about 3.7 ounces (115 grams). Their head-to-tail length is 12.6 to 13 inches (32 to 33 centimeters).

Geographic range: Common cuckoos are found throughout Europe and Asia. They also live in Siberia and parts of Africa.

Habitat: Common cuckoos live in various habitats. They're found in wooded areas, including rainforests where heavy rain produces many trees. They also live in meadows and grassland areas like steppes, where there are few trees.

Common cuckoos leave their eggs in the nest of any one of over 125 species of birds that act as hosts, hatching the cuckoo's egg and taking care of the young. (Roger Wilmshurst/ Bruce Coleman Inc. Reproduced by permission.)

Diet: Common cuckoos are insectivores, primarily eating insects. Their diet includes hairy caterpillars, dragonflies, beetles, and crickets.

Behavior and reproduction: Common cuckoos are solitary and polygamous (puh-LIH-guh-mus). Both males and females breed with many different partners. There is no nest where the female lays eggs. Instead she relies on birds of other species to incubate the eggs and feed the young birds. After mating, the cuckoo looks to see which birds are building nests. The cuckoo may destroy one or more eggs in the "host" bird's nest. The cuckoo does this to make room for her egg. The host is usually fooled because the cuckoo chooses a bird that lays an egg similar to her own. While each cuckoo lays only one type of egg, cuckoos lay eggs of so many sizes and colors that their eggs resemble those of over 125 different host species.

Common cuckoos and people: The common cuckoo has long fascinated people because the female's behavior is so different from that of a traditional mother who cares for her young. A form of the bird's name is used to describe the victim of a dishonest act. Initially, a "cuckold" was man whose wife cheated on him—a "cuckold" is now someone who was deceived. In addition, "cuckoo" is a term used to describe someone who acts strangely.

Not all references to cuckoos, however, are negative. The birds' call is imitated in the chimes of the cuckoo clock. And in England, people say that when they hear a cuckoo in nature that the season of spring will soon arrive.

Conservation status: Common cuckoos do not face extinction; their species is not in danger of dying out. ∎

Greater roadrunner *(Geococcyx californiana)*

Resident

GREATER ROADRUNNER
Geococcyx californiana

Physical characteristics: Greater roadrunners are ground cuckoos, terrestrial birds that live primarily on the ground. They rarely fly, traveling on their sturdy legs instead of using their wings. Birds can fly for a short distance and will do so when in danger or traveling downhill.

The roadrunner's head-to-toe length is 22.1 inches (56 centimeters) long. The white-tipped tail accounts for about half of that length. Male roadrunners weigh 0.64 pounds (320 grams). Females weigh about 0.58 pounds (290 grams). Their plumage is black, white, and brown.

The female greater roadrunner builds a flat nest out of sticks and twigs in a cactus, tree, or shrub. (© C.K. Lorenz/Photo Researchers, Inc. Reproduced by permission.)

Geographic range: Greater roadrunners live in Mexico and the southwestern United States.

Habitat: Greater roadrunners live in the dry brush and scrub in the Mojave (moe-HAH-vay) and Sonoran deserts in the United States.

Diet: The greater roadrunner is an omnivore, which means one that eats both meat and vegetation. The bird is fast enough to catch lizards, snakes, spiders, insects, birds, and rabbits.

The roadrunner is among the few animals that hunt rattlesnakes. The bird moves so quickly that it can grab the snake by the tail. The roadrunner holds the rattler in its mouth and shakes it, hitting the snake's head on the ground until it dies. The roadrunner then swallows its prey.

The roadrunner's diet changes in winter when there are fewer animals in the desert. The bird will then eat plants.

Behavior and reproduction: Roadrunners are monogamous and mate for life. They live in pairs and breed in the spring. The male and female gather sticks and twigs for the birds' nest. The female builds a flat nest in a cactus, tree, or shrub. She then lays from two to twelve eggs. Laying eggs may take up to three days.

Both parents incubate the eggs; the male usually sits on them at night. The incubation period lasts from eighteen to twenty-one days. Eggs don't hatch at one time, and a week may pass between hatchings. Rain and food supply influences breeding patterns. Birds in California's Mojave and Sonoran Deserts breed only in the spring. Summer rains in the Arizona portion of the Sonoran increases the food supply, and birds breed in August and September.

Greater roadrunners and people: Greater roadrunners face the risk of being struck by vehicles as they run along desert roads.

Conservation status: Roadrunner populations are not in danger of extinction. However, some populations' numbers are dropping as areas develop. ∎

FOR MORE INFORMATION

Books:

Stuart, Chris and Tilde. *Birds of Africa, from Seabirds to Seed Eaters.* Cambridge, MA: The MIT Press, 1999.

Wade, Nicholas, ed. *The New York Times Book of Birds.* New York: The Lyons Press, 2001.

Web sites:

The Bird Site, Los Angeles Natural History Museum. http://www.nhm.org/birds/guide (accessed April 25, 2004).

"Avian Orders: Cuculiformes." BIRDNET. http://www.nmnh.si.edu/BIRDNET/ORDERS/Cuculiformes.html (accessed May 8, 2004).

OWLS
Strigiformes

Class: Aves
Order: Strigiformes
Number of families: 2 families

PHYSICAL CHARACTERISTICS

Owls are easy to recognize. They have an almost human appearance, with upright posture, large rounded heads, and large eyes that face forward (most birds have eyes on the sides of their heads). All owls are carnivores, or meat-eaters, and several adaptations make them effective hunters, including a hooked beak for tearing flesh and strong feet tipped with sharp talons, or claws. The toes can be used in a two-forward, two-backward arrangement for a good grip on prey (most birds have three toes pointing forward and one pointing backward). Feathers are unusually soft, allowing for silent flight, so owls can hear their prey and approach it without warning.

Most owls are nocturnal, active at night and asleep by day. Adaptations for night hunting include eyes that can see in low-light conditions and very sensitive hearing. The eyes are enclosed in a ring of bone and cannot move freely, so owls must turn the entire head to look sideways. They do have extra flexible necks that allow the head to turn 270°, so an owl can see what's behind its back. Many owls have ears positioned asymmetrically on the head, with one higher than the other. This arrangement helps owls locate the source of a sound. Feathers on the face are arranged in a flat circle called a facial disk. It works much like a satellite dish, focusing sound waves on the ear openings.

Most owls have subdued, or dull, color. The feathers are usually gray or brown with spotted or streaky patterns that create a camouflage effect, allowing the owl to blend in with its surroundings. This is useful when owls are sleeping during the day. The owls avoid being noticed by predators such as hawks. Male and female owls usually look alike but females are often are slightly larger.

The heaviest owl is the Eurasian eagle-owl, which weighs 9.25 pounds (4.2 kilograms). At 28 inches (71 centimeters), however, it is a little shorter in length than the great gray owl, which measures 33 inches (84 centimeters) long. The smallest owl is the elf owl, which weighs 1.4 ounces (40 grams) and is about 5 inches (13 centimeters) long.

GEOGRAPHIC RANGE

Owls are found on every continent except Antarctica. The tropics support the greatest variety of owl species.

HABITAT

The vast majority of owl species are forest dwellers. Few species live at high elevations or in very dry habitats. Most owls are sensitive to disturbance, but a few species adapt well to living among humans in suburban or urban areas. The eastern screech-owl is a good example. Members of the group called fishing owls are unusual for their habit of living near forest streams or in mangrove swamps and feeding mostly on fish. Only a few owl species undergo true migrations. Most species live in the same place year round. In winters when populations of small rodents such as lemmings or voles are low, northern owls may leave their usual home ranges and invade southern regions.

DIET

All owls are carnivores. They catch small animals with their feet, kill them with a bite to the neck, and swallow them head-first. Most owls hunt from a raised perch. They sit, watch, and listen, then swoop or glide to their prey. At the last minute, they swing their legs forward and spread their talons to strike. Very large owls (such as eagle-owls) take medium-sized mammals such as rabbits, skunks, and monkeys. Medium-sized owls take mostly small mammals, such as voles, rats, mice, and shrews. Small owls feed mostly on insects along with other invertebrates such as snails, spiders, scorpions, moths, or crickets. Many owls occasionally take bats, birds, small reptiles, and amphibians in addition to their preferred prey. Many species cache (KASH), or store, extra prey to eat later. In cold climates cached prey may freeze. The owl just sits on it to thaw it. Owls swallow their prey whole but cannot digest hard bones, fur, and feathers. These materials are later coughed up in a neat package called an owl pellet.

BEHAVIOR AND REPRODUCTION

Most owls are active at night and sleep by day. Usually owls roost in sheltered spots—thick foliage or a branch close to a tree trunk. Some people think owls are "tame" because roosting owls may allow humans to come quite close. Actually, this behavior is an adaptation for avoiding detection by predators. If they're disturbed, owls pull their feathers in tight to look slim and lean close to the tree trunk to avoid being noticed. A few species are active by day, notably the snowy owl. This species lives in the Arctic, where daylight lasts twenty-four hours in the breeding season.

Because owls are active at night, they depend more on their ears than their eyes to communicate with other owls. Males mostly use vocalizations (sounds), rather than colorful feathers or flight displays, to get a female's attention. Owls also call to defend their territory and to stay in touch with each other. In most species, both sexes vocalize but the male calls more than the female.

Most owls are solitary. They hunt and roost alone, except during the breeding season. Most owls breed just once a year. They do not build their own nests. The smallest owls often nest in abandoned woodpecker holes. Larger owls use old crow or raptor nests, the top of a snag (a dead tree, standing, with the top broken off), a tree hole, a natural cave, or an abandoned building. A few species nest on the ground, including snowy owls and short-eared owls. Burrowing owls nest underground in prairie dog, badger, or ground squirrel burrows. Female owls do not gather any nest material. Eggs are laid on bare ground or the floor of the tree cavity.

A male and female owl bond by preening each other, straightening and cleaning their feathers. In many species, the male offers a gift of food to his mate. Owl eggs are white and more round than oval. A typical clutch ranges in size from two to four eggs for small owls to five to eight eggs for larger owls. In most species, the female lays one egg a day until the clutch is complete. But where many songbirds start to incubate the eggs after the clutch is complete, female owls start incubating with the first egg. That means the owlets hatch on different days and are of different sizes. Often, the youngest, smallest nestlings do not survive.

OWLS AND PEOPLE

Owls have always inspired the human imagination. A Paleolithic rock painting of an owl is one of the oldest known human drawings. The Bible describes owls as birds of waste places and forbids eating them. In many cultures owls are considered bad omens or creatures of the underworld, probably because they fly at night and have spooky-sounding calls. The sight or sound of an owl is thought to warn of death. This idea is seen repeatedly in the plays of William Shakespeare.

Not every culture has feared owls. In ancient Greece the owl was the symbol of Athena, the goddess of wisdom. In their nighttime activity, owls were thought to be like hard-working scholars. Owls continue to be a symbol of education in the United States in the twenty-first century.

CONSERVATION STATUS

As of 2003, the IUCN lists seven owl species as Critically Endangered, facing an extremely high risk of extinction, or dying out, in the wild; nine species as Endangered, facing a very high risk of extinction in the wild; and eleven species as Vulnerable, facing a high risk of extinction in the wild. A number of owl species occur on only one small island or in one small area. That makes these species particularly vulnerable to extinction.

In the United States two owl species are protected under the Endangered Species Act. The ferruginous pygmy-owl is listed as Endangered and the spotted owl is listed as Threatened.

Habitat loss because of logging or agriculture is the biggest problem for owls. Other causes of mortality include illegal shooting, collisions with cars and human-built structures, electrocution on power lines, and poisons used against rats and mice.

BIRDS OF PREY?

For a long time, owls were thought to be close relatives of birds in the order Falconiformes (the hawk-like birds). The two groups do have a lot in common. Both are hunters with excellent eyesight. They have strong legs and sharp talons for catching prey. They have hooked beaks for killing and eating their prey. The term "birds of prey" is still often used to describe the two groups. In 1985, however, researchers took a careful look at bird DNA. They decided owls are most closely related to birds in the order Caprimulgiformes, or nightjars. Besides the genetic evidence, there are other similarities between these two groups. Both are active at night, their voiceboxes are similar, and their feathers are arranged in the same way.

FOR MORE INFORMATION

Books:

BirdLife International. *Threatened Birds of the World*. Barcelona and Cambridge, U.K.: Lynx Edicions, 2000.

Duncan, James R. *Owls of the World: Their Lives, Behavior and Survival*. Buffalo, NY: Firefly Books, 2003.

Johnsgard, Paul A. *North American Owls: Biology and Natural History*. Washington, DC: Smithsonian Institution Press, 2002.

Kaufman, Kenn. *Lives of North American Birds*. New York: Houghton Mifflin Company, 1996.

König, Claus, Friedhelm Weick, and Jan-Hendrik Becking. *Owls: A Guide to the Owls of the World*. New Haven, CT: Yale University Press, 2002.

Web sites:

Lewis, Deane P. The Owl Pages. http://www.owlpages.com (accessed on June 25, 2004).

BARN OWLS
Tytonidae

Class: Aves
Order: Strigiformes
Family: Tytonidae
Number of species: 16 species

PHYSICAL CHARACTERISTICS

Like "typical" owls in the family Strigidae, barn owls have forward-facing eyes, excellent vision in dim light, and very sensitive ears. (Research shows that the common barn owl can locate prey by sound alone in complete darkness.) Tytonids differ from "typical" owls in having long, compressed bills, rather short tails, and rather long legs. The facial disk is heart-shaped instead of round. They lack the feather structures called ear tufts that many typical owls display. Their dark eyes are comparatively small and oval-shaped. The inner edge of the middle claw is serrated, like a comb. Barn owls use this claw to preen their feathers.

Most species in this group have a pale belly contrasting with a darker gray or brown back. The feathers show a beautiful all-over speckling. Females tend to be larger, heavier, and darker in color than males.

The smallest member of this family is the Oriental bay owl, just 9 inches (23 centimeters) long. Common barn owls vary widely in size, and some members of this species are also very small. They may weigh as little as 6.6 ounces (187 grams). The longest and heaviest barn owls are female Australian masked owls at 2.8 pounds (1.3 kilograms) and 22.4 inches (57 centimeters).

GEOGRAPHIC RANGE

Barn owls are widely distributed. The species for which the family is named, the barn owl, is the world's most widespread species of land bird. Barn owls are found on every continent

LIFE ON THE FARM

Barn owls seem to be declining in numbers in the United States, Britain, and Canada. The likely reason for these declines is the loss of farmland, which makes very good habitat for barn owls. Barns and silos provide nest sites, and the owls can hunt for rodents in nearby fields. In the last few decades, however, many farms have been converted to housing developments or industrial parks. To help owl populations, conservationists are putting up nest boxes for owls in some areas. The boxes look like jumbo birdhouses. One reason to help owls is that they provide free pest control. One study by the Connecticut Department of Environmental Protection reports a barn owl family will eat more than 1,000 rats and mice in one nesting season.

except Antarctica and on many islands. No members of the family are found in Earth's coldest regions, however. No barn owls live in the Arctic or in the northernmost parts of Europe, Asia, or North America. Barn owls are also absent from the driest desert regions such as the Sahara and the Middle East.

HABITAT

Barn owls need a mix of wooded areas and open space. They also require tree cavities, caves, or other protected areas for nest sites.

DIET

Barn owls eat mostly small mammals such as voles and mice. They will also take birds, reptiles, amphibians, and large insects, however. In Australia, where there are no native mammals, barn owls prey on small marsupials. Barn owl pellets have a distinctive dark coating of mucus.

BEHAVIOR AND REPRODUCTION

Most barn owls are solitary in their habits, but some of the smallest species will gather in groups to hunt and roost when prey is plentiful. Usually they hunt from perches, but some of the smallest species hunt on the wing. Barn owls are almost exclusively nocturnal. They return to their roosts at dawn, often calling as they do so. They sleep by day, usually balancing on one leg with the wings closed and hunched forward to hide the pale belly.

Large species defend large home ranges. Small species are less territorial and defend only a small area around the nest site. When confronted with an intruder, barn owls perform distinctive defensive displays. A disturbed owl will make bowing movements, tilting forward with the tail raised, wings spread to the sides, and head lowered and swinging from side to side. At the same time it hisses and snaps its bill. If the intruder doesn't back off, the owl may strike with one foot or even spray feces.

Many typical owls make hooting calls, but no barn owls hoot. Their calls sound like screams, screeches, twitters, and whistles. A courting pair will engage in a trilling duet.

Most barn owls nest in sheltered locations such as tree holes and abandoned buildings. Grass owls are the exception—they tunnel into tall grass. The female incubates the eggs and broods the hatchlings while the male brings food to her and her young. Barn owls in temperate climates typically raise one brood per year. Species in warmer climates may raise two to three broods per year. Clutch size varies from one or two in sooty owls to seven or eight in barn owls and grass owls. Females lay more eggs when prey is abundant. After leaving the nest, the owlets may depend on their parents for food for several more weeks to months.

BARN OWLS AND PEOPLE

With their pale feathers and eerie calls, barn owls are sometimes called "ghost owls" or "spirit owls." In many cultures, they are regarded as associates of witches. They have a long history of living in association with humans. Evidence from Pleistocene cave dwellings shows that owls and humans shared the same caves.

CONSERVATION STATUS

Three species are listed as Endangered, facing a very high risk of extinction, on the IUCN Red List, the Madagascar red owl, Africa bay owl, and the Taliabu masked owl. One barn owl species, the Minahassa masked owl, is listed as Vulnerable, facing a high risk of extinction.

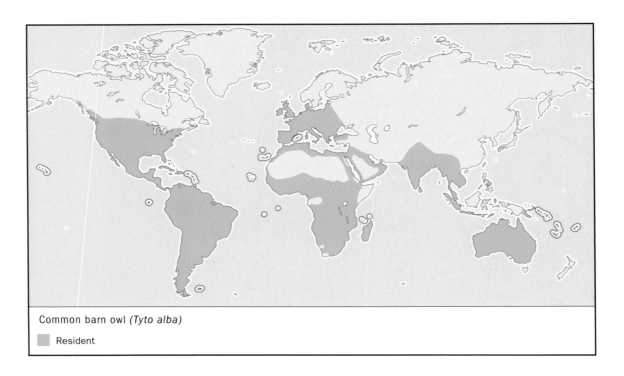

Common barn owl (Tyto alba)

▨ Resident

COMMON BARN OWL
Tyto alba

Physical characteristics: Sometimes called simply the barn owl, this species is widely distributed. Populations in different locations can be quite different in size and appearance. They range in length from 11 to 17 inches (29 to 44 centimeters) and vary in weight from 0.4 to 1.5 pounds (0.2 to 0.7 kilograms). The North American subspecies is the largest. The feathers are subtly colored but quite beautiful seen up close. They are mottled gray and buff-brown on the back and pale on the belly, with fine spots overall. Members of island populations tend to be darker in color than mainland populations. Males and females look alike.

Geographic range: This is the most widely distributed owl species. Barn owls occur on every continent except Antarctica.

Habitat: Barn owls prefer areas of open woods, grasslands, and brushy areas. Areas near cliffs offer nest sites. They will live near

humans on farms or in urban areas as long as there are nest sites (for example, barns, silos, or church steeples) and open space for hunting.

Diet: Barn owls take whatever prey is available, the right size, and active at night. They seem to choose the slowest and fattest species among all the possible prey, usually specializing in small rodents such as voles, mice, and shrews. Small birds, amphibians, reptiles, and fish are occasionally taken, and invertebrates such as insects are rarely eaten.

Though most owls are "sit and wait" predators, barn owls often hunt by flying low and slow over open ground. They use their sense of hearing more than sight to locate prey. They usually hunt alone, but if prey is plentiful, they may hunt in groups.

Barn owls are monogamous (muh-NAH-guh-mus). At the beginning of the breeding season, males make courtship flights, patrolling their territories while calling loudly. Sometimes a male and female will fly together, or the male will chase the female while both scream loudly. One courtship display is the moth flight. The male hovers in mid air in front of a female. Another is the in-and-out flight. The male flies into and out of the nest sight as if showing it off. The female shows her interest with a snoring call, and the male responds with a gift of food.

Barn owls adjust their nesting efforts to the amount of prey that is available. If food is plentiful, the female lays a large number of eggs and may even nest a second time in the same year. She lays one egg every two or three days till the clutch is complete but starts incubating the eggs right away. This means the first owlet may hatch two to three weeks before the last. Young owls leave the nest when they are fifty-six to sixty-two days old. A female may start to lay more eggs before the last owlet from her first clutch has fledged.

Barn owls and people: One nickname for the common barn owl is monkey-faced owl. Some people actually believed they were flying monkeys. Barn owls have been introduced to some islands as a form of natural pest control. Grape growers in California are among the farmers that now welcome barn owls to their properties by hanging up nesting boxes. The owls help to control rodent pests.

Conservation status: Barn owls in North America have been declining slightly in numbers for the past four decades. Similar small declines are documented in Canada, Britain and Europe. So far, wildlife experts are not concerned that the species is threatened. ∎

FOR MORE INFORMATION

Books:

BirdLife International. *Threatened Birds of the World.* Barcelona and Cambridge, U.K.: Lynx Edicions and BirdLife International, 2000.

Duncan, James R. *Owls of the World: Their Lives, Behavior and Survival.* Buffalo, NY: Firefly Books, 2003

Johnsgard, Paul A. *North American Owls: Biology and Natural History.* Washington, DC: Smithsonian Institution Press, 2002.

Kaufman, Kenn. *Lives of North American Birds.* New York: Houghton Mifflin Company, 1996.

König, Claus, Friedhelm Weick, and Jan-Hendrik Becking. *Owls: A Guide to the Owls of the World.* New Haven, CT: Yale University Press, 2002.

Web sites:

BirdLife International. http://www.birdlife.net (accessed on June 28, 2004).

Lewis, Deane P. The Owl Pages. http://www.owlpages.com (accessed on June 28, 2004).

family

phylum

class

subclass

order

monotypic order

suborder

▲ **family**

PHYSICAL CHARACTERISTICS

These owls are often called the "typical" owls. They have typical owl traits including a large, rounded head and forward-facing eyes set in a facial disk, an arrangement of feathers that focuses sound into the ears. They are adapted for night hunting, with eyes that see well in low-light conditions, very sensitive hearing, strong feet, and sharp talons (TAL-unz). Many members of this family have ear tufts on top of their heads. These are just feathers, not used for hearing. Typical owls differ from the family Tytonidae, barn owls, in several ways. Many have yellow eyes, and the facial disk is round rather than heart-shaped.

GEOGRAPHIC RANGE

Representatives of the family can be found on every continent except Antarctica. In contrast to tytonids, which are found only in regions where the climate is mild, some typical owls live in very cold climates.

HABITAT

Typical owls can be found in almost every type of habitat, but 95 percent are forest dwellers. The term "forest" covers a wide range of habitats, from tropical rainforest to boreal evergreen forest.

DIET

Small mammals such as voles are the most important food item for many typical owls. The type of prey taken varies with size. Small owls eat mostly insects but may also take small birds, reptiles, and amphibians. The largest owls, the eagle-owls, may take such large animals as rabbits, hares, and pheasants. The group called fishing owls eats fish almost exclusively.

BEHAVIOR AND REPRODUCTION

Most typical owls hunt by sitting on an elevated perch while watching and listening for prey. Exceptions to this hunting style include Northern hawk owls, which hunt like falcons, chasing other birds on the wing. Long-eared and short-eared owls patrol for prey by flying low and slowly over fields. In winter, great gray owls detect voles not by sight, but by the sounds they make under the snow, then plunge-dive. They can break through snow crusts thick enough to support a man.

Many typical owls make classic owl "hoo-hoo" vocalizations, but also use a variety of other vocalizations to communicate. Most typical owls are solitary night hunters. A few, such as long-eared owls, gather in groups in winter to roost. A few are active by day, including burrowing owls.

NEW OWLS DISCOVERED

Owls are not well studied because they fly at night, and many species live in remote places, far from human dwellings. Scientists have had some owl surprises in recent years. One species of barn owl, the Congo Bay owl, was thought to be extinct. Then it was rediscovered in 1996 in Rwanda. In 2001, researchers discovered an entirely new species, never before known to science, in Brazil. It is called the Pernambuco pygmy-owl. Yet another new species, the Sumba hawk owl, was also discovered in 2001, on the Indonesian island of Sumba. All three species live in areas where forest is being cut down, however. Conservationists hope the news of owl discoveries will not be followed by news of their extinction.

About 10 percent of all typical owls undergo true seasonal migration. The northern saw-whet owl is one example. Many species in northern regions move south in winters when their rodent prey are scarce.

Most strigids are monogamous (muh-NAH-guh-mus; having only one mate). In a few species (the boreal owl is one example), a male may take two mates simultaneously if food is plentiful. Most members of the group nest in tree cavities, shallow caves, or the abandoned nests of crows or hawks. A few species nest on the ground. Burrowing owls nest in the underground burrows of prairie dogs and other mammals.

The average clutch size is two to four, though eagle owls typically lay a single egg and burrowing owls can have clutches of ten or more when food is plentiful. The female incubates the eggs and broods the chicks while the male feeds the family. The young often leave the nest before they can fly to clamber around in the nest tree. At this stage they are called branchers.

OWLS AND PEOPLE

Through the ages, owls have been the subjects of myth, folklore, and art. People have used owls in different ways. Snowy owls are a subsistence food for Arctic people. Owl body parts are used by traditional healers in Southeast Asia. They have been revered in some cultures. In ancient Babylon, for example, pregnant women wore protective owl amulets. In many cultures, however, owls have been feared. The Swahili believed owls made children sick. Some Arab cultures believed owls were evil spirits that carried children off. In the twenty-first century, conservationists are working to overcome old superstitions and protect owls threatened by loss of habitat.

CONSERVATION STATUS

Six species in this family are considered Critically Endangered, facing an extremely high risk of extinction, six species are Endangered, facing a very high risk of extinction, and eight are Vulnerable, facing a high risk of extinction.

Eastern screech-owl *(Otus asio)*

☐ Resident

EASTERN SCREECH-OWL
Otus asio

Physical characteristics: Eastern screech-owls have ear tufts but often fold them flat, so they appear to have smooth, rounded heads. Individuals may be gray or rufous (red) in color. Rufous owls are more common in warm and moist climates such as the southern Appalachians. Gray owls are more common in northern regions and dry southern areas such as Texas. Research suggests gray birds survive better in heavy snow and cold temperatures.

Eastern screech-owl parents continue to feed their young for eight to ten weeks after the owlets fledge, grow feathers necessary for flying. (Joe McDonald/Bruce Coleman Inc. Reproduced by permission.)

Individuals range in length from 6.3 to 9.8 inches (16 to 25 centimeters). Females are slightly larger than males, and owls from northern regions tend to be larger than individuals in southern regions.

Geographic range: Eastern screech-owls are found throughout the eastern half of the United States and north into southern Canada.

Habitat: Screech-owls occupy a variety of habitats, from young to mature forests, and from lowlands and river valleys to mountain slopes. They also live alongside humans in suburbs and cities.

Diet: These small owls eat small prey, mostly invertebrates including insects, earthworms, and crayfish. Screech-owls in northern climates are more likely to take small mammals and songbirds.

Behavior and reproduction: The primary call is a distinctive, horse-like whinny that increases in pitch, then falls off gradually, ending with a trembling sound. When they are courting, males and females sing loud trilled duets.

Screech-owls usually nest in abandoned woodpecker holes. The female may lay two to six eggs. She incubates them for twenty-six to thirty-four days while the male brings food. The owlets fledge (grow feathers necessary for flying) twenty-five to twenty-seven days after hatching. Their parents continue to feed them for another eight to ten weeks.

Eastern screech-owls and people: Eastern screech-owls do well in suburban areas with mature trees and will use wooden nest boxes.

Conservation status: Populations tend to cycle naturally from high to low and back. Temporary declines are sometimes misinterpreted as evidence the species is in trouble. However, the IUCN does not consider this species to be threatened. ■

Barred eagle-owl (*Bubo sumatranus*)

▨ Resident

BARRED EAGLE-OWL
Bubo sumatranus

Physical characteristics: The dark back is marked with reddish brown bars, contrasting with the barred, grayish white belly. The eyes are brown and the beak and feet are yellow. Barred eagle-owls have very noticeable ear tufts.

The group called "eagle-owls" includes the largest owls in the world. This species is a fairly small member of the group, 15.7 to 18.1 inches long (40 to 46 centimeters), a little smaller than the great horned owl.

Geographic range: Southern Myanmar, peninsular Thailand, south to Sumatra and Bangka Island.

Habitat: Tropical forests intersected by streams, secondary growth, plantations, and forested gardens.

Diet: Barred eagle-owls feed on large insects such as grasshoppers and beetles, along with small rodents, birds, and snakes.

Behavior and reproduction: The main call is a low-pitched "hoo." Pairs are thought to mate for life and may return to the same nest site year after year, often a natural tree cavity.

Barred eagle-owls and people: No particular significance to humans is known.

Conservation status: This species tolerates disturbed habitat and will nest around human homes. It is not considered threatened by the IUCN. ■

Barred eagle-owls live in tropical rainforests in Southeast Asia. (Illustration by Patricia Ferrer. Reproduced by permission.)

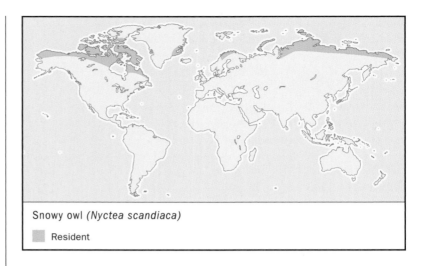

Snowy owl (*Nyctea scandiaca*)

Resident

SNOWY OWL
Nyctea scandiaca

Physical characteristics: This is the only mostly white owl. Males may be completely white; females have black bars on the back and belly. These heavy-bodied owls have very large, rounded heads and no ear tufts. The eyes are yellow and the dark beak may be hidden by feathers. Snowies are particularly well adapted to the cold. The legs and feet are completely covered with feathers. The feathers are unusually stiff, to keep out Arctic winds.

Geographic range: Snowy owls are found in a ring of habitat that circles the North Pole. In summer they breed on the tundra. In winter they may move as far south as the northern Great Plains of North America or north central Europe and Asia.

Habitat: Snowy owls nest on tundra. On their southward wanderings, they often frequent open, grassy areas such as airfields and golf courses.

Diet: Snowy owls feed almost exclusively on several kinds of Arctic voles and lemmings, species that undergo regular boom-and-bust population cycles. They sometimes take much larger prey, including ptarmigans and snowshoe hares, and often steal food from Arctic foxes. In a region where daylight can last for twenty-four hours during the summer months, they routinely hunt by day.

Behavior and reproduction: Snowy owls rarely vocalize outside of the breeding season. The typical call is a gruff, low-pitched hoot. They nest right on the ground, usually on a raised mound. A typical clutch has five eggs. The female incubates the eggs for thirty-one to thirty-three days while the male feeds her. The young leave the nest after twenty to twenty-eight days but cannot fly well until they are about fifty days old.

Snowy owls and people: In years that snowy owls wander south, their presence thrills bird watchers. A subsistence food for the Inuit, snowy owls may legally be hunted by all Alaska residents. In the twenty-first century, the snowy owl has been made popular by the success of the Harry Potter books and movies.

Conservation status: Snowy owls are not considered threatened by the IUCN, although populations in northern Europe seem to be declining somewhat. Populations are not well monitored. ◼

Snowy owls spend their summers on the tundra, and head south for the winter, to areas such as the Great Plains of North America. (Robert J. Huffman/Field Mark Publications. Reproduced by permission.)

FOR MORE INFORMATION

Books:

Birdlife International. *Handbook of the Birds of the World.* Vol. 5, *Barn-owls to Hummingbirds.* Barcelona: Lynx Edicions, 1992.

BirdLife International. *Threatened Birds of the World.* Barcelona and Cambridge, U.K.: Lynx Edicions and BirdLife International, 2000.

Duncan, James R. *Owls of the World: Their Lives, Behavior and Survival.* Buffalo, NY: Firefly Books, 2003.

Johnsgard, Paul A. *North American Owls: Biology and Natural History.* Washington, DC: Smithsonian Institution Press, 2002.

Kaufman, Kenn. *Lives of North American Birds.* New York: Houghton Mifflin Company, 1996.

König, Claus, Friedhelm Weick, and Jan-Hendrik Becking. *Owls: A Guide to the Owls of the World.* New Haven, CT: Yale University Press, 2002.

Web sites:

Lewis, Deane P. The Owl Pages. http://www.owlpages.com (accessed on June 27, 2004).

Class: Aves
Order: Caprimulgiformes
Number of families: 5 families

order
CHAPTER

PHYSICAL CHARACTERISTICS

The order Caprimulgiformes is known as nightjars and "night-jar" is also the name of the largest family in the order. An order consists of animals with similar characteristics. Caprimulgiformes have large heads, and their large eyes help them see at night. Also large is the gape, the width of the mouth when open. Around the mouths of some birds are whisker-like bristles. The birds have short legs, and many birds have one toe on each foot that points backward, forward, or away from the foot.

Caprimulgiformes have plain plumage. Adults' feathers are brown, gray, brownish yellow, and rufous, a reddish brown. Plumage is patterned, and this protective coloration helps Caprimulgiformes blend in with trees and hide from predators. Members of this order are also known as night birds because they are nocturnal, active at night.

The nightjar family, Caprimulgidae, consists of nineteen genera and seventy-seven species. Birds range in length from 6 to 16 inches (15 to 40 centimeters) and weigh from 0.7 to 6.6 ounces (20 to 188 grams). Members of this family have long wings and tails. They do not have bristles around their mouths. Furthermore, on the middle toe is a claw that is serrated, segments of the claw resemble the teeth of a comb.

The oilbird family, Steatornithidae, has one genus and one species. The birds have hooked bills and are about 17 to 19 inches (43 to 49 centimeters) long. They weigh from 13 to 16 ounces (375 to 455 grams). They are similar to nightjars, and have long wings and tails.

The frogmouth family, Podargidae, consists of two genera and thirteen species. The family name comes from the frogmouth's huge gape and the large beak, which resemble the mouth of a frog. Birds range in length from 7.5 to 24 inches (19 to 60 centimeters) and weigh from 1.5 to 23.6 ounces (43 to 670 grams). Wings and tails are rounded.

The owlet-nightjar family, Aegothelidae, is sometimes called the owlet-frogmouth family. The family consists of one genus and eight species. Owlet-nightjars range in length from 7 to 12 inches (18 to 30 centimeters) and weigh from 1 to 3.5 ounces (29 to 98 grams). Birds' eyes face forward, and the gapes are as wide as birds' heads. Owlet-nightjar wings and tails are long.

The potoo family, Nyctibiidae, consists of one genus and seven species. Birds range in length from 8 to 23 inches (21 to 57 centimeters) and weigh from 1.6 to 2.2 ounces (46 to 624 grams). Birds resemble frogmouths, but are thinner and have smaller bills. Wings and tails are long.

GEOGRAPHIC RANGE

Nightjars, the largest family in the order Caprimulgiformes, are located throughout much of the world. There are twenty-five Caprimulgidae species in Africa, and nightjar species live in countries in North and South America, Europe, Asia, and Australia. These birds are not found in the Arctic and Antarctic.

Oilbirds are found in Central and South America. They live in countries including Panama and Bolivia. Birds also range in Trinidad and Tobago.

Frogmouth species live in Asian countries including India, Vietnam, Java, and the Philippines. They also range in Australia and South Pacific countries including Tasmania, New Guinea, and the Solomon Islands.

Owlet-nightjars range in the South Pacific on Australia, Tasmania, New Caledonia, northern Moluccas, the Solomon Islands, and New Guinea.

Potoos live in Central and South America, and are found in countries from Mexico to Uruguay. They also range in Hispaniola and Jamaica.

HABITAT

Habitats are as varied as the families in this large order. Some members of the nightjar family live in rainforests, where heavy rainfall throughout the year produces abundant growth. They also range in grasslands and savannas, where there are fewer trees. Nightjars also live in semi-arid deserts and forests.

Oilbirds live in caves along coasts and in the mountains. They range in forests including coniferous or evergreen forests, where trees do not shed leaves. Frogmouths live in rainforests and other wooded areas. Owlet-nightjars live in tropical forests, savannas, open woodland, and scrub, areas with under-sized vegetation. Potoos live in tropical forests and in trees in savannas.

DIET

Oilbirds eat fruit that they pluck from trees. All other caprimulgiforms eat arthropods, animals with no backbones. These include insects, spiders, and millipedes. Larger birds eat vertebrates, creatures with backbones, like frogs, mice, small birds, and bats.

BEHAVIOR AND REPRODUCTION

Caprimulgiformes are nocturnal, meaning they are active at night. Some families are also crepuscular (kri-PUS-kyuh-lur), becoming active at twilight. Birds in this order communicate with calls.

Most species are monogamous (muh-NAH-guh-mus), mating with one partner. Nightjars do not build nests, and the female lays one to two eggs. She and the male incubate the eggs, sitting on them until they hatch. In some species, both parents feed the young birds. Female oilbirds have a clutch of two to four eggs, and both parents incubate them. Female frogmouths lay from one to three eggs, and both parents incubate. Owlet-nightjars lay three to four eggs. Females incubate and both parents feed the young. Potoos usually have a clutch of one egg. Both parents incubate and care for the young.

While frogmouths, owlet-nightjars, oilbirds, and potoos live their lives in one area, some nightjar species travel great distances. European nightjars breed in Europe and migrate to Africa for the winter.

CAPRIMULGIFORMES AND PEOPLE

In the Caprimulgiformes order, some family names reflect the relationship between birds and people. Nightjars have been called "goatsuckers" because people believed that the nocturnal birds flew down and sucked the milk from goats and cows. When animals died, people mistakenly blamed the birds. However, nightjars do not drink milk.

The name "nightjar" comes from Europe. The bird's loud call can last several minutes. Since birds are nocturnal, their noise "jarred" or startled sleeping people and woke them up.

Furthermore, oilbirds received their names because the birds eat fruit containing oil and fat. In the past, people captured the birds and boiled them to collect the oil. They used the oil for cooking or as fuel to light their lamps. Now people are interested in observing oilbirds. People visit caves where these unique birds roost during the day.

CONSERVATION STATUS

There is concern about the future of some Caprimulgiformes species, according to the World Conservation Union (IUCN). These species are threatened by loss of habitat as forests are cleared for farming and development.

The Puerto Rican nightjar is Critically Endangered, facing an extremely high risk of extinction in the wild in the immediate future. However, conservation efforts could result in the ranking being changed to Endangered, facing a very high risk of extinction in the near future.

The Itombwe nightjar and the white-winged nightjar are Endangered. Only one specimen of the Itombwe nightjar was found in the Democratic Republic of the Congo. White-winged nightjars live in Bolivia and Brazil. When this species was discovered in Paraguay, it was a sign that the population was larger. The species ranking was changed from Critically Endangered to Endangered.

Two Indonesian species, the satanic-eared nightjar and Bonaparte's nightjar, are Vulnerable, facing a high risk of extinction in the wild.

FOR MORE INFORMATION

Books:

Stuart, Chris and Tilde. *Birds of Africa From Seabirds to Seed Eaters* Cambridge, MA: The MIT Press, 1999.

GUIDED BY ECHOES

Oilbirds move safely in dark caves by making clicking sounds. The birds listen to the echoes made when the sounds bounce off surfaces like cave walls. Oilbirds know to fly away from the echoes or they will crash into something. The guiding process oilbirds use is called echolocation. Bats, porpoises, and whales also use echolocation.

Periodicals:

Pratt, Thane K. "Evidence For A Previously Unrecognized Species of Owlet-Nightjar." *The Auk* (January 2000): 1–11.

Web sites:

"Australian Owlet-Nightjar." Australian Museum Online. http://www.amonline.net.au/factsheets/owlet_nightjar.htm (accessed on June 1, 2004).

"White-throated nightjar." Environmental Protection Agency/Queensland Parks and Wildlife Service. http://www.epa.qld.gov.au/nature_conservation/wildlife/nocturnal_animals/birds/whitethroated_nightjar/ (accessed on June 1, 2004).

OILBIRD

Steatornithidae

Class: Aves

Order: Caprimulgiformes

Family: Steatornithidae

One species: Oilbird (*Steatornis caripensis*)

family

CHAPTER

PHYSICAL CHARACTERISTICS

Oilbird plumage (feathers) is the color of cinnamon, and the bird's reddish brown feathers are dotted with white spots. The long tail is colored by faint black bars, lines of color. Males and female birds have similar coloring, and females are slightly smaller than males.

The oilbird is the only member of the Steatornithidae family. While they resemble owls, order Strigiformes, oilbirds belong to the Caprimulgiformes order. Like other families in the Caprimulgiformes order, the oilbird has a large gape, the width of the mouth when it's open.

Birds in the Caprimulgiformes and Strigiformes orders are nocturnal, active at night, and their large eyes provide the strong vision needed to see at night. Both owls and oilbirds have hooked bills, but the owl has sharp claws on its feet. The owl uses these talons (TAL-unz) to capture prey, animals hunted as food. Oilbirds have small feet and eat only fruit.

Oilbirds eat fruit that is rich in fat and oil, which provides the energy needed to fly. When chicks are fed these fruits before they are able to fly, they become very fat, often growing larger than the adults. While adult birds weigh from 13 to 16 ounces (375 to 455 grams), a seventy-day-old oilbird chick weighs approximately 21 ounces (600 grams). As the young bird develops, the parents feed it less often. The combination of less food and growing into adulthood causes the oilbird to lose weight. Oilbirds got their name from the fact that in the past chicks were captured and boiled down in order to make oil.

phylum

class

subclass

order

monotypic order

suborder

▲ **family**

Adult oilbirds measure 17 to 19 inches (43 to 49 centimeters) in length. The bird has blue eyes and a yellow beak with whisker-like bristles on both sides. The oilbird uses its bill to pluck fruit from trees.

Since oilbirds have short feet, they do not perch or stand on trees. Instead, the bird rests, which is like sitting. At rest, the head of the oilbird is lower than its tail. Furthermore, their feet are so weak that they do very little walking, instead they fly to get from one place to another.

Their wingspan, the distance between the fully spread wings, is approximately 37.5 inches (95 centimeters). The wings are wide and slotted so that the oilbird can fly slowly while carrying loads into the dark caves where they live during the day. At night, oilbirds use their powerful wings to fly as far as 75 miles (120 kilometers) in search of food.

GEOGRAPHIC RANGE

Oilbirds live mainly in South America and are found in the countries of Guyana, Trinidad, Venezuela, Colombia, Ecuador, Peru, Brazil, and Bolivia. Oilbirds also range in the Central American countries of Costa Rica and Panama, and the islands of Tobago and Aruba.

HABITAT

Oilbirds live in caves along coasts and in the mountains. Birds make their homes in areas near coniferous or evergreen forests, where trees do not undergo seasonal changes. While generally found in caves, oilbirds also live inside gorges, deep, narrow areas.

DIET

Oilbirds are frugivores, animals that eat fruit. Oilbirds eat the fruits of palm trees, laurel trees, and avocado trees.

Groups of oilbirds forage at night, looking for food. They fly down, pluck fruit from the trees, and swallow it whole. Oilbirds eat the soft pulp inside the fruit. During the day, birds digest their food and then regurgitate (re-GER-jih-tate) the

seeds. Regurgitation is the process of vomiting, removing food in the stomach through the mouth.

BEHAVIOR AND REPRODUCTION

The Spanish name for oilbird is *guácharo*, meaning "one who cries." Oilbirds can be noisy. If people invade their caves, the birds will shriek or squawk loudly to warn other oilbirds and frighten the invaders. The oilbird family is social, and colonies, groups of birds, live together in caves.

A large cave in Caribe, Venezuela, is said to house about ten thousand oilbirds. A protected population lives in Dunston Cave in Trinidad's Asa Wright Nature Centre. The center tracks the bird population by doing a bird count several times each year. The bird census in November of 1998 was 119 adults. In June of 2003, there were 120 adults, twenty chicks, and two eggs. The following December, the center counted 154 adult oilbirds.

Oilbirds become active at twilight, and the colony flies out at night to forage for food. Birds usually look for fruit in pairs and groups. Their vision is strong enough to hunt for food at night. However, the birds rely on sound to guide themselves inside dark caves.

Oilbirds enter the cave and make clicking sounds at a frequency low enough to be heard by people. They click at the

Oilbird *(Steatornis caripensis)*

▨ Resident

rate of ten to twelve clicks per second, with the number of clicks increasing as oilbirds get closer to an obstacle. Oilbirds know to click faster because they listen to the echo of the click as the sound bounces off surfaces like walls and rocks. Their brain compares the echo with the sound of the original click. The brain analyzes how close the echo is, and the birds adjust their flight so they will not crash into something. This navigation system, called echolocation (eck-oh-loh-KAY-shun), is also used by porpoises, whales, and bats.

During the day, oilbirds roost, rest in caves. Oilbirds are thought to be monogamous (muh-NAH-guh-mus), with a single male and single female bird staying together permanently. The two birds roost together on flat surfaces like ledges.

Oilbirds often breed during the rainy season, but this may vary by location. In Venezuela's Caribe Cave, females lay eggs in April and May. The timing is believed to be connected with the abundance of laurel tree fruit. In Trinidad, the population of nestlings, birds without feathers, is highest in May and June.

Breeding oilbirds build nests far inside caves and away from predators. Nests are usually on ledges located 33 to 66 feet (10 to 20 meters) above the floor of a cave. The oilbird nest resembles a saucer and is made of material including regurgitated seeds and fruit pulp. Birds use their saliva as a glue to hold the nest together.

Female oilbirds lay a clutch of two to four white eggs. Both parents incubate the eggs, sitting on them until they hatch in thirty-two to thirty-five days. The chicks weigh from 0.4 to 0.5 ounces (12 to 15.5 grams). They are born with their eyes closed and have few feathers. Parents feed the chicks fruit, and the young birds become plump. They weigh almost twice as much as adult birds at seventy days old. The nestlings have feathers, but their tails and wings are smaller than adults. At they grow into adulthood, their feathers develop and they lose weight. Young oilbirds leave the nest when they are 110 to 120 days old.

OILBIRDS AND PEOPLE

Oilbirds were once hunted as food or a source of oil. In the twenty-first century, the birds are legally protected in many countries, which means that it is against the law to injure or kill oilbirds in those nations. Furthermore, oilbirds are a tourist attraction. People vacation and visit oilbird caves in places like Caribe, Venezuela, and Trinidad.

CONSERVATION STATUS

Oilbirds are not in danger of extinction, dying out. However, they may become endangered if forests are cut down, since trees provide the only source of food for these fruit-eating birds.

FOR MORE INFORMATION

Web sites:

"Oilbirds." Asa Wright Nature Centre & Lodge. http://www.asawright.org/ nature/oilbirds.html (accessed on June 1, 2004).

Querna, Betsy. "Native Son Captures Beauty of Trinidad's 'Eden.'" National Geographic Today. http://news.nationalgeographic.com/news/2001/05/0508_trinidadphotographer.html (accessed on June 1, 2004).

Thomas, Betsy T. "Family STEATORNITHIDAE (OILBIRD)" *Handbook of the Birds of the World.* Online at http://www.hbw.com/hbw/volume5/famil501.html (accessed on June 1, 2004).

FROGMOUTHS
Podargidae

Class: Aves
Order: Caprimulgiformes
Family: Podargidae
Number of species: 13 species

PHYSICAL CHARACTERISTICS

Frogmouths received their name because their large beaks look like the mouths of frogs. Like others in the order Caprimulgiformes, frogmouths have large heads and large eyes. Members of this order are nocturnal, and their large eyes help the birds see at night. Their middle toe is longer than their other toes. Unlike other Caprimulgiformes, frogmouths do not have a toe on each foot that is serrated, separated into parts like the teeth of a comb.

Frogmouths have been said to resemble owls. While both owls and frogmouths are nocturnal, active at night, and have large eyes, there are some differences. Frogmouths have wide, curved bills. Owls have short, hooked bills. Frogmouths have short legs and small feet. Frogmouths do not have talons, the sharp claws that characterize birds of prey like owls.

Prey is the animal or plant that predators hunt for food. The bill and mouth help frogmouths capture food. Their wide-bill reveals a large gape, open mouth. Around the bill are bristles. These whisker-like hairs are believed to guide the prey into the bird's mouth.

Frogmouths have soft plumage, feathers, and weigh from 1.5 to 23.6 ounces (43 to 670 grams).

There are three species in the Australian frogmouth genus (JEE-nus; group of related animals within a family), *Podargus*. Feather colors include various shades of brown and gray. Patterns in the plumage such as white spots and black streaks help to camouflage birds. With this protective coloring, birds blend

phylum

class

subclass

order

monotypic order

suborder

▲ **family**

in with the trees where they perch. Birds range in length from 12.8 to 15.2 inches (32 to 38 centimeters). Their tails and wings are long.

The remaining ten species belong to the Asian frogmouth genus, *Batrachostomus*. Plumage is mostly brown on males of some species. Females are bright rufous, reddish brown. The Asian frogmouths are smaller than Australian frogmouths. The length of Asian frogmouths ranges from 9.2 to 16 inches (23 to 40 centimeters.) Most Asian species have wider bills and longer tails than their Australian relatives. Their wings are more rounded than Australian frogmouths.

GEOGRAPHIC RANGE

Australian frogmouths live in Australia, New Guinea and surrounding islands, Tasmania, and the Solomon Islands. Asian frogmouths live in Asian countries including India, Vietnam, Sri Lanka, the Philippines, Borneo, and Java.

HABITAT

Frogmouths live in a range of habitats where there are trees. Some species live in rainforests where heavy rain produces plenty of trees. Other birds live in grassland and scrub areas where there are fewer trees. Species live in plantations, where people plant trees, and birds also live in neighborhoods.

DIET

Frogmouths are insectivores, insect eaters. Their diet includes caterpillars, beetles, and millipedes, insects with many legs. Some species eat spiders, frogs, and mice. They fly to the ground to capture food or chase after flying prey like moths.

BEHAVIOR AND REPRODUCTION

Frogmouths are crepuscular (kri-PUS-kyuh-lur) and nocturnal, meaning they become active at twilight, just before dark, and in the evening. They rest in trees during the day and hunt for food at night. Birds roost in trees during the day, camouflaged (KAM-uh-flajd) by their color. Since birds hide so well, there is still a lot to learn about some species of frogmouths.

Australian frogmouths build platform-like nests made of sticks. Nests are located in trees, and female Australian frogmouths lay from one to three eggs. The female sits on the eggs, incubating them until they hatch. Both parents feed the chicks.

The Asian frogmouths build a small nest on a branch or tree stem. The nest is constructed of soft feathers called down. Spider webs and tiny lichen plants are placed around the nest to camouflage it. Female Asian frogmouths lay one egg. In some species, the male incubates the egg, sitting on it during the day.

FROGMOUTHS AND PEOPLE

For the most part, frogmouths remain hidden from people and have little relationship with them.

CONSERVATION STATUS

Although frogmouths are not in danger of dying out, loss of habitat could cause a decrease in some frogmouth populations. According to the World Conservation Union (IUCN), changes such as deforestation, cutting down trees, could have an effect on species including the large frogmouth, Gould's frogmouth, and the Bornean frogmouth.

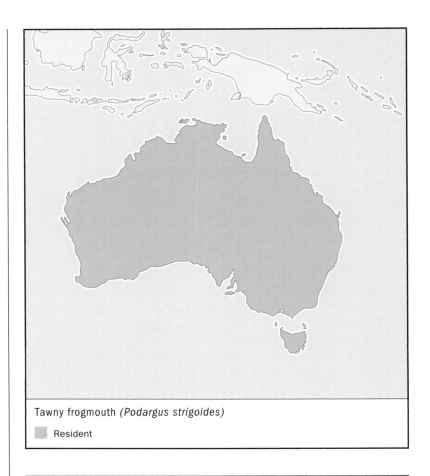

Tawny frogmouth *(Podargus strigoides)*

▨ Resident

SPECIES ACCOUNT

TAWNY FROGMOUTH
Podargus strigoides

Physical characteristics: Tawny is a brownish yellow color, and this frogmouth species has variations of those colors in their patterned plumage. Like other members of the Caprimulgiformes order, feather colors blend in with the color of trees. This form of camouflage is known as protective coloration.

The upper feathers of male tawny frogmouths are usually gray with black streaks. Lower plumage is a lighter gray, with black streaks and white bars. There may be various shades of brown in the plumage. Female tawny frogmouths have more brown and rufous in their plumage.

Tawny frogmouths have yellow eyes and light brown bills surrounded by bristles. The birds have small legs and feet. The middle toe of each foot is longer than other toes. Tawny frogmouths range in length from 13.5 to 21 inches (34 to 53 centimeters). They weigh from 6 ounces to 1.5 pounds (180 to 670 grams).

Both tawny frogmouth parents incubate their eggs, and both parents feed the chicks. (© M.P. Kahl/VIREO. Reproduced by permission.)

Geographic range: Tawny frogmouths are found in Australia and Tasmania.

Habitat: Tawny frogmouths live in all Australian habitats except rainforests where heavy rain produces an abundance of trees that do not shed leaves and deserts where there are no trees. They can be found in grassland areas where there are few trees, deciduous forests where trees shed leaves, plantations of trees planted by people, and tree groves. Tawny frogmouths also live in the gardens of suburban neighborhoods.

Diet: Tawny frogmouths eat insects, worms, slugs, and snails. They also eat frogs, small mammals, reptiles, and birds. The choice of food for these nocturnal birds is based on what prey they can find at night.

Tawny frogmouths usually get their prey by swooping down, flying quickly from their tree perches. Birds use their strong bills to capture prey and then swallow it.

Hungry tawny frogmouths may also fly from their perches and try to capture flying insects like moths. This chase in the air is not just dangerous for the prey, which could be captured in flight. The tawny frogmouth may chase insects illuminated by the car headlights. While the lights help the predator see its prey, the birds often collide with the cars and die.

Behavior and reproduction: Tawny frogmouths usually breed from August to December. However, birds in dry areas may breed after heavy rains. Birds build a platform nest of loose sticks in the fork of a tree branch. The female lays two or three eggs. Both parents incubate the eggs. The male usually incubates during the day. The male may do this because the female is more colorful and would be seen by predators during daylight.

Eggs hatch in about thirty days. Both parents feed the chicks. The young birds fledge, grow their feathers, after thirty to thirty-five days. Tawny frogmouths usually only breed once a year. However, female birds in southern Australia sometimes have two broods, sets of chicks.

Tawny frogmouths and people: People driving at night may unintentionally kill tawny frogmouths that fly in front of their car while hunting flying insects.

Conservation status: Tawny frogmouths are not in danger of extinction, dying out. ■

FOR MORE INFORMATION

Web sites:

"Red List Text." BirdLife International. http://www.birdlife.org/datazone/downloads/red_list.txt (accessed on June 5, 2004).

"Tawny Frogmouth." Australian Museum Online. http://www.amonline.net.au/factsheets/tawny_frogmouth.htm (accessed on June 1, 2004).

"Tawny Frogmouth." Environmental Protection Agency/Queensland Parks and Wildlife Service. http://www.epa.qld.gov.au/nature_conservation/wildlife/nocturnal_animals/birds/tawny_frogmouth/ (accessed on June 1, 2004).

"Tawny Frogmouth." Honolulu Zoo. http://www.honoluluzoo.org/tawny_frogmouth.htm (accessed on June 1, 2004).

OWLET-NIGHTJARS
Aegothelidae

Class: Aves
Order: Caprimulgiformes
Family: Aegothelidae
Number of species: 7 species

PHYSICAL CHARACTERISTICS

The name "owlet-nightjar" refers to the characteristics that these birds share with owls, members of the Strigiformes order, and with nightjars, other members of the Caprimulgiformes order. Owlet-nightjars and other members of this order have large heads and large eyes that provide strong vision at night.

Owlet-nightjars also look somewhat like small owls. Both owlet-nightjars and owls have long, narrow tails and wings. The eyes of owlet-nightjars and owls face forward like a human's eyes do. The owl's eyes are in a facial disk, an arrangement of facial feathers that focuses sounds to its ears. The round shape of the owl's face is very clear; the facial disk is not as clear on the owlet-nightjar.

Owlet-nightjars have short legs, a characteristic of the Caprimulgiformes order. However, their legs are not as short of those of other bird families in this order. Furthermore, owlet-nightjars have long toes and claws on their feet, which is similar to the owls, who have sharp claws called talons (TAL-unz). Some other families in the Caprimulgiformes order have a toe that is serrated like the teeth of a comb.

Frogmouths have wide, curved bills, and owls have a short, hooked bill. Owlet-nightjars have tiny bills surrounded by whisker-like bristles. Their small bill opens to a gape, width of the open mouth, which is as wide as their head.

All members of the owlet-nightjar family have dark eyes and soft plumage, feathers, in various shades of brown. Other plumage colors include gray, tan, and rufous, a reddish brown color. Feathers are patterned with streaks of color. Owlet-nightjars range from 7 to 12 inches (18 to 30 centimeters) in length. They weigh from 1 to 3.5 ounces (29 to 98 grams).

Little is known about some owlet-nightjar species because the birds are nocturnal and remain hidden during the day. However, researchers have been able to observe the Australian owlet-nightjar. Females are usually rufous and males are gray. Both have paler coloring on their undersides. There are pale black bars on the undersides, and they have two black stripes on their heads. Australian owlet-nightjars are 8.3 to 10 inches long (20 to 23 centimeters) and weigh 1.4 to 2.1 ounces (39 to 60 grams).

GEOGRAPHIC RANGE

Owlet-nightjars live in Australia, Moluccas, New Guinea and nearby islands, Tasmania, and New Caledonia.

HABITAT

Owlet-nightjars live in various types of forests. Species in New Guinea range in rainforests, where rain throughout the year produces abundant growth. Owlet-nightjar species live in mountain forests, and in scrubland where there are fewer trees.

DIET

Owlet-nightjars are insectivores, animals that eat insects. Their diet also includes small invertebrates, spineless creatures like millipedes and spiders. The mountain owlet-nightjar of New Guinea eats insects and earthworms.

The diets of some owlet-nightjar species are not known. The birds remain hidden from people during the day and are not always seen at night when they hunt for food.

Owlet-nightjars usually hunt and catch their prey by flying from their tree perches to the ground. Sometimes the owlet-nightjars chase and catch food while flying. The birds catch prey with their bills and swallow it whole.

BEHAVIOR AND REPRODUCTION

Australian owlet-nightjars hunt for food within a specific territory. Birds usually pair up to forage, look for food, at night. During the day, birds remain hidden in nests.

Owlet-nightjars are hole-nesters, building nests in holes in trees and openings in rocks.

Australian owlet-nightjars breed from July through December. The male and female birds build a nest out of green leaves. They build the nest in openings such as the hollow of a tree or the crevice in a rock. The female lays two to five eggs in the nest. Both parents incubate the eggs, sitting on them to keep them warm. The eggs hatch after about four weeks. Owlet-nightjar chicks stay in the nest for about three to five weeks. These owlet-nightjars have one brood, set of chicks, each year.

Threats to owlet-nightjars include predators like domestic cats that hunt the birds and eat them. In addition, when owlet-nightjars hunt for food, they may be killed by drivers who do not see the birds flying at night.

OWLET-NIGHTJARS AND PEOPLE

Owlet-nightjars have little contact with people.

CONSERVATION STATUS

The New Caledonian owlet-nightjar is Critically Endangered, facing an extremely high risk of extinction in the wild, according to the World Conservation Union (IUCN). The New Caledonian owlet-nightjar population was thought to be extinct.

The New Caledonian owlet-nightjar was identified in 1880 when a specimen, a single bird, was collected. No other birds were seen and the New Caledonian owlet-nightjar was declared extinct. However, the species had not died out. A New Caledonian owlet-nightjar was seen in 1998, and the conservation status was changed.

Australian owlet-nightjars live throughout Australia and New Guinea, are not considered endangered.

Other species hide so well that it is not known whether they are endangered. However, owlet-nightjar populations will be affected if habitat is lost due to deforestation, the removal of trees from forests.

Feline owlet-nightjar (*Aegotheles insignis*)

▨ Resident

FELINE OWLET-NIGHTJAR
Aegotheles insignis

Physical characteristics: Feline owlet-nightjars look somewhat like cats. Their faces have a feline shape. Tufts of feathers above the eyes look like cats' ears, and they have whiskery bristles around the bill. Feline owlet-nightjars have long feathers that appear fluffy. Plumage color ranges from rufous to brown. Feather patterns include brown and black vermicular, twisted, lines and white spots on the body. There are two white stripes on the head, and birds have white bars on their tails.

Feline owlet-nightjars are about 12 inches (30 centimeters) long. They weigh from 2.1 to 3.5 ounces (59 to 98 grams).

Geographic range: Feline owlet-nightjars live in New Guinea.

Habitat: Feline owlet-nightjars live in montane, or mountain, rainforests. The trees are evergreen, and do not change with the seasons.

Diet: Feline owlet-nightjars eat beetles and other insects.

Behavior and reproduction: There is no information available regarding feline owlet-nightjars' behavior or breeding and nesting patterns.

Feline owlet-nightjars and people: There is no known relationship between feline owlet-nightjars and people. However, research may change that and provide additional information about feline owlet-nightjars.

Conservation status: Feline owlet-nightjars are not in danger of extinction.   ■

Feline owlet-nightjars live in the mountain rainforests of New Guinea, and feed on beetles and other insects.
(© W. Peckover/VIREO. Reproduced by permission.)

FOR MORE INFORMATION

Periodicals:

Brigham, R. Mark, Gerhard Körtner, Tracy A. Maddocks, and Fritz Geiser. "Seasonal Use of Torpor by Free-Ranging Australian Owlet-Nightjars." *Physiological and Biochemical Zoology* (September/October 2000): 613–620.

Pratt, Thane K. "Evidence For a Previously Unrecognized Species of Owlet-Nightjar." *The Auk* (January 2000): 1–11.

Web sites:

"Australian Owlet-Nightjar." Australian Museum Online. http://www.amonline.net.au/factsheets/owlet_nightjar.htm (accessed on June 1, 2004).

"New Caledonian Owlet-Nightjar (*Aegotheles savesi*)." BirdLife International. http://www.birdlife.org/datazone/search/species_search.html?action=SpcHTMDetails.asp&sid=2328&m=0 (accessed on June 5, 2004).

family
CHAPTER

phylum

class

subclass

order

monotypic order

suborder

▲ **family**

PHYSICAL CHARACTERISTICS

Like other members of the Caprimulgiformes order, the potoo (poe-TOO) has a large head and large eyes that provide the stronger vision needed for birds that are active at night. Caprimulgiformes have large gapes, which is the width of the mouth when open. A large gape allows birds to catch prey, creatures like insects hunted for food. The potoo's gape is as wide as its head.

While most members of the Caprimulgiformes order have whisker-like bristles on their faces, some potoo species lack bristles, or their bristles are not well-developed. The visible portion of all potoos' bills is small. Potoos have long wings and long, pointed tails. They have short legs and strong toes.

From head to tail, potoos measure from 8 to 23 inches (21 to 57 inches). They weigh 1.6 to 22 ounces (46 to 624 grams). The birds' soft feathers are usually gray, yellowish brown, blackish brown, and white. The rufous potoo is a combination of orange and rufous (reddish brown). Wing color is described in the name of the white-winged potoo.

Bands of colors in the potoo family's feathers form patterns so that potoos resemble the trees where they live. Adult males and females have similar plumage (feather) coloring.

During the nineteenth century, birds in the Nyctibiidae family were called "tree nighthawks." They are now known by the name of one of the species. People thought it sounded like birds in the species were saying the word "potoo."

GEOGRAPHIC RANGE

Potoos live in Mexico, Costa Rica, Panama, Uruguay, Nicaragua, Colombia, Venezuela, French Guiana, Guyana, Ecuador, Peru, Brazil, Bolivia, Argentina, Tobago, Jamaica, Hispaniola, and Trinidad.

HABITAT

Potoos live in rainforests, where rain throughout the year produces abundant growth. The birds live in coniferous or evergreen forests, where trees don't undergo seasonal change and shed leaves. Potoos also live in trees in grassland areas called savannas, where there are only a few trees.

DIET

Potoos eat flying insects like beetles, moths, termites, crickets, grasshoppers, and fireflies. Birds fly after their prey and catch it in the air. However, they sometimes take prey off of a plant or tree.

BEHAVIOR AND REPRODUCTION

Potoos are nocturnal, becoming active at night. They are solitary feeders, traveling alone while they hunt for food.

During the day, potoos perch on a tree branch or trunk. The bird stands very still on a broken branch or one that slopes. In this motionless position, with its tree-like coloration, the potoo looks like a part of the tree and predators can't see the bird.

Predators that hunt and kill potoos for food include hawks, monkeys, and other mammals that can climb trees.

Even when asleep, the potoo is on the alert for predators. The potoo holds its head so that its bill is pointed upward. Its eyes appear shut, but the potoo looks out from partially open eyes. If predators get too close, the potoo flies away. The bird returns to the same perches for weeks or months.

At night, the potoo hunts for food. The bird chases prey, catching food in its mouth. The potoo then returns to its perch and eats.

Members of the potoo family are noisy at night. They sing loudly, and their calls vary by species. Calls are similar to whistles.

Potoos are monogamous (muh-NAH-guh-mus), a male and female pair up for long-term breeding. The birds build a nest

BIRDS WITHOUT NESTS

Potoos do not build nests for their young. Instead of gathering twigs or other nesting material, potoos choose an indented area in a tree for the one egg that the female bird lays. Locations include a broken branch, the forked part of a branch, or a tall tree stump.

After the female lays the egg, both parents incubate it. The potoos are motionless during the daytime, a behavior that young potoos quickly learn.

in the hollow of a tree, a branch, or in a broken branch. The female lays usually one white egg there. Both parents incubate the egg, keeping it warm until it hatches. Unlike birds that sit when they incubate, potoos stand upright during incubation. The egg hatches in about thirty days, and the bird grows feathers in forty to fifty-five days.

POTOOS AND PEOPLE

People rarely see the well-hidden potoos. In the past, the birds were the subject of legends and superstition. Some people thought it was bad luck to mock a potoo's call. The call of the great potoo was supposed to be a sign of upcoming trouble or a death.

Today, people interested in the environment visit potoo habitats. They try to view and photograph the birds.

CONSERVATION STATUS

Potoos are not in danger of extinction (dying out), according to guidelines from the World Conservation Union (IUCN). However, the number of birds has dropped as habitat is lost when trees are cut down.

Gray potoo *(Nyctibius griseus)*

█ Resident

GRAY POTOO
Nyctibius griseus

Physical characteristics: The gray potoo's plumage is brown with streaks of other colors that include gray, black, and reddish brown. The bird has black streaks on the crown (top) of the head and the lower part of the body. The potoo's patterned plumage resembles the tree branches where potoos perch, so the birds can roost (rest) during the day without being seen by predators. Male and female potoos have similar coloring.

Gray potoos live in the rainforests and grasslands of Mexico and Central and South America, where they eat moths, grasshoppers, beetles, termites, and fireflies. (Patricio Robles Gil/Bruce Coleman Inc. Reproduced by permission.)

The most colorful part of the gray potoo is the iris when the bird is seen at night. The iris is the round portion of the eye surrounding the pupil. If light is shined on the gray potoo, its irises look yellow or orange.

The head-to-tail length of gray potoos ranges from 13 to 16 inches (33 to 41 centimeters). Gray potoos weigh from 5 to 7 ounces (145 to 202 grams). The gray potoo looks much like the northern potoo. However, their calls are so different that each was placed in a separate species.

The gray potoo's call consists of five notes described by people as sounding mournful, or sad.

The gray potoo is also known as the common potoo, the giant nightjar, and poor-me-one.

Geographic range: Gray potoos live in Mexico and Central and South America. Birds are found in the countries of Costa Rica, Panama, Uruguay, Nicaragua, Colombia, Venezuela, French Guiana, Guyana, Ecuador, Peru, Brazil, Bolivia, Argentina, Tobago, Jamaica, Hispaniola, and Trinidad.

Habitat: Gray potoos live in rainforests, coniferous or evergreen forests, and in grassland where there are few trees. Birds also live on plantations, land where people plant trees.

Diet: Gray potoos eat moths, grasshoppers, beetles, termites, and fireflies.

Behavior and reproduction: Gray potoos are solitary and monogamous birds. The breeding season when birds mate varies by location for this species found throughout much of Latin America. In Tobago, gray potoos mate between March and May. The female potoo lays one egg. Both parents incubate the egg that hatches in thirty to thirty-three days. The chick fledges, grows its flying feathers, in forty to fifty-one days.

Gray potoos and people: In Brazil, people thought the mournful song of the gray potoo was actually the sound of a person who had been unlucky in the love. According to the legend, either the love was unrequited (the other person wasn't interested), or the relationship was ended by death or separation. The potoo's sad call was thought to be the song of the unhappy person who had died and had been brought back to life in another form (reincarnated).

Conservation status: Gray potoos are not at risk of extinction. ∎

FOR MORE INFORMATION

Books:

Attenborough, David. *The Life of Birds.* Princeton, NJ: Princeton University Press, 1998.

Periodicals:

Young, Bruce E., and James R. Zook. "Nesting of Four Poorly-Known Bird Species on the Caribbean Slope of Costa Rica." *Wilson Bulletin* (March 1999): 124.

Web sites:

Tobago Home Folklore and History of Trinidad and Tobago. http://www.tobago.hm/folk/bm001bird-c-l.htm#g (accessed on May 25, 2004).

Class: Aves
Order: Caprimulgiformes
Family: Caprimulgidae
Number of species: 77 species

family

CHAPTER

phylum
class
subclass
order
monotypic order
suborder
▲ family

PHYSICAL CHARACTERISTICS

The Caprimulgidae family is the largest family in the order Caprimulgiformes. Nightjars measure 6 to 16 inches (15 to 40 centimeters) from head to tail. Their weight ranges from 0.7 to 6.6 ounces (20 to 188 grams). Plumage (feather) color includes brown, gray, brownish yellow, and rufous (reddish brown). Those colors form patterns that help nightjars hide in trees.

The nightjar has a large head with large eyes that provide the strong vision needed to see during the night. The bird's small bill opens to reveal a large gape, which is the width of the mouth when open. Nightjars have short legs and long wings and tails.

Nighthawks, a group of nightjars, don't have bristles, and they usually have longer tails and wings than nightjars.

GEOGRAPHIC RANGE

Nightjar species are found throughout most of the world. No species live in the Arctic, Antarctic, and some oceanic islands.

Some nightjar species migrate across continents. These include European nightjars that breed in Europe and spend the winter in Africa.

HABITAT

Nightjars live in habitats ranging from semi-arid deserts to rainforests, where abundant rainfall produces plentiful growth. The birds occur in deciduous forests where trees shed leaves and coniferous forests that do not undergo seasonal changes. Nightjars also live in grassland areas with fewer trees.

DIET

Nightjars fly after prey or hunt on the ground for food such as insects, flies, beetles, ants, and caterpillars. Birds sometimes eat spiders. Larger nightjars may eat frogs and small birds.

BEHAVIOR AND REPRODUCTION

Nightjars spend the daytime roosting, sitting quietly in trees. Many species are nocturnal, meaning that they are active at night. Some species are crepuscular (kri-PUS-kyuh-lur), starting their activities at twilight, the time between sunset and darkness. During active times, nightjars hunt for food, eat, and mate. Nightjars are noisy at night. Males sometimes call to attract females, while other calls are territorial songs to warn other birds to stay away from a location.

WHY BIRDS HAVE WHISKERS

Many nightjars have whisker-like bristles around their mouths, but opinion is divided about why the birds have bristles. Some researchers think that the bristles help the birds capture prey while flying by helping to push insects into nightjars' mouths. Others disagree with that explanation, saying the bristles may protect the nightjars' eyes from being injured by prey struggling to escape.

The start of the breeding season depends on when there is a large amount of insects to feed young birds. In most climates, there are fewer insects during winter months, so breeding takes place in the spring or summer. Females of some species breed twice during the season and have two broods (sets of young).

Most nightjar species are monogamous (muh-NAH-guh-mus). Some species mate for life. In other species, male and female stay together for the breeding season.

Nightjars do not build nests. Females lay one to two eggs on the ground or in a tree branch. They incubate the eggs, sitting on them to keep them warm. Males of some species also help with incubation. Eggs hatch in seventeen to twenty-one days, and in some species, both parents feed chicks. The young fledge, grow feathers, in about two weeks. Two weeks later, the birds are able to fly and feed themselves.

Nightjars are hunted by predators including owls, crows, hawks, foxes, rats, and snakes. To make it difficult for predators to see them, the birds take advantage of their coloration and remain motionless, perched in trees, during the daytime.

NIGHTJARS AND PEOPLE

Nightjars received their name because their loud night call jarred (disturbed) sleeping people. The birds are also known as "goatsuckers" because people wrongly thought the birds drank milk from goats and cows. Nightjars actually hunt insects near the animals.

CONSERVATION STATUS

Several nightjar species are at risk as their habitat is lost when trees are cut down, according to World Conservation Union (IUCN). The Puerto Rican nightjar is Critically Endangered, facing an extremely high risk of extinction, dying out. That ranking could be changed to Endangered, facing a very high risk of extinction, due to conservation programs.

The white-winged nightjar's status has changed from Critically Endangered to Endangered, reflecting the new discovery of birds in Paraguay. Also Endangered is the Itombwe nightjar. Just one bird has been found in the Democratic Republic of the Congo.

Rated Vulnerable, facing a high risk of extinction, are the satanic-eared nightjar and Bonaparte's nightjar.

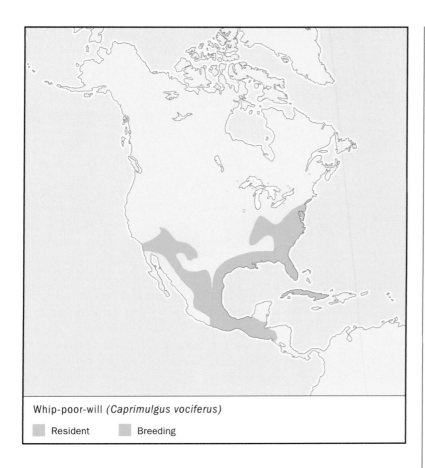

Whip-poor-will *(Caprimulgus vociferus)*

■ Resident   ■ Breeding

WHIP-POOR-WILL
Caprimulgus vociferus

Physical characteristics: Whip-poor-wills range in length from 9 to 10 inches (23 to 26 centimeters). They weigh from 1.5 to 2.4 ounces (42 to 69 grams). Their patterned plumage is brown, gray, and, white.

These birds have rounded wings. Their feet are so tiny that whip-poor-wills perch on trees length-wise, as if lying on their sides.

The whip-poor-will is named for its call. People thought they heard the bird, say, "whip-poor-will." Birds make this call as the sky becomes dark at night and just before dawn when skies lighten. Whip-poor-wills also call their name at night, especially when the moon is visible.

The whip-poor-will is named for its call, which sounds like "whip-poor-will." Birds make this call as the sky becomes dark at night and just before dawn when skies lighten. (© A. Morris/VIREO. Reproduced by permission.)

Geographic range: Whip-poor-wills live in the United States, Canada, Mexico, Cuba, and Central American countries including Honduras.

Habitat: Whip-poor-wills live in pine forests, deciduous forests, and open land where there are fewer trees.

Diet: Whip-poor-wills eat moths, beetles, ants, grasshoppers, and other insects.

Behavior and reproduction: Whip-poor-wills are nocturnal. Their breeding season starts at the beginning of May. Birds mate in areas ranging from Canada to Mexico, and then migrate south for the winter.

After mating, the female whip-poor-will nests on the ground and lays two eggs on leaves. The female incubates the eggs. The male sometimes incubates, too. The eggs hatch in nineteen to twenty days. The female cares for the chicks, and the male brings them food at night. When the chicks are twenty days old, they can fly.

The female and male may breed again and produce a second clutch of two eggs. If the female is caring for the first brood, the male looks after the second clutch.

Whip-poor-wills and people: The whip-poor-will hides so well that people know the bird mainly by its call.

Conservation status: Whip-poor-wills are not in danger of extinction. ■

Gray nightjar *(Caprimulgus indicus)*

■ Resident   ■ Breeding   ■ Nonbreeding

GRAY NIGHTJAR
Caprimulgus indicus

Physical characteristics: Gray nightjars are gray with other plumage coloring that includes brown, black, reddish brown, brownish yellow, and white. Birds range in length from 8.3 to 11.4 inches (21 to 29 centimeters). They weigh from 2.4 to 3.8 ounces (69 to 107 grams). The birds are also called jungle nightjars.

Geographic range: Gray nightjars breed in Asian countries including India, China, and Japan. Birds in the north migrate to Java in the winter. Gray nightjars were seen in Alaska in 2001.

Habitat: Gray nightjars live in rainforests, areas thick with trees and other growth. Birds also live in trees on farms and in other areas.

The female gray nightjar lays her eggs on the ground. The male may or may not help her incubate the eggs. (© A. J. Knystautas/VIREO. Reproduced by permission.)

Diet: Gray nightjars eat insects.

Behavior and reproduction: The female gray nightjar lays two eggs on the ground. She incubates the clutch and may be helped by the male. The eggs hatch in sixteen to seventeen days. The young have reddish brown down (soft feathers). They grow feathers in approximately eighteen days.

Gray nightjars and people: Gray nightjars are rarely seen, but people hear them. The territorial song is said to sound like knocking.

Conservation status: Gray nightjars are not threatened, but are considered rare in India. ■

FOR MORE INFORMATION

Books:

Baicich, Paul J., and Colin J. O. Harrison. *A Guide to the Nests, Eggs and Nestlings of North American Birds.* San Diego, CA: Academic Press, 1997.

Sibley, David, Allen. *The Sibley Guide to Birds.* New York: Alfred A. Knopf, 2000.

Stuart, Chris and Tilde. *Birds of Africa From Seabirds to Seed Eaters.* Cambridge, MA: The MIT Press, 1999.

Periodicals:

Burt, William. "Nightjars Are Everywhere But Just Try Finding One." *Smithsonian* (July 2000): 74.

Web sites:

Global Registry of Migratory Species. http://131.220.109.5/groms/Species_HTMLs/Cindicus.html (accessed on May 29, 2004).

Williams, Ted. "Night Bard of Spring." National Audubon Society earth-almanac. http://magazine.audubon.org/earthalmanac/almanac0405.html#night (accessed on May 25, 2004).

order

CHAPTER

phylum

class

subclass

● order

monotypic order

suborder

family

PHYSICAL CHARACTERISTICS

The name Apodiformes is based on the Greek words "a pous," meaning "without foot." Apodiforms have small feet and their legs are short. Many birds in this order cannot walk, and they are unable to escape quickly by simply walking and then flying away if they land on the ground.

Although their feet are weak, apodiforms are strong fliers because they have thick shoulder bones and long, powerful breastbones. Because of their neck muscles, these birds can move their heads quickly.

Some physical differences and behavioral differences separate the three families in the Apodiformes order. A family is a group of birds that have similar characteristics.

Birds in the swift family (Apodidae) eat, mate, and sleep in the air. These birds, also called typical swifts, have long, pointed wings. Their head-to-tail length ranges from 3.4 to 9.6 inches (9 to 25 centimeters). They can weigh from 0.2 to 7.6 ounces (5 to 205 grams). The swift has a short bill and a large gape, which is the width of the mouth when it is open. The swift opens its mouth to catch prey, or insects hunted for food.

Swifts' feathers are brown or black, with white patterns in some birds. Male and female birds have similar plumage (feather color).

Tree swifts belong to the Hemiprocnidae family. Unlike swifts, these birds can perch in trees. Birds range in length from 5.8 to 11.5 inches (15 to 30 centimeters), and weigh from 0.8 to 2.9 ounces (21 to 79 grams). Tree swifts have small, flat bills, large gapes, and whiskers. They have long wings and forked tails.

Tree swifts are also called crested swifts because of the crest (clump of feathers) on their foreheads. Plumage is brown or light gray, other colors may include blue, green, and white. The plumage color of the male and female birds differs.

Hummingbirds belong to the Trochilidae family. They are named for the humming sound made by their quickly vibrating wings. Hummingbirds can fly backwards and hover, staying in one place by flapping their wings.

Hummingbirds range in length from 2 to 8.7 inches (5 to 22 centimeters), and weigh from 0.07 to 0.7 ounces (1.9 to 21 grams). These birds have long, thin bills and long, forked tongues.

The hummingbird family is the most colorful member of the Apodiforme family. Plumage colors include red, green, pink, blue, yellow, and purple. Usually, female birds are less colorful than males, which helps the females hide their young from predators, animals that hunt prey for food.

GEOGRAPHIC RANGE

Swifts are found throughout most of the world. They live on every continent except Antarctica and do not live in polar regions.

Tree swifts can be found in India, Sri Lanka, Bangladesh, Thailand, Cambodia, Vietnam, Malaysia, Sumatra, Borneo, the Philippines, Indonesia, New Guinea, Bismarck, and the Solomon Islands.

Hummingbirds live in the United States, Canada, Central American countries including Costa Rica and Guatemala, South American countries including Venezuela and Brazil, and the Caribbean Islands.

HABITAT

Swifts and hummingbirds live in coniferous forests that do not undergo seasonal changes. They also live in deciduous forests where trees lose their leaves during cold or dry weather. Hummingbirds live in deserts, and members of both families inhabit grassland areas where there are few trees. Hummingbirds also live in wetlands, areas where the land is low and wet.

Tree swifts live in rainforests, areas where heavy rain produces abundant growth.

Members of all three families live in trees. Swifts sometimes make nests in chimneys and on cliffs. Some hummingbirds and swiftlets live in caves. In addition, some swifts and hummingbirds migrate, traveling to another area where food is more plentiful. The chimney swift lives in North America and spends its winters in Central and South America.

DIET

Swifts and tree swifts are insectivores, birds that eat insects. Swifts catch most prey while flying with their mouths open. The type of insects eaten depends on where the swifts are and the weather. On warm days, there are more insects in the air. Swifts' prey includes mayflies, termites, and ants, and sometimes even spiders.

Tree swifts perch in trees and watch for prey, such as flies, bugs, and ants. They fly after prey and after catching it, they swallow it whole.

Hummingbirds use their long tongues to drink nectar, a sweet liquid found in flowers. Since hummingbirds live in many countries around the world, members of this family drink nectar from thousands of different flowers. Hummingbirds are likely to feed on flowers that are red, orange, and yellow. The birds may also eat insects.

BEHAVIOR AND REPRODUCTION

Swifts are sociable and live in large groups of birds called colonies. Tree swifts are usually found alone or in pairs. They may, however, form a group of ten to twelve individuals. Both birds, swifts and tree swifts, are noisy birds and may create quite a bit of noise when congregating.

Hummingbirds are solitary, pairing up only to breed. Male hummingbirds are territorial and chase other birds away from the area where they feed. When food is scare, swifts and hummingbirds may hibernate.

Swifts and hummingbirds are active during the day. Tree swifts are crepuscular (kri-PUS-kyuh-lur), meaning that they become active at twilight or just before sunrise.

Apodiformes use various materials for their nests. The birds "glue" their nests together with saliva, a watery solution in their mouths, thereby hardening and holding the nest. Swifts make nests out of twigs, feathers, and other materials that they catch as it floats through the air. Tree swifts use feathers and bark from trees for their nests. Hummingbirds weave spider webs into their nests.

Collocalia swiftlets in Asia use only saliva to make their nests. People eat these nests in bird's nest soup.

Swifts and tree swifts are monogamous (muh-NAH-guh-mus), meaning that they mate with only one partner. Hummingbirds are polygamous (puh-LIH-guh-mus) and do not mate with the same partner, but instead have a number of different partners. After mating, the male hummingbird leaves and the female lays two eggs.

The tree swift lays one egg, while the swift lays a clutch of one to six eggs. Males from both families help care for the young.

Swifts spend so much time in the air that they are usually safe from mammal predators. The birds fly rapidly, but sometimes are caught by hawks. In addition, brown tree snakes eat swifts on some islands.

FLIGHT PATTERNS OF MIGRATING BIRDS

Migratory swifts and hummingbirds fly great distances, often without stopping until they reach winter homes where there is more food. In the wild, swifts may travel at a speed of more than 100 miles (160 kilometers) per hour. The smaller hummingbirds timed in laboratories flew at speeds ranging from 30 to 53 miles (48 to 85 kilometers) per hour.

Swifts alternate between wing movement and gliding, allowing the wind to assist in moving them along. Hummingbirds can stop in mid-air by flapping their wings up and down, allowing them to hover and feed.

SWIFTS, HUMMINGBIRDS, AND PEOPLE

For thousands of years, people in Asia have used cave swiftlet nests as the main ingredient for bird's nest soup. There is no known significant relationship between people and tree swifts.

People place hummingbird feeders in their yards because they enjoy watching them fly about and drink flower nectar. The birds pollinate the flowers when they drink the nectar, by transferring flower pollen (male sex cells) from the stamen to the pistil, the organ that bears the seeds. This eventually leads to the production of more flowers.

CONSERVATION STATUS

Some species of swifts and hummingbirds face threats to their survival, according to the World Conservation Union (IUCN). Nine hummingbird species are Critically Endangered, facing an extremely high risk of extinction, as their habitat is lost due to development, farming, and logging. Six hummingbird and swift species are Endangered, facing a very high risk of extinction. Brown tree snakes accidentally brought to Guam by ships ate many of these birds on the island. Other swiftlets died when pesticides were sprayed to kill insects.

FOR MORE INFORMATION

Books:

Attenborough, David. *The Life of Birds*. Princeton, NJ: Princeton University Press, 1998.

Baicich, Paul J., and Colin J. O. Harrison. *A Guide to the Nests, Eggs and Nestlings of North American Birds*. San Diego, CA: Academic Press, 1997.

Sibley, David, Allen. *The Sibley Guide to Birds*. New York: Alfred A. Knopf, 2000.

Wells, Diana. *100 Birds and How They Got Their Names*. Chapel Hill, NC: Algonquin Books, 2002.

SWIFTS
Apodidae

Class: Aves
Order: Apodiformes
Family: Apodidae
Number of species: 99 species

family

CHAPTER

phylum

class

subclass

order

monotypic order

suborder

▲ **family**

PHYSICAL CHARACTERISTICS

Swifts are aerial birds, meaning that they spend much of their lives in the air. Birds eat, drink, mate, and are believed to sleep while flying. Swifts are powerful flyers because they have strong breast muscles and long wings that are large and narrow. Their legs and feet are so small that they cannot walk. When swifts are on the ground, they are unable to quickly take off and fly. As a result, swifts land on tall trees or structures like chimneys. Swifts cling to surfaces by using their four strong toes on each foot.

The head to-tail length of swifts ranges from 3.4 to 9.6 inches (9 to 25 centimeters), and they can weigh from 0.2 to 7.6 ounces (5 to 205 grams). Most birds have black feathers, with some brown and blue coloration. Some birds have white rumps, chests, and bellies. Male and female birds have similar plumage (feathers).

The swift has a narrow body and a large head with large eyes. The bird has a short bill and a large gape, which is the width of the open mouth. The gape, being as large as the swift's head, allows it to catch and swallow insects while flying.

The word "swift" means fast, and swifts can fly at a speed of more than 100 miles (160 kilometers) per hour!

GEOGRAPHIC RANGE

Swifts are found throughout most of the world, on every continent except Antarctica.

HABITAT

Swifts' habitats vary from coniferous and deciduous forests to grasslands where there are few trees.

WAITING OUT THE BAD WEATHER

Swifts depend on the weather for their food supply. They rely on breezes to blow insects in their direction. During a storm, rain washes the insects away, depleting the swifts' food supply. Cold weather also decreases the number of insects for the birds to feed on. For swift nestlings too young to fly, the solution is becoming torpid. Nestlings enter torpor, a state in which their body temperature drops and their heartbeat slows. In this state, birds can go for ten days without food.

Swifts need to build nests in locations where it is easy for them to take flight. Swiftlets build nests in caves. Some birds make nests on cliffs, in chimneys or other tall structures.

DIET

Swifts are insectivores, animals that eat insects. Flying swifts catch and eat insects including flies, ants, beetles, and sometimes spiders. Adults eat one to three times an hour, and some birds eat ten thousand insects a day.

BEHAVIOR AND REPRODUCTION

Swifts become active at dawn. They are noisy and live in large groups called colonies. Some species migrate, flying from an area with harsh winter weather to a warmer climate where there is a larger food supply.

Swifts are monogamous (muh-NAH-guh-mus), mating with one partner. Birds make nests out of twigs, feathers, and items they find while flying. To hold the material together, swifts use their saliva, the liquid solution in their mouths, which hardens around the nest material.

The female swift lays one to six eggs. Both parents incubate the eggs, sitting on them to keep them warm in order for them to hatch. Eggs hatch in nineteen to twenty-eight days. Both parents feed the young. Other swifts, called cooperative breeders, may assist the parents in feeding. The adults carry insects for the young in pouches located below their tongues.

Cave swiftlets use only saliva when building their nests. People in Asia take the nests of some swiftlets and use them as the main ingredient in bird's nest soup. Since caves are dark, cave swiftlets use echolocation (eck-oh-loh-KAY-shun) to guide them as they move around in the caves. The birds make a sound and listen to the echoes that bounce off the surfaces.

SWIFTS AND PEOPLE

People harvest swiftlet nests for use in bird's nest soup. Bird watchers enjoy watching colonies of swifts fly across the sky. Some people track their migration and report the birds' progress on the Internet.

CONSERVATION STATUS

The World Conservation Union (IUCN) lists several species as threatened. The Guam swiftlet is Endangered, facing a very high risk of extinction, dying out. The bird population dropped by 80 percent after birds were killed by pesticides, chemicals that were sprayed to eliminate insects. Their populations have also declined due to being preyed on by the brown tree snake, a species introduced to Guam from ships by accident. The birds, being unable to take flight quickly from the ground, were vulnerable to this ground-dwelling snake.

IUCN ranks some swift species as Vulnerable, facing a high risk of extinction. Low populations make the dark-rumped swift, Aitu swiftlet, and the Polynesian swiftlet Vulnerable. Loss of habitat as trees are cut down makes the Congo swift Vulnerable. The Seychelles swiftlet is Vulnerable because birds nest at only three locations.

Chimney swift *(Chaetura pelagica)*

■ Resident   ■ Breeding

CHIMNEY SWIFT
Chaetura pelagica

Physical characteristics: The chimney swift is often described as a "cigar with wings." The swift's cylindrical body looks like a cigar. Its plumage is sooty brown (black-brown), and its underparts are gray-brown. The bird's wings are slightly curved and the tail only shows when it is spread.

Chimney swifts range in length from 4.6 to 5.4 inches (12 to 14 centimeters), and weigh from 0.8 to 1.0 ounces (20 to 23 grams).

Geographic range: Chimney swifts live and breed in the United States and Canada. They are found east of the Rocky Mountains in both countries. The swifts migrate through Central America and spend winters in South American countries including Peru and Chile.

Habitat: Chimney swifts live in forests and in cities. Birds once nested in hollow trees, but they now build nests in empty chimneys, well shafts, silos, and sometimes in building attics. Nests are located just below the opening of the structure.

Diet: Chimney swifts eat flying insects such as flies, ants, and beetles. They sometimes eat spiders.

Behavior and reproduction: Chimney swifts are sociable and travel with a colony. Birds may stay in the air until they are ready to nest.

These birds are monogamous. In the nesting season, chimney swifts build nests with twigs that they break from trees. They use saliva to attach the nest vertically (with the opening lengthwise) to the side of a hollow tree or chimney.

The female lays two to seven eggs between May and July, and the eggs hatch within nineteen to twenty-one days. Chicks fledge (grow flying feathers) in twenty-eight to thirty days. The young swifts may leave the nest a week before growing their feathers.

Chimney swifts and people: People have long watched the swifts fly south for the winter. In addition, the North American Chimney Swift Nest Research Project in Texas is tracking the birds' migration. The group wants to develop towers where swifts can roost.

Conservation status: Chimney swifts are not in danger of dying out. ■

African palm swift *(Cypsiurus parvus)*

◼ Resident

AFRICAN PALM SWIFT
Cypsiurus parvus

Physical characteristics: The African palm swift is about 6.1 inches long (16 centimeters) and weighs from 0.4 to 0.5 ounces (10 to 14 grams). The palm swift has gray-brown plumage. The head and wings are darker than the pale under parts, and some birds have streaks of color on their throats. In male birds the throat is whiter than in female swifts.

Geographic range: African palm swifts live in sub-Saharan Africa, south of the Sahara Desert. These nations include Namibia, Madagascar, and South Africa.

African palm swifts build their nests on the underside of palm leaves, and sometimes underneath other structures such as bridges. (© D. & M. Zimmerman/VIREO. Reproduced by permission.)

Habitat: African palm swifts live in grassland and other areas where there are palm trees. Birds build nests on the underside of palm leaves, and sometimes on structures like bridges.

Diet: African palm swifts eat insects, flying ants, beetles, termites, and spiders.

Behavior and reproduction: African palm swifts are active during the daytime and return at sunset to their nests in the leaves of palm trees. Birds mate and nest on the underside (back) of palm fronds.

These swifts build nests with feathers that they collect while flying, and use saliva to attach the feathers to the palm. The nest is a vertical platform. During the night, the male and female birds roost (rest). They hold onto the nest with their toes when they mate.

The female goes to the top of the platform to lay eggs. After laying an egg, she pushes it into the nest and "glues" it to the palm leaf with her saliva. She then lays another egg and repeats the process.

The female lays a clutch of one to three eggs. The eggs hatch in about twenty days. Young palm swifts fledge, or grow feathers in thirty-one to thirty-three days.

Risks to palm swifts include loss of habitat when people strip (remove) palm leaves.

African palm swifts and people: African palm swifts eat insects that people regard as pests, and the birds are a tourist attraction in Namibia.

Conservation status: African palm swifts are not in danger of extinction. ∎

FOR MORE INFORMATION

Books:

Attenborough, David. *The Life of Birds.* Princeton, NJ: Princeton University Press, 1998.

Baicich, Paul J., and Colin J. O. Harrison. *A Guide to the Nests, Eggs and Nestlings of North American Birds.* San Diego, CA: Academic Press, 1997.

Sibley, David Allen. *The Sibley Guide to Birds.* New York: Alfred A. Knopf, 2000.

Wells, Diana. *100 Birds and How They Got Their Names.* Chapel Hill, NC: Algonquin Books, 2002.

Web sites:

North American Chimney Swift Nest Research Project. http://www.concentric.net/~dwa/page6.html (accessed on May 26, 2004).

"Palm Stripping Destroys Swifts' Nesting Places." *The Free Press of Namibia* (February 27, 2003) Online at http://www.namibian.com.na/2003/February/environment/03B8B156C8.html (accessed on May 26, 2004).

TREE SWIFTS
Hemiprocnidae

Class: Aves
Order: Apodiformes
Family: Hemiprocnidae
Number of species: 4 species

family

CHAPTER

phylum

class

subclass

order

monotypic order

suborder

▲ **family**

PHYSICAL CHARACTERISTICS

The head-to-tail length of tree swifts ranges from 5.8 to 11.5 inches (15 to 30 centimeters). Birds weigh from 0.8 to 2.9 ounces (21 to 79 grams). Tree swifts have long wings and tails that are forked and divided into two sections so that they resemble the letter V turned on its side. Tree swifts fly quickly when hunting food, but they live in one area and usually do not migrate.

Tree swifts belong to the Apodiformes order that also includes swifts and hummingbirds. While all the birds share some physical characteristics, swifts and hummingbirds have weak feet and do little perching, sitting or standing on a surface. Instead, they spend much of their time in the air. Tree swifts have stronger legs and are able to perch in trees.

Swifts have mostly gray plumage, feathers. Tree swifts and hummingbirds are more colorful. Tree swifts have patches of color in their plumage. Some birds have whiskers. Other birds have a crest, a group of feathers that stand upright on their foreheads.

Some species characteristics are described by the birds' names. The crested tree swift has a crest. The gray-rumped tree swift has gray plumage on its rump. The moustached tree swift has a white "moustache," white plumage that extends from the chin to the back of the neck. The whiskered tree swift has long feathers that extend from the face like whiskers. The bird is also known as the lesser tree swift.

GEOGRAPHIC RANGE

Tree swifts live in Asia in the countries of India, Nepal, Sri Lanka, Malaysia, Bangladesh, Myanmar, Thailand, Bali, China, Cambodia, and Vietnam. They also range in New Guinea, Bismarck, the Philippines, and the Solomon Islands.

HABITAT

Tree swifts live in various types of tree habitats. They live in forests with deciduous trees that lose their leaves during cold or very dry seasons. Tree swifts also live in forests with coniferous or evergreen trees that generally stay green all winter. They range in rainforests where abundant rainfall produces a lot of growth. The birds also range in grassland areas called savannas where there are fewer trees and grasses grow. They range near forest openings and are sometimes found near the edge of rivers. Some species also live in towns and are found in gardens.

DIET

Tree swifts eat flying insects like ants, beetles, wasps, and bees. Tree swifts are aerial feeders; they fly after prey, insects hunted for food. The birds also eat spiders.

BEHAVIOR AND REPRODUCTION

Tree swifts are usually sedentary, staying in one area throughout the year. Birds roost, rest, during the daytime and perch standing up on branches. Tree swifts are crepuscular (kri-PUS-kyuh-lur) and nocturnal; they become active at twilight or in the evening.

Tree swifts form small groups, but they have been seen in flocks of up to fifty gray-rumped tree swifts. Birds flock to chase flying insects.

Tree swifts are monogamous (muh-NAH-guh-mus), they have only one mate. Tree swifts build tiny nests out of feathers and pieces of bark. Like other Apodiformes, tree swifts build nests with saliva, the watery liquid in their mouths. Their salvia hardens as it dries, so swifts use saliva to glue the saucer-shaped

SOCIAL SWIFT SPECIES

Some tree swift species are more social than others. Crested tree swifts form groups of six to twelve birds. They have little to do with other species. Whiskered tree swifts may be alone, in pairs, or in groups of six birds. However, the whiskered birds do not mind sharing their tree with gray-rumped tree swifts. Gray-rumped tree swifts just perch higher in the trees, which probably helps the two species get along.

nest together. The female lays one egg. Both parents incubate the egg, keeping it warm, until it hatches after approximately three weeks. Birds fledge, grow feathers needed for flight, about three weeks later.

Predators that hunt tree swifts for food include snakes and larger birds.

TREE SWIFTS AND PEOPLE

People enjoy watching flocks of tree swifts. Gray-rumped birds are active at dusk and can be seen flying down to drink from pools and other bodies of water.

CONSERVATION STATUS

Tree swifts are not in danger of extinction, dying out.

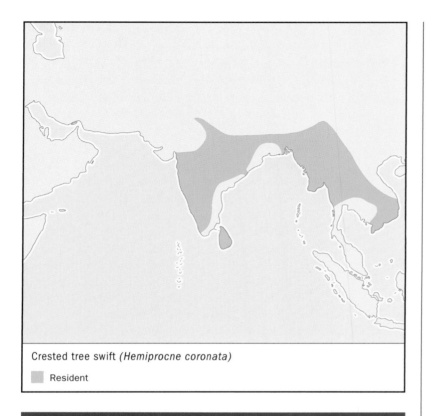

Crested tree swift (*Hemiprocne coronata*)

■ Resident

CRESTED TREE SWIFT
Hemiprocne coronata

Physical characteristics: Crested tree swifts range in length from 8.2 to 9 inches (21 to 22.6 centimeters) and weigh 0.7 to 1.0 ounces (20 to 26 grams). They have long, narrow wings and forked tails. All birds have blue-gray plumage, green-blue crests on their foreheads, and coloring that looks like black eye patches.

Male crested tree swifts have a pale rufous, brownish red, patch below the eye. That coloring extends to ear coverts, small feathers near the ears. On male bodies, feathers are white below the breasts. Wings are mainly blackish brown. Some wing feathers are pale gray and blue. Tails are blue-gray on top and pale gray on the back side.

Female crested tree swifts have black plumage in the area between their eyes and bills. That black coloring extends to their ear coverts. Below the black plumage is a thin line of white plumage that looks

Crested tree swifts live in forests and gardens in Southeast Asia. (Illustration by Bruce Worden. Reproduced by permission.)

like a moustache. The line extends from the face to the sides of the head below the ears. Female crested tree swifts have dark gray throats.

Crested tree swifts were once thought to belong to the same species as the gray-rumped tree swift. However, the crested swifts do not have pale gray plumage on their rumps.

Geographic range: Crested tree swifts live in India, Nepal, Sri Lanka, Bangladesh, Myanmar, Thailand, China, Cambodia, and Vietnam.

Habitat: Crested tree swifts live in deciduous forests, in open areas near trees, and in home gardens. Most birds live in areas with altitudes, heights, of no more than 1,197 feet (365 meters). However, birds also range at higher altitudes of 3,937 to 4,593 feet (1,200 to 1,400 meters).

Diet: Crested tree swifts eat flying insects like the small, two-winged midge.

Behavior and reproduction: While crested tree swifts are sedentary, don't migrate, the birds in India sometimes fly to different parts of the country when seasons change. Crested tree swifts are nocturnal and are active in the later part of the night. Birds look for food in pairs or in small groups of six to twelve birds. They fly in circles to feed, and their call is described as harsh.

Crested tree swifts often perch upright on branches with no leaves. They have favorite perches and stand with the tips of their wings crossed.

The breeding season varies by location, but birds usually mate between December and July. The male and female birds build a tiny nest out of pieces of bark, feathers, and saliva. Birds attach the nest to a branch with saliva, and the female lays one gray egg. Both parents incubate the egg. They do this by perching upright and covering the egg with their feathers.

The egg hatches after about three weeks. Both parents care for the chick. The young bird fledges approximately fifty days after the egg was laid.

Crested tree swifts and people: Since the crested tree swift population is large and found in many countries, they are often studied to learn more about the family.

Conservation status: Crested tree swifts are not at risk of extinction. ■

FOR MORE INFORMATION

Books:

Ali, Sálim. *The Book of Indian Birds.* Oxford, U.K.: Oxford University Press, 1996.

Chantler, Phil. *Swifts: A Guide to the Swifts and Tree Swifts of the World,* 2nd ed. New Haven, CT: Yale University Press, 2000.

Kennedy, Robert S., et al. *A Guide to the Birds of the Philippines.* Oxford, U.K.: Oxford University Press, 2000.

Robson, Craig. *Birds of Thailand.* Princeton, NJ: Princeton University Press, 2002.

Web sites:

Lockwood, Burleigh. "Apodiformes." Chaffee Zoological Gardens of Fresno. http://www.chaffeezoo.org/animals/apodiformes.html (accessed on June 25, 2004).

CHAPTER

phylum

class

subclass

order

monotypic order

suborder

▲ **family**

PHYSICAL CHARACTERISTICS

Hummingbirds received their name because of the humming sound their wings make. They have powerful wings and can fly backwards, upside down, and quickly change direction. Hummingbirds hover when feeding, remaining motionless in the air. They feed by dipping their long bills and long, forked tongues into flowers.

Hummingbirds range in size from the bee hummingbird, which is 2.25 inches (5.7 centimeters) long, to the giant hummingbird, which is 8.5 inches (21.6 centimeters) long.

Hummingbirds are sometimes called "flying jewels" because of their colorful plumage, feathers. Some feathers are iridescent, which means the colors appear to change depending on where light shines on the plumage. Males are usually more colorful than females. Plainer coloring helps the female stay hidden from predators that would hunt the female and young.

GEOGRAPHIC RANGE

Hummingbirds live in North, Central, and South America.

HABITAT

Hummingbirds live in coniferous forests where trees do not undergo seasonal change. They range in rainforests where year-round rain produces abundant growth and in deciduous forests where trees shed leaves during certain seasons. They are also found in grasslands, deserts, and wetlands like swamps.

DIET

Hummingbirds drink nectar, a sweet liquid inside flowers. They are attracted to red, orange, and yellow flowers. When hummingbirds feed, they pollinate flowers. Pollination is the transfer of flower pollen, the male sex cells, from the stamen to the pistil, the organ that bears seeds. This transfer allows seeds to form and new flowers to grow. Hummingbirds pollinate thousands of flowering plants.

Hummingbirds also eat insects. The size of this prey, creature hunted for food, depends on the size of the hummingbird.

BEHAVIOR AND REPRODUCTION

Hummingbirds are active during the day. They are solitary, alone, pairing up only to breed. The birds are polygamous (puh-LIH-guh-mus), having more than one mate at the same time. After the birds mate, the male leaves. The female lays one to two eggs. The female incubates, sits on, the eggs to keep them warm. Eggs hatch in two to three weeks, and young birds leave the nest three weeks later.

Some hummingbirds are territorial and chase other birds away from their feeding area. Cold weather causes hummingbirds to enter torpor, a type of hibernation in which their heartbeat and other body functions slow down.

HUMMINGBIRDS AND PEOPLE

For centuries, hummingbirds have fascinated people. In Latin America, people once thought the sun disguised itself as a hummingbird. In some countries, people thought they would find romance or wealth if they used a powder made of hummingbird bodies. Europeans used to decorate hats with hummingbird feathers.

During the twentieth century, laws were passed to protect hummingbirds, and modern people appreciate the beauty of the "flying jewels."

CONSERVATION STATUS

Nine hummingbird species are listed by the World Conservation Union (IUCN) as Critically Endangered, facing an extremely high risk of extinction, dying out, in the wild. Eleven species are Endangered, facing a very high risk of extinction in the wild, and nine are Vulnerable, facing a high risk of extinction. Threats to hummingbirds include loss of habitat as trees are cut down for lumber or land is used for farming.

Hairy hermit *(Glaucis hirsuta)*

◼ Resident

HAIRY HERMIT
Glaucis hirsuta

Physical characteristics: Hairy hermits are also called rufous-breasted hermits. Rufous is the reddish brown color on the hummingbirds' chests and lower feathers. Upper feathers are green. Males have darker chests, and their wings are longer than female birds. All birds' bills curve down, but males' bills curve more.

Hairy hermits measure 4 to 4.7 inches (10 to 12 centimeters). Males weigh 0.21 to 0.28 ounces (6 to 8 grams). Females weigh from 0.19 to 0.26 ounces (5.5 to 7.5 grams).

Geographic range: Hairy hermits live in South America and are found in countries including Brazil, Peru, Venezuela, Suriname, Panama, Colombia, Trinidad and Tobago.

Habitat: Hairy hermits live in rainforests, other wooded areas, and wetland.

Diet: Birds drink nectar and sometimes eat small spiders.

Behavior and reproduction: Hairy hermits are solitary unless breeding. During the day the birds eat. They also bathe by hovering close to water and then diving in partly or all the way.

Hairy hermits are trapliners, they look for food in a large area instead of a small territory. Trapliners usually follow a regular route, line, to flowers, their traps.

During the breeding season, males form a lek, a group of up to twelve birds. Males sing so that females will choose them for mating. After breeding, the male leaves. The female flies to a nest located under leaves, hidden from predators like snakes and larger birds.

The cone-shaped nest is made of plant material. The female lays two eggs. Sometimes two females will share a nest, so there may be more eggs in the nest. The female incubates the eggs, which hatch after seventeen to nineteen days. Chicks are black with gray down, soft "baby" feathers. Birds fledge, growing feathers needed for flight, in twenty to twenty-five days. Fledglings stay with their mother for three to four weeks.

The breeding season varies by location. Birds mate in September through May in Brazil and from January to July in Trinidad.

Hairy hermits and people: People travel to see hairy hermits in places like Machu Picchu, the ruins of an ancient city in Peru.

Conservation status: Hairy hermits are not threatened with extinction. ■

Hairy hermits mostly drink nectar, but may also eat small spiders. (Illustration by Patricia Ferrer. Reproduced by permission.)

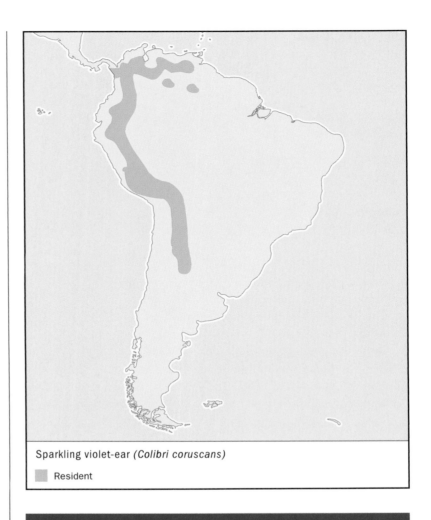

Sparkling violet-ear *(Colibri coruscans)*

■ Resident

SPARKLING VIOLET-EAR
Colibri coruscans

Physical characteristics: Sparkling violet-ears are part of a genus (JEE-nus), group of animals with similar characteristics, of hummingbirds named for the bluish purple color of feathers near their ears. These large feathers are long and stiff. The sparkling violet-ear's upper body feathers are metallic green. Lower feathers are green, and the bird has a blue stomach. The tail is iridescent green with a blue band.

Male and female birds have similar coloring. Birds range in length from 5.1 to 5.5 inches (13 to 14 centimeters). This length includes the tail that is about 2.2 inches (6 centimeters) long. The hummingbird's black bill curves down and is approximately 1 inch (2.5 meters) long.

Male birds weigh 0.27 to 0.3 ounces (7.7 to 8.5 grams). Females weigh from 0.24 to 0.26 ounces (6.7 to 7.5 grams).

Geographic range: Sparkling violet-ears live in Argentina, Bolivia, Brazil, Chile, Colombia, Guyana, Peru, and Venezuela.

Habitat: Sparkling violet-ears live near coniferous or evergreen eucalyptus forests, gardens, and plains areas.

Diet: Sparkling violet-ears drink nectar. These birds will also catch and eat insects in flight.

Behavior and reproduction: Sparkling violet-ears are solitary and aggressive. Birds declare their territory by singing. The birds sing much of the day, and sub-groups develop their own calls.

Sparkling violet-ears have iridescent, or shiny, body and tail feathers. (© J. Fuhrman/VIREO. Reproduced by permission.)

Breeding seasons vary by region. Birds in Venezuela mate from July through October. Birds find mates at leks, areas where groups of males try to attract a female to mate. After mating, the male leaves. The female lays two eggs in a tiny, cup-shaped nest made of twigs and other plant material. Eggs hatch in seventeen to eighteen days. The young fledge in three weeks.

According to reports, male sparkling violet-ears were seen twice caring for their young. Normally, male hummingbirds have little to do with their young.

Sparkling violet-ears and people: People travel to Latin America to see and photograph sparkling violet-ears.

Conservation status: Sparkling violet-ears are not in danger of extinction. ■

Anna's hummingbird (*Calypte anna*)

█ Resident

ANNA'S HUMMINGBIRD
Calypte anna

Physical characteristics: Anna's hummingbirds have tube-shaped bodies, long foreheads, and short, straight bills. All birds have green feathers. The male has a black bill, and a red crown, top of the head, and throat. The female has a gray head. The male has gray tail feathers; there are white tips on the female's tail feathers.

Birds range in length from 3.9 to 4.3 inches (10 to 11 centimeters). Males weigh from 0.12 to 0.2 ounces (3.5 to 5.8 grams). Females weigh from 0.12 to 0.17 ounces (3.3 to 4.7 grams).

This hummingbird was named for the wife of a nineteenth-century bird collector, Duke Victor Massena.

Geographic range: Anna's hummingbirds range in southwest Canada, the western United States, and northwest Mexico. Birds migrate during the winter, traveling south from locations such as Oregon to Arizona and Mexico.

Habitat: Birds live in forests, grasslands, and in towns and neighborhoods near gardens and parks.

Diet: Anna's hummingbirds drink nectar. They eat flies, wasps, bees, spiders, and insects. Hummingbirds take prey off plants or catch it while flying.

Behavior and reproduction: Anna's hummingbirds are solitary, and males defend their territory. The breeding season lasts from November to May, sometimes extending to July. During that time, the female may have two or three broods, groups of young birds hatched at the same time.

The male leaves after mating. The female lays two eggs in a nest located on the branch of a tree or bush. The nest is made of material including leaves, feathers, and spider webs. The female incubates the eggs that hatch in fourteen to nineteen days. The birds fledge in eighteen to twenty-six days.

Anna's hummingbirds and people: Many people in North America put feeders containing sugar water in their yards so they can watch Anna's hummingbirds.

Conservation status: Anna's hummingbirds are not threatened with extinction. ■

FOR MORE INFORMATION

Books:

Burton, Robert. *The World of the Hummingbird.* Kingston, Canada: Firefly Books, 2001.

Howell, Steve N.G. *Hummingbirds of North America.* San Diego, CA: Academic Press, 2002.

Periodicals:

Dunn, Terry. "Hummingbirds: Frantic and Fascinating." *Zoogoer* 31, no. 2 (2002). Online at http://natzoo.si.edu/Publications/Zoogoer/2002/1/ hummingbirds.cfm (accessed on July 19, 2004).

Web sites:

"Hummingbird." San Diego Zoo.org Animal Bytes. http://www.sandiegozoo.org/animalbytes/t-hummingbird.html (accessed on June 24, 2004).

MOUSEBIRDS
Coliiformes

Class: Aves
Order: Coliiformes
One family: Coliidae
Number of species: 6 species

PHYSICAL CHARACTERISTICS

The mousebird order received its name because the birds look like mice when they creep around on the ground and tree branches. Mousebirds have gray or brown plumage (feathers) and patches of other coloring. These birds, also known as colies (KOHL-eez), range in head-to-tail length from 10.2 to 15.7 inches (26 to 39.8 centimeters). Mousebirds' pointed tails make up more than half of that length.

Mousebirds have crests, clumps of feathers on their head. Birds have short red legs and feet. Mousebirds' small, curved bills are strong enough to break the skin off fruit.

GEOGRAPHIC RANGE

Mousebirds live in sub-Saharan Africa, in countries south of the Sahara Desert. Bar-breasted mousebirds range throughout most of that area. White-headed mousebirds live in Kenya and Tanzania. Chestnut-backed mousebirds live in the region of the Democratic Republic of the Congo and Angola. White-backed mousebirds and red-faced mousebirds live in southern Africa. Blue-naped mousebirds live in western, central, and eastern Africa.

HABITAT

Mousebirds live in forests where deciduous trees lose their leaves during dry or cold seasons. The birds live in grassland areas where there are fewer trees and grass grows. Some birds live in parks and in garden trees.

phylum

class

subclass

order

● **monotypic order**

suborder

family

DIET

Mousebirds eat fruit, flowers, leaves, and buds. They sometimes eat insects.

BEHAVIOR AND REPRODUCTION

Mousebirds are social and noisy. They live in flocks of six to twenty-four birds. The birds are sedentary, not usually migrating from one area to another. During the day, birds eat, drink water, and take dust baths. Mousebirds travel in flocks to feed. Some birds climb to the top of a tree or bush to begin their flights. Birds fly quickly and land by crashing head-first into plants.

At night, a group of twenty or more birds roost (rest) in a tree. When the temperature drops, the birds enter a form of hibernation called torpor.

Mousebirds divide into pairs to breed. The birds are monogamous (muh-NAH-guh-mus), and breed with the same partner. The mousebird is an asynchronous (ay-SIN-kruh-nus) breeder, one that doesn't lay all eggs at the same time. The female lays a clutch of two to five eggs. However, sometimes there are seven eggs in a nest. The additional eggs usually belong to another female sharing the nest.

Mousebirds usually build nests in hidden places like leaf-covered branches or in thick bushes. The birds sometimes locate their nests near the nests of wasps, insects that have painful stings. Wasps provide protection against predators like snakes and larger birds. These predators hunt mousebirds for food.

After mousebirds breed, the male and female incubate the eggs, sitting on eggs to keep them warm. The mousebird's community behavior can extend to breeding. The couple that mated may be helped by "helper" birds. This is called cooperative breeding. Sometimes other males help guard the nest. These helpers are often the older offspring of the parents.

The eggs hatch in eleven to twelve days, and the birds fledge (grow flying feathers) within ten days to two weeks.

MOUSEBIRDS AND PEOPLE

Mousebirds damage trees, and that upsets people. They may poison or shoot the birds. Mousebirds sometimes die when pesticide is sprayed to kill insects. Not all birds are disliked; some people have bar-breasted mousebirds as cage birds.

CONSERVATION STATUS

Mousebirds are not in danger of extinction (dying out).

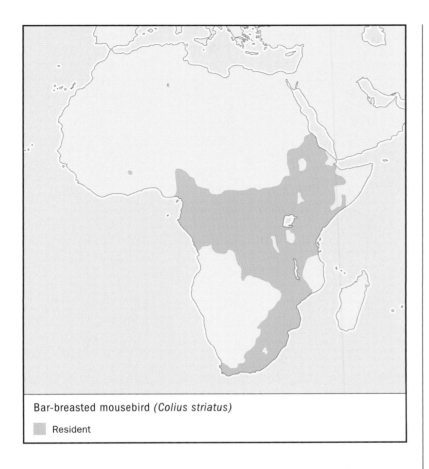

Bar-breasted mousebird (*Colius striatus*)

Resident

BAR-BREASTED MOUSEBIRD
Colius striatus

Physical characteristics: Bar-breasted mousebirds, also called speckled mousebirds, have mostly brownish gray plumage, and their crests are the same color. The length of the long-tailed birds ranges from 10.2 to 14.2 inches (26 to 36 centimeters). Weight ranges from 1.3 to 2.8 ounces (36 to 80 grams).

The white-eared bar-breasted mousebirds of East Africa have white feathers on the sides of their heads. A subspecies in the northern range has a white spot on its upper mandible (jaw). Birds in one subspecies have bills that are black on top and pink on the bottom. Some groups of birds have white or blue marks on their bills.

During the day, bar-breasted mousebirds feed, bathe, and preen, cleaning their feathers with their beaks. (© R. Cartmell/ VIREO. Reproduced by permission.)

Another difference is the color of the iris, the round part of the eye surrounding the pupil. Iris colors in subspecies include white, brown, and green. In addition, the iris may be two-toned, with the color above the pupil different from the color below it.

Geographic range: Bar-breasted mousebirds live in countries including Angola, Botswana, Cameroon, the Central African Republic, Eritrea, Ethiopia, Gabon, Mozambique, Nigeria, Somalia, Sudan, South Africa, Tanzania, Uganda, and Zimbabwe.

Habitat: Bar-breasted mousebirds live in grassland, deciduous forests, parks, gardens, and orchards where fruit trees grow.

Diet: Bar-breasted mousebirds eat fruit, berries, and plant buds and leaves. The type of food varies by habitat. Birds eat items native to an area along with fruits such as strawberries and tomatoes. The birds sometimes eat insects.

Behavior and reproduction: Bar-breasted mousebirds live in flocks of from six to thirty birds. The smaller group is usually a family of birds. Larger flocks consist of birds that look for food together and spend nights in the same trees. During the day, mousebirds feed and bathe. They also preen, cleaning their feathers with their beaks. At night, the flock roosts in tree branches.

Bar-breasted mousebirds can breed throughout the year. When birds breed depends on factors such as whether food is available to feed the young. During this season, birds pair off. The female lays one to five eggs. Both parents incubate the eggs.

The breeding pair may be helped by other birds. These cooperative breeders help with incubation and feeding. The helpers consist of one to three young birds of the same sex. Males are older offspring of the parents; females may not be related.

Bar-breasted mousebird eggs hatch in about twelve days, and chicks have yellow tongues. After the birds fledge, the parents may breed again. A female can lay up to eight clutches in a year.

Since mousebirds live in groups, this provides some protection from predators. Automobile drivers are a greater danger to bar-breasted mousebirds because the birds fly in a line one after the other. While flying in this pattern, drivers may accidentally kill the birds.

Bar-breasted mousebirds and people: People have various relationships with bar-breasted mousebirds. They sometimes resent the birds for ruining crops and taking fruit. People also admire the birds. The country of Gabon honored the bird with a 1992 stamp, and people in England bred captive mousebirds in 1912. Since then, people in countries including the United States keep bar-breasted mousebirds as cage, or captive, birds.

Conservation status: Bar-breasted mousebirds are not in danger of extinction.   ■

FOR MORE INFORMATION

Books:

del Hoyo, Josep, et al., eds. *Handbook of the Birds of the World.* Barcelona: Lynx Edicions, 1992.

Dickinson, Edward C., ed. *The Howard and Moore Complete Checklist of the Birds of the World,* 3rd ed. Princeton, NJ and Oxford, U.K.: Princeton University Press, 2003.

Forshaw, Joseph, ed. *Encyclopedia of Birds,* 2nd ed. San Diego, CA: Academic Press, 1998.

Harrison, Colin James Oliver. *Birds of the World.* London and New York: Dorling Kindersley, 1993.

Stuart, Chris and Tilde. *Birds of Africa From Seabirds to Seed Eaters.* Cambridge, MA: The MIT Press, 1999.

Periodicals:

McKechnie, Andrew E., and Barry G. Lovegrove. "Thermoregulation and the Energetic Significance of Clustering Behavior in the White-Backed Mousebird (*Colius colius*)." *Physiological and Biochemical Zoology* (March 2001): 238.

Web sites:

Kenya Birds. "Speckled Mousebird." Kenya Birds. http://www.kenyabirds.org.uk/s_mbird.htm (accessed on June 8, 2004).

TROGONS

Trogoniformes

Class: Aves

Order: Trogoniformes

One family: Trogonidae

Number of species: 37 species

monotypic order
CHAPTER

phylum

class

subclass

order

● **monotypic order**

suborder

family

PHYSICAL CHARACTERISTICS

Trogons (TROH-gahnz) are medium-sized, compact, brightly plumaged (feathered) birds that live mostly in trees; possess thin, delicate skin; soft and dense plumage; short necks; short, heavy, broad-hooked bills; short, rounded wings; long, broadly squared tails; and small, weak legs and feet. They are 9 to 16 inches (23 to 41 centimeters) long (excluding the tail streamer, the central part of the tail that is extra-long) and weigh between 1.2 and 7.3 ounces (35 and 210 grams).

Broad bills and weak legs are due to the trogon diet and arboreal (tree living) habits. In some species, bills are not curved but have serrated (saw blade-like) cutting edges. Trogon feet are described as heterodactyl (het-ur-oh-DAK-tuhl), with the first and second inner front toes turned backward and the third and fourth toes turned forward. This unusual toe arrangement allows them to cling vertically to trees. Their weak feet are unable to turn without the help of their wings.

Adult males are among the most brilliantly colored of all tropical birds. Their plumage is a brilliant green with some yellow, blue, or violet on the upper body, head, breast, and back; and yellow, orange, pink, or carmine (deep red) on the belly. Since trogon skin is delicate, feathers are easily lost. Central tails are long and broad, and hide three outer feathers usually with black or white bars; the outer feathers can be twice the length of inner tails. Females are duller in appearance, with browns and grays replacing the blues and greens of males. Female under parts, however, are often as brightly colored as those of males. Many trogons have distinctive bar-like or wavy wing sections, colored white-on-black in males and buff-on-black in females. Juveniles are irregularly brown patched with white and buff spots.

GEOGRAPHIC RANGE

Trogons are distributed throughout central and southern Africa, Southeast Asia, Central America, and north and central South America.

HABITAT

Trogons usually live in tropical forests, being found from rainforests to tropical woodlands. Most species are scattered within the tropics and subtropics, usually inhabiting the middle elevations of forests. On the northern and southern edges of their habitat, trogons live in drier climates including thorn forests, bamboo thickets, and savannas (flat grasslands).

DIET

Trogons eat fruits and insects, and sometimes small vertebrates (animals with backbones), although diets vary depending on the continent. African species are either exclusively insectivorous (feeding solely on insects) or carnivorous (feeding solely on meat), while species in Asia and the Americas eat both foods. Moths, butterflies, stick insects, beetles, small lizards, snails, frogs, and other similar creatures are also eaten. Trogons capture most food by hovering over prey before grabbing it from the air or off of branches. They swallow their food whole usually while sitting on a perch.

BEHAVIOR AND REPRODUCTION

Trogons fly with a graceful up and down motion, but are reluctant to fly far. Because trogons have short legs and weak feet, they are unable to walk. Normally, they sit still, making them difficult to find. They generally do not migrate.

Trogons pair monogamously (muh-NAH-guh-mus-lee; each bird having just one mate), and become territorial while breeding. They are solitary during the nonbreeding season. The breeding season occurs during the dry season in the tropics when food is more common. Spring and summer breeding is typical among species in temperate (mild) and arid (dry) areas. Males will call out a "wac-wac" sound in order to attract a mate after finding a nest site. Nest sites are usually made in cavities (hollow areas) of live trees or by roughing out holes in decaying tree trunks, but also in epiphyte (EPP-uh-fyte) root masses (plants that grow on others) and termite nests. Females answer with a call and with a show of a lowered tail. Males dig out a nest mostly with the bill, and then sing out for a female to join him. The agreeable female then helps with further construction. Nest cavities are either rising tunnels that lead to chambers, or shallow depressions that leave the occupying bird exposed. Nests are usually reused.

Two to four white or pastel-colored round eggs are laid in the unlined nest cavity. Usually only one brood (young birds born and raised together) occurs each year. The incubation period (time it takes to sit and hatch eggs) is sixteen to twenty-one days, being shared by both sexes but with the female usually sitting during the night. Chicks are hatched helpless, naked, and blind. They are raised by both parents, who feed them regurgitated (food brought up from the stomach) fruit and whole insects. They quickly grow down, and learn how to fly at fifteen to thirty-one days. Chicks breed for the first time at one or two years of age.

TROGONS AND PEOPLE

Hunters and collectors have targeted trogons for their brilliant tail feathers. Trogans, especially the quetzal (kett-SAHL), have often been given special status among ancient peoples. Today, many trogon species are very popular with tourists and nature lovers.

CONSERVATION STATUS

Trogons are relatively common but are still adversely affected by habitat destruction from humans. Ten trogons are identified as Near Threatened, in danger of becoming threatened with extinction, on the World Conservation Union (IUCN) Red List in 2002.

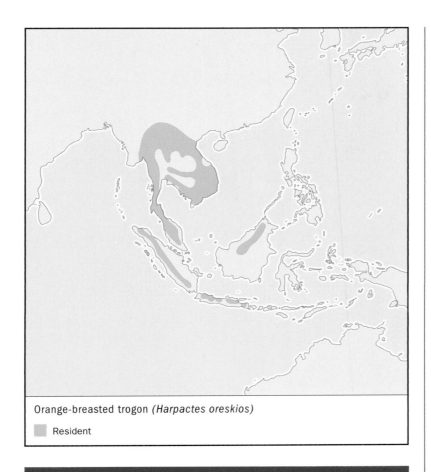

Orange-breasted trogon *(Harpactes oreskios)*

▢ Resident

ORANGE-BREASTED TROGON
Harpactes oreskios

Physical characteristics: Orange-breasted trogons generally have an olive-yellow head with feathers that are bristled and upright, chestnut upperparts, orange breast that changes to bright yellow on upper and lower portions, white bars on wing sections, and a blue bill. Males have a dull olive-yellowish head with a blue ring; rufous (reddish brown) upperparts and upper tail with paler rump (lower part of back); broad white bars on wing sections; and yellow (gray-based) upper breast with some white along the mid-line. Females have additional gray-brown on head and upperparts; pale buffy-brown rump, gray breast; and yellow lower underparts. Juveniles are similar to females, with young males having warmer brown upperparts. They are

Orange-breasted trogons sometimes feed in flocks containing several other species of birds. They eat fruit and insects. (Illustration by Bruce Worden. Reproduced by permission.)

9.8 to 10.2 inches (25 to 26 centimeters) long and weigh about 2 ounces (57 grams).

Geographic range: Orange-breasted trogons are found in southern China, the Malaysian Peninsula, Java, Sumatra, and northern Borneo.

Habitat: Orange-breasted trogons are found in humid, lower-to-middle elevation evergreen forests, lowlands and swampy forests, open dry forests, bamboo forests, thin tree jungles, and sometimes among clumps of trees near forests.

Diet: Orange-breasted trogons feed on fruits and insects including ants, beetles, caterpillars, cicadas (suh-KAY-duhz), crickets, grasshoppers, lizards, spiders, and various vegetable materials. They feed on the ground more often than other trogons, but appear to also feed high off the ground within forests. They sometimes feed in flocks containing several species.

Behavior and reproduction: Orange-breasted trogons perch on shorter trees in the middle and upper canopy (uppermost layer of vegetation) of the forest. They perch by themselves or in pairs, usually not moving. They breed January to June, but usually in February and March. These birds build nests in hollow stumps that are low to the ground, usually less than 3 feet (1 meter) from the ground. Females can lay one to four eggs, but two or three eggs are most common. Little information is available on rearing techniques with regards to incubation and nestling periods (time when young birds are still unable to leave the nest).

Orange-breasted trogons and people: There is no known significance between orange-breasted trogons and people.

Conservation status: Orange-breasted trogons are not globally threatened. ∎

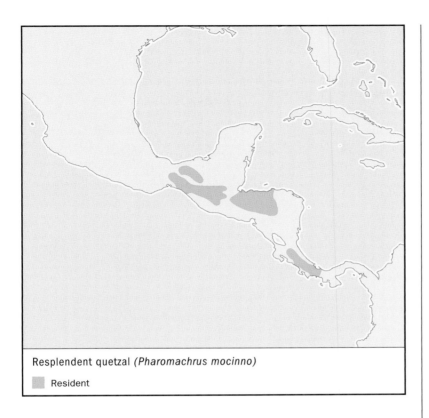

Resplendent quetzal *(Pharomachrus mocinno)*

Resident

RESPLENDENT QUETZAL
Pharomachrus mocinno

Physical characteristics: Resplendent quetzals generally have brilliant glittering gold-green upperparts, including the head and upper chest, which change to bluish colors depending on the direction they are seen in the sunlight. Their underparts are crimson in color from the middle to lower sections of the breast. Flight feathers are blackish, with parts beneath the tail being white. Males have a yellow bill, which is partly hidden by green feathers that circle around the eyes. Females have a blackish to yellow bill; bronze-green head; green upperparts, throat, and upper breast; gray from the mid-breast to the mid-belly; blackish upper portions of the tail; and grayish black and white under parts of the tail. Male young are similar to females, except with a yellow bill, more bronze on the upperparts, and additional white under the tail. Resplendent quetzal adults are 14.2 to 15.7

inches (36 to 40 centimeters) long, with tail streamers that are a length of up to 25.6 inches (65 centimeters). They weigh between 6.3 and 7.4 ounces (180 and 210 grams).

Geographic range: Resplendent quetzals are found in areas of Central America, from southern Mexico to western Panama.

Habitat: Resplendent quetzals occur in forests and along forest edges, mostly in the canopy and sub-canopy (below the treetops), but can be found in lower areas. Specifically, they are found in mountainous evergreen forests, densely vegetated ravines and cliffs, park-like clearing and pastures, and open areas with scattered trees next to forests.

Diet: Resplendent quetzals eat fruit, insects, small reptiles (such as lizards), and amphibians (such as frogs).

Behavior and reproduction: Resplendent quetzals are territorial by nature. They nest in a deep, unlined cavity with one entrance. The nest is usually 14 to 90 feet (4.3 to 27 meters) off the ground in a rotting trunk or stump in the forest or in a nearby clearing. During the breeding season, which lasts from March to June, male resplendent quetzals show off to females with flying displays. Females lay one to two eggs, incubate them for seventeen to nineteen days, and then fledge them (raise them until they can fly) for twenty-three to thirty-one days.

Resplendent quetzals and people: The ancient Maya and Aztec cultures of Central America have long honored resplendent quetzals. Their plumes were used for decoration well into the twentieth century. Their colorful plumage is very popular with birdwatchers.

Conservation status: Resplendent quetzals are Near Threatened mostly due to poachers and habitat disturbances. Threats include habitat clearance, poaching, lack of law enforcement, and local exploitation of forest resources. ■

FOR MORE INFORMATION

Books:

del Hoyo, Josep, A. Elliott, J. Sargatal, et al., eds. *Handbook of the Birds of the World.* Barcelona: Lynx Edicions, 1992.

Dickinson, Edward C., ed. *The Howard and Moore Complete Checklist of the Birds of the World,* 3rd ed. Princeton, NJ and Oxford, U.K.: Princeton University Press, 2003.

Elphick, Chris, John B. Dunning, Jr., and David Allen Sibley, eds. *The Sibley Guide to Bird Life and Behavior.* New York: Alfred A. Knopf, 2001.

Forshaw, Joseph, ed. *Encyclopedia of Birds,* 2nd ed. San Diego, CA: Academic Press, 1998.

Harrison, Colin James Oliver. *Birds of the World.* London and New York: Dorling Kindersley, 1993.

Perrins, Christopher M., and Alex L. A. Middleton, eds. *The Encyclopedia of Birds.* New York: Facts on File, 1985.

Stattersfield, Allison J., and David R. Capper, eds. *Threatened Birds of the World: The Official Source for Birds on the IUCN Red List.* Cambridge, U.K.: BirdLife International, 2000.

Class: Aves

Order: Coraciiformes

Number of families: 8 families

order

CHAPTER

PHYSICAL CHARACTERISTICS

Kingfishers, todies, hoopoes, and relatives (also called coraciiforms) include some interesting bird families with many of the most beautiful species in the world. The eight families in the order Coraciiformes include: kingfishers (Alcedinidae), todies (Todidae), motmots (Momotidae), bee-eaters (Meropidae), rollers (Coraciidae), hoopoes (Upupidae), woodhoopoes (Phoeniculidae), and hornbills (Bucerotidae). Appearance between adult males and females are similar in most species, except for most hornbills and some kingfishers. The bird families are very distinct from each other, and at first glance would not appear to be related except that they have a common foot structure. All members of the order look like each other with regards to their syndactylous (sin-DACK-tuh-lus) toes. That is, all birds have two, and sometimes three, forward pointing toes on their feet that are joined together partially at the base. The middle toe is connected to the inner toe at its base and to the outer toe for most of its length. The fused-together toes are most notable among bee-eaters and kingfishers.

Generally, all species are small- to medium-sized birds with short legs, rather small and weak feet, and short toes. Coraciiforms are 4 to 31 inches (10 to 79 centimeters) long, and weigh between 0.2 ounces and 8 pounds (6 grams and 4 kilograms). One of the smallest birds is the Puerto Rican tody, which has a length of 4 inches (10 centimeters) and a weight of about 0.2 ounces (6 grams). Two of the largest species are the Southern ground-hornbill and Abyssinian ground-hornbill. Both birds

phylum

class

subclass

● **order**

monotypic order

suborder

family

are about 31 inches (79 centimeters) in length and about 7 pounds (3 kilograms) in weight.

Coraciiforms are also recognized as having large heads, short necks, and somewhat large bills. Most have bills that are long, pointed, and colorful. Bills are enormous in the hornbills, often resembling New World toucans (tropical birds with a large beak). Most species have long tails and tall crests, with bright, colorful plumage (feathers).

Coraciiforms share other, less noticeable characteristics, including the structure of the palate bones (the bones on the roof of the mouth), lack of the ambiens muscle in the leg (the muscles that control the movement of toes), and the feather tracts (the spacing of feathers in a pattern).

GEOGRAPHIC RANGE

Coraciiformes are found on all continents except Antarctica. Members of the kingfisher family are most widely distributed of all the families, being found on all ice-free continents, but are most commonly found from New Guinea to tropical Asia. Only a few kingfishers are found in the Americas, with the belted kingfisher being the species most widespread in the United States. The other families have more limited distributions. Motmots and todies are found only in the New World, with motmots found in Mexico and into South America, and todies found in the islands of the Greater Antilles (in the West Indies of the Caribbean).

The other families occur only in the Old World, ranging widely across Africa, Eurasia, and into Australia, New Zealand, New Guinea, and neighboring islands of the South Pacific. All woodhoopoes and most bee-eaters and rollers are found in Africa, usually in the warmer central and southern regions. The rest of the bee-eaters are found in other temperate and tropical regions of the Old World. Hoopoes are found in Africa and Eurasia. Hornbills are spread out between tropical Africa and Asia, with small populations in the Philippines and Malaysia.

HABITAT

Most coraciiform species are found in the tropical rainforests. Kingfishers usually inhabit tropical forests or woodlands, and are often found near water. Bee-eaters are found in temperate and tropical regions. Other regions of habitat outside of the tropics include coniferous and deciduous forests and grasslands.

They are often found along rivers and streams, seacoasts, and wetlands. Many species that live near inland waters in the summer will travel to the seacoast when inland waters freeze over in the winter.

DIET

Coraciiforms eat small animals, especially small vertebrates, or animals with a backbone, (such as fishes, reptiles, amphibians, and small mammals), and invertebrates, or animals without a backbone (such as insects, worms, and crustaceans). For instance, the shovel-billed kingfisher eats mainly earthworms. Some species, such as many forest hornbills, eat fruit and berries as their primary source of food, only adding meat when raising their young.

Although most species search for food within trees, some species hunt for food on the ground. They catch their prey primarily by dropping down to the ground from a perch (as with true rollers and bee-eaters) or into water (as with kingfishers). When birds drop down to their prey, they may hover while targeting onto food (as in kingfishers), or they may take the food as they fly (as in bee-eaters and broad-billed rollers). Some families, such as todies and motmots, use both terrestrial (on the ground) and aerial (in the air) techniques for the capture of prey. A few species gather their food while they walk or run about on the ground, such as the common hoopoes and some African hornbills.

BEHAVIOR AND REPRODUCTION

Coraciiforms share the behavior of digging cavity nests in earthen banks, sandy banks, insect and termite hills, or rotten trees. They are considered primitive perching birds. Most members of the order are partly arboreal; that is, they primarily live, feed, and breed in trees. Many members are social in their habits and are somewhat noisy when communicating among themselves and warning others of their presence. In fact, the laughing kookaburra, one of the best known birds of Australia, is famous for its "laughing" song.

Most species nest in cavities, crevices, or holes in a tree, rock face, building, or within the ground (such as a tunnel with the nesting chamber at the end). Kingfishers, todies, motmots, and bee-eaters usually dig their own earthen burrows, which often occur in sandy banks, rotten trees and other wooden places, or insect nests. Nests become very smelly as body waste and the remains of food accumulate inside. Only hornbills maintain tidy nests, going to the effort of directing body waste outside the nest and removing food remains.

Male and female pairs mate for life. Most species are territorial when breeding, meaning that they keep other birds away from their nest. In addition, most species breed as a single male-female pair. In some families, there are species that live and breed as groups (usually a mating pair plus one or a few helpers); some species even nest in large colonies (large groups of birds that live together and are dependent on each other). Males and females generally share duties of nest construction, chick defense, and food delivery (with males providing most of the early gathering of food, and females sharing more feeding duties after the chicks have grown).

Eggs are normally laid inside a cavity that is thinly lined with plant materials. Females produce white or pale eggs, except hoopoes, whose eggs are tinted light blue-green. The eggs are rounded and shiny, except for the oval ones of the hoopoes and hornbills. In most species, the female performs most or all of the incubation (sitting on) of eggs and the raising of young chicks. The eggs hatch after two to four weeks of incubation. The length of time is different for each species. The newborns are hatched helpless, blind, and naked, except in hoopoes, whose newborns have patches of fine down. The upper jaw in newborn chicks is visibly shorter than the lower one. They depend on their parents when very young. They have waxy sheaths (tube-shaped coverings that protect feathers) on their feathers up until the time that they are able to fly.

KINGFISHERS, TODIES, HOOPOES, RELATIVES, AND PEOPLE

People generally enjoy the colorful appearance of coraciiforms. In fact, the area of Sarawak (in north-central Malaysia) is known as "The Land of the Hornbill" and the state of Sabah (in northeast Malaysia) has a kingfisher on its national coat of arms. However, with the continued unrestricted spread of human development into their habitats, the birds continue to be threatened in their abilities to live freely in their natural environments. For the most part, when they have a large geographical range, the birds are commonly seen and not adversely affected by the presence of people.

CONSERVATION STATUS

Twenty-five species of Coraciiformes are threatened with extinction. There are three Critically Endangered species, facing an extremely high risk of extinction in the wild; five listed as Endangered, facing a very high risk of extinction in the wild; and seventeen species are Vulnerable, facing a high risk of extinction in the wild.

FOR MORE INFORMATION

Books:

Alsop, Fred J. III. *Birds of North America.* New York: Dorling Kindersley, 2001.

AOU Check-list of North American Birds, 7th ed. Washington, DC: The Union (The American Ornithologists' Union), 1998.

del Hoyo, Josep, et al., eds. *Handbook of the Birds of the World.* Barcelona, Spain: Lynx Edicions, 1992.

Dickinson, Edward C., ed. *The Howard and Moore Complete Checklist of the Birds of the World,* 3rd ed. Princeton, NJ and Oxford, U.K.: Princeton University Press, 2003.

Elphick, Chris, John B. Dunning Jr., and David Allen Sibley. *The Sibley Guide to Bird Life and Behavior.* New York: Alfred A. Knopf (distributed by Random House), 2001.

Harrison, Colin James Oliver. *Birds of the World.* London and New York: Dorling Kindersley (distributed by Houghton Mifflin), 1993.

Forshaw, Joseph, ed. *Encyclopedia of Birds,* 2nd ed. San Diego, CA: Academic Press, 1998.

Kaufman, Kenn. *Birds of North America.* New York: Houghton Mifflin, 2000.

Perrins, Christopher M., and Alex L. A. Middleton, eds. *The Encyclopedia of Birds.* New York: Facts on File, 1985.

Stattersfield, Allison, J., and David R. Capper, eds. *Threatened Birds of the World: The Official Source for Birds on the IUCN Red List.* Cambridge, U.K.: BirdLife International, 2000.

Class: Aves
Order: Coraciformes
Family: Alcedinidae
Number of species: 91 species

family

CHAPTER

PHYSICAL CHARACTERISTICS

Kingfishers are vibrant birds both in appearance and behavior, with a long pointed bill, small weak feet, large head, compact body, short neck, and very short legs. The bill and feet are usually black or brown but may be yellow, orange, or red. The bill's shape depends on feeding habits: narrow and flattened at the sides in species that hunt prey by water diving; broad and flattened with distinct upper and lower surfaces in species that catch small ground animals; or especially wide in forest species that search for prey in soil and leaf litter. The feet have three front toes that are fused at their bases. In some species, the second toe is shortened or absent. The metallic-looking plumage is often black, white, or reddish brown, with areas of iridescent blue, purple, or green. Wings are short and rounded, while the tail varies from extremely short to very long. Kingfishers are 4 to 18 inches (10 to 48 centimeters) long, and weigh between 0.3 and 16.4 ounces (9 and 465 grams).

GEOGRAPHIC RANGE

Kingfishers are found on all continents except Antarctica, but are unevenly distributed with regard to species. Most species that live in forests are found in Australia, New Guinea, and Indonesia east of Bali and Sulawesi. Others are found on the islands of the Pacific, in western Indonesia, the islands of Java, Borneo, Sumatra, and the Philippines. A few species are found on the Asian mainland, in India, and the Middle East. Species that live in savannas, grasslands, are found mostly in the tropical region of sub-Saharan Africa and Madagascar.

HABITAT

Kingfishers are found throughout aquatic or wooded habitats, avoiding open country. They range from arid savannas to dense rainforests, and from low seacoasts to high mountains. Species that feed on aquatic animals are found from arid (dry, little rainfall) seashores to small mountain streams. Species that feed on land animals are found from arid savannas to dense rainforests.

DIET

Most kingfishers consume relatively large invertebrates, especially grasshoppers, earthworms, and crustaceans, as well as small vertebrates, especially reptiles, fishes, and amphibians. A few species eat fruit. They spend much time perched in a stationary position on the lookout for prey, animals they hunt for food, swooping down to grab prey from the ground, water, air, or leaves.

BEHAVIOR AND REPRODUCTION

Most species are sedentary (tending not to move), and nearly all are diurnal (active during the day). Many of them bathe by diving repeatedly into water. The majority of species roost alone within vegetation. They all are highly vocal. Loud calls warn visitors that they have ventured into kingfisher territories, while softer calls are communications between mates or with offspring.

To attract females, male kingfishers perform courtship rituals such as aerial displays, plumage, feather, exposure, and feeding of females. Both sexes play roles in selecting and digging nest sites, usually in earthen banks, but also in rotten wood, termite nests, or tree hollows. They dig by flying into the surface bill-first, then loosening debris with the bill, and later by kicking out loosened materials with feet. A tunnel is built that can extend from 3 to 26 feet (1 to 8 meters), ending in an unlined nest cavity.

The white, round, shiny eggs are laid one a day with two to seven eggs in a clutch. Both sexes take part in incubation and care of young. Females remain on the nest overnight. Incubation takes from two to four weeks, and the nestling period is from three to eight weeks. Babies are born blind and naked. Feathers emerge with quills (hollow feather shafts). They become independent a few days to about a week after learning to fly, and become sexually mature within a year.

KINGFISHERS AND PEOPLE

Some people hunt kingfishers when the birds eat fish commercially raised on farms. In the past, some kingfishers were stuffed for the beauty of their plumes and feathers, and other feathers were worn as hair decorations. Often the call of kingfishers was seen as an omen. The laughing kookaburra is an important symbol of Australia.

CONSERVATION STATUS

The main threats to kingfishers are the clearing, draining, or polluting of rainforest habitats. Twelve species are considered threatened by extinction, dying out, and at least two subspecies have become extinct. Threatened species are found in Southeast Asia and the Pacific Islands, including New Zealand and Australia.

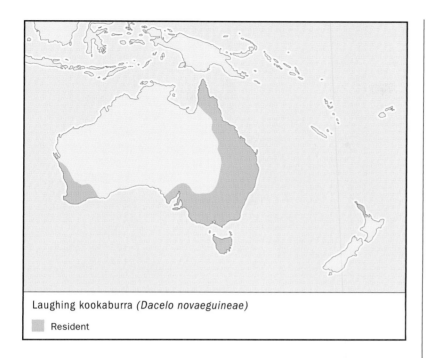

Laughing kookaburra (*Dacelo novaeguineae*)

☐ Resident

LAUGHING KOOKABURRA
Dacelo novaeguineae

Physical characteristics: Laughing kookaburras are the largest of the kingfishers, with a dark brown and white body, blue rump, and reddish tail with white-tipped outer tail feathers and blue-tipped wing coverts (feathers between flight feathers of the wing and tail). They have a dark stripe through their eyes. The blunt, heavy bill is black in color above and horn-colored below. Their small feet are used mainly for perching. They are from 15 to 17 inches (39 to 42 centimeters) long, and weigh between 7 and 16 ounces (190 and 465 grams).

Geographic range: Laughing kookaburras are located in eastern and southwestern Australia.

Habitat: Laughing kookaburras are found in dry and open eucalyptus forests and woodlands, and often are seen in parks and gardens that border such areas.

Diet: Laughing kookaburras eat mostly insects, beetles, grasshoppers, and spiders, but also eat small vertebrates, such as snakes,

Laughing kookaburras get their name from the cackling sounds they make. (Kike Calvo/Bruce Coleman Inc. Reproduced by permission.)

lizards, mice, and small birds. When spotting prey, they swoop down to pick up small animals. They usually eat alone.

Behavior and reproduction: A breeding pair and its mature off-spring are often heard cackling at dawn. When in defense of their ter-ritory, laughing kookaburras often have their heads stretched up and tails raised while making cackling sounds. During the day, they are often seen perched motionless in dense foliage, looking for prey.

The male and female breed for life, and share the raising of their latest brood with older offspring. Nests are usually made in natural cavities, but can be formed from termite nests or soft dead wood. Fe-males lay from one to five eggs. The incubation period is between twenty-four and twenty-nine days, with the female performing most of the duties, and other members performing other chores. The nestling period is from thirty-two to forty days. Young birds stay with their parents for several years as helpers.

Laughing kookaburras and people: People in Australia are very familiar with the life of laughing kookaburras, and the birds are a well-known emblem of the country.

Conservation status: Laughing kookaburras are not threatened, being widespread and common. In fact, the species grows in numbers when humans develop previously undeveloped areas such as parks and gardens, where the birds can safely look for food under leaf litter and mulch. ■

Rufous-collared kingfisher *(Actenoides concretus)*

■ Resident

RUFOUS-COLLARED KINGFISHER
Actenoides concretus

Physical characteristics: Rufous-collared kingfishers are medium-sized, plump kingfishers, with a green crown (top of the head); blue (in males) and buff-spotted green (in females) back; and rufous (red) coloring on and below the collar. The bill is black above and yellow below. Rufous-collared kingfishers are 9 to 9.5 inches (22.9 to 24.1 centimeters) long, and weigh between 2.1 and 3.2 ounces (59.5 and 90.7 grams).

Geographic range: Rufous-collared kingfishers are commonly found on the Malay Peninsula, Borneo, and Sumatra.

Habitat: Rufous-collared kingfishers are usually found in dense, lowland rainforests, and sometimes in secondary forests (that is, in forests where new vegetation has formed after the original vegetation of the forest has been destroyed either by nature or by humans). They are found up to 5,600 feet (1,700 meters) above sea level.

Diet: They feed on various arthropods; mostly insects and large scorpions, but also fish, snails, small snakes, and lizards. They catch prey by dropping from a low perch to snatch the prey off the water surface or off the ground. Occasionally, they turn over leaves in search of food.

Rufous-collared kingfishers usually catch prey by dropping from a low perch to snatch the prey off the water surface or off the ground. (Illustration by Brian Cressman. Reproduced by permission.)

Behavior and reproduction: When calling out, rufous-collared kingfishers produce a loud, long whistle that rises in tone. They perch mostly in the middle and lower levels of forests. When perched, they will regularly show a slow bobbing head and pumping tail.

Monogamous (muh-NAH-guh-mus) pairs, birds mated only with each other, usually dig nest burrows in earthen banks, but also use rotten tree trunks. They dig out tunnels that end in a nest chamber about 8 inches (20 centimeters) in diameter. Females usually lay two eggs, which are incubated for about twenty-two days.

Rufous-collared kingfishers and people: There is no known significance between people and rufous-collared kingfishers.

Conservation status: Rufous-collared kingfishers are considered Near Threatened, in danger of becoming threatened with extinction, due to extensive removal of lowland forests, but continue to survive in hill forests and in conserved tracts. ∎

Belted kingfisher *(Megaceryle alcyon)*

■ Resident ■ Breeding ■ Nonbreeding

BELTED KINGFISHER
Megaceryle alcyon

Physical characteristics: Belted kingfishers are large kingfishers with a stocky blue-gray body, white breast and collar, and large head. It is one of the few North American birds in which females are more colorful than males. Males have blue-gray upperparts with a plain blue-gray band across the breast and appear to have a big head with a large bill and shaggy, double-pointed crest. A white spot appears around its eyes. Females have a blue-gray breast band with a rufous band below. In flight, it shows a white patch on the upper wing. Juveniles of both sexes resemble adult females. They are 11 to 13 inches (28 to 33 centimeters) long, about 20 inches (51 centimeters) in wing span, and weigh between 4 and 6.3 ounces (113 and 178 grams).

Geographic range: Belted kingfishers are found across the north-central United States and southern Canada, and south throughout the United States, except for southwestern and far south-central regions and southern Florida. During the summer breeding season, belted kingfishers migrate from about 65° north latitude to nearly the Arctic Circle. During nonbreeding winter, the birds migrate to the southwestern United States and central America, south to the Galápagos Islands and Guyana.

Habitat: Belted kingfishers are found around wooded freshwater bodies such as lakes, rivers, streams, ponds, and estuaries or calm marine waters. They range from the seashore to 8,200 feet (2,500 meters) above sea level. During nonbreeding seasons, they gather in mangroves, coasts, watercourses in open country, marshes, and offshore islands.

Diet: Belted kingfishers eat fish, but also take amphibians, reptiles, insects, crustaceans, crayfish, mollusks, small mammals, young birds, and berries. They hunt in the late morning or afternoon. Sometimes the birds follow egrets for prey that they disturb. They hunt for food by either perching from trees or by hovering from 20 to 49 feet (6 to 15 meters) above streams or ponds. Often, they plunge headfirst into waters, catching most prey within 2 feet (60 centimeters) of the surface. They pound captured prey against their perch with sideways head movements.

Behavior and reproduction: Belted kingfishers fly with irregular wing beats. They are easily seen in tree perches that overlook water or on coastal rocks. Their territorial call is a long, uneven rattle. They also have a higher, shorter, more musical trill sound.

Belted kingfishers are monogamous birds, with both parents helping to dig out a tunnel and nest in an earthen bank that is within easy reach of water. They usually dig down from 3 to 7 feet (1 to 2 meters) below the ground surface but can go down to 15 feet (4 meters), with a nest cavity of 8 to 12 inches (20 to 30 centimeters) in diameter. Females lay from five to eight eggs, which are incubated between twenty-two and twenty-four days and nested between twenty-seven and thirty-five days. Males and females share incubation (sitting on eggs), brooding (providing warmth and shelter by gathering chicks under the breast or wing), and feeding duties. They have from one to two broods (groups of young birds) per year.

Belted kingfishers and people: Before regulations, people sometimes hunted belted kingfishers when they fed on fish stocks at fish hatcheries and along trout streams.

Conservation status: Belted kingfishers are not threatened. They are widespread and common in many areas, being more resistant to pollution than most other kingfishers. ■

FOR MORE INFORMATION

Books:

Alsop, Fred J. III. *Birds of North America*. New York: Dorling Kindersley, 2001.

AOU Check-list of North American Birds, 7th ed. Washington, DC: The American Ornithologists' Union, 1998.

Elphick, Chris, John B. Dunning Jr., and David Allen Sibley, eds. *The Sibley Guide to Bird Life and Behavior.* New York: Alfred A. Knopf, 2001.

Forshaw, Joseph, ed. *Encyclopedia of Birds,* 2nd ed. San Diego, CA: Academic Press, 1998.

Kaufman, Kenn. *Birds of North America.* New York: Houghton Mifflin, 2000.

Perrins, Christopher M., and Alex L. A. Middleton, eds. *The Encyclopedia of Birds.* New York: Facts on File, 1985.

Web sites:

Coraciiformes Taxon Advisory Group. http://www.coraciiformestag.com (accessed on July 19, 2004).

TODIES

Todidae

Class: Aves

Order: Coraciiformes

Family: Todidae

Number of species: 5 species

family

CHAPTER

PHYSICAL CHARACTERISTICS

Todies are tiny, delicate, rather chunky kingfisher-like birds. They have a broad head; a long, narrow, and somewhat flattened bill that is colored red or orange-red below and black above; sky-blue to gray cheeks; bright scarlet-red throat patch; short, slightly rounded tail; and shining green wings. All species have brilliant emerald-green feathers on their upper bodies, with various colors on the breast, sides, and stomach depending on the species, some pale (whitish, cream, or grayish) and others having mixtures of pink, yellow, green, and blue. Individual species are identified most often by the different colors of their sides, stomach, and cheeks.

The shape of the bill is designed for efficient eating. It easily snaps up insects from the undersides of leaves in short, sweeping movements. Most species have short, rounded wings and loosely fluffed plumage (feathers). The short wings are efficient for their short flights. Other species fly longer distances, and have longer wings. Males and females are similar in physical characteristics. Adult todies show no changes in feather color between the seasons. The five species are: Cuban tody, narrow-billed tody, Puerto Rican tody, Jamaican tody, and broad-billed tody.

Todies somewhat resemble miniature kingfishers and often are mistaken for hummingbirds. They are 4 to 4.6 inches (10.1 to 11.7 centimeters) long, and weigh between 0.19 and 0.27 ounces (5.4 and 7.7 grams).

phylum

class

subclass

order

monotypic order

suborder

▲ **family**

GEOGRAPHIC RANGE

Todies range through the larger islands of the Caribbean, including the Greater Antilles in the West Indies. Cuba, Jamaica, and Puerto Rico each have one species, while Hispaniola holds two species.

HABITAT

Todies inhabit primary (original) and secondary (vegetation has regrown after the original forest is cut down) tropical forests and woodlands, including dry lowlands, lush mountain rainforests, pine groves, streamside vegetation, pasture borders, limestone regions, cactus deserts, and shaded coffee plantations. Within these environments, their population is limited by the amount of vegetation, number of insects, and other requirements, especially good nesting locations. They occupy environments ranging from 160 feet (50 meters) below sea level to elevations above 9,800 feet (3,000 meters). They seek out brushy lands and forests with plenty of foliage (leaves, flowers, and branches), epiphytes (EPP-uh-fytes; plants that grow while attached to another plant, usually high in the air), and vines. They often are found along the edges of streams or rivers.

DIET

Todies eat large amounts of food with respect to their tiny body size, often eating one insect or more during every minute of the daytime hours. They eat a wide variety of insect families, but chiefly consume ants, bugs, butterflies, cockroaches, damselfies, flies, grasshoppers, mantids, and mayflies. They also eat lizards, seeds, and spiders.

BEHAVIOR AND REPRODUCTION

Todies generally appear as vivid green birds that fly rapidly with bounce-like actions through the woods in pairs while chirping to each other. They often accompany such behaviors with loud nasal beeps, grating and monotonous "neet" or "prrrrreeet," or harsh chatter. Their calls help to distinguish the various species. They are generally territorial (protecting an area from other birds), but will temporarily join other species that are feeding within their territories. They spend much of the day, either alone or in pairs, sitting motionless on perches of small twigs. They normally perch with their bills in an uplifted position.

Todies catch their prey by a graceful stunt-plane-like technique in which the head is directed upward while the bird scans the undersides of leaves and twigs. While jerking its head and moving its eyes, it darts upward at a shallow angle and flies at a short curved path in order to grab an insect and continue the end of its flight at another perch. They may also hover in mid-air in order to catch prey.

Todies are homeotherms; that is, they have body temperatures like humans in which metabolic rates and temperatures are controlled. At times, todies can become very inactive to conserve energy. Such dormant periods occur when they cannot eat because of the darkness at night and during long periods of heavy rain. Females also become dormant in order to save their energy while breeding. Todies do not migrate.

Todies often show courtship displays of hovering and zooming that involve great amounts of whirling and crackling of the wings. The flapping of the wings (sometimes called wing-rattling) is similar to the noise heard when pulling a finger quickly across a comb. Males and females pursue each other at very fast speeds, weaving around foliage. Once paired, both will exchange freshly caught insects.

When ready to start a family, they dig tube-shaped, angled tunnels in vertical soil embankments from February to May. One tunnel may take eight weeks to finish. Bills chisel out the soil, while their feet push the soil away. Tody eggs are much larger than eggs of other similarly sized birds, with eggs weighing about 26 percent of the adult's body weight (with typical egg-to-body weight in birds from 2 to 11 percent). Tody females lay one clutch, or set of eggs, per year, with two to five eggs per clutch. If destroyed, females will produce another clutch.

Eggs are tiny, white, glossy, and roundish. Incubation periods (time spent sitting on eggs) last twenty-one to twenty-two days, while nestling periods (time a young bird spends at the nest after hatching) are between nineteen and twenty days. Each parent spends only two to three daylight hours incubating. Hatching occurs usually in the late afternoon. Nestlings are born naked, with cushioned heels that cover the feet. Young remain in the nest until they can fly.

TODIES AND PEOPLE

People degrade the territory of todies when they enter and alter the natural forests they prefer. They are often an attraction for birdwatchers, allowing people to approach them as closely as 6 feet (2 meters).

CONSERVATION STATUS

Todies, generally, are not threatened. However, in 2001, population densities decreased due to habitat destruction. The narrow-billed tody is considered Near Threatened, in danger of becoming threatened with extinction.

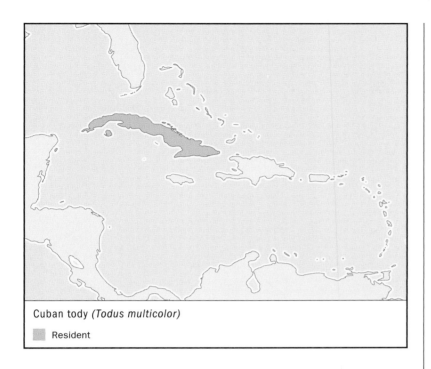

Cuban tody *(Todus multicolor)*

▨ Resident

CUBAN TODY
Todus multicolor

**SPECIES
ACCOUNT**

Physical characteristics: Cuban todies are brilliantly colored, primarily green in body color, with a big head, no neck, and the smallest bill of all todies. They have rosy pink sides, whitish stomach, yellow undertail coverts (feathers between flight feathers of the wing and tail), red throat, and sky-blue cheek patch. The flattened bills have notched edges and a yellow base. Their eyebrows are an almost brilliant yellow-green. They have a wingspan of about 4.3 inches (10.8 centimeters) in length, with a weight of between 0.21 and 0.23 ounces (6.0 and 6.5 grams).

Geographic range: Cuban todies range throughout Cuba, including the Isle of Pines (Isle of Youth) and four large cays (KEYS or KAYS; low islands or reefs) off of Cuba's north coast.

Habitat: Cuban todies are found in dry lowlands, dry mountainous scrublands, tropical deciduous forests, tropical lowland evergreen forests, mountainous evergreen forests, pine forests, and along

Cuban todies are colorful birds whose most characteristic call is a soft "pprreeeee-pprreeeee." (© Doug Wechsler/VIREO. Reproduced by permission.)

seashores (near coastal vegetation). Specifically, they are found in shady areas, usually along streams and rivers.

Diet: Cuban todies eat mostly small adult and larval insects, but have been known to eat caterpillars, spiders, and small lizards. They sometimes (but rarely) eat small fruits.

Behavior and reproduction: Cuban todies are rather inactive birds that search for prey from a perch. They forage, search for food, in arid scrub at an average height above the ground of 9 feet (2.7 meters). They often look for food from twigs and undersides of leaves. They make a characteristic rattling with their wings. When perched, they sometimes repeat a peculiar short "tot-tot-tot-tot" sound. Their most characteristic call is a soft "pprreeeee-pprreeeee."

Cuban todies pair for life, and have striking courtship patterns, including showing their bright pink sides. They breed from April to June, first digging burrows in earthen banks, within rotten logs, and in natural limestone cavities. Tunnels are usually about 1 foot (0.3 meters) in length, with a chamber at the end. The walls of the tunnel and the egg chamber are often lined with a thick glue-like substance mixed with algae (AL-jee), grass, lichens (LIE-kenz), small feathers, and other materials. Though infrequent, they also build at cave entrances. The white eggs produced by the female, usually three to four in number, are the smallest of the todies.

Cuban todies and people: People in poor areas sometimes eat Cuban todies. Otherwise, they are a delight to people who enjoy watching them.

Conservation status: Cuban todies are not threatened by extinction, being common and widely distributed throughout its range. However, Cuba's poverty and unstable economy may affect tody populations, especially with regards to pesticide use, which may harm the todies. ∎

FOR MORE INFORMATION

Books:

Clements, James F. *Birds of the World: A Checklist*. Vista, CA: Ibis Publishing Company, 2000.

Elphick, Chris, John B. Dunning Jr., and David Allen Sibley, eds. *The Sibley Guide to Bird Life and Behavior.* New York: Alfred A. Knopf, 2001.

Forshaw, Joseph, ed. *Encyclopedia of Birds,* 2nd ed. San Diego, CA: Academic Press, 1998.

Perrins, Christopher M., and Alex L. A. Middleton, eds. *The Encyclopedia of Birds.* New York: Facts on File, 1985.

Class: Aves
Order: Coraciiformes
Family: Momotidae
Number of species: 9 species

family

CHAPTER

phylum

class

subclass

order

monotypic order

suborder

▲ family

PHYSICAL CHARACTERISTICS

Motmots are impressive-looking, robust birds that look somewhat like kingfishers. Male and female motmots have a similar appearance. The birds have bright shades of green and blue colors, a black mask, and a long racquet-tipped tail in most species.

The longish, powerful bill curves slightly downward at the tip, and, in most species, the bill has notches like saw teeth along the edges that are used for cutting. The tongue is somewhat long. Legs are short, with each foot having three front toes and a rear toe. The middle front toe is almost completely joined to the inner toe.

The short wings are rounded. Plumage (feathers) is bright green or turquoise green on the back and tail of all species, with specks of soft blue or reddish brown on the wings and tail. Some species have brilliant blue or emerald stripes along the side of the head. There is a mixture of browns and greens on the underbody.

Several species have green or brown crowns (feathers at the top of the head) but most species have crowns of turquoise, blue, or black. Several species have a black spot on the breast. All birds have a black mark through or near the eyes; in some species, the mark is accented by thin turquoise stripes above and below. A group of black feathers at the chin and throat is characteristic of all motmots.

The tail is broad and long and sharply tapers at the base. The central pair of feathers is extra long. Barbs (parts of a feather) near the tail fall off readily, resulting in the shaft looking bare in spots. At these empty spots, a small oval disk remains.

Motmots are 6 to 21 inches (16 to 53 centimeters) long, and weigh between 0.9 and 7.4 ounces (25 and 210 grams).

GEOGRAPHIC RANGE

Motmots are found from northeastern Mexico through most of tropical South America, as far as northern Argentina. Honduras contains seven species, while Mexico, Guatemala, and Nicaragua each have six species. Venezuela, the Guianas, and Suriname have only one species.

HABITAT

Motmots are mainly found in tropical or mountainous forests and woodlands. Although most species are lowland dwellers, the blue-throated motmot ranges from 4,900 to 10,000 feet (1,500 to 3,100 meters) in middle America, and the highland motmot ranges between 4,100 and 7,200 feet (1,250 and 2,200 meters) in the South American Andes. Most motmots inhabit the midstory or understory (rather than the overstory, or highest trees) of forests or woodlands.

DIET

Motmots eat invertebrates, or animals without a backbone (such as beetles, butterflies, caterpillars, centipedes, cicadas [suh-KAY-duhz], crabs, dragonflies, earthworms, mantids, millipedes, spiders, scorpions, and snails), small vertebrates, or animals with a backbone (such as frogs, lizards, nestling birds, small fishes, and small snakes), and fruits (such as the fruit of figs, heliconia, incense, palms, and nutmegs). It appears that the larger the species, the more fruit it has in its diet.

Motmots secure food in different ways, depending on the size of the species. Smaller species use sit-and-wait strategies and secure prey that is flying, while larger species fly in their search for prey that is usually on the ground. Once caught, prey is beaten against a perch with their strong bills in order to crush it. Indigestible food is regurgitated (re-GER-jih-tate-ud) as pellets. Some species follow trains of army ants that disturb insects, allowing them to grab the insects.

BEHAVIOR AND REPRODUCTION

Motmots appear to be solitary (living alone), but maintain pair bonds (bonds between a mated pair) throughout their lives.

When disturbed, a motmot twitches its tail. Motmots are not very active, and are hard to see when they remain still within the forest. They are inactive at night and active during dawn and dusk. Calling is most active during the early morning. Short migrations sometimes occur for motmots; they may leave breeding areas for a month or so. Motmots have a wide range of calls, from soft, rhythmical hoots to squawk-like and cooing noises, which are sounded singly or in a series. Voices can carry for long distances. Males and females sing together as a mating ritual, which also helps to strengthen the bond during the non-breeding season and to maintain the security of their territory.

Mating pairs build nests usually by themselves, but sometimes in the company of other nests, sometimes with more than forty pairs of breeding birds. Nests are usually in burrows in earthen banks, but are sometimes in crevices in rocks. Motmot male-female pairs dig out underground chambers, taking turns at loosening soil and kicking dirt out of the opening. The chamber may be from 5 to 16 feet (1.5 to 5 meters) long in the larger species. Eggs are laid on bare soil, but may also be laid on re-gurgitated insect parts. Rounded, shiny, and white eggs are usually laid three to five per clutch. Only one clutch per year is normal, unless the clutch is lost to predators or the weather. In those cases, a second clutch is laid after ten to twenty-one days. Eggs are incubated by both sexes during long shifts of up to twenty-four hours at a time. The incubation period is between seventeen and twenty-two days, depending on the species. Chicks hatch blind, featherless, and dependent on their parents. Both sexes care for the brood, feeding them butterflies, moths, other insects, partially digested food, and protein-rich fruits. Young leave the nest from twenty-four to thirty-two days after hatching.

MOTMOTS AND PEOPLE

People use motmot tail feathers and wings for ornamentation.

CONSERVATION STATUS

One species is Vulnerable, facing a high risk of extinction, dying out: the keel-billed motmot. Habitat destruction is a concern for all species as the destruction of forests and woodlands continues unabated.

Blue-crowned motmot (*Momotus momota*)

■ Resident

BLUE-CROWNED MOTMOT
Momotus momota

Physical characteristics: Blue-crowned motmots have a large head with down curved, short, broad beaks, which are serrated along the upper edge. They have bluish black crowns that are bordered with violet and turquoise, and have a black mask with turquoise above and below. The back of the neck is rufous (reddish brown), and its upper

Blue-crowned motmots capture prey by sitting quietly on wires, fence posts, or tree branches, and then suddenly flying toward the prospective meal, taking it while it flies or while its on the ground. (Michael P. L. Fogden/ Bruce Coleman Inc. Reproduced by permission.)

body parts are green to olive brown. They have olive green to dull cinnamon under body parts, with one or more spots on the chest.

The plumage of the blue-crowned motmot is composed of shades of blue and green. The center tail feathers are greenish blue, and have bare spines at the tip. Their legs are particularly short. The feet have a middle toe that is almost completely fused to the inner toe, but not to the rear toe. Blue-crowned motmots are 15 to 16 inches (38 to 41 centimeters) in length (including the tail) and weigh between 2.7 and 6.2 ounces (77 and 175 grams). The bill is about 1.6 inches (4.1 centimeters) in length.

Geographic range: Blue-crowned motmots have the widest distribution of any motmots. They are found from northeastern Mexico to northern Argentina.

Habitat: Blue-crowned motmots occupy a variety of habitats, including tropical evergreen and deciduous forests, coastal forests, mountainous forests, and secondary vegetation. They live on the edges of rainforest, secondary growth forests, and plantations. They range to altitudes up to 4,300 feet (1,300 meters), living near water for drinking and bathing.

Diet: Blue-crowned motmots eats insects and other invertebrates, including earthworms, centipedes, and snails. They sometimes eat mice and small reptiles and amphibians, and occasionally some fruits.

They capture prey by sitting quietly on wires, fence posts, or tree branches looking for prey. Sighting possible food, they suddenly fly toward the prospective meal, taking it while it flies or while on the ground. Before swallowing its prey, they hit it repeatedly against the ground or branches to kill or stun it. Insects are often eaten after trains of army ants disturb them. Fruits are often plucked while the birds hover in the air.

Behavior and reproduction: Blue-crowned motmots can sometimes appear to be solitary birds, but in reality they maintain pair bonds. They are not very active and often go undetected. The tail often twitches like the pendulum of a clock when the motmot is disturbed. They make a sound like a double hoot with a resonance similar to that of an owl. They are inactive at night and active during twilight at both dawn and dusk, and most active at the early morning light.

Pairs of blue-crowned motmots, who are believed to mate for life, dig holes during the rainy months from August to October when the soil is soft. The tunnel holes are 5 to 14 feet (1.5 to 4 meters) long and about 4 inches (10 centimeters) in diameter. The nest cavity usually measures 10 inches high (25 centimeters), 10 inches (25 centimeters) in width, and 14 inches (36 centimeters) in length. They are normally dug into the sides of cliffs or in the ground, but will use rock crevices on occasion. They reappear at the holes during the beginning of the breeding season, from March to April.

After a courtship ritual involving the carrying of leaves by the male to the female, mating begins. One adult incubates the eggs from early afternoon to dawn, and then the partner takes its place. Incubation lasts about twenty-one days. Lowland motmots stop covering their young at night when they are a week old. Young resemble adults in coloration, but lack long racket-like tail feathers.

Blue-crowned motmots and people: People have successfully bred blue-crowned motmots in captivity.

Conservation status: Blue-crowned motmots are not threatened. Because of their ability to live in a wide geographical range and in many different forest types, and to tolerate intrusion by humans, blue-crowned motmots are commonly found. However, when forests are destroyed, their survival may become threatened.   ■

FOR MORE INFORMATION

Books:

Clements, James F. *Birds of the World: A Checklist.* Vista, CA: Ibis Publishing Company, 2000.

Elphick, Chris, John B. Dunning, Jr., and David Allen Sibley, eds. *The Sibley Guide to Bird Life and Behavior.* New York: Alfred A. Knopf, 2001.

Forshaw, Joseph, ed. *Encyclopedia of Birds,* 2nd ed. San Diego: Academic Press, 1998.

Perrins, Christopher M., and Alex L. A. Middleton, eds. *The Encyclopedia of Birds.* New York: Facts on File, 1985.

Web sites:

"Blue-crowned Motmot (*Momotus momota*)." Coraciiformes Taxon Advisory Group, TAG website. http://www.coraciiformestag.com/Motmot/history.htm (accessed on 20 March 2004).

BEE-EATERS
Meropidae

Class: Aves
Order: Coraciiformes
Family: Meropidae
Number of species: 22 to
                        24 species

phylum

class

subclass

order

monotypic order

suborder

▲ **family**

PHYSICAL CHARACTERISTICS

Bee-eaters are small- to medium-sized birds that are graceful in appearance and actions, and with an alert, upright posture when perched. They are active, colorful, and social birds with a large head; short neck; long, narrow, down-curved bill; green wings with a broad black tailing edge; long, simply patterned tail; long-looking central feathers (in many species); very short legs; and weak feet. Most bee-eaters have bright green upperparts; buff or chestnut colored underparts; various colorful head and facial patterns; and black, blue, or reddish purple eye mask. They usually have a black band on the upper breast, and the chin and throat are snowy, bright yellow, red, or blue. Wings are rounded in forest species, and long and pointed in open country species.

In all species, males and females are similar, though males can be brighter in color than females and usually have longer tail streamers (long central tail feathers). Young bee-eaters are generally less colorful than adults. Adults are 6.7 to 13.8 inches (17 to 35 centimeters) long (including the tail) and weigh between 0.5 and 3.0 ounces (15 and 85 grams).

GEOGRAPHIC RANGE

Bee-eaters range throughout the tropics of the Old World, with their center of population in northern and tropical Africa. They are also found in Madagascar, Southeast Asia, New Guinea, and Australia.

HABITAT

Bee-eaters live in areas of open, lightly wooded country such as savannas (flat grasslands), woodlands, steppes (large, often treeless, plains), and scrub deserts. Some species prefer rainforests. They are often found near water.

DIET

Bee-eaters eat bees, mostly honey bees, other venomous (poisonous) insects such as wasps, as well as ants, sawflies, and other flying insects. A few species eat large insects, small lizards on the ground, and small fish. They find bees near their hives or around flowering trees and herbs. Most bee-eaters catch their prey in a "sit-and-wait" position, sitting on a perch, finding likely prey, and chasing them down in flights that might cover distances from 150 to 180 feet (50 to 60 meters). They normally return to their perch in order to consume food.

BEHAVIOR AND REPRODUCTION

Bee-eaters are, for the most part, lively birds. Only about five species prefer to live alone. They usually live in colonies (large groups that live dependently together), and prefer to have close contact with each other, often huddling together on a common perch in groups of six or seven. When perched, they move the tail backwards and forwards in a small sweeping motion. They migrate seasonally between breeding and wintering grounds. Their calls sometimes have melodies, while at other times are hoarse cawings.

Reproduction by bee-eaters depends on the species. Some use solitary nesting activities, while others depend on large colonies to help in nesting. Cooperative breeding within colonies is more normal than unaided pair nesting. Courtship rituals between bee-eaters do not exist other than some shared feeding between courting (getting ready to mate) females and males. Males will chase away any rival males when necessary, and call out to neighboring pairs not to approach too closely.

All bee-eaters dig nesting burrows into earthen banks or flat sandy ground, often along rivers, ditches, gullies, and even into aardvark or warthog dens. Nests may be solitary, in groups of two or three, in regular or irregular arrangements along banks, or in large colonies containing up to one thousand or more holes. Burrows may be 1.5 to 9 feet (0.5 to 3 meters) long, depending

BEE-RUBBING

Because their prey is poisonous, bee-eaters undertake a complicated process to assure poison is removed before eating. After taking caught prey back to the perch, bee-eaters toss it into the air, catching it with its bill tip. They strike it several times against the perch. In an action called bee-rubbing, bee-eaters grab the insect's tail tip, quickly rubbing the body against the perch to squeeze out the bee's fluid. They gradually grab the insect around its abdomen in order to expel leftover venom, eventually tearing out the stinger and poison glands. The food is then safely swallowed whole.

on the species and soil type. The burrow ends in an unlined chamber nest.

Females lay two to four white eggs in the tropics, and up to seven eggs in drier climates. The incubation period (the time spent sitting on eggs) is eighteen to twenty-three days. Females do most of the incubating at night, while both share sitting duties during the day. Both parents share feeding of the young along with any helpers. Hatchlings are pink, blind, and naked. Their skin soon turns gray, eyes open, and spiny feathers appear. The nestling period (the time it takes young to leave the nest after hatching) is between twenty-four and thrity-two days. After one year, bee-eaters either breed or become a helper to a breeding pair.

BEE-EATERS AND PEOPLE

Overall, people do not affect bee-eaters in any significant way. However, bee-eaters are a great source of enjoyment to birdwatchers.

CONSERVATION STATUS

Bee-eaters are not threatened. However, because they eat only poisonous insects, which are often controlled by humans with the use of pesticides (chemicals used to control pests), they are vulnerable to the effects of such chemicals.

Purple-bearded bee-eater *(Meropogon forsteni)*

Resident

PURPLE-BEARDED BEE-EATER
Meropogon forsteni

Physical characteristics: Purple-bearded bee-eaters are easily identified from other bee-eaters because they have a purple-blue head,
throat, and breast. They are colorful birds, with dark green upperparts, wings, and tail streamers; dark brown lower belly; green and
russet (reddish brown) tail feathers; blackish forehead and crown (the
top of a bird's head); chocolate on the sides and back of the neck.
The long, broad throat feathers hang over the breast, and the neck
and nape feathers form a coat that is sleeked down or fluffed out.
When flying, they look mostly green, with broad rounded wings, a
longish tail, and short-to medium tail streamers. Purple-bearded bee-
eaters are 9.8 to 10.2 inches (25 to 26 centimeters) long without

tail streamers that can add up to 2.4 inches (6 centimeters) to its length.

Geographic range: Purple-bearded bee-eaters are the most restricted species, occurring only on the island of Sulawesi (formerly called Celebes), Indonesia.

Habitat: Purple-bearded bee-eaters are found in open areas of rainforests, often in the mid- and upper-canopy (treetop) levels of the forest, on the edges of forests, and in the lowlands where forests meet well-timbered farmland. They range from sea level to 6,070 feet (1,850 meters) in altitude.

Diet: They eat flying insects, including bees, beetles, wasps, and dragonflies. Most of their feeding begins from perches located at the middle and upper canopy of forests. After capturing their food, purple-bearded bee-eaters return to their perch where they beat their prey a few times against the perch.

Behavior and reproduction: Purple-bearded bee-eaters are sedentary birds (tending not to migrate), although they sometimes move to coastal areas for the rainy seasons, and then return to interior areas for dry seasons. They call out a quiet, shrill, high-pitched "szit," or "peet." They excavate burrows in steep banks located near forest streams, cliffs, high-level roads, or banks by forest paths. Little information is available on the reproduction processes used by the birds. However, it is believed that females reproduce at any time of the year.

Purple-bearded bee-eaters and people: Purple-bearded bee-eaters have no special significance to humans.

Conservation status: These bee-eaters are not globally threatened.   ■

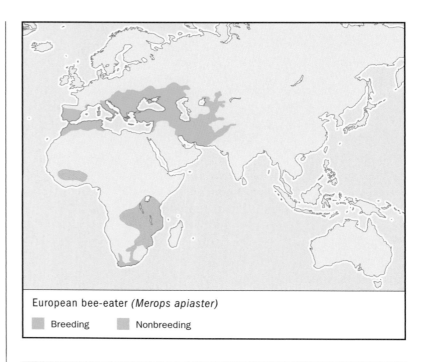

European bee-eater (Merops apiaster)

■ Breeding   ■ Nonbreeding

EUROPEAN BEE-EATER
Merops apiaster

Physical characteristics: European bee-eaters are considered one of the loveliest bee-eaters, with bright color patterns: blue underneath; bronze above; chestnut on top of the head; and golden-yellow around the throat and shoulder. Since this bird is usually seen flying, this color combination is not often seen clearly. Females are slightly paler than males. Juveniles are mainly green and lack any chestnut or gold in their feathers, but still possess pale yellow throats. Adults also have a dark eye stripe; a slender, pointed bill; small feet; and pointed central tail feathers. Adults are 9 to 10 inches (23 to 25 centimeters) long, excluding tail streamers that are about 0.8 inches (2 centimeters) long. European bee-eaters weigh between 1.6 and 2.8 ounces (44 and 78 grams).

Geographic range: European bee-eaters are found in northwest Africa from Morocco to Libya, Mediterranean islands, countries of the northern Mediterranean east through the Middle East to Pakistan, northern India and Afghanistan. A few birds are found in South Africa. Large numbers of European bee-eaters migrate seasonally between breeding areas in Europe and Asia and their wintering grounds in tropical Africa and western India.

Habitat: European bee-eaters like warm, open habitats with rivers, sandy soils, pasturelands, scattered trees, and bushes. They are found in grasslands, open woodlands, pasturelands with scattered trees, and forests in drier habitats.

Diet: European bee-eaters eat mostly insects, mainly bumble bees, honeybees, and wasps, but over 300 species of insect prey have been recorded. They feed primarily from a perch, but may also feed while in flight. They usually hunt within 0.6 miles (1 kilometer) of their nest, but can be found up to 7.2 miles (12 kilometers) away.

Behavior and reproduction: European bee-eaters are sociable birds, giving out loud but attractive "quilp," "prruip," and "kruup" sounds, along with many others. They spend most of their time hunting for food, in graceful flight, but also spend some time perched on bare twigs and telephone wires. They are sometimes a solitary nester, but are more commonly found breeding in colonies, sometimes along with up to 400 other nests. Nests are located in earthen banks or cliffs, and usually consist of an unlined chamber at the burrow's end up to 5 feet (1.5) meters in length. Females lay eggs during May in the southern part of their range, and in June and early July in Russia. South African populations begin breeding in October. Clutch sizes are the largest of any bee-eater, with up to ten eggs, but generally with a range of five or six. Cooperative breeding is common, with about 20 percent of nesting pairs using a helper.

European bee-eaters eat mostly insects, mainly bumble bees, honeybees, and wasps. They can feed while they're flying, or fly off of a perch to catch their food. (© R. Tipper/VIREO. Reproduced by permission.)

European bee-eaters and people: People persecute European bee-eaters more than any other species of bee-eaters, especially when their territories overlap areas where beekeeping (keeping bees to harvest honey) is common. It is generally considered a pest in all of its range.

Conservation status: European bee-eaters are not globally threatened. ■

FOR MORE INFORMATION

Books:

del Hoyo, Josep, et al., eds. *Handbook of the Birds of the World.* Barcelona: Lynx Edicions, 1992.

Dickinson, Edward C., ed. *The Howard and Moore Complete Checklist of the Birds of the World,* 3rd ed. Princeton, NJ and Oxford, U.K.: Princeton University Press, 2003.

Forshaw, Joseph, ed. *Encyclopedia of Birds,* 2nd ed. San Diego, CA: Academic Press, 1998.

Fry, C. Hilary, and Kathie Fry. *Kingfishers, Bee-Eaters and Rollers: A Handbook.* Princeton, NJ: Princeton University Press, 1992.

Harrison, Colin James Oliver. *Birds of the World.* London and New York: Dorling Kindersley, 1993.

Perrins, Christopher M., and Alex L.A. Middleton, eds. *The Encyclopedia of Birds.* New York: Facts on File, 1985.

Stattersfield, Allison, J. and David R. Capper, eds. *Threatened Birds of the World: The Official Source for Birds on the IUCN Red List.* Cambridge, U.K.: BirdLife International, 2000.

ROLLERS
Coraciidae

Class: Aves
Order: Coraciiformes
Family: Coraciidae
Number of species: 18 species

PHYSICAL CHARACTERISTICS

Rollers include three subfamilies: true rollers, ground-rollers, and the cuckoo roller. The three groups are medium-sized, brightly colored, and fairly large, stocky birds with a short necks; broad, strong syndactylous (sin-DACK-tuh-lus) feet, merged toes with no web in between; rounded wings; and short tails, though some species have tail streamers, a longer, central tail part. Sexes are similar or identical in color, depending on species. Rollers are 9 to 20 inches (22 to 50 centimeters) long, and weigh between 2.8 and 8.8 ounces (80 and 250 grams).

True rollers have plumage, feathers, of blue, blue-green, green, brown, or lilac, with olive, chestnut, or pink markings. Bills may be strong, arched, and hook-tipped, suited for grasping ground prey; or may be short and wide, suitable for catching flying insects. True rollers' wings are long and rounded, with tails that may be squared, slightly rounded, or somewhat forked, sometimes with longer outermost feathers.

Ground-rollers are more brown, buff or black in the plumage. They have rufous (reddish) or dark-green upperparts, simply patterned underparts, and bold facial patterns. Ground-rollers have large heads, strong bills, heavy bodies, short, rounded wings, long legs, and pointed tails.

Male cuckoo rollers are velvety gray; with a dark shiny green back, tail and wings; and a black eye stripe. Females and young birds are brown, with darker streaks.

GEOGRAPHIC RANGE

Rollers range within Africa, southern Europe, and southern Asia to northeastern and southeastern Asia, and Australasia, east to the Solomon Islands.

HABITAT

Rollers live in forests, woodlands, savannas (flat grasslands), and within urban areas, preferring the tropics and subtropics.

DIET

Rollers eat a variety of foods such as insects, spiders, lizards, small mammals, and small birds. True rollers perch to wait for prey like arthropods, invertebrate animals with joined limbs, found around leaf litter or flying through the air. Ground-rollers eat mostly food found on the ground, capturing small vertebrates, animals with backbones, such as frogs and lizards hidden in the leaf litter or probing for prey with their bills into soft soils. Cuckoo rollers eat large insects and small reptiles that they find among trees and shrubs.

BEHAVIOR AND REPRODUCTION

Rollers perch evenly spaced within groups. True rollers gather into migrating flocks, and are territorial most of the year. They are usually seen singly or in pairs, sometimes in post-breeding families. When breeding, they are noisy with loud cackling calls that occur during daring maneuvers. During non-breeding seasons, the birds are quiet and slow. Ground-rollers are territorial, especially when feeding. When in danger, they sit quietly in a well-concealed position. They make brief, gruff-sounding calls mostly during breeding.

During courtship, true rollers use loud sounds while rolling during through the air. Bowing is performed between male and female pairs while perched and facing each other, with mating occurring afterwards. Unlined nests are usually located within tree holes, but also found in crevices (narrow cracks in rocks), rocky parts of mountains, and buildings. Clutches, groups of eggs hatched together, are three to six unmarked white eggs, with an incubation period, time needed to sit on eggs, of eighteen to twenty days. Females do the sitting, but males help out. Newly hatched chicks are naked and helpless, with small feathers first appearing around seven days. Full feathers occur between seventeen and twenty-two days. Both parents feed nestlings, young birds unable to leave nest, for around thirty days, and for up to twenty days after fledging, learning to fly.

Ground-rollers breed during summers. Pairs defend their nesting territories, and courtship feeding of females by males is common. Nests are made in tree hollows, but some nest in chambers at the end of a burrow excavated, dug, by the birds. Two to four white eggs are laid. Incubation appears to be performed by the female, and both parents feed nestlings.

ROLLERS AND PEOPLE

People generally have little interest in rollers. Some exceptions occur; for instance, body parts of rollers are used in love potions, drinks supposedly used to increase sexual desire. Rollers have also been viewed as good omens. People hunt ground-rollers for food because they are easy targets.

CONSERVATION STATUS

True rollers are common throughout all or part of their ranges, with one species considered Vulnerable, facing a high risk of extinction in the wild. Ground-rollers have four species that are considered Vulnerable due to deforestation. Cuckoo rollers are generally common and survive in small, fragmented forest patches. However, they are being adversely affected by widespread land clearing.

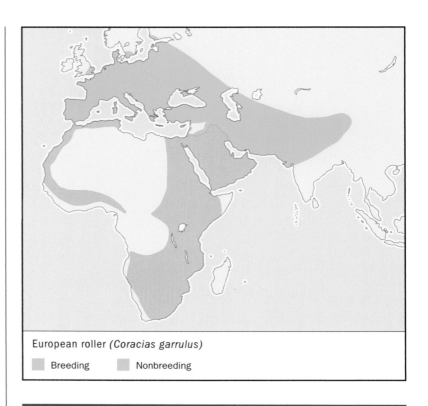

European roller (*Coracias garrulus*)

■ Breeding   ■ Nonbreeding

EUROPEAN ROLLER
Coracias garrulus

Physical characteristics: European rollers are heavily built, large rollers with no tail streamers. Their head, neck, and underparts are bright pale blue, with rufous to chestnut upperparts, blue square-tipped tail, and vivid blue wing patch. The throat and breast are streaked with white. They have a short black streak through the eye, and a brownish black bill with a white base. The two central tail feathers are dark olive-gray, with the remaining feathers greenish blue with darker bases. They are 12.2 to 12.5 inches (31 to 32 centimeters) long and weigh between 3.9 and 6.7 ounces (110 and 190 grams). Females and males look alike.

Geographic range: They breed throughout Europe, western and southwestern Asia, and the Middle East; and, while not breeding, live in the eastern half of Africa, and along the northern and central coasts of western Africa, and as far south as South Africa.

Habitat: They exist in open woodlands, wooded grasslands, cultivated fields, oak forests, pinewoods, river valleys, urban parks, and gardens of lowlands. They range from sea level up to about 2,000 feet (600 meters). They do not like open water; steppes, treeless, grass-covered plains; and plains, dry land with few trees. During breeding season, they are attracted to sunny lowlands.

Diet: European rollers eat mostly insects such as beetles, grasshoppers, locusts, crickets, cicadas (suh-KAY-duhz), mantids, wasps, bees, ants, termites, flies, butterflies, and caterpillars. Occasionally, they eat scorpions, centipedes, spiders, worms, frogs, lizards, snakes, and birds. While on their perches, European rollers watch for ground prey. Seeing food, they expose long, broad wings as they attack. They then return to the perch. Before eating prey, they repeatedly strike the food against the perch. They also catch insects in midair. Undigested remains are regurgitated (re-GER-jih-tate-ud; brought up from the stomach) in pellets.

European rollers form pairs that defend their nests. The females sit on the eggs, but both parents help feed the chicks. (© H. & J. Eriksen/VIREO. Reproduced by permission.)

Behavior and reproduction: European rollers are often seen hunched on a lookout perch on a tree, post, or telephone wire. They migrate seasonally to Africa, mainly in the east and south. They are noisy birds, often calling out a short gruff "rack," a chattering "rack rack rackrak ak," or a screeching "aaaarrr" (which is a sound of warning). They are noticeable while in their breeding territories. During wintering periods, they are quiet and slow moving birds. They breed in pairs, but loose flocks migrate together. They are active on warm days, but less active during rainy ones.

They form monogamous (muh-NAH-guh-mus) pairs, having only one mate, and they strongly defend their nests. Their courtship displays involve deep ascents followed by spectacular twisting dives that show off their wing colors. Croaking and rattling calls (like "ra-ra-ra-raa-raa-aaaaaa-aaaar") accompany the display. They breed from May to June, with females laying two to six (usually four) eggs in an unlined, usually pine or oak, tree hollow, crevice in rock faces, or hole in walls of buildings. The incubation period is between seventeen and nineteen days, performed totally by the females. Both parents feed chicks. The fledgling period, time while the young grow their flying feathers, is twenty-five to thirty days.

European rollers and people: People admire European rollers for their beauty and like them because they eat insects, pests to humans. However, they are still often hunted for food, sport, and taxidermy, the stuffing and mounting of animals in a lifelike state.

Conservation status: European rollers are not threatened—they still number in the millions—however their numbers continue to decrease in Europe. ■

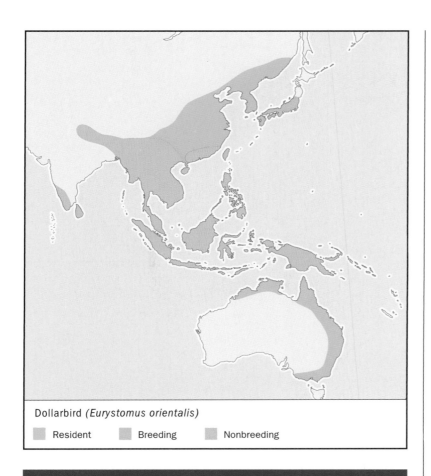

Dollarbird *(Eurystomus orientalis)*

■ Resident   ■ Breeding   ■ Nonbreeding

DOLLARBIRD
Eurystomus orientalis

Physical characteristics: Dollarbirds are stocky, dark greenish-blue or purplish birds with a large head; short, thick neck; short legs; short-looking, square-ended tail; and short but broad, heavy red bill. They have broad and long wings with central tail feathers that are blackish with dark blue bases and outer feathers that are blackish with purple-blue edges and greenish-blue bases. Dollarbirds have white-silvery or pale blue "dollar"-like circles on their open wings, which is noticeable while flying. The forehead and chin are blackish brown; back of the neck and ears are very dark olive-brown; and back and rump are bluish olive. The throat is purple with narrow blue streaks; while the breast, sides, belly, undertail, and underwing areas are

Dollarbird females lay their eggs in high tree hollows, sometimes in woodpecker holes. They often use the same nest several years in a row. (© J. Warham/VIREO. Reproduced by permission.)

green-blue. Their eyes are dark brown, while legs and feet are bright red. They are 9.8 to 11.0 inches (25 to 28 centimeters) long, and weigh between 4.0 and 5.6 ounces (115 and 160 grams).

Geographic range: Dollarbirds are located from southeastern Asia to the Philippines, Indonesia and the northern and eastern coastal lands of Australia.

Habitat: Dollarbirds reside in deciduous woodlands, evergreen forests, forest margins, savannas, farmlands (such as rubber and coffee plantations), urban parks, and gardens, up to elevations of 4,900 feet (1,500 meters). They favor hot lowlands and foothills.

Diet: They eat large insects that are captured in flight, especially beetles, crickets, mantids, grasshoppers, cicadas (suh-KAY-duhz), shield-bugs, moths, and termites. Dollarbirds occasionally take insects from the ground. Once crushed by their bills, they are swallowed. They feed mostly in the late afternoon and evening.

Behavior and reproduction: Dollarbirds live alone or in pairs. For much of the day they sit inactively on a perch. They often wag their tail up and down when about to fly, but otherwise sit quietly, moving only the head. The birds migrate to higher latitudes from their normal residences in the tropics. They are rather silent, but occasionally are noisy, uttering a hoarse, raspy "chak," or a series of "krak-kak-kak" or "kek-ek-ek-ek-ek-k-k". Dollarbirds are noticeable with their high, rotating flights or when perched on top of high trees. They fly in large flocks when migrating or when feeding on swarms of flying insects.

They are monogamous birds that breed in the summer. The breeding pair will defend their nesting territory. Dollarbirds use loud calling and aerobatics, spectacular flying stunts, in courtship rituals. Females lay three or four eggs, which are laid in high tree hollows, sometimes in woodpecker holes. Nests are often used several years in a row. The incubation period is twenty-two to twenty-three days. Both parents feed the chicks. Parents and chicks leave for wintering areas when chicks are able to fly.

Dollarbirds and people: Dollarbirds have no known significance to humans.

Conservation status: Dollarbirds are not threatened.   ■

FOR MORE INFORMATION

Books:

del Hoyo, Josep, Andrew Elliott, Jordi Sargatal, Jose Cabot, et al., eds. *Handbook of the Birds of the World.* Barcelona: Lynx Edicions, 1992.

Dickinson, Edward C., ed. *The Howard and Moore Complete Checklist of the Birds of the World,* 3rd ed. Princeton, NJ and Oxford, U.K.: Princeton University Press, 2003.

Forshaw, Joseph, ed. *Encyclopedia of Birds,* 2nd ed. San Diego, CA: Academic Press, 1998.

Fry, C. Hilary, and Kathie Fry. *Kingfishers, Bee-Eaters and Rollers: A Handbook.* Princeton, NJ: Princeton University Press, 1992.

Harrison, Colin James Oliver. *Birds of the World.* London, U.K. and New York: Dorling Kindersley, 1993.

Perrins, Christopher M., and Alex L. A. Middleton, eds. *The Encyclopedia of Birds.* New York: Facts on File, 1985.

Stattersfield, Allison J., and David R. Capper, eds. *Threatened Birds of the World: The Official Source for Birds on the IUCN Red List.* Cambridge, U.K.: BirdLife International, 2000.

family
CHAPTER

PHYSICAL CHARACTERISTICS

Hoopoes (HOO-pooz) are medium-sized perching and ground birds that are especially popular because of their highly patterned plumage, feathers. They also have very long, thin, de-curved, slightly bent, bills; small head; large, stiffened fan-like crest, tuft on top of head; broad, rounded wings; short, squared tails; and short legs. Bold plumage on the chest can vary in color between pinkish brown, pinkish orange, chestnut, and rufous (reddish), while feathers on the wings, back, and tail are black with bold white stripes. The particular widths of stripes depend on which continent the hoopoe is located. The crest and head are both tipped with black. The bill is shaped specifically so its muscles can move to easily open and close its bill while the bird searches for food. Males and females are very similar in appearance. Juveniles are duller in color than adults; with white wings that show a small amount of cream color and a crest and bill that is relatively short. Adult hoopoes are 10.2 to 12.6 inches (26 to 32 centimeters) long, and weigh between 1.3 and 3.1 ounces (38 and 89 grams).

GEOGRAPHIC RANGE

Hoopoes are widely found in northern, central, and southern Africa, Madagascar, Europe, and Asia.

HABITAT

Hoopoes inhabit lightly timbered temperate climates that have cold winters and warm summers. They prefer open and

phylum
class
subclass
order
monotypic order
suborder
▲ **family**

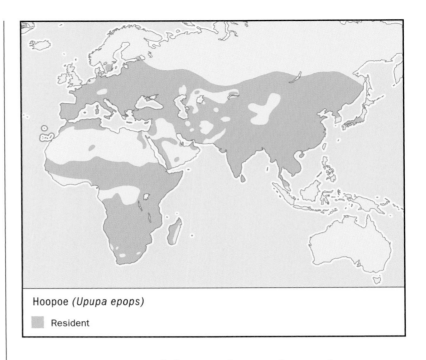

Hoopoe (*Upupa epops*)

■ Resident

semi-open country with bare earthen patches or short grasses, usually with some trees. Such country include pastures, cultivated grounds, wooded farmlands, parklands, orchards, gardens, vineyards, woodlands, edges and clearings, steppes (treeless plains), plains (large amount of dry lands with few trees), dry and wooded savannas (flat grasslands), river valleys, foothills, scrublands, semi-deserts, and, in Southeast Asia, coastal dune scrublands. Within these areas, they look for cavities (hollow areas) in trees, walls, rocks, dirt banks, or termite mounds for their nests. Hoopoes stay away from damp areas. They range elevations up to 10,170 feet (3,100 meters), but normally are found below 6,560 feet (2,000 meters).

DIET

Hoopoes eat mostly insects, particularly soft larvae (LARvee; active immature insects) and pupae (PYOO-pee; developing insects found inside cocoons). Prey includes primarily ants, beetles, bugs, butterflies, dragonflies, flies, grasshoppers, grubs, termites, and worms. They also eat earthworms, centipedes, spiders, and woodlice, and sometimes eat frogs, lizards, and small snakes. Hoopoes hunt for prey primarily on the ground in short grasses and on bare soil by walking short distances, stopping

Hoopoes eat mainly insects. They usually search for them on the ground, but may sometimes make a short flight to catch their prey. (John A. Snyder/Bruce Coleman Inc. Reproduced by permission.)

to insert its long slender bill into the ground with the hope of finding food, and then walking off in a different direction. They sometimes probe under and between bark on trees; and other times dig small holes and turn over leaf litter, dry animal droppings, and other material on the ground in search of prey. Hoopoes also make short flights in the air to catch prey. Hoopoes feed alone or in pairs during the spring and summer breeding season. At other times, they feed in small groups of other hoopoes.

BEHAVIOR AND REPRODUCTION

Hoopoes fly with a distinctive pattern of irregular (often erratic), butterfly-like flapping of its wings. When coming to rest, they raise their crest, which remains flat during the time of flight. The crest, which normally rests folded within the back of its neck, is also raised when they become excited. Also when alarmed, they make a quiet chattering sound. They are able to easily climb upward even on rough surfaces. Hoopoes are diurnal birds (active only during the day), roosting in cavities at night. Hoopoes give out a soft "hoo-poo" and "oop-oop-oop" calls, which is easily heard over long distances, while puffing out of its neck feathers. During the breeding season, they are usually found singly or in pairs, but at other times they are seen in family groups or loose flocks of up to ten birds. They are migratory birds over the northern parts of their range, and partially migratory elsewhere within their range. Northern populations of hoopoes winter in tropical areas of Africa, India, and Southeast Asia. The birds in the southernmost parts of their range rarely migrate.

Hoopoes are monogamous (muh-NAH-guh-mus), having one mate, and are strongly territorial while breeding. Breeding starts usually in late April. Males begin the courtship process several weeks before actual breeding, using a song to attract his female partner in a series of two to five loud "hoop" notes, which are often sung on posts. Males chase females, bringing food, and showing off possible nest sites. Male hoopoes locate holes in trees, walls, cliffs, banks, termite mounds, woodpecker holes, flat ground, and crevices, narrows cracks or openings, between rocks in order to use as nests. The entrance is narrow, forcing hoopoes to squeeze inside. Once located, males chase away all intruders on the ground and in the air, making this area his protected territory. Such locations use little or no nesting materials, but can be made up of plants, feathers, wool, and other similar substances, eventually making the nest cavity, hollow area, very smelly and unsanitary. Suitable nests may be reused for several years.

During courtship, males will feed the female partner just before mating. Afterwards, the pair often flies slowly throughout their territory, one behind the other, while raising and lowering their crests. Females usually produce one egg each day, with a clutch size, number of eggs hatched together, of four to seven eggs in tropical areas and five to nine eggs in temperate regions, with a maximum number of twelve eggs. The smooth, non-glossy eggs can vary in color from grayish, yellowish, greenish, or brownish. They are about 1.02 by 0.71 inches (2.6 by 1.8 centimeters) in size. The incubation period, time in which birds sit on hatched eggs, is from twenty-five to thirty-two days, with females performing the entire process of sitting on the eggs. Eggs are hatched at different times. At first, females feed and take care of newborn chicks, but later both parents feed and take care of the young. Males feed females while she is caring for the eggs and for the first week after the young have hatched. Fledglings, young birds that have grown feathers that are necessary to fly, begin to feed on their own after six days, but remain with parents for many weeks, usually around twenty-eight days after hatching. Usually only one brood, young that are born and raised together, is raised each year, however up to three broods have been recorded. In the beginning young birds fly very clumsily in irregular curves, and walk awkwardly.

The young nesting birds use hissing sounds, poking upward with their bills, and striking with one wing in order to defend themselves from enemies. They also use very smelly secretions from body glands and sprayings of feces, solid body waste, to fend off attacks. To defend against predators, adults flatten themselves against the ground by spreading their wings and tails onto the ground, with their head raised backward and bill raised.

HOOPOES AND PEOPLE

People like hoopoes because they eat many insects that are agriculture and forestry pests. Thus, hoopoes are widely protected by a variety of national laws. However, many hoopoes are still hunted in southern Europe and parts of Asia.

CONSERVATION STATUS

Hoopoes are not threatened, and are common and abundant in most of their range. They have, however, suffered diminished populations at the boundaries of their ranges, especially in Europe where most of their populations have declined over the twentieth century and into the twenty-first century. Their numbers have declined in Africa, Madagascar, and Asia due to previously productive land that has gradually turned into deserts and other lands that have been turned into farmland. A previous species, the giant hoopoe, has been extinct probably since the year 1600.

FOR MORE INFORMATION

Books:

del Hoyo, Josep, et al., eds. *Handbook of the Birds of the World.* Barcelona: Lynx Edicions, 1992.

Dickinson, Edward C., ed. *The Howard and Moore Complete Checklist of the Birds of the World,* 3rd ed. Princeton, NJ and Oxford, U.K.: Princeton University Press, 2003.

Forshaw, Joseph, ed. *Encyclopedia of Birds,* 2nd ed. San Diego, CA: Academic Press, 1998.

Fry, C. Hilary, and Kathie Fry. *Kingfishers, Bee-Eaters and Rollers: A Handbook.* Princeton, NJ: Princeton University Press, 1992.

Harrison, Colin James Oliver. *Birds of the World.* London and New York: Dorling Kindersley, 1993.

Perrins, Christopher M., and Alex L. A. Middleton, eds. *The Encyclopedia of Birds.* New York: Facts on File, 1985.

Stattersfield, Allison, J., and David R. Capper, eds. *Threatened Birds of the World: The Official Source for Birds on the IUCN Red List.* Cambridge, U.K.: BirdLife International, 2000.

Web sites:

"Hoopoe." *Wikipedia, The Free Encyclopedia.* http://en.wikipedia.org/wiki/Hoopoe (accessed on April 24, 2004).

"*Upupa epops.*" Animals Online. http://www.animals-online.be/birds/hoppen/hoopoe.html (accessed on April 24, 2004).

WOODHOOPOES
Phoeniculidae

Class: Aves
Order: Coraciiformes
Family: Phoeniculidae
Number of species: 6 species

phylum

class

subclass

order

monotypic order

suborder

▲ **family**

PHYSICAL CHARACTERISTICS

Woodhoopoes (WOOD-huu-puuz) are small- to medium-sized birds. Some species have a long, slender decurved, slightly bent, bill; others have straight bills; and still others have greatly down-curved bills. They have plumage, feathers, that is mainly black with glossy green or purple undertones; and have broad, rounded wings and a long, graduated, divided in steps of different lengths, tail. Some species have a white or brown head. Most species have patches, either bars or spots, of white across the wing and on the tips of the tail feathers. Woodhoopoes have long toes, short legs, and strong, thick hooked claws. They have dark brown irises, colored part, within their eyes. Females usually have shorter bills and tails than males, and young birds are duller in color than adults. Juveniles of all species have bills and feet that are black. In three species, the bill turns orange-red as they mature, as do the feet in two species. Adults are 8 to 15 inches (20 to 38 centimeters) long and weigh between 0.6 and 3.5 ounces (18 and 99 grams).

GEOGRAPHIC RANGE

Woodhoopoes range throughout sub-Saharan Africa, with a small number of birds in northeast Africa. They are one of the few bird families that are confined to Africa.

HABITAT

Woodhoopoes live in rainforests, forests, woodland, savannas (flat grassland), thornbush country, and arid steppes (dry plains that are often grass-covered) that contain adequate amounts of scattered trees. They avoid treeless areas, and only two species occur in the more northern areas of tropical forests. Woodhoopoes require areas that are heavily forested in order to roost and nest in tree holes, and to use its bark and twigs to hide their food.

DIET

They eat invertebrates, animals without a backbone, mainly insects and arachnids, eight-legged animals that includes spiders, scorpions, and mites, and their larvae (LAR-vee), active immature insects; along with some fruits and small vertebrates, animals with a backbone. Probing into crevices, narrow openings, and cracks, or prying off bark on the trunks and limbs of trees are their means of locating prey. Strong feet allow woodhoopoes to hunt at all angles, including hanging upside down, with the tail used as a brace. Larger species tend to search on larger branches; species with thicker, straighter bills dig and pry more often; and smaller species probe into the smallest holes on the smallest of twigs. Some species will also feed on the ground or catch flying insects in midair. Woodhoopoes do not drink water on a regular basis because they receive most of their needed moisture from their prey.

BEHAVIOR AND REPRODUCTION

Smaller-sized species of woodhoopoes are somewhat sedentary, tending not to migrate, but larger species tend to migrate more. Some larger species live in groups of five to twelve birds, making themselves noticeable when they interrupt their eating to make noisy sounds among the group. After a short period of time, they quietly return to foraging, searching for food. The small species tend to live only as pairs. All birds defend their territory with loud cackling calls, exaggerated bowing of the body, and rising of the tail. Such cackling sounds helps to maintain the identity and togetherness of the group, which usually consists of an extended family of parents, helpers, and young. Their broad, rounded wings and long, graduated tail allow skillful and, at times, rapid flights.

Woodhoopoes nest in tree cavities. Most cavities are natural holes, but old nest holes previously dug out by barbets and woodpeckers are also used. Barbets are small tropical birds that are brightly colored, with a large head, thick hairy bill, short rounded wings, and short tail; related to the toucan. They rarely use holes in the ground or in buildings. Nests are unlined. Mating pairs are monogamous (muh-NAH-guh-mus), having only one mate. A male will feed the breeding female as a courtship ritual. Such feeding will continue throughout the nesting period, along with feedings from helpers. The female lays and incubates, sits on to provide warmth, a clutch, group of eggs hatched together, of two to five gray or blue-green eggs that are oval and pitted. The incubation period is seventeen to eighteen days, with a nestling period, time necessary to take care of young, of about thirty days. The female hatches the young chicks but later leaves and helps the others bring the chicks food. The nestlings have a prickly appearance due to growing feathers. Juveniles stay with the parents for several months after fledging, growing the feathers needed for flight, and sometimes act as helpers.

WOODHOOPOES AND PEOPLE

Woodhoopoes have no known significant importance to humans.

CONSERVATION STATUS

Woodhoopoes are not threatened. In some areas, woodhoopoes have been reduced by the collection of timber for fuel and building material.

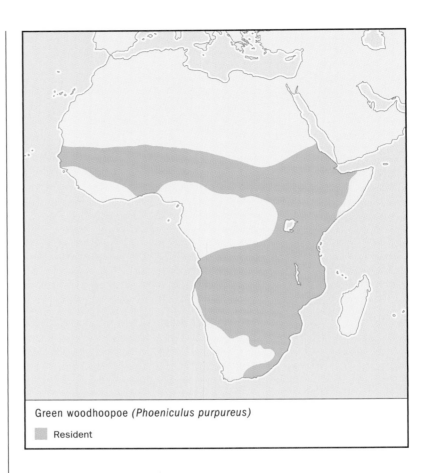

Green woodhoopoe (*Phoeniculus purpureus*)

▨ Resident

GREEN WOODHOOPOE
Phoeniculus purpureus

Physical characteristics: Green woodhoopoes, considered the largest of the woodhoopoes, are primarily black in color with variable green and purple glossy overtones. They have a blue head and throat; violet on the back of the neck; white spots on their flight feathers and at the tip of its tail; a white bar across the middle of the wings; and red bill and feet, with bills being black in some populations. They have short, strong legs and sharp claws for gripping bark firmly. The long, graduated tail is used, either closed or spread, as a support.

Green woodhoopoe bills are long, slender, and slightly curved. The bill of males is longer than that of females, with a male weight about

18 to 20 percent more than females. Juveniles do not contain iridescence, glossy, colors like the adults, and have short dark bills and dark feet. Most juvenile males and some females have brown or buff throats, with smaller number of tail spots than what are found on adults. Adults are 13 to 15 inches (32 to 37 centimeters) long and weigh between 2.0 and 3.5 ounces (54 and 99 grams).

Geographic range: Green woodhoopoes are one of the most widespread of all woodhoopoes. They range throughout much of sub-Saharan Africa.

Habitat: Green woodhoopoes are found in open woodlands, savannas, palm groves, along rivers within forests, wooded gardens, and dry, mixed scrublands that contain at least a few larger trees. They are found from near sea level to altitudes well over 6,560 feet (2,000 meters). Green woodhoopoes must live in areas that contain large enough trees, except for thick rainforests, in order to find cavities for roosting and nesting. They are not found in arid zones and dense forests.

Green woodhoopoes are social birds. They will often exchange food as part of their social behavior. (Kerry T. Givens/Bruce Coleman Inc. Reproduced by permission.)

Diet: Green woodhoopoes eat caterpillars, beetle larvae, spiders and spider eggs, adult and larval moths, and winged and un-winged termites. They occasionally eat centipedes, millipedes, small lizards, and small fruits. They are well suited for climbing on tree trunks and branches in search for food. Most often, they forage by probing within cracks or bark of tree trunks, branches, and twigs. Males search lower down on the tree, while females tend to forage higher where smaller branches, limbs, and twigs are located. Sometimes green woodhoopoes dig in animal dung found on the ground, catch insets in flight, or steal food from nests of other species. Prey is often pounded and rubbed against a branch before being eaten.

Behavior and reproduction: Green woodhoopoes are territorial birds. They live in social groups, often in groups of four to eight members, but occasionally in much larger groups of up to sixteen birds. They often follow one another in single file in short flights from one tree to another. Green woodhoopoes will often exchange food as part of their social behavior. They are frequently noisy birds, often defending their territory with loud cackling calls; rapid, exaggerated bowing movements; and strong movements of the tail up and down.

Breeding activities can occur in every month, but are more frequent in months that are wet. They will often nest in tree holes, either natural or old woodpecker holes, but sometimes in the ground. When nests occur in trees, the nest is usually up to 72 feet (22 meters) above the ground. When the weather is abnormally wet, usually in late summer, they will nest in buildings. The female will lay two to five eggs, and then incubate them for seventeen to eighteen days. The nestling period lasts about thirty days. Adult and juvenile helpers will assist the mating pair in feeding and other duties.

Green woodhoopoes and people: People and green woodhoopoes have little significance to each other. However, the birds are often found in gardens and parks.

Conservation status: Green woodhoopoes are not threatened. They are widespread and common throughout their range, including a number of large national parks. ■

FOR MORE INFORMATION

Books:

del Hoyo, Josep, Andrew Elliott, Jordi Sargatal, Jose Cabot, et al., eds. *Handbook of the Birds of the World.* Barcelona: Lynx Edicions, 1992.

Dickinson, Edward C., ed. *The Howard and Moore Complete Checklist of the Birds of the World,* 3rd ed. Princeton, NJ and Oxford, U.K.: Princeton University Press, 2003.

Forshaw, Joseph, ed. *Encyclopedia of Birds,* 2nd ed. San Diego, CA: Academic Press, 1998.

Fry, C. Hilary, and Kathie Fry. *Kingfishers, Bee-Eaters and Rollers: A Handbook.* Princeton, NJ: Princeton University Press, 1992.

Harrison, Colin James Oliver. *Birds of the World.* London, U.K. and New York: Dorling Kindersley, 1993.

Perrins, Christopher M., and Alex L. A. Middleton, eds. *The Encyclopedia of Birds.* New York: Facts on File, 1985.

Stattersfield, Allison J., and David R. Capper, eds. *Threatened Birds of the World: The Official Source for Birds on the IUCN Red List.* Cambridge, U.K.: BirdLife International, 2000.

HORNBILLS

Bucerotidae

Class: Aves

Order: Coraciiformes

Family: Bucerotidae

Number of species: 54 species

family

CHAPTER

phylum

class

subclass

order

monotypic order

suborder

▲ family

PHYSICAL CHARACTERISTICS

Hornbills are medium- to large-sized, stocky, and highly vocal birds that are described as flamboyant, very showy. They have long, oversized but lightweight, slightly decurved (down-curved) bills. The bills are located below noticeable casques (KASKS), horny growths. The casques come in various sizes; shapes, including bumps, ridges, or horns; and colors such as brilliant orange, yellow-gold, deep crimson, or shiny black. Experts think casques might be used to help support large bills, make calls louder, or attract mates.

Hornbills have patches of bare skin around the eyes and throat and long eyelashes on their upper lids. To support their head and large bill, they have strong neck muscles and two neck vertebrae, bones in the spinal column, connected together. Hornbill plumage, feathers, is not very colorful, usually with areas of black, white, gray, or brown. The color and size of plumage and the shape of the casque identifies the age and sex. Hornbills vary in size and shape, from 11.8 to 47.3 inches (30 to 120 centimeters) long, and weigh between 3.5 ounces and 13.25 pounds (100 grams and 6 kilograms). Males are larger and heavier than females and have bills that are up to 30 percent longer.

GEOGRAPHIC RANGE

Hornbills are found in sub-Saharan Africa; from India and continuing east through south and Southeast Asia; onto the Indonesian and Philippine archipelagos including New Guinea; and east to the Solomon Islands.

HABITAT

Hornbills inhabit deserts, rainforests, steppes (treeless plain, often semiarid and grass-covered), woodlands, savannas (flat grasslands), and mountains, but prefer forested areas to other locales. Hornbills must be near large trees in order to nest and feed. Different species prefer various habitats, allowing many species to live in the same area.

DIET

Hornbills eat a variety of food, from animals to fruits and seeds. They are omnivorous, eating both meat and fruit in their meals.

BEHAVIOR AND REPRODUCTION

Hornbills generally groom their feathers as their first activity after dawn, and then begin searching for food. They move in pairs, but some species move in family groups of three to twenty. When plenty of food is available, larger groups may come together. Bills are used for various functions including feeding, grooming, and nest-sealing. They are not considered as migratory birds, but are territorial for many species.

Hornbills display sounds that are described as the noise made by an approaching train. The sound is possible because hornbills do not have small feathers that cover their flight feathers; so wings allow air to pass through, producing train-like vibration sounds. These "whooshing" sounds come in different intensities depending on wing size, and are used to defend the territory and to maintain contact with group members.

Hornbills are believed to be monogamous (muh-NAH-guh-mus), having only one mate. Usually one breeding pair will be joined by earlier offspring who help raise the latest brood. Courtship begins when pairs fly together through the air, perch close to each other, groom one another, and exchange food.

Hornbills use an interesting nesting pattern. They build nests in holes, mostly natural cavities, hollow areas, in trees or rock crevices. However, unlike most other birds, all hornbills, except a few, seal the cavity entrance, leaving only a slit through which the female, and later her young, receive food from the male. The male brings mud to the female who use it, along with her saliva, to seal the opening. If mud is not available, the female will substitute her own feces, solid waste. Egg size and number, and incubation period, the time needed to sit and hatch the eggs, depends on female body size. Clutch size, number of eggs hatched together, ranges from two to three eggs in large hornbills, and up to eight for smaller hornbills. Incubation periods run between twenty-three and forty-nine days. Eggs hatch in intervals, with the chicks emerging naked, pink, and blind. Feather growth begins in a few days, with the skin turning black. Fledglings, young who have grown enough feathers to be able to fly, have underdeveloped casques and small bills, but after about one year, their appearance is like the adults.

HORNBILLS AND PEOPLE

People hunt hornbills for food and as a treatment for ailments. The birds play an important role in the customs and traditions of local people. Their feathers, heads, and casques are valued. They are often adopted as local mascots or state birds.

CONSERVATION STATUS

Two hornbill species are Critically Endangered, facing an extremely high risk of extinction in the wild. Two species are Endangered, facing a very high risk of extinction in the wild. Five species are Vulnerable, facing a high risk of extinction in the wild, and twelve species are Near Threatened, may become threatened with extinction.

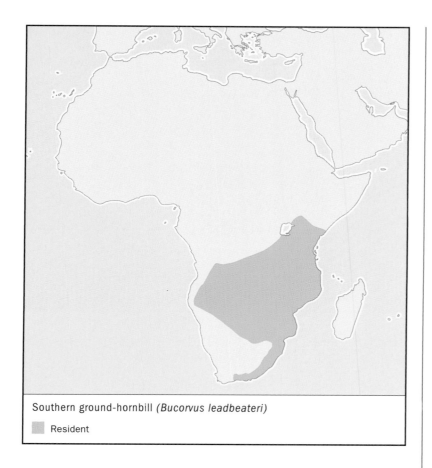

Southern ground-hornbill (*Bucorvus leadbeateri*)

■ Resident

SOUTHERN GROUND-HORNBILL
Bucorvus leadbeateri

Physical characteristics: Southern ground-hornbills are the largest in size and darkest in color of hornbill species. They are black with white primary feathers, the largest flight feathers, and red throat skin. Males have bare facial skin, and throat skin that can expand. Females have a blue patch on their red throat skin. When flying, white wing patches are visible. Juveniles are browner than adults, with black flecks in the primary wings, gray sides that reach to the bill, and pale gray-brown facial skin. Adults are 35.4 to 39.4 inches (90 to 100 centimeters) long. The male weighs between 7.6 and 13.6 pounds (3.5 and 6.2 kilograms) and the female weighs between 4.9 and 10.1 pounds (2.2 and 4.6 kilograms).

Southern ground-hornbills eat mostly small animals, and hunt in groups on the ground by walking, probing, pecking, and digging at the ground. (© Karl Ammann/Corbis. Reproduced by permission.)

Geographic range: They are found in eastern South Africa, Botswana, northern Namibia, Angola, and southern Burundi and Kenya.

Habitat: Southern ground-hornbills live in woodlands, savannas, and grasslands next to forests. They are found at elevations up to 9,800 feet (3,000 meters), preferring moist habitats.

Diet: Southern ground-hornbills are mostly carnivorous, eating only meat. They eat insects, grasshoppers, beetles, scorpions, and termites. During the dry season, they also eat insect larvae (LAR-vee), snails, frogs, and toads. Sometimes southern ground-hornbills eat larger prey, such as snakes, lizards, rats, hares, squirrels, and tortoises. At times, they will eat carrion (decaying animals), fruits, and seeds. The birds are able to eat these animals by using their powerful dagger-like bills to cut and tear their prey. Southern ground-hornbills hunt in groups from the ground by walking, probing, pecking, and digging.

Behavior and reproduction: Southern ground-hornbills roost in trees. They live in groups of up to eight birds, with each bird of the group sharing and defending a territory. The territory may be as large as 36 square miles (100 square kilometers). Nests are holes in trees or rock faces, lined with dry leaves brought by males. The entrance is not sealed. Females lay one to three eggs at intervals of three to five days, usually from September to December. The incubation period is thirty-seven to forty-three days. Adult and immature helpers usually assist the dominant pair, and feed the nesting female. Chicks are hatched with pink skin that turns black within three days. At about eighty-six days, young birds fledge, or grow the feathers necessary for flight. Southern ground-hornbills remain with the parents at least until maturity, about four to six years.

Southern ground-hornbills and people: Local people think highly of southern ground-hornbills, but also eat them for food and medicinal, healing, purposes.

Conservation status: Southern ground-hornbills are not threatened. They are widespread and common throughout their geographic range except in some areas of South Africa and Zimbabwe where their populations are declining. ■

Helmeted hornbill (*Rhinoplax vigil*)

■ Resident

HELMETED HORNBILL
Rhinoplax vigil

Physical characteristics: Helmeted hornbills are large, dark brown and white birds with short red bills. They have high, nearly solid, heavy casques, and long, white tail feathers. Adults are 37.4 to 41.4 inches (110 to 120 centimeters) long, with females weighing between 5.7 and 6.3 pounds (2.6 and 2.8 kilograms) and males weighing about 6.7 pounds (3.1 kilograms).

Geographic range: Helmeted hornbills are found in South Myanmar and south Thailand, Malaysia, Sumatra, and Borneo.

Habitat: They prefer rainforests primarily at a habitat below an altitude of 4,900 feet (1,500 meters).

Diet: Helmeted hornbills eat many different types of figs.

Behavior and reproduction: They are believed to be territorial. The species has a distinctive loud call that includes a series of introductory "tok," followed by a flowing laughter-like sound. Both sexes regularly engage in strange, aerial hammering and head-butting behaviors with the use of their casque, especially near fruiting fig trees.

Little is known about the reproduction of helmeted hornbills. Females breed throughout the year, but in southern Sumatra, fledglings are usually found between May and June.

Helmeted hornbills and people: People in Southeast Asian cultures consider the helmeted hornbill to be one of their most significant species. They are widely hunted for their feathers and casques ("ivory") that are valued for traditional dances and ceremonial decoration. Illegal carved casques are still traded internationally.

Conservation status: Helmeted hornbills are considered Near Threatened and listed on Appendix I of the Convention in International Trade in Endangered Species (CITES). They are common where its range is left undisturbed. However populations are declining throughout most of its range due to hunting and forest destruction. ∎

Helmeted hornbills eat almost nothing else but figs. They eat figs from up to twelve species of fig trees. (© T. Laman/VIREO. Reproduced by permission.)

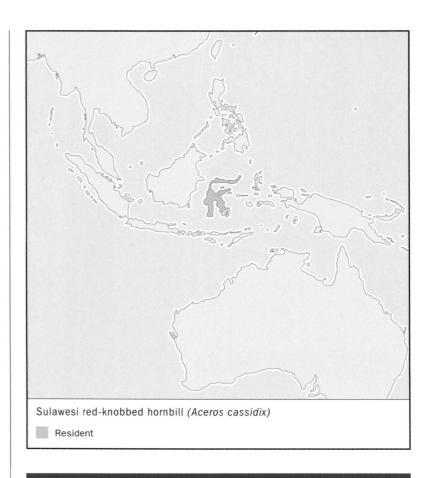

Sulawesi red-knobbed hornbill *(Aceros cassidix)*

☐ Resident

SULAWESI RED-KNOBBED HORNBILL
Aceros cassidix

Physical characteristics: Sulawesi red-knobbed hornbills are black with a white tail. They have a high, wrinkled, red casque. Necks are rufous, reddish, in males, and black in females. Their beaks are ridged and yellow with blue throat skin. Adults are 27.6 to 31.5 inches (70 to 80 centimeters) long. Female weight is unknown, and male weight is between 5.2 and 5.5 pounds (2.4 and 2.5 kilograms).

Geographic range: They are found in the Indonesian island of Sulawesi and nearby islands of Lembeh, Togian, Muna, and Buton.

Habitat: Sulawesi red-knobbed hornbills prefer lowland rainforests, particularly at altitudes below 3,600 feet (1,000 meters).

Diet: They eat a very wide range of fruits, mostly off of the top of the forest's canopy.

Behavior and reproduction: The Sulawesi red-knobbed hornbill is a non-territorial bird, that ranges across a wide area of land. They are usually seen in pairs, but also observed in large numbers, usually fewer than 120 individuals, while feeding at fruiting figs trees. They emit a loud barking call that can be heard for more than 1.2 miles (2 kilometers). Sulawesi red-knobbed hornbills assist in the scattering of seeds and growth of plants because they eat many fruits.

Nesting begins in June or July, at the end of the rainy season so young can feed during the fruit season. Nests may be built near others, often up to ten mating pairs per 0.4 square miles (1 square kilometer). Females usually lay two to three eggs, with an incubation period of between thirty-two and thirty-five days and nestling period of about 100 days.

Sulawesi red-knobbed hornbills and people: People believe that the feathers and casques of Sulawesi red-knobbed hornbills are filled with powers that give the owner protection from all types of problems. Their feathers and casques are, therefore, used to decorate headdresses and drums for traditional warrior dances. Their meat is also eaten by people.

Conservation status: Sulawesi red-knobbed hornbills are not threatened. They are locally found with densities of up to 130 birds per square mile (51 birds per square kilometer). Distribution is slowly becoming more restricted due to the decline in forested areas. ■

FOR MORE INFORMATION

Books:

del Hoyo, Josep, et al., eds. *Handbook of the Birds of the World.* Barcelona: Lynx Edicions, 1992.

Dickinson, Edward C., ed. *The Howard and Moore Complete Checklist of the Birds of the World,* 3rd ed. Princeton, NJ and Oxford, U.K.: Princeton University Press, 2003.

Fry, C. Hilary, and Kathie Fry. *Kingfishers, Bee-Eaters and Rollers: A Handbook.* Princeton, NJ: Princeton University Press, 1992.

Harrison, Colin James Oliver. *Birds of the World.* London and New York: Dorling Kindersley, 1993.

Forshaw, Joseph, ed. *Encyclopedia of Birds,* 2nd ed. San Diego, CA: Academic Press, 1998.

Perrins, Christopher M., and Alex L. A. Middleton, eds. *The Encyclopedia of Birds.* New York: Facts on File, 1985.

Stattersfield, Allison, J., and David R. Capper, eds. *Threatened Birds of the World: The Official Source for Birds on the IUCN Red List.* Cambridge, U.K.: BirdLife International, 2000.

WOODPECKERS AND RELATIVES

Piciformes

Class: Aves

Order: Piciformes

Number of families: 6 families

PHYSICAL CHARACTERISTICS

Woodpeckers and their relatives make up the order Piciformes, which includes six families of birds that nest in cavities (hollow areas within a rock or tree): jacamars (Galbulidae); puffbirds (Bucconidae); barbets (Capitonidae); honeyguides (Indicatoridae); woodpeckers, wrynecks, and piculets, (Picidae); and toucans (Ramphastidae).

Although the six families look very different, most piciform birds share a common adaptation that helps them live in trees. This special feature is zygodactylous (zye-guh-DACK-tuhl-us; "yoke-toed" or "X-shaped") feet, which have two toes in front and two toes behind. With this arrangement, the birds can easily grab onto bark while hopping along branches and running up and down tree trunks. Along with this special feature, woodpeckers and their relatives also have similar jaw muscles and tongues, and do not have down feathers (except the jacamars). The tongue is capable of sticking out of its bill up to 4 inches (10 centimeters) in the green woodpecker, allowing it to take insects from deep cracks and crevices.

Piciforms are small- to medium-sized birds. They also share similar skeletal features, especially with the bones of the vertebrae (spinal column), sternum (breastbone), and ribs. Many members have heavy, sturdy bills, but the general size and shape of the bills varies widely. Jacamars have longish pointed bills; puffbirds have large, broad, often hooked bills; barbets have largish, generally heavy, sometimes notched bills; woodpeckers have strong, tapering, often chisel-tipped bills; honeyguides

phylum

class

subclass

● **order**

monotypic order

suborder

family

have relatively short bills that can be either stubby or pointed; and toucans have huge, colorful bills. The colorful plumage (feathers) found on most of the birds is very different among all of the piciform birds. However, they almost always contain combinations of black and white with accents of red and yellow.

Males and females usually look alike, but with some small differences in the color of nape (back part of neck) patches and the presence or absence of feathers around the bill, or what is called their "moustaches." One exception is Neotropical barbets, which show a great difference between males and females with regard to plumage color and pattern. Woodpeckers (one of three groups in the family Picidae) are unique within the family, order, and, in fact, among all birds in that they have strong, extra-stiff tail feathers that are used to brace themselves against tree trunks while climbing vertically or hammering with their beaks. Barbets also use their tail as a brace, but only while digging nest cavities. Woodpeckers and relatives are 3 to 22 inches (8 to 56 grams) long and weigh between 0.3 and 20 ounces (8 and 569 grams).

GEOGRAPHIC RANGE

Even though they do not migrate, piciform birds make up one of the most widespread bird orders, mostly due to the woodpeckers that are found on all the world's continents except for Antarctica and Australia. The other piciform families are less widely distributed; the jacamars, toucans, and puffbirds are only found in the New World tropics, and honeyguides only found in Southeast Asia and Africa. Barbets are found in both the tropics of the New World and the Old World.

HABITAT

Piciforms inhabit forests and woodlands, mostly in tropical environments. They are arboreal—that is, they live in trees. Many of the species prefer mature forests with a closed canopy, meaning the tallest trees' leaves let little light onto the forest floor. However, some species prefer open, fragmented forests and woodland savannas (flat grasslands) while other species like forest edges, stream banks, grasslands, orchards, and parks.

DIET

Woodpeckers and their relatives eat a variety of foods and therefore, have a big difference in bill structure. Woodpeckers, jacamars, honeyguides, and puffbirds eat mostly insects and their larvae (LAR-vee; active immature insects), but some woodpeckers also eat fruit and nuts. Honeyguides also eat beeswax from beehives. Toucans and barbets eat mainly fruits, but do feed insects and other similar foods to young. Jacamars and puffbirds locate prey while in the air, eating mostly butterflies (for jacamars) and flying beetles (for puffbirds). Woodpeckers and their relatives also catch their prey with different techniques: taking them from leaves, branches, and tree trunks; probing into bark crevices and removing bark; drilling holes to insert tongues; carving off large pieces of bark; pecking funnel-shaped holes into ants' nests; or catching prey in flight. Their sturdy, stout beaks allow them to find prey in wood and other similar materials.

BEHAVIOR AND REPRODUCTION

Woodpeckers and relatives are not considered very social birds, except for a few species. They are rarely seen on the ground or flying in the air, but are mostly found searching for food, eating captured prey, nesting, raising young, and roosting in trees. Most piciform birds do not migrate, move seasonally, but remain in their home range throughout the year. However, a few species migrate many miles between their breeding and wintering areas. A male-female pair will breed alone, but will maintain their bond—especially for woodpeckers, puffbirds, and barbets—throughout the year as they protect their territory. Some species of toucans form small flocks while foraging for food, and honeyguides and barbets come together at times when there is plenty of food available.

Piciforms are good climbers but weak flyers, except for honeyguides who are strong, acrobatic birds. Woodpeckers and relatives communicate in many different ways. They ruffle their crown feathers, spread their wings, sway the head, hop and dance about, and tap and drum their bill on tree trunks and branches.

Piciforms have two unique and very unusual behaviors that are unknown anywhere else in the bird community. First, woodpeckers and a few species of barbets communicate to one another by "drumming" (that is, tapping or hammering) rhythmically on hollow trees or other such structures in particular ways (depending on the species). Second, honeyguides, as their name says, "guide" animals such as honey badgers, baboons, and humans to bees' nests with the use of calls and short flights to the nests. When one of these animals is drawn to a beehive

DRUMS OF WOODPECKERS

All woodpeckers tap or "drum" their bills rapidly against wood in order to defend their territory and to attract mates. This drumming is used instead of songs in most species. The length, speed, frequency, and loudness at which a particular woodpecker drums often identify a particular species. However, the quality of the drumming sound often depends on the type of wood on which the woodpecker is tapping.

and breaks it open, the honeyguides help themselves to the beeswax.

Woodpeckers and their relatives are territorial, living in individual, pair, or family territories. They often defend a territory even from their own species. They display several courtship activities; among them, drumming and tapping on trees in specific patterns, flights into the air, and expressive calls to attract a mate. In fact, the black woodpecker taps about forty-three times within a two and a half-second period. They nest (and roost) in cavities, with some families laying their eggs in the nests of other hole-nesting species such as woodpeckers and barbets. The type of cavity used varies among the six families. Some species of jacamars and puffbirds dig out decayed trees among former termite nests, while other species dig burrows in soil, often along riverbanks. Barbets and woodpeckers use their strong, sharp beaks to hammer out nest cavities in rotting trees. Other birds often take over such nests, making woodpeckers and their relatives helpful to such birds. The large species of toucans use natural holes in trees, while the smaller species often drive out woodpeckers from newly dug holes, and then enlarge the holes to suit their needs. They will reuse the nests for many years.

Almost all woodpeckers and their relatives lay white eggs. During the incubation period, the mating pair will nest at intervals of thirty to 150 minutes. The nestling period is eighteen to thirty-five days. The whole family breaks up from one to eight weeks after the young leaves the nest.

WOODPECKERS, RELATIVES AND PEOPLE

People have historically used feathers from toucans and woodpeckers for ceremonial ornaments. Humans hunt many of the larger species for food. Woodpeckers and relatives play an important role in the forest ecosystem, helping to control insects and the cycle of decay and regrowth of plants and animals. The blue toucan is well known in some countries as the mascot for a popular breakfast cereal, while Woody the Woodpecker has been a popular cartoon character for many decades.

Many homeowners, however, consider woodpeckers as pests because of the damage done to homes and other building structures by the use of their bills. For the most part, scientists regard piciform birds as beneficial to the environment. Toucans and barbets greatly help to scatter seeds. Woodpeckers help to control pest insects in forests, while holes pecked out in trees help other birds and some animals such as squirrels in finding nest locations.

CONSERVATION STATUS

According to recent research, fifteen species (of a total of 383 species) of piciform birds are classified as Critically Endangered, Endangered, or Vulnerable, at an extremely high, very high, or high risk of extinction. Another twenty-eight species are classified as Near Threatened. Experts on the birds warn that even though fewer than 4 percent of the birds are threatened, continued loss of habitat greatly harms the ability of the birds to reproduce and live. Decreased numbers of piciformes have also occurred due to hunting and capture for pets and other human activities. In fact, collecting of some species for museums is believed to have contributed to the extinction of some of those species.

FOR MORE INFORMATION

Books:

Alsop III, Fred J. *Birds of North America.* New York: Dorling Kindersley, 2001.

Baughman, Mel M., ed. *Reference Atlas to the Birds of North America.* Washington, DC: National Geographic, 2003.

del Hoyo, J., A. Elliott, J. Sargatal, J. Cabot, et al., eds. *Handbook of the Birds of the World.* Barcelona: Lynx Edicions, 1992.

Dickinson, Edward C., ed. *The Howard and Moore Complete Checklist of the Birds of the World,* 3rd ed. Princeton, NJ and Oxford, U.K.: Princeton University Press, 2003.

Field Guide to the Birds of North America, 4th ed. Washington, DC: National Geographic Society, 2002.

Forshaw, Joseph, ed. *Encyclopedia of Birds,* 2nd ed. San Diego, CA: Academic Press, 1998.

Harrison, Colin James Oliver. *Birds of the World.* London and New York: Dorling Kindersley, 1993.

Kaufman, Kenn, et al. *Birds of North America.* New York: Houghton Mifflin, 2000.

Sibley, David. *The Sibley Guide to Birds.* New York: Alfred A. Knopf, 2000.

JACAMARS
Galbulidae

Class: Aves
Order: Piciformes
Family: Galbulidae
Number of species: 17 species

phylum

class

subclass

order

monotypic order

suborder

▲ **family**

PHYSICAL CHARACTERISTICS

Jacamars (ZHAK-uh-mahrz) are glossy, graceful-appearing birds that look like hummingbirds but are really related to woodpeckers, puffbirds, and toucans. They are very noticeable birds because of their jewel-like colors and long, sharp bill. Their bright plumage (feathers) consists of metallic green or blue upperparts, light patches on their throat or breast, a metallic green head, and reddish to dull brown or blackish underparts. Some species have color differences ranging from purple to red or chestnut brown. In many species, the bill is three times as long as the head.

The birds have short legs (except for one species) and zygodactyl (zye-guh-DACK-tuhl) feet (two toes face forward and two point backwards), which helps them grab branches and food while hunting. Unique features of this family include a long appendix (small outgrowth from large intestine), no gall bladder (sac that stores bile), a bare preen gland (oil-secreting sac at tail base), and a long, thin tongue. They have a long tail with ten to twelve tail feathers that are of different lengths and short wings with ten primary feathers. Males and females have similar plumage, although some female species are less colorful on head and neck. Adults are 5.1 to 12.2 inches (13 to 31 centimeters) long.

GEOGRAPHIC RANGE

Jacamars range from southern Mexico in Central America to northern Argentina in South America.

HABITAT

Jacamars live near tropical rainforests, stream or riverine (around a river) forests, and savanna (flat grassland) woodlands. They especially prefer Neotropical rainforests, the geographic area of plant and animal life east, west, and south of Mexico's central plateau that includes Central and South America and the West Indies. They are found generally at low altitudes, at the edges of forests, areas of fallen trees and clay or sandy stream banks, and within areas that contain colorful butterflies.

DIET

Jacamars prefer to eat large, showy, flying insects such as blue morpho butterflies, hawk moths, and venomous insects such as wasps, ants, and sawflies. Their diet also consists of other types of butterflies and moths, dragonflies, and flying beetles. They grab prey out of the air with their long, sharp (forceps-like) bill. They do not like butterflies that use body chemicals to defend themselves.

BEHAVIOR AND REPRODUCTION

Jacamars make expert maneuvers (mah-NOO-verz) as they swoop down from perches to capture colorful prey in mid-air. They spend most time on branches, staying alert for flying insects. After catching prey, jacamars grab the winged insect away from its wings or stinger in order not to become blinded by its fluttering wings or injured by its stinger. After perching, they beat it against a tree branch to kill it, and then remove the wings and stingers before eating it. They live generally in pairs, perching and hunting in the same area. Some species join in small family groups. Jacamars use a variety of calls to communicate, such as trills, squeals, whistles, and short songs, which are generally considered pleasant.

Male jacamars use a series of sharp calls during breeding season to attract a mate. The monogamous (muh-NAH-guh-mus; having one mate) pair builds nest holes in some species, while in other species only females do the work. The birds sometime drill holes for nests in deep riverbanks, using their bill to break up the soil and then their feet to remove soil by kicking it backwards. Other nest locations are on earthen banks or roots of fallen trees, while some use termite nests if other sites are unavailable. The nest occurs at the end of the tunnel in a horizontal, oval-shaped chamber. Tunnels are 12 to 36 inches (30

to 91 centimeters) long and about 2 inches (5 centimeters) wide. No materials are used for the nest, although eggs are often covered with a layer of partially digested food brought up from the parents' stomachs. Nests are used many times.

Females lay one to four round, glossy, white eggs that are not marked. Both parents incubate (sit on) the eggs during the day for one to three hours at a time. At night, the female incubate alone while the male defends the nest. Jacamars seldom leave eggs alone. While the female sits on the eggs, the male will feed his mate several times a day. The incubation period (time that it takes to sit on eggs before hatching) is twenty to twenty-three days. Newborn jacamars are born with white down. Both parents feed the young with insects. The nestling period, or the time it takes to take care of the young unable to leave the nest, is nineteen to twenty-six days. When they are ready to leave the nest, their plumage looks like the parents.

JACAMARS AND PEOPLE

The name jacamar is derived from the Tupi word *jacama-ciri*, which is used by Brazilian natives.

CONSERVATION STATUS

The three-toed jacamar is listed as Endangered, facing a very high risk of extinction, and another species, the coppery-chested jacamar, is listed as Vulnerable, facing a high risk of extinction. All species of jacamars are threatened by habitat loss. For example, in Brazil intensive clearing of vegetation in forests has caused a decline in populations.

Rufous-tailed jacamar (*Galbula ruficauda*)

Resident

RUFOUS-TAILED JACAMAR
Galbula ruficauda

Physical characteristics: Rufous-tailed jacamars have metallic coppery green upperparts, pale buffy chins, a white or buff patch on the throat, which is sometimes speckled green, rufous (reddish) to chestnut underparts, blackish primary feathers, and long graduated central

Rufous-tailed jacamars catch flying insects in midair. (© Doug Wechsler/VIREO. Reproduced by permission.)

tail feathers. Females are slightly duller and paler than males, with a cinnamon-buff chin and throat and dark cinnamon-buff underwing coverts (small feather around base of quill). They have a very long, slender bill, sometimes called "needle beak", that is about 2 inches (5.1 centimeters) long. Adults are about 7.5 to 9.8 inches (19 to 25 centimeters) long and weigh between 0.6 an 1.0 ounces (18 to 28 grams).

Geographic range: Rufous-tailed jacamars are probably the most widespread jacamars with a distribution from southern Mexico to northern Argentina including Mexico, Costa Rica, Ecuador, Colombia, Brazil, Argentina, and Trinidad and Tobago.

Habitat: Rufous-tailed jacamars are found on the edge of forests, in woodlands and thickets, and near streams and rivers.

Diet: Their diet includes flying insects that are caught in midair. Once caught, they beat the food against a branch before eating it.

Behavior and reproduction: Rufous-tailed jacamars live alone or in pairs, and like to forage from shrubbery near the ground. They do not migrate, but they do make short journeys. The birds signal danger or anxiety with a sharp trill. Males regularly feed females during courtship. They use former termite nests or earthen banks for their breeding sites. Both mates and females dig out nests to a depth of 7.9 to 19.7 inches (20 to 50 centimeters). Females lay one to four white eggs in ground-hole nests. The incubation period is nineteen to twenty-three days, while the nestling period is nineteen to twenty-six days. Both males and females incubate and take care of young. Nestlings hatch with whitish down feathers and are fed insects, especially butterflies.

Rufous-tailed jacamars and people: There is no known significance between people and rufous-tailed jacamars.

Conservation status: Rufous-tailed jacamars are not threatened. They are widespread and common, being able to change the way they live while in different habitats. ■

Coppery-chested jacamar (*Galbula pastazae*)

Resident

COPPERY-CHESTED JACAMAR
Galbula pastazae

Physical characteristics: Coppery-chested jacamars have metallic green upperparts, a dark rufous colored-throat, dark brown eyes, a distinctive yellowish orange eye ring, a copper-colored tail, and grayish feet. Males and females look alike except that females have a dark rufous-colored throat, and less visible coloring around the eyes. Their

Male and female coppery-chested jacamars sit on their eggs and care for the chicks when they hatch. (Illustration by Wendy Baker. Reproduced by permission.)

heavy bill is about 2 inches (5.1 centimeters) long. Adults are 9.0 to 9.5 inches (23 to 24 centimeters) long, and weigh about 1.1 ounces (31 grams).

Geographic range: Coppery-chested jacamars are not seen very often because there are not very many of them. They have been seen at a few sites in Ecuador, southern Colombia, Amazonian Brazil, and along the eastern slopes of the Ecuadorian Andes at altitudes of up to 5,100 feet (1,550 meters), the highest elevations of all jacamars.

Habitat: They are found in montane (mountain) tropical rainforests.

Diet: Their diet consists of a wide variety of flying insects. They prefer to hunt from one favorite perch, watching carefully for possible prey. When seeing a possible target, they capture the flying insect as it flies through the air.

Behavior and reproduction: Coppery-chested jacamars are very alert hunters, as are all jacamars. They give a series of three to five loud calls such as "pee pee-pee-pe-pe-pee-pee-pee." Females lay one to four white eggs in curved ground-hole nests that are carefully hidden. When born, young are covered with white down. The incubation period is twenty to twenty-three days. Males and females share in incubation activities, along with taking care of the chicks as they grow.

Coppery-chested jacamars and people: There is no known significance between people and coppery-chested jacamars.

Conservation status: Coppery-chested jacamars are listed as Vulnerable. There are few areas where coppery-chested jacamars are found and their populations are low. They are found mostly in Colombia and the eastern slope of the Andes. Their populations are being reduced due to habitat loss, mainly from the loss of forested areas. ■

FOR MORE INFORMATION

Books:

del Hoyo, Josep, et al., eds. *Handbook of the Birds of the World.* Barcelona: Lynx Edicions, 1992.

Dickinson, Edward C., ed. *The Howard and Moore Complete Checklist of the Birds of the World,* 3rd ed. Princeton, NJ and Oxford, U.K.: Princeton University Press, 2003.

Forshaw, Joseph, ed. *Encyclopedia of Birds,* 2nd ed. San Diego, CA: Academic Press, 1998.

Harrison, Colin James Oliver. *Birds of the World.* London and New York: Dorling Kindersley, 1993.

Perrins, Christopher M., and Alex L. A. Middleton, eds. *The Encyclopedia of Birds.* New York: Facts on File, 1985.

Web sites:

Steve Metz Photography. "Rufous-tailed Jacamar." http://www.stevemetzphotography.com/photo%20pages/Trinidad&Tobago/Rufous-tailed%2 0Jacamar.htm (accessed on July 19, 2004).

Class: Aves
Order: Piciformes
Family: Bucconidae
Number of species: 32 species

family

CHAPTER

PHYSICAL CHARACTERISTICS

Puffbirds are related to jacamars, but lack the iridescent (brilliant, shiny) colors of those birds. Puffbirds have a small- to medium-sized body, a large head, large eyes, short neck and a sturdy, flattened, slightly curved or hook-tipped bill (bills are more streamlined in some species). They have short and rounded wings, and a short and narrow tail, although some species have broader and longer tails. The swallow-winged puffbird has more tapered wings and a shorter bill than that of the other puffbird species.

Their mostly brown plumage (feathers) is soft and loose, and is not as colorful as jacamars' plumage. However, it has a very attractive pattern consisting of white, buff, rufous (reddish), brown, and black colors, especially with its sharp breast bands and streaked, barred, or spotted underparts. Their feet are small and zygodactylous (zye-guh-DACK-tuhl-us; two toes facing forward and two turned backward). Males and females look nearly the same, except for two species. Adults are 5.1 to 11.4 inches (13 to 29 centimeters) long and weigh between 0.5 and 3.7 ounces (14 and 106 grams).

GEOGRAPHIC RANGE

Puffbirds range from southern Mexico in Central America to northern Argentina and Paraguay in South America. They are not found on any islands off the coasts of these countries.

HABITAT

Puffbirds are found from dry to humid forests, lowlands, open woodlands, and wooded savannas (flat grasslands). They are not often found within the deep parts of the forest. The birds are usually found in areas below 3,280 feet (1,000 meters) in elevation, but some species are found in areas that rise up to 9,500 feet (2,900 meters). Puffbirds are found mainly in northern South America, particularly in the area surrounding the Amazon River. Most birds are found around the forest edges, in areas where trees have fallen, along streams and lakes, and inside clearings. They especially like locations where plenty of perches are available and many vines hang down from the trees.

DIET

Because puffbirds are difficult to locate, little is known about their eating habits. It is believed that they eat mostly insects. Most species also eat arthropods (invertebrate animals with jointed limbs), along with small frogs, lizards, and snakes. Some species eat small amounts of fruits, berries, and buds, but mostly only in species that live at high elevations. They hunt for food only within the trees, going up to 65 feet (20 meters) to catch prey.

BEHAVIOR AND REPRODUCTION

Puffbirds are arboreal birds, meaning that they live in trees. They perch motionless in trees for long periods waiting for prey to approach. When flying, puffbirds fly quickly and swiftly on whirl-sounding wings. They defend their territory throughout the year with sounds that tell outsiders they are close by and to stay away. They are generally solitary birds, although some species are found in small family groups. Vocal sounds are also used to attract mates. Their voice is thin and ring-like, and can range from weak to loud, rarely being pleasant. Puffbirds do not seem to be migratory birds, yet some species that live at high altitudes or at the southernmost edge of their geographic range do migrate in response to changes in seasons.

Puffbirds are monogamous (muh-NAH-guh-mus), meaning that they have only one mate. They breed at various times throughout their ranges, depending on the amount of rainfall. It is believed that nests are made from cavities that are dug out of former termite and ant beds and sometimes out of abandoned nests of other birds. Some nests are burrowed into sand or soil, while others are made in tree holes. Both members of the mating

PUFFED UP PUFFBIRDS

Puffbirds were given their name because of their ability to "puff up" their feathers when alarmed. The combination of their large head, short tail, and often loose feathers also gives them a "puffy" look.

pair generally dig nests. Nest cavities vary in length from 20 to 60 inches (50 to 150 centimeters) with larger species digging longer cavities. Cavities end in a rounded chamber that is usually not lined with any materials but can be lined at times with leaves or grass. Some species place leaves around the entrance, probably to hide the opening.

Their small, white unmarked eggs can vary from dull to glossy and are usually laid in clutches (groups of eggs hatched together) of two to three, sometimes four. The incubation period (length of time needed to sit on eggs and warm them in order to hatch them) is unknown in most species. Both sexes incubate the eggs and only one brood (young birds that are born and raised together) is raised each year. Hatchlings (newly born birds) are born blind and naked, but are still able to crawl to the entrance on their first day of life in order to take food from their parents. The fledgling period (time it takes for feathers to develop in order to fly) is believed to be twenty to thirty days. Young birds remain in their birthing territory for about one year.

PUFFBIRDS AND PEOPLE

There is no significant relationship between people and puffbirds.

CONSERVATION STATUS

One species, the sooty-capped puffbird, is listed as Near Threatened, in danger of becoming threatened with extinction. Generally, all puffbird populations are declining throughout South and Central America mostly because their forested areas are growing smaller.

White-necked puffbird (*Notharchus macrorhynchos*)

■ Resident

WHITE-NECKED PUFFBIRD
Notharchus macrorhynchos

Physical characteristics: White-necked puffbirds look a little bit like kingfishers, being identified mainly by their white forehead and wide, glossy black breast band. They have glossy black-blue upperparts, a white collar, throat, sides of face, and belly. The bill is

black, there is variable dark barring on the flanks, the tail is narrow with white tips and the feet are black. As one of the largest puffbirds, adults are about 11 inches (25 centimeters) long and weigh between 2.9 and 3.7 ounces (81 and 106 grams).

Geographic range: They range from Mexico in Central America to Venezuela, Colombia, Ecuador, eastern Peru, northern Bolivia, and northern and western Brazil (to the Amazon River) in South America.

Habitat: White-necked puffbirds live in mostly humid to semi-arid (somewhat dry) secondary forests, mixed pine and oak woods, forest edges and clearings, and plantations; from sea level to 3,940 feet (1,200 meters).

Diet: Their diet consists of large insects and small vertebrates (animals with backbone), along with some vegetable materials. They hunt from the ground to the tops of the trees.

Behavior and reproduction: The mating pair defends their territory. They do not migrate. White-necked puffbirds spend much of their time perching without motion on high open branches. Female and male pairs dig nests in former termite nests built in trees usually 40 to 50 feet (12 to 15 meters) off the ground, but can range from 10 to 60 feet (3 to 18 meters). Holes in the ground are also used as nests. Information about incubation and nestling periods and activities are not known.

White-necked puffbirds and people: There is no known significant relationship between people and white-necked puffbirds.

Conservation status: White-necked puffbirds are not threatened. There are few in Central America, but they are fairly numerous in South America. ■

Rufous-capped nunlet (*Nonnula ruficapilla*)

■ Resident

RUFOUS-CAPPED NUNLET
Nonnula ruficapilla

Physical characteristics: Rufous-capped nunlets have a small body, slender bill, deep chestnut crown (top of head), a gray face, nape (back of neck), and sides of the breast. They have plain dull-brown upperparts, rufous (reddish) underparts, a whitish belly, and dark brownish gray feet. Adults are 5.3 to 5.5 inches (13.5 to 14.0 centimeters) long and weigh between 0.5 and 0.8 ounces (14 and 22 grams).

Geographic range: They range (east and west) from eastern Peru to western Brazil south of the Amazon River, and (north and south) from northern Brazil to northern Bolivia.

Habitat: Rufous-capped nunlets live in the mid-levels and undergrowth of humid forest edges, secondary forests, streamside forests, and the banks of the black waters (igapó) of the Amazon River area. They prefer areas that surround rivers and contain bamboo trees.

Diet: It is believed that they eat mostly insects.

Behavior and reproduction: Rufous-capped nunlets are usually found alone or in pairs. They are generally found sitting quietly in low vegetation where they search for food. The birds give out a long series of sharp, clear, short whistles sounding like "fwick!-fwick!" that are softer and lower in sound near the beginning and end. Little information is available about reproduction. It is known that nests are often made in holes in earthen banks or trees.

Rufous-capped nunlets and people: There is no known significant relationship between people and rufous-capped nunlets.

Conservation status: Rufous-capped nunlets are not threatened. They seem to be fairly common in most of their habitat. ∎

Rufous-capped nunlets are usually found alone or in pairs. They are generally found sitting quietly in low vegetation where they search for food. (Illustration by Dan Erickson. Reproduced by permission.)

FOR MORE INFORMATION

Books:

del Hoyo, Josep, Andrew Elliott, Jordi Sargatal, Jose Cabot, et al., eds. *Handbook of the Birds of the World.* Barcelona: Lynx Edicions, 1992.

Dickinson, Edward C., ed. *The Howard and Moore Complete Checklist of the Birds of the World,* 3rd ed. Princeton, NJ and Oxford, U.K.: Princeton University Press, 2003.

Forshaw, Joseph, ed. *Encyclopedia of Birds,* 2nd ed. San Diego, CA: Academic Press, 1998.

Harrison, Colin James Oliver. *Birds of the World.* London and New York: Dorling Kindersley, 1993.

Perrins, Christopher M., and Alex L. A. Middleton, eds. *The Encyclopedia of Birds.* New York: Facts on File, 1985.

Web sites:

Mangoverde World Bird Guide. "White-necked Puffbird *Notharchus macrorhynchos*." http://www.mangoverde.com/birdsound/spec/spec 100-1.html (accessed on July 19, 2004).

BARBETS
Capitonidae

Class: Aves
Order: Piciformes
Family: Capitonidae
Number of species: 92 species

PHYSICAL CHARACTERISTICS

Barbets are colorful, small- to medium-sized birds. They have a thick, stout bill that is cone-shaped and sharply tipped, bristles (in most species) around the mouth and bill, and tufts over the nostrils. They have a rather large head, a forked or brush-tipped tongue, short and rounded wings, a short tail, and a zygodactyl (zye-guh-DACK-tuhl) foot structure (two toes pointing forward and two toes backward). The bill is heavy and strong, being short but solid in smaller species and rather long and pointed in larger ones.

Males and females look alike in African and Asian species, but look different in color and patterns in South American species. Many African species are mostly black and white with patches of yellow, red, or both in various patterns. Asian barbets are mostly green with patterns of yellow, red, purple, brown, and blue in the chest, head-top, and cheek. South American barbets are often showy-looking birds with black, white, red, and yellow present. Others have orange breast shields or red breast bands. Adults are 3.2 to 13.8 inches (8 to 35 centimeters) long and weigh between 0.3 and 7.2 ounces (8.5 and 203 grams).

GEOGRAPHIC RANGE

Barbets are found in northern South America, southern Central America, sub-Saharan Africa, and south and Southeast Asia. They are found mainly within tropical Africa.

phylum

class

subclass

order

monotypic order

suborder

▲ **family**

HABITAT

Barbets inhabit lowland tropical forests and forest edges. Some species, especially the African ones, are found in secondary forests, parklands, and urban areas that contain fruiting trees. Other species live in drier thornbush habitats with large termite mounds. Barbets like dead wood for digging out nesting holes and to perch on all year-round.

DIET

Barbets are fruit eaters, but young barbets need high protein diets and therefore feed on insects. Where available, the fruit, nectar, and blossoms from avocado, banana, fig, mango, papaya, and pepper trees are eaten. Also, ants, beetles, larvae (LAR-vee), bird eggs, centipedes, lizards, locusts, snails, spiders, termites, worms, and young birds are eaten. They are often found foraging around thickets, ditches, and outbuildings.

BEHAVIOR AND REPRODUCTION

Their zygodactyl foot structure allows them to perch, grasp, and climb in near-vertical motions. The outer toe is moved forwards or sideways to provide a better hold. Barbets hop and climb quickly but awkwardly on trees, and move slowly through low bushes and on the ground. They often perch silently for long periods of time. Larger species are less active than smaller ones. Barbets fly well, but look a little awkward in the air, mostly flying only short distances. They do not support themselves with their tail, except when digging nests. They have a monotonous voice and make a fast series of notes resembling honks, chirps, or hammer-tapping. Mating pairs call out to each other in a pattern of notes, which may be also used by other group members. The larger species are social birds, with helpers to assist in raising young. Others are more territorial, with only the mating pair helping out in the caring of young. They roost in nest holes all year round.

Barbets are monogamous (muh-NAH-guh-mus; having one mate), with some species mating for life. Most of the birds have breeding territories which they defend by singing, often having ten to twelve different calls sung individually or between the mating pair and the helpers. Breeding birds also show color patches on the head, wings, rump, tail, and bill, with feathers erected to emphasize the effect. Male and female pairs often preen each other (groom feathers with the bill). The nest is usually a hole in decayed or dead trees (in branches for smaller species), but can also be former termite mounds or burrows within sand or earthen banks. The hole enters a vertical shaft and ends in a widened chamber where females lay two to five white eggs. The incubation period (time to sit on eggs before hatching) varies, but is twelve to fourteen days in some species, while it is eighteen to nineteen days in other species. The nestling period (time needed to care for young) also varies with species: periods of twenty to twenty-one days, twenty-four to twenty-six days, and thirty-three to thirty-five days. The shorter periods are associated with the smaller species, while the longer periods generally accompany larger species.

BARBETS AND PEOPLE

There is no known significant relationship between people and barbets.

CONSERVATION STATUS

One species, the white-mantled barbet is listed as Endangered, facing a very high risk of extinction, dying out, and nine species are Near Threatened, not currently threatened, but could become so. Habitat loss from logging and other human activities continue to threaten populations of barbets.

Coppersmith barbet *(Megalaima haemacephala)*

▨ Resident

COPPERSMITH BARBET
Megalaima haemacephala

Physical characteristics: Coppersmith barbets are small, plump barbets with a short neck, large head, and short tail. They have dark green upperparts, a red forehead, yellow sides of the throat and head, one black stripe through the eyes and another one that runs below the eyes and onto the bill. They have pale greenish-white under parts with broad dark green streaks and a red patch across the upper breast, and reddish legs. Females are a duller red than the bright males. Juveniles lack all red colorings, with streaky patterns on the throat and a much paler bill. Adults are 5.9 to 6.7 inches (15 to 17 centimeters) long and weigh between 1.1 and 1.8 ounces (30 and 52 grams).

Geographic range: Coppersmith barbets are found from peninsular and northern India, northeastern Pakistan, Bangladesh, Nepal, and Sri Lanka, to southwestern China, Malaysia, Sumatra, and the Philippines.

Habitat: Coppersmith barbets prefer dry deciduous woodlands, forest edges, teak forests, irrigated orchards and plantations with fruiting trees, urban areas that contain trees, and mangroves.

Diet: Their diet consists of figs, custard-apples, guavas, mangos, and papal fruits, along with smaller berries and many types of insects such as beetles, crickets, mantids (plural of mantis; large, predatory insects), and various insect larvae. They tap and chip away tree bark in order to find invertebrates (animals without a backbone).

Behavior and reproduction: Coppersmith barbets sing frequently with a long call. While singing, they bob their head, jerk their body, and flick their

Both parents feed young coppersmith barbets while they're at the nest. (© V. Sinha/ VIREO. Reproduced by permission.)

tail. Their call is a series of "tuk-tuk-tuk," which sounds like a copper sheet being beaten (which gives the bird its name). Females lay two to four eggs in a hole dug from a tree. The incubation period is twelve to fourteen days, and the fledgling period (time for young to grow feathers necessary to fly) is about five weeks. Both parents feed the young, but once chicks learn to fly the parents leave them to brood again (young born and raised together).

Coppersmith barbets and people: People often enjoy hearing coppersmith barbets sing their "hammering" song.

Conservation status: Coppersmith barbets are not threatened. They are common in most of their range. ∎

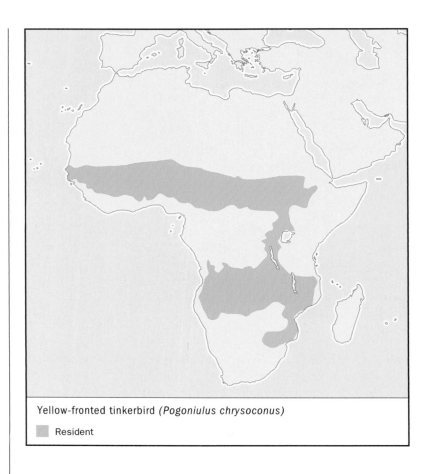

Yellow-fronted tinkerbird (*Pogoniulus chrysoconus*)

▨ Resident

YELLOW-FRONTED TINKERBIRD
Pogoniulus chrysoconus

Physical characteristics: Yellow-fronted tinkerbirds are small, strong-billed, short-tailed tinkerbirds that have a yellow to orange forecrown and center of crown bordered in black. They have a black hindcrown with white streaks, black upperparts with white to yellow-white streaks, gray under parts washed with lemon yellow, a black tail with yellow-white edges, blackish brown wings edged in white or yellow-white, and a mostly pale yellow rump. Adults are 4.3 to 4.7 inches (11 to 12 centimeters) long and weigh between 1.9 and 2.2 ounces (8 and 20 grams).

Geographic range: They are found in the sub-Saharan Africa, from the Atlantic Ocean to southern Sudan (but not found near the coast of the Red Sea), south from Sudan to Lake Victoria, and most of Central Africa south to Mozambique. They are not found in central West Africa.

Habitat: The birds live in many types of forests and riverside woodlands. They like dry, bushy lands from small patches of forests to tall clumps and scattered trees in grasslands and scrublands.

Yellow-fronted tinkerbirds eat small berries and fruits, as well as insects, beetles, and other invertebrates. (P. Ward/Bruce Coleman Inc. Reproduced by permission.)

Diet: Yellow-fronted tinkerbirds eat small berries and bright red, orange, and purple fruits, such as mistletoe berries and figs, as well as insects, beetles, and other invertebrates. They move quietly through foliage and dead leaves while pecking at prey or taking off berries and fruits.

Behavior and reproduction: Yellow-fronted tinkerbirds do not regularly migrate. They usually are found alone or in pairs, but will sometimes join flocks of many bird species. The birds fly fast from spot to spot. During breeding season, they dig cavities in many places such as dead stumps or branches. During this time, breeding birds become aggressive to other barbets that try to approach. In order to defend their territory, males erect their crown feathers, swing their head, flutter their wings, flick their tail, and call out with popping sounds. Females lay two to three white eggs. The incubation period is about twelve days, while the nestling period is about twenty-one days. They breed in all seasons, and have three to four broods each year.

Yellow-fronted tinkerbirds and people: People enjoy listening to the song of yellow-fronted tinkerbirds.

Conservation status: Yellow-fronted tinkerbirds are not threatened. They are generally common throughout their geographical range. ■

Toucan barbet (*Semnornis ramphastinus*)

Resident

TOUCAN BARBET
Semnornis ramphastinus

Physical characteristics: Toucan barbets are patterned and colorful birds with a short bill that is large at the base. Males have black around the bill base, a stiff black tuft on the nape (back of neck), and a broad white line behind the eyes. Females are similar to males, but do not have the stiff tuft on the nape. Juveniles are duller in color. Adults are about 7.5 to 9.8 inches (19 to 25 centimeters) long and weigh between 3.0 and 3.9 ounces (85 and 110 grams).

Geographic range: They are found in southwestern Colombia and western Ecuador in South America.

Habitat: Toucan barbets prefer wet subtropical forests and montane (mountainous) tropical forests, secondary growth, and forest edges and open pastures that contain scattered fruit trees.

Diet: Their diet is made up of mostly fruits (sixty-two species of plants have been recorded), but they also eat insects and other invertebrates when fruit is limited or not available.

Behavior and reproduction: Toucan-barbets are found around fruiting trees and bushes. They forage in groups of up to six birds, usually a territorial pair and their young. The birds hop on branches and climb through low bushy growth from about ground level to the forest canopy. They sometimes remain motionless on a perch. Their

The toucan barbet gets its name from its colorful bill—toucans are birds that have brightly colored bills. (Illustration by Joseph E. Trumpey. Reproduced by permission.)

song is a series of short, foghorn-like notes repeated many times, such as "hawnk" followed by "ag." During this song, the tail is often cocked. A territory is found around a roosting and nesting hole in a dead tree. The breeding pair will drive away all visitors, including older off-spring and other group adults, except for one or two helpers. The number of eggs laid is unknown. The incubation period is about fifteen days. The male and helpers will help the female incubate the eggs. The young are fed for forty-three to forty-six days. If another brood is laid, the earlier offspring will help out.

Toucan barbets and people: People may trap toucan barbets.

Conservation status: Toucan barbets are Near Threatened. They are common in parts of their small range of about 7,700 square miles (20,000 square kilometers). Some birds suffer from trapping and loss of their habitat. ■

FOR MORE INFORMATION

Books:

del Hoyo, Josep, et al, eds. *Handbook of the Birds of the World.* Barcelona: Lynx Edicions, 1992.

Dickinson, Edward C., ed. *The Howard and Moore Complete Checklist of the Birds of the World,* 3rd ed. Princeton, NJ and Oxford, U.K.: Princeton University Press, 2003.

Forshaw, Joseph, ed. *Encyclopedia of Birds,* 2nd ed. San Diego, CA: Academic Press, 1998.

Harrison, Colin James Oliver. *Birds of the World.* London and New York: Dorling Kindersley, 1993.

Perrins, Christopher M., and Alex L. A. Middleton, eds. *The Encyclopedia of Birds.* New York: Facts on File, 1985.

Web sites:

"Coppersmith Barbet *Megalaima haemacephala.*" Delhibird: The Northern India Bird Network. http://www.delhibird.org/species/sp03557.htm (accessed on August 24, 2004).

TOUCANS
Ramphastidae

Class: Aves
Order: Piciformes
Family: Ramphastidae
Number of species: 41 species

PHYSICAL CHARACTERISTICS

Toucans are the symbol of the American tropics and very easy to recognize. They are large, brightly colored birds with very large bills that are also brightly colored. You are not likely to confuse a toucan with any other bird.

A toucan's bill often curves downward at the tip. Though large, it is very lightweight. Serrations along the edge look like teeth. Toucans are distinctive in other ways. They have a long tongue with a brushy tip. The feet have two toes pointing forward and two pointing backward, like a woodpecker's. (Most birds have three toes pointing forward and one toe pointing back). The skin around the eye is bare, without feathers, and often brightly colored. The joint at the base of the tail is unusually flexible. Males and females look much alike, although the male usually is heavier and has a longer bill.

GEOGRAPHIC RANGE

Toucans are found from north-central Mexico south through Central America to northern Argentina in South America. Colombia has the largest number of toucan species, twenty-one in all. Venezuela, Ecuador, and Brazil each are home to seventeen toucan species. Rivers often form barriers separating different species because toucans don't like to make long flights over water.

HABITAT

Most toucans live in tropical rainforest, usually at low elevations. They require mature forest with full-grown trees, big

phylum

class

subclass

order

monotypic order

suborder

▲ **family**

enough and old enough to develop cavities, holes, that toucans can use as nest sites. They also need forests with plenty of fruit trees.

DIET

Back in the eighteenth century, the first European naturalists to see toucan specimens (animals collected for study) concluded these birds must catch fish with their massive, serrated bills. In fact, forest fruits make up 95 percent of the toucan diet. Common foods include guavas, figs, red pepper fruits, and palm fruits. To eat, a toucan holds a fruit in the tip of its beak, then tosses its head backward so the fruit falls down its throat. After digesting the pulp, the toucan regurgitates (re-GER-jih-tates; throws up) the hard pits and seeds. In this way, forest seeds are spread to new places.

Along with fruit, toucans also catch and eat small animals including songbirds, crickets, cicadas (suh-KAY-duhz), spiders, termites, lizards, toads, frogs, and snakes. They raid eggs and nestlings from other birds' nests. Some species catch bats as they sleep in daytime roosts. Some follow columns of army ants to eat the insects stirred up by the ant swarms.

BEHAVIOR AND REPRODUCTION

Most toucans live year round in the same area. A few species make annual migrations between mountainside forests, where they spend spring and summer, and lowlands, where they spend fall and winter. Their main predators, animals that hunt them for food, are forest eagles, hawks, and owls. Monkeys, snakes, and weasels raid toucan nests. Small songbirds will mob or chase after the toucans that raid their nests.

Toucans prefer to stay high in the treetops. They don't like to descend to the forest floor. They drink rainwater from treetop plants called bromeliads and bathe by fluttering against wet leaves. They also like to take sunbaths. Most species avoid flying over open water. They are weak flyers and can tire, fall into the water, and drown.

Toucans often live in small flocks of about a dozen birds or fewer. It's common to see a group gather high in a tree to vocalize together, in the early morning, evening, or after a rainstorm. The calls sound like harsh grunts and croaks. Group members also interact by preening each other. To cross an open space, birds go one at a time. Many toucans roost in tree cavities. A sleeping toucan turns its head so its bill rests on its back, then bends its tail forward over the back so that it looks like a ball of feathers.

Members of larger species do not breed until they are three or four years old. Males often court females by feeding them berries. Often, the pair also preens one another. Most toucans nest in tree holes. They may remove chunks of very rotten wood but do not really dig a hole like woodpeckers do. Large toucans often use natural holes. Small toucans use abandoned woodpecker holes. One pair may use the same hole year after year. Both parents incubate the white eggs for about sixteen days. They also share the work of brooding the nestlings and bringing insects. The young birds fledge, grow their flying feathers, after about fifty days, but the parents keep feeding them for another eight to ten days.

TOUCAN TALK

Hollywood movies often use toucan sounds in the background. These weird-sounding calls create a jungle atmosphere. The calls are very loud and will carry through the dense forest. And they are very strange. Channel-billed toucans croak. Emerald toucanets grunt. White-throated toucans yip like dogs. Other species rattle and squawk and even purr. Often, a pair of birds will perch high in a tree to call for an hour or more, twice a day, at dawn or dusk. Their duet is a classic rainforest sound.

TOUCANS AND PEOPLE

Brazilian rulers once wore ceremonial robes of toucan feathers. Amazonian Indians still use toucan feathers and bills as decorations. Toucans are also hunted for food and taken from nests to be raised as pets. In some areas they are considered pests on orchard crops. In Great Britain, a toucan was the mascot for a popular beer, and in the United States a blue toucan is the mascot for a well-known breakfast cereal.

CONSERVATION STATUS

One species, the yellow-browed toucanet of Peru, is listed as Endangered, facing a very high risk of extinction, by the World Conservation Union (IUCN). Three other species are considered Near Threatened, in danger of becoming threatened with extinction: the saffron toucanet of central South America, the plate-billed toucan, and the gray-breasted mountain-toucan. Habitat loss to logging and agriculture is a problem because most species need undisturbed forest. Selective logging sounds environmentally responsible but removes large trees that would support strangler figs, an important source of fruit. New roads being built through the forest could isolate populations, because toucans don't like to cross wide open spaces.

Gray-breasted mountain toucan (*Andigena hypoglauca*)

■ Resident

GRAY-BREASTED MOUNTAIN TOUCAN
Andigena hypoglauca

Physical characteristics: This is one of four species of mountain toucan. All are a mix of blue, gray, and brown overall and have red feathers under the tail. This species can be identified by its colorful bill: red and black at the tip and yellow-green at the base, where there is a black, thumbprint-shaped mark. The black head is set off from the chestnut-brown back by a pale gray collar. Individuals may be 18 to 19 inches (46 to 48 centimeters) long and weigh 8.6 to 13.1 ounces (244 to 370 grams).

Geographic range: These birds live in the west slope of the north-central Andes from central Colombia through Ecuador to southeast Peru.

Habitat: This species lives at higher elevations than other toucans, in humid mountaintop forests. Birds spend much of their time in the tallest trees.

Diet: Fruits and berries. This species is more willing than most to leave the high canopy, leaves of the tallest trees, to feed on raspberries in the understory, area beneath the tallest trees.

Behavior and reproduction: The behavior has not been well studied. Birds feed alone or in small groups of up to six individuals. They move quietly, not like most toucans. They have been seen feeding with other bird species including tanagers, thrushes, and blackbirds. Little is known about their breeding habits.

Gray-breasted mountain toucans and people: This species lives in remote areas and is of little significance to humans.

Conservation status: Considered Near Threatened by the IUCN. In some areas its high-altitude forest habitat is being cleared for farms, mining, grazing, or wood-cutting for fuel. ■

Toco toucan *(Ramphastos toco)*

Resident

TOCO TOUCAN
Ramphastos toco

Physical characteristics: This is the largest of the toucans and very easy to identify. Toco toucans are black overall except for a white throat. The truly enormous bill is orange with a black oval spot at the tip. The skin around the eyes is also orange. Individuals average 21.5 to 23.8 inches (55 to 61 centimeters) long and may weigh 17.7 to 30.4 ounces (500 to 860 grams).

The toco toucan's most distinctive feature is its colorful bill. Pairs preen each other and fence with their bills like swordfighters. (© K. Schafer/ VIREO. Reproduced by permission.)

Geographic range: These toucans live from the mouth of the Amazon River in Brazil southward to Paraguay, northern Bolivia, and northern Argentina.

Habitat: Toco toucans can live both in undisturbed forest and in secondary forests as well as plantations and palm groves.

Diet: Like all toucans, toco toucans eat a variety of fruits, but mostly figs. They also eat caterpillars, termites, and eggs and nestlings of other birds.

Behavior and reproduction: Toco toucans are more likely than other species to drop down to the forest floor to feed on fallen fruit. They are more willing to fly across open water and through open areas. The voice is a deep grunt. Individuals may feed alone or in small flocks. They are very agile and often hang head-down like oversized chickadees to get at hard-to-reach fruits.

Pairs preen each other and fence with their bills like swordfighters. They often nest in palm-tree cavities and can dig the hole a little deeper. They also nest in burrows, which they dig in soft, sandy riverbanks, or nest in tree-termite nests that have been opened by woodpeckers. A typical clutch is two to four white eggs. The male and female take turns incubating for eighteen days. The nestlings are fed insects at first. They fledge after forty-three to fifty-two days.

Toco toucans and people: This species is often depicted in art. It is the classic symbol of the rainforest. Toco toucans are still hunted for food and young birds are taken as pets.

Conservation status: This species is not considered to be threatened. It is adapted to living in secondary forests and plantations, and there is some evidence that toco toucans are moving into newly cleared areas in Amazonia. ■

FOR MORE INFORMATION

Books:

del Hoyo, Josep, Andrew Elliott, and Jordi Sargatal, eds. *Handbook of the Birds of the World.* Vol. 7, *Jacamars to Woodpeckers.* Barcelona: Lynx Edicions, 2002.

Fjeldså, Jon, and Niels Krabbe. *Birds of the High Andes.* Copenhagen: University of Copenhagen Zoological Musuem, 1990.

Short, Lester L., and Jennifer F. M. Horne. *Toucans, Barbets and Honeyguides.* Oxford, U.K.: Oxford University Press, 2001.

Skutch, A. F. *Trogons, Laughing Falcons, and Other Neotropical Birds.* College Station, TX: Texas A & M University Press, 1999.

Stotz, Douglas F., John Fitzpatrick, Theodore A. Parker II, and Debra K. Moskovits. *Neotropical Birds: Ecology and Conservation.* Chicago: University of Chicago Press, 1996.

HONEYGUIDES

Indicatoridae

Class: Aves
Order: Piciformes
Family: Indicatoridae
Number of species: 17 species

family

CHAPTER

PHYSICAL CHARACTERISTICS

Honeyguides are fairly small tropical birds that are related to woodpeckers and barbets. Their most visible features are the dark stripe on the cheeks (on some species) and the white on the outer tail feathers (on all species). They have drab-colored plumage (feathers) of olive-greens, grays, browns, black, and white, with some signs of yellow, depending on the species. Males and females look alike with respect to their plumage, except for three species. Two species have yellow wing patches, and one species has orange on the head and rump. Honeyguides have a short and sturdy bill (with most species having a raised rim on the nostrils to prevent liquid foods from entering), a long tail with very short feathers, which is marked with white bars and tipped in a dark color, and strong legs with strong zygodactyl (zye-guh-DACK-tuhl) toes (two toes [second and third] pointing forward and two toes [first and fourth] facing backward). They have long and hooked claws and long, narrow, and pointed wings. They also have very good senses of sight, sound, and smell. Adults are 4 to 8 inches (10 to 20 centimeters) long and weigh between 0.4 and 1.9 ounces (10 and 55 grams).

GEOGRAPHIC RANGE

Honeyguides are found in the temperate (mild) and tropical parts of Africa south of the Sahara. In addition, two species are found along the southern foothills of the Himalayas and in Southeast Asia.

HABITAT

Honeyguides live in dense primary forests, secondary forests, gallery forests in semiarid country, open woodlands and scrublands that include a mix of broadleaved trees, shrubs, and grassland. Generally, darker-colored species tend to live in broadleaved forests, while paler ones live in drier woodlands. They live from sea level to near the top of trees in mountainous areas.

DIET

Their diet is mostly made up of beeswax, but the birds also eat insects, ants, spiders, bee larvae (LAR-vee; active immature insects), waxworms, termites, flies, and caterpillars. They sometimes eat fruits and other plant matter. All honeyguides eat live prey, animals they hunt for food, by catching it while in the air. The bill is adapted to feeding on wax and probing for insects in tree bark. They feed on beeswax by flying up to a bee nest, gripping the tree's surface alongside the outer comb, and biting off and swallowing pieces of wax. The body of honeyguides is strong enough to be protected from most bee stings, but they can be killed if enough bees attack. A few species lead animals or humans to honey sources by flying close to them and calling "churr-churr-churr-churr" or "tirr-tirr-tirr-tirr" in order to get them to open up the food source.

BEHAVIOR AND REPRODUCTION

The behavior of honeyguides makes them one of the most interesting birds to watch, especially the way they eat beeswax and actually lead other animals to wax sources. They are also aggressive birds in that they harass other birds and mob around wax sources. They are solitary birds most of the time, although when foraging for food, dozens of honeyguides may show up at a wax source. Many species will fly around human settlements (such as campgrounds) hoping to find food.

All honeyguides sing, except for one species. Their singing consists of a wide variety of sounds that are sung for particular situations. While singing, the birds also arch their necks, fluff out rump feathers (and other feathers), and quiver the tail. The rustling sound of waving wings is often heard with aggression or mating sounds. White tail bars are often displayed while the birds fly. They have strong wings that allow them to do complicated maneuvers in the air. For courtship, males sing and make aerial displays directed toward females.

All honeyguides are brood parasites, meaning that females lay fertile eggs among the eggs of other bird species in order for the nesting birds to incubate their eggs. Honeyguides do not build nests and are unable to raise their own young. Most female honeyguides lay about six eggs, but will leave only one or two eggs per nest. The female honeyguide invades a nest while the parents are gone, deposits a white thick-shelled egg (blue in one species), sometimes punctures or removes a host's egg, and leaves within seconds. All host nests are in cavities, such as in trees, in the ground, in termite mounds, or in ant nests. The most frequently used host birds are barbets, tinkerbirds, kingfishers, bee-eaters, hoopoes, and woodpeckers. When honeyguides are born, they break host eggs that have not hatched or kill host hatchlings with their hooked bills and claws. Their breeding season is tied to the breeding season of their host species. The incubation period (time to sit on eggs before hatching) is twelve to thirteen days and the nestling period (time to take care of young unable to leave nest) is thirty-eight to forty days.

HONEYGUIDES AND PEOPLE

Some species of honeyguides guide humans to honey sources.

CONSERVATION STATUS

No species are currently listed as Threatened by the World Conservation Union (IUCN). Three species, the Malaysian honeyguide, yellow-rumped honeyguide, and dwarf honeyguide, are listed as Near Threatened, in danger of becoming threatened. Most species in Africa and Asia are threatened by deforestation.

Malaysian honeyguide (*Indicator archipelagicus*)

Resident

MALAYSIAN HONEYGUIDE
Indicator archipelagicus

Physical characteristics: Malaysian honeyguides have brownish gray plumage with small, bright yellow shoulder patches, dark olive-brown upperparts, a light gray breast, and red eyes. They have a brown pointed bill, white under parts, and black legs and feet. Females do not have the yellow shoulder patch. Adults are about 2.5 inches (16 centimeters) long and weigh between 0.8 and 1.4 ounces (23.0 and 38.5 grams).

Geographic range: These honeyguides live in the Malaysian Peninsula, Sumatra, and Borneo.

Habitat: Malaysian honeyguides inhabit tropical rainforests and broadleaved, lowland evergreen forests from sea level to 3,280 feet (1,000 meters) in elevation. They also are found in open country, secondary forests, and in hill-slope forests.

Diet: They eat beeswax, bee larvae, bees, and other insects.

Behavior and reproduction: Malaysian honeyguides call out with harsh, cat-like "miaow," followed by a churring "miaow-krruuu" or "miao-miao-krruuu," which rises in pitch. Males that are mating with females will sing. Little else is known about their reproduction behavior except that they are thought to be brood parasites like other honeyguides. Breeding seasons are believed to occur from February to May in Malaya, during August in Thailand, May into June in Sumatra, and from January into March in Borneo.

Malaysian honeyguides and people: There is no known significant relationship between people and Malaysian honeyguides.

Conservation status: Malaysian honeyguides are listed as Near Threatened due to deforestation. ■

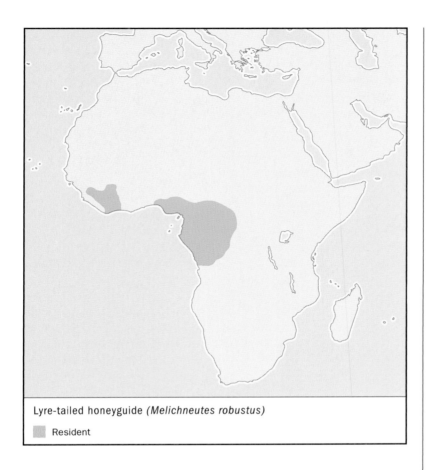

Lyre-tailed honeyguide *(Melichneutes robustus)*

☐ Resident

LYRE-TAILED HONEYGUIDE
Melichneutes robustus

Physical characteristics: Dull-colored lyre-tailed honeyguides have a long, lyre-shaped tail (U-shaped), and two middle pairs of retrices (RET-rihs-uhs) paired flight feathers of the tail, which extend from the tail edges) that are curved outward at distal ends (away from the point of attachment), while the outermost retrices are narrow and short. The birds also have a white undersurface about the tail (which is shown while in flight), olive-green upperparts, and whitish under parts. Males and females look different with respect to their plumage (unlike most honeyguides whose sexes look alike). Females show some gray streaks on the rear underbelly, and their tail is not as large

The lyre-tailed honeyguide is named after the lyre, a stringed instrument that is played by plucking the strings. Its tail looks similar to the U-shaped instrument. (Illustration by Wendy Baker. Reproduced by permission.)

as the male, but has the same shape. Adults are about 6 inches (17 centimeters) long and weigh between 1.7 and 2.2 ounces (47.0 and 61.5 grams).

Geographic range: They are found in two primary locations in western Africa: one location that includes Liberia, Sierra Leone, and the Ivory Coast, and the other location that includes a larger area around Cameroon.

Habitat: Lyre-tailed honeyguides are located in lowland tropical rainforests, primary forests and their edges, secondary forests, and plantations.

Diet: They eat beeswax, bee larvae, termites, insects, spiders, and fig fruits.

Behavior and reproduction: Lyre-tailed honeyguides are not believed to migrate. The mating display of lyre-tailed honeyguides is very interesting. Males fly around while singing several "pee-pee" notes, which go into "ve-bek, ve-vek." They then go into a rapid and steep dive with their tail feathers spread out. These feathers brush against the wind to make a "kwa-ba kwa-ba" series of sounds. Males may also fly up and down in spiral movements.

Lyre-tailed honeyguides and people: There is no known significant relationship between people and lyre-tailed honeyguides.

Conservation status: Lyre-tailed honeyguides are not currently threatened.   ■

FOR MORE INFORMATION

Books:

del Hoyo, Josep, et al., eds. *Handbook of the Birds of the World.* Barcelona: Lynx Edicions, 1992.

Dickinson, Edward C., ed. *The Howard and Moore Complete Checklist of the Birds of the World,* 3rd ed. Princeton, NJ and Oxford, U.K.: Princeton University Press, 2003.

Forshaw, Joseph, ed. *Encyclopedia of Birds,* 2nd ed. San Diego, CA: Academic Press, 1998.

Harrison, Colin James Oliver. *Birds of the World*. London and New York: Dorling Kindersley, 1993.

Perrins, Christopher M., and Alex L.A. Middleton, eds. *The Encyclopedia of Birds*. New York: Facts on File, 1985.

Web sites:

Creagrus at Monterey Bay. "Honeyguides: Indicatoridae." http://www.montereybay.com/creagrus/honeyguides.html (accessed on July 13, 2004).

WOODPECKERS, WRYNECKS, AND PICULETS
Picidae

Class: Aves
Order: Piciformes
Family: Picidae
Number of species: 213 species

phylum

class

subclass

order

monotypic order

suborder

▲ **family**

PHYSICAL CHARACTERISTICS

Woodpeckers, wrynecks, and piculets, together called picids (PISS-ids), are small- to medium-sized birds that are primarily arboreal (live in trees). They have patterns of brown, green, or black-and-white. Most picids have zygodactyl (zye-guh-DACK-tuhl) toes (two toes facing forward and two backward). Woodpeckers and piculets usually have just two feather colors, with males having red or yellow on the head and females lacking it or with less of it; while wrynecks have similar looking sexes.

Woodpeckers have stiff rectrices (RET-rihs-uhs; paired tail feathers). Wrynecks and piculets do not have rectrices. Woodpeckers have a relatively large head that is often called a "shock-absorber" due to its hammering into wood, a straight, sharply pointed to chisel-tipped bill, long cylindrical tongue that is often tipped like a brush, short legs, and strongly curved claws. The major tail feathers are mostly black.

Wrynecks have brown, gray, and black upperparts, a slender, pointed bill, rounded wings, lightly colored under parts, a relatively long tail with rounded tail feathers, and short legs. Piculets look like small woodpeckers except that tail feathers are pointed but not stiff. Piculet plumage is soft and mostly brown and black in color patterns.

Woodpeckers are 4.7 to 24.0 inches (12 to 60 centimeters) or more long and weigh between 0.6 and 21.0 ounces (17 and 600 grams). Wrynecks are 6.3 to 7.5 inches (16 to 19 centimeters) long and weigh between 0.78 and 2.10 ounces (2 and 59 grams). Piculets are 3.0 to 6.3 inches (7.5 to 16.0 centimeters) long and weigh between 0.24 and 1.20 ounces (6.8 and 33.0 grams).

GEOGRAPHIC RANGE

Picids are found around the world except Australia, New Zealand, New Guinea, Madagascar, Ireland, many oceanic islands, and polar regions. Wrynecks are found only in Eurasia and Africa. Piculets are located only in Asia, South and Central America, and Hispaniola.

HABITAT

Picids are found in any environment that contains woody vegetation, preferring forests, woodlands, and savannas (flat grasslands). Some species are located in grasslands and deserts. Picids need high relative humidity, frequent precipitation, and the presence of standing or running water to make moist wood so that it will decay in order to help the birds more easily dig into the wood.

DIET

Their diet is mostly insects and other arthropods (invertebrate animals with jointed limbs). It also includes fruits, nuts, and tree sap. A chisel-like bill of many species helps to find wood-boring beetle larvae (LAR-vee; active immature insects), ants, and termites, along with sap stored inside trees. Its long worm-shaped tongue has a barbed tip that, together with sticky saliva, is used to catch prey.

BEHAVIOR AND REPRODUCTION

Picids fly with both wavy and straight movements, with larger species preferring straighter motions. Since wings are short, picids are able to maneuver (mah-NOO-ver) easily throughout forests. Most picids do not migrate, but some species do make seasonal migratory trips.

Vocalizations are single notes often used to communicate between breeding mates. "Winny" and "rattle" calls are often heard, but with many differences heard from different species. Picids also communicate by making mechanical sounds by tapping on wood.

Picids are monogamous (muh-NAH-guh-mus; have a single mate), and nest in cavities, holes. Most dig their own cavities, sometimes with the assistance of helpers. All females lay shiny white eggs. Clutch size (eggs hatched together) varies within and among species, but averages three to five eggs. The incubation period (time needed to sit on and warm eggs in order for them to hatch) is ten to twelve days, and is shared by both parents. Young stay helpless, naked, and blind from birth to about four to seven days. The nestling period (time to take care of young unable to leave nest) lasts from three to six weeks.

WOODPECKERS, WRYNECKS, AND PICULETS AND PEOPLE

The bright red feathers of many male woodpeckers are important to the culture of natives. Various species have been hunted for their scalps, bills, tongues, and skins. Several species have been eaten by local cultures. Woodpeckers help to control pest insect populations. However, woodpeckers are also blamed for damage to buildings and agricultural crops.

CONSERVATION STATUS

Nineteen woodpeckers and five piculet species were included on the 2003 World Conservation Union (IUCN) Red List of Threatened Species. Three species are listed as Critically Endangered, facing an extremely high risk of extinction; one species as Endangered, facing a very high risk of extinction; seven species as Vulnerable, facing a high risk of extinction; and thirteen species as Near Threatened, in danger of facing a risk of extinction. Habitat destruction and modification are the largest threats to picids.

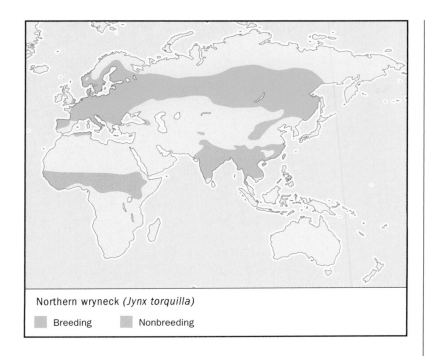

Northern wryneck (*Jynx torquilla*)

■ Breeding   ■ Nonbreeding

NORTHERN WRYNECK
Jynx torquilla

Physical characteristics: Northern wrynecks have a gray appearance without the stiff tail feathers of most picids. Their upperparts are gray mottled with brown and buff, with a diamond-shaped dark patch on the back extending to the nape (back of neck). The breast is light gray. Experts report that they have the longest tongue of any bird in proportion to its body. Sexes look alike, and juveniles look similar to adults. Adults are 6 to 7 inches (15 to 18 centimeters) long and weigh between 0.8 and 1.9 ounces (22 and 54 grams). Their wingspan is 11 to 12 inches (28 to 30 centimeters) long.

Geographic range: Some species breed from northern Eurasia south through temperate Eurasia to Japan. Other species breed in western Asia and northwestern Africa. Nonbreeding populations are found wintering in the warmer climates of central Eurasia south to drier areas of central and West Africa, India, Southeast Asia, southern China, and southern Japan.

Northern wrynecks build nests in old woodpecker holes, nest boxes, and other natural and artificial cavities, sometimes enlarging them. (Hans Reinhard/ Bruce Coleman Inc. Reproduced by permission.)

Habitat: They live in open deciduous or mixed forests, clearings, wooded pastures, and edge habitats with scattered ground cover.

Diet: They eat arthropods, ants, and insect larvae and pupae (PYOO-pee; developing insect inside cocoon). They forage by hopping on the ground and capturing prey with its sticky tongue.

Behavior and reproduction: Northern wrynecks have a call similar to "kew-kew-kdw-kew." They travel at night about their home range, alone during the nonbreeding season, as pairs during breeding season, or as post-breeding family groups. The birds build nests in old woodpecker holes, nest boxes, and other natural and artificial cavities, sometimes enlarging them. Nests are 3 to 49 feet (1 to 15 meters) off the ground, while the nest bottom is sometimes lined with grass or moss. The clutch size is seven to twelve eggs. The incubation period is twelve to fourteen days and the fledgling period (time for young to grow flight feathers) is eighteen to twenty-two days. Both parents take care of young for ten to fourteen days after birds are able to fly. A second nest may follow after the first.

Northern wrynecks and people: No known significant relationship exists between northern wrynecks and people.

Conservation status: Northern wrynecks are not threatened. Their numbers are declining in Europe as their habitat is converted by humans and as conifer forests replace native trees. ■

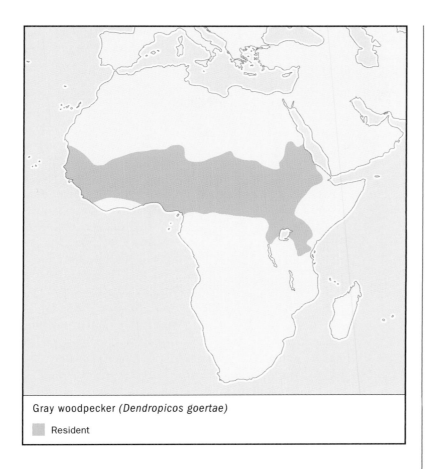

Gray woodpecker (*Dendropicos goertae*)

◼ Resident

GRAY WOODPECKER
Dendropicos goertae

Physical characteristics: Gray woodpeckers are small woodpeckers with a long, straight, rather wide bill, unbarred green or brownish green upperparts, a red rump, a brownish black tail, and gray under parts with an orange-to-yellow belly patch and some barring on the flanks. Males have a pale, striped, gray head with red on the back of the head and neck, while females lack the red on the head. Adults are about 8 inches (20 centimeters) long and weigh between 1.4 and 1.9 ounces (40.5 and 52.5 grams).

Gray woodpeckers eat insects, ants, termites, beetle larvae, and other arthropods. They search for their food on the ground, in the air, and on live and dead trees. (Illustration by Gillian Harris. Reproduced by permission.)

Geographic range: They range throughout the forests and savanna habitats in central and west Africa; from sea level to 9,800 feet (3,000 meters).

Habitat: Gray woodpeckers inhabit wooded and savanna areas, thickets with large trees, riverine (near rivers) forests, gardens, and mangroves.

Diet: Their diet consists of insects, ants, termites, beetle larvae, and other arthropods. They forage on the ground, in live and dead trees, and in the air.

Behavior and reproduction: Gray woodpeckers are found in pairs and family groups. They move quickly through its habitat, and often remain near forest edges. Their call is a loud and fast "peet-peet-peet-peet." The nesting period is from December to June in west Africa; December to February and July to September in the Democratic Republic of the Congo; and February to July and September to November in eastern Africa. The breeding pair digs out the nest cavity from a tree, usually 1 to 60 feet (0.3 to 18.3 meters) off the ground. Clutch size is two to four eggs. There is no known information about incubation, parental care, or fledging.

Gray woodpeckers and people: There is no known significant relationship between gray woodpeckers and people.

Conservation status: Gray woodpeckers are not threatened. They are fairly common to common in the areas where they live. ∎

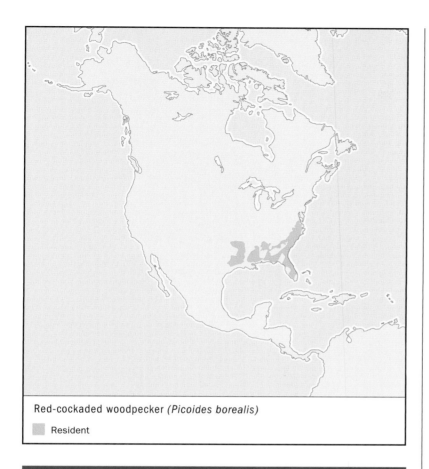

Red-cockaded woodpecker (*Picoides borealis*)

Resident

RED-COCKADED WOODPECKER
Picoides borealis

Physical characteristics: Red-cockaded woodpeckers are medium, black-and-white woodpeckers with large white cheek patches and back plumage that has alternating, horizontal stripes of black and white. They have a black forehead and the back of the neck is also black with a small red streak on each side of the forehead (called a cockade, thus its name), a black stripe behind eyes, whitish under parts, and a black tail with black-spotted white outer feathers. They have black wings and wing coverts (small feather around quill base) with white spots. Males have several tiny red feathers between white cheek patches and a black crown (top of head), while females do not have red coloring. Young males have a patchy-looking red section on

Red-cockaded woodpeckers live in family groups of a mated pair, current young, and unmated adult helpers. (John Snyder/ Bruce Coleman Inc. Reproduced by permission.)

the forehead, while young females have white flecks on the lower forehead. Adults are 7.1 to 8.7 inches (18 to 22 centimeters) long and weigh between 1.4 and 1.9 ounces (40 and 55 grams). Their wingspan is about 16 inches (40.6 centimeters) long.

Geographic range: They are scattered in eastern Texas, southeastern Oklahoma, southern Missouri, south central Kentucky, central

Tennessee, to southeastern Maryland, south to southern Florida and across the Gulf coast.

Habitat: They are widely found in open, mature pine forests and forests of pine mixed with oak, especially long-leaf pines and loblolly pines.

Diet: Red-cockaded woodpeckers eat ants, beetles, caterpillars, roaches, wood-boring insects, and spiders found on tree surfaces, especially pine trees, and by scaling back loose bark. They eat earworms off of corn in the summer, along with berries and nuts. Males forage on limbs and trunk of pines above the lowest branches. Females forage on trunk below the lowest branch.

Behavior and reproduction: Red-cockaded woodpeckers are noisy birds, with calls of "yank-yank," "sripp," and "tsick." They are monogamous, with a family clan of the mated pair, current young, and unmated adult helpers. They nest in the roost cavity of the breeding male, which sometimes takes the male one year to finish (but may be used for years). Only living pine trees are used for the roost/nest. They spend a lot of time maintaining the flow of tree sap, which is used to stop predator snakes. Females lay two to five eggs. The incubation period is ten to fifteen days, and the fledgling period is twenty-two to twenty-nine days. Both parents and helpers care for young, with only one brood each year.

Red-cockaded woodpeckers and people: Because of red-cockaded woodpeckers' dependence on pine forests, they are in conflict with the logging industry. Bird watchers enjoy watching these birds.

Conservation status: Red-cockaded woodpeckers are listed as Vulnerable. They are also listed as Endangered under the U.S. Endangered Species Act. They have declined in numbers because of deforestation. Conservation measures have been enacted to help the birds recover. ■

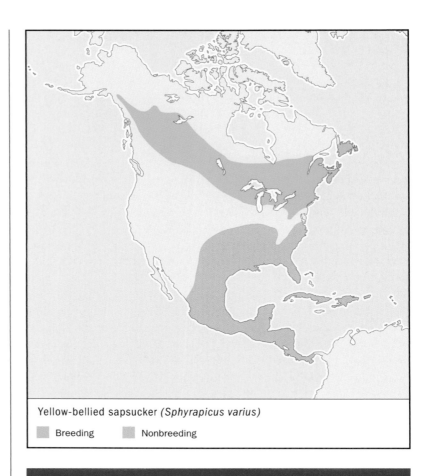

Yellow-bellied sapsucker *(Sphyrapicus varius)*

☐ Breeding ☐ Nonbreeding

YELLOW-BELLIED SAPSUCKER
Sphyrapicus varius

Physical characteristics: Yellow-bellied sapsuckers are small black-and-white woodpeckers with a short, chisel-tipped bill and a white stripe that goes down the wing. Adult males have a red throat, forehead, and forecrown, a black bib (area under bill), a bold black-and-white patterned face, a white shoulder patch, and black-and-white barring on the back. There is a pale yellow wash on the under parts, the yellow breast changes to whitish on the lower belly, and is streaked about the flanks, leading to a white rump. Females have a white throat and a paler red forehead and crown. Juveniles have more brown and buff than adults, and less white and red on crown. Adults are 7.5 to 8.7 inches (19 to 22 centimeters) long and weigh between

1.4 and 22 ounces (40 and 62 grams). Their wingspan is 16 to 18 inches (40.6 to 45.7 centimeters) long.

Geographic range: They breed in northern North America east of the Rocky Mountains across Canada from northeastern British Columbia to southern Labrador and Newfoundland, south to North Dakota and Connecticut. They have separated populations in the Appalachian Mountains of eastern Tennessee and northern Georgia. They winter in the eastern United States through eastern and southern Mexico and Central America, Bahamas, and West Indies.

Habitat: Yellow-bellied sapsuckers are found in deciduous and mixed forests, especially around aspen, birch, and hickory trees.

Diet: Their diet consists of beetles and their larvae, insects, ants, other arthropods, tree sap, fruits, tree buds, and berries. Young are fed a mixture of sap and insects by both sexes.

Yellow-bellied sapsucker mates perform loud drumming duets during breeding season along with cries of "hoih-hoih." They build nests with small entrances, just large enough for them to enter. (Illustration by Gillian Harris. Reproduced by permission.)

Behavior and reproduction: Yellow-bellied sapsuckers generally are found alone. They are usually found near a group of trees (often near water) where they obtain sap for food. Both sexes migrate, but males migrate shorter distances than females and return earlier to the breeding territory. They are often silent birds, but do make low, growling "mew" cat-like sounds. When alarmed, they give out calls of "cheee-er, cheee-er." Mates perform loud drumming duets during breeding season along with cries of "hoih-hoih." Most nests are built in living trees that are infected with a fungus that rots the tree's center. The entrance is made very small, just allowing them to enter. Clutch size is four to five eggs, with more eggs produced as the birds go north. The incubation period is twelve to thirteen days and the fledgling period is twenty-five to twenty-nine days; both parents incubate and fledge. There is one brood each year.

Yellow-bellied sapsuckers and people: People consider yellow-bellied sapsuckers pests when they damages trees in search of sap.

Conservation status: Yellow-bellied sapsuckers are not threatened. ■

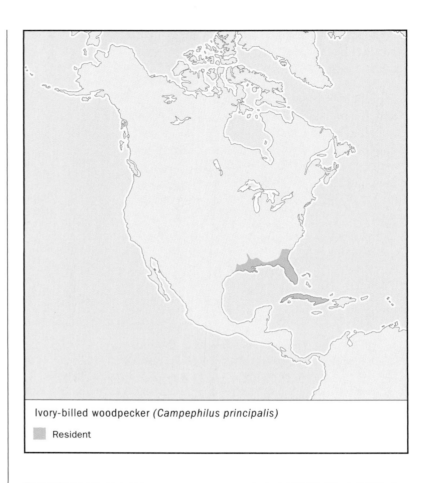

Ivory-billed woodpecker *(Campephilus principalis)*

Resident

IVORY-BILLED WOODPECKER
Campephilus principalis

Physical characteristics: Ivory-billed woodpeckers are a very large woodpeckers that are mostly black with white streaks going down the neck on each side to the upper wing bases, a robust, chisel-tipped, ivory-white bill, a black forecrest, a white patch on the folded wing, and white secondary feathers and inner primary feathers. Males have a pointed crest (growth on top of head) that is black in front and scarlet behind. Females have a longer, more pointed, somewhat re-curved solid black crest. Adults are 18.5 to 21.0 inches (47 to 54 centimeters) long and weigh between 15.5 and 18.3 ounces (440 and 570 grams). Their wingspan is 30 to 32 inches (76.2 to 81.3 centimeters) long.

Geographic range: The birds are found in the southeastern United States from eastern Texas to North Carolina and south throughout Florida, and in Cuba.

Habitat: Ivory-billed woodpeckers inhabit old-growth forests, especially bottomlands, swamp forests and cypress swamps, pine uplands, and areas with dead trees.

Diet: They eat arthropods, especially larvae of large wood-boring beetles, and fruits.

Behavior and reproduction: Ivory-billed wood-peckers have a territory of about 6 square miles (15.5 square kilometers). They are often seen in family groups. Their call is a sad-sounding single-or double-note tooting; one such sound is a clarinet-like "yank-yank-yank." The birds are monogamous. They breed from January through April in North America and March through June in Cuba. They build nest cavities in large dead trees or in live trees with fungus. Nests are usually built 24 to 50 feet (7.3 to 15.2 meters) off the ground with a cavity often 2 feet (6 meters) in depth. Females lay two to four eggs. The incubation and fledgling periods are not known, but both parents incubate and take care of young.

Ivory-billed woodpeckers and people: Ivory-billed woodpeckers have been important to the cultures of Native Americans (especially their head and bill), as good-luck charms, and in the trade of skins and eggs for early European settlers in North America. The birds have been captured for food. They helped to limit the number of pest insects on farmlands and in forests.

Conservation status: Ivory-billed woodpeckers are listed as Critically Endangered, and may already be extinct. Their rarity is due mostly to loss old-growth forests and the killing of the birds over many centuries. ■

Ivory-billed woodpeckers may be extinct, but researchers remain hopeful that the bird still survives. (Illustration by Gillian Harris. Reproduced by permission.)

FOR MORE INFORMATION

Books:

Alsop, Fred J. III. *Birds of North America.* New York: Dorling Kindersley, 2001.

Baughman, Mel M., ed. *Reference Atlas to the Birds of North America.* Washington, DC: National Geographic, 2003.

del Hoyo, Josep, et al., eds. *Handbook of the Birds of the World.* Barcelona: Lynx Edicions, 1992.

Dickinson, Edward C., ed. *The Howard and Moore Complete Checklist of the Birds of the World,* 3rd ed. Princeton, NJ and Oxford, U.K.: Princeton University Press, 2003.

Field Guide to the Birds of North America, 4th ed. Washington, DC: National Geographic Society, 2002.

Forshaw, Joseph, ed. *Encyclopedia of Birds,* 2nd ed. San Diego, CA: Academic Press, 1998.

Harrison, Colin James Oliver. *Birds of the World.* London and New York: Dorling Kindersley, 1993.

Kaufman, Kenn, with collaboration of Rick and Nora Bowers and Lynn Hassler Kaufman. *Birds of North America.* New York: Houghton Mifflin, 2000.

Sibley, David. *The Sibley Guide to Birds.* New York: Alfred A. Knopf, 2000.

Terres, John K. *The Audubon Society Encyclopedia of North American Birds.* New York: Knopf, 1980.

Web sites:

About.com. "Endangered Red-cockeyed Woodpecker: Only 1 Percent of its Habitat Left." http://birding.about.com/library/weekly/aa012301a.htm (accessed on July 19, 2004).

Nutty Birdwatcher. "The Ivory-billed Woodpecker." http://www.birdnature.com/mar1898/ivorybilledwood.html (accessed on July 19, 2004).

Species List by Biome

CONIFEROUS FOREST
African broadbill
African pitta
American cliff swallow
American goldfinch
American robin
Anna's hummingbird
Barn swallow
Barred eagle-owl
Belted kingfisher
Black-and-red broadbill
Black-and-white warbler
Black-capped chickadee
Black-capped vireo
Black-crowned barwing
Blue-gray gnatcatcher
Bornean bristlehead
Brown creeper
Brown kiwi
Cedar waxwing
Chaffinch
Chimney swift
Crag martin
Cuban tody
Dollarbird
Dunnock
Dusky woodswallow
Eastern bluebird
Eastern screech-owl
Emu

Fan-tailed berrypecker
Fiery minivet
Fire-breasted flowerpecker
Gray butcherbird
Gray nightjar
Gray parrot
Gray potoo
Green magpie
House sparrow
House wren
Ivory-billed woodpecker
Japanese white-eye
Kirtland's warbler
Kokako
Laughing kookaburra
Little slaty flycatcher
Malaysian honeyguide
Northern bobwhite quail
Northern wryneck
Nuthatch
Oilbird
Orange-breasted trogon
Osprey
Palmchat
Peregrine falcon
Red crossbill
Red-breasted nuthatch
Red-cockaded woodpecker
Resplendent quetzal
Rifleman

Rose-throated becard
Rufous treecreeper
Rufous-browed peppershrike
Rufous-capped nunlet
Rufous-tailed jacamar
Satyr tragopan
Scarlet macaw
Sparkling violet-ear
Spotted nutcracker
Striated pardalote
Whip-poor-will
White-necked puffbird
White-throated fantail
Winter wren
Wrentit
Yellow-bellied sapsucker
Yellow-breasted chat

CONTINENTAL MARGIN
Blue-footed booby
Brown pelican
Great cormorant
Northern gannet

DECIDUOUS FOREST
African broadbill
African pitta
American cliff swallow
American goldfinch

American robin
Anna's hummingbird
Arctic warbler
Asian fairy-bluebird
Australian magpie-lark
Baltimore oriole
Bar-breasted mousebird
Barn owl
Barn swallow
Baywing
Black bulbul
Black guan
Black-and-white warbler
Black-capped chickadee
Black-capped vireo
Blue jay
Blue-crowned motmot
Blue-gray gnatcatcher
Brown creeper
Brown kiwi
Bushtit
Cedar waxwing
Chaffinch
Chimney swift
Coppersmith barbet
Crag martin
Crested tree swift
Cuban tody
Dollarbird
Dunnock
Dusky woodswallow
Eastern bluebird
Eastern screech-owl
Emu
Eurasian golden oriole
European bee-eater
European roller
Fire-breasted flowerpecker
Gray catbird
Gray nightjar
Gray-crowned babbler
Great tit
House sparrow
House wren
Ivory-billed woodpecker
Jacky winter

Japanese white-eye
Leaf-love
Northern wryneck
Nuthatch
Orange-breasted trogon
Osprey
Painted buttonquail
Peregrine falcon
Peruvian plantcutter
Plain chachalaca
Red-breasted nuthatch
Red-cockaded woodpecker
Rifleman
Rose-ringed parakeet
Rufous scrub-bird
Rufous vanga
Rufous-capped nunlet
Rufous-tailed jacamar
Satyr tragopan
Scarlet macaw
Southern scrub robin
Spotted flycatcher
Striated pardalote
Tawny frogmouth
Toucan barbet
Whip-poor-will
White-breasted mesite
White-helmet shrike
White-necked puffbird
Wild turkey
Willie wagtail
Willow ptarmigan
Winter wren
Wood duck
Yellow-bellied sapsucker
Yellow-breasted chat
Yellow-fronted tinkerbird
Yellowhead
Yellow-rumped thornbill

DESERT
American cliff swallow
American mourning dove
Barn swallow
Cactus wren

California condor
Collared pratincole
Crab plover
Crested caracara
Crimson chat
Egyptian vulture
Emu
Gray catbird
Gray hypocolius
Greater hoopoe-lark
Greater roadrunner
Harris's hawk
House sparrow
Malleefowl
Namaqua sandgrouse
Northern lapwing
Ostrich
Pallas's sandgrouse
Peregrine falcon
Peruvian plantcutter
Rock pigeon
Snow finch
Splendid fairy-wren
Striated grasswren
Verdin
Western scrub-jay
Willie wagtail

GRASSLAND
African broadbill
African palm swift
African paradise-flycatcher
American cliff swallow
American mourning dove
American robin
Anna's hummingbird
Arctic skua
Australasian lark
Australian magpie-lark
Australian pratincole
Bar-breasted mousebird
Barn owl
Barn swallow
Baya weaver
Baywing

Black rail
Black-capped chickadee
Black-capped vireo
Black-crowned barwing
Black-faced sheathbill
Blue bustard
Blue jay
Blue-black grassquit
California condor
Cape sugarbird
Cattle egret
Cedar waxwing
Collared pratincole
Common cuckoo
Common myna
Common waxbill
Corncrake
Crag martin
Crested caracara
Crimson chat
Dollarbird
Eastern phoebe
Eclectus parrot
Egyptian vulture
Emu
Eurasian bittern
European bee-eater
European roller
European starling
European white stork
Fan-tailed berrypecker
Golden-winged sunbird
Gray go-away-bird
Gray hypocolius
Gray potoo
Gray woodpecker
Gray-crowned crane
Great blue heron
Great bustard
Great kiskadee
Green woodhoopoe
Gyrfalcon
Hammerhead
Harris's hawk
Helmeted guineafowl
Hoopoe

Horned lark
House sparrow
Jacky winter
Killdeer
King vulture
Laysan finch
Lesser rhea
Loggerhead shrike
Long-billed curlew
Malleefowl
Northern bobwhite quail
Northern lapwing
Northern raven
Northern wryneck
Ostrich
Painted buttonquail
Pallas's sandgrouse
Palmchat
Peregrine falcon
Peruvian plantcutter
Purple sunbird
Rainbow lorikeet
Red-billed oxpecker
Red-legged seriema
Red-winged blackbird
Rock pigeon
Roseate spoonbill
Rose-ringed parakeet
Rosy-breasted longclaw
Rufous-capped nunlet
Sacred ibis
Sandhill crane
Savanna sparrow
Secretary bird
Shoebill
Small buttonquail
Snowy owl
Song sparrow
Southern ground-hornbill
Southern red bishop
Southern scrub robin
Spotted munia
Sprague's pipit
Stonechat
Tawny frogmouth
Village weaver

White-helmet shrike
White-necked puffbird
Wild turkey
Wrentit
Yellow-fronted tinkerbird
Yellow-rumped thornbill
Zebra finch

LAKE AND POND
African jacana
American anhinga
American cliff swallow
American white pelican
Australian magpie-lark
Barn swallow
Baya weaver
Belted kingfisher
Black tern
Black-and-red broadbill
Black-capped donacobius
Canada goose
Chaffinch
Common iora
Common loon
Crag martin
Eurasian bittern
Gray wagtail
Great blue heron
Great cormorant
Great crested grebe
Greater flamingo
Greater thornbird
Hammerhead
Hoatzin
Mallard
Mute swan
Northern wryneck
Osprey
Peregrine falcon
Pheasant-tailed jacana
Red-throated loon
Roseate spoonbill
Rosy-breasted longclaw
Rufous hornero
Sacred ibis

Shoebill
Song sparrow
Sunbittern
Sungrebe
Village weaver
Western grebe
Wood duck
Yellow-breasted chat
Zebra finch

OCEAN
Arctic skua
Blue-footed booby
Chatham mollymawk
Common diving-petrel
Common iora
Common loon
Common murre
Emperor penguin
Great auk
King eider
Laysan albatross
Laysan finch
Macaroni penguin
Magellanic penguin
Magnificent frigatebird
Manx shearwater
Northern fulmar
Northern gannet
Puffin
Red-throated loon
White-tailed tropicbird
Wilson's storm-petrel

RAINFOREST
African paradise-flycatcher
African pitta
Albert's lyrebird
Amazonian umbrellabird
American cliff swallow
Apapane
Arctic warbler
Asian fairy-bluebird
Australasian figbird
Baltimore oriole

Barn owl
Barn swallow
Barred antshrike
Bishop's oo
Black-naped monarch
Blue-crowned motmot
Bornean bristlehead
Buff-spotted flufftail
Cape batis
Common bulbul
Common cuckoo
Common iora
Common sunbird-asity
Common trumpeter
Coppery-chested jacamar
Crag martin
Cuban tody
Dodo
Eclectus parrot
Fan-tailed berrypecker
Feline owlet-nightjar
Fiery minivet
Golden whistler
Golden-winged sunbird
Gray antbird
Gray nightjar
Gray potoo
Gray-breasted mountain-
  toucan
Gray-necked picathartes
Great blue turaco
Greater racket-tailed drongo
Greater thornbird
Guianan cock-of-the-rock
Hairy hermit
Helmeted hornbill
Highland tinamou
Hooded pitta
House sparrow
Kagu
King bird of paradise
King vulture
Kokako
Little slaty flycatcher
Long-tailed manakin
Luzon bleeding heart

Lyre-tailed honeyguide
Malaysian honeyguide
Maleo
Mauritius cuckoo-shrike
Osprey
Peregrine falcon
Purple sunbird
Purple-bearded bee-eater
Rainbow lorikeet
Red-billed scythebill
Ribbon-tailed astrapia
Roseate spoonbill
Rose-ringed parakeet
Ruby-cheeked sunbird
Rufous scrub-bird
Rufous vanga
Rufous-collared kingfisher
Rusty-belted tapaculo
Satin bowerbird
Sharpbill
Southern cassowary
Southern logrunner
Spangled cotinga
Spotted quail-thrush
Square-tailed drongo
Striated pardalote
Stripe-headed rhabdornis
Sulawesi red-knobbed
  hornbill
Sunbittern
Toco toucan
Toucan barbet
Variable pitohui
Victoria's riflebird
Wattled curassow
White-breasted mesite
Willie wagtail
Wire-tailed manakin

RIVER AND STREAM
African broadbill
African pitta
American anhinga
American cliff swallow
American dipper
American white pelican

Australian magpie-lark
Baltimore oriole
Barn swallow
Baya weaver
Black-and-red broadbill
Black-capped donacobius
Canada goose
Cedar waxwing
Chaffinch
Common loon
Crag martin
Crested caracara
Cuban tody
Dusky woodswallow
Eurasian dipper
European bee-eater
European roller
Gray catbird
Gray hypocolius
Gray wagtail
Gray woodpecker
Great blue heron
Great cormorant
Great crested grebe
Green woodhoopoe
Gyrfalcon
Hoatzin
Mute swan
Northern wryneck
Peregrine falcon
Red-breasted nuthatch
Red-throated loon
Roseate spoonbill
Rosy-breasted longclaw
Rufous-capped nunlet
Rufous hornero
Rufous-tailed jacamar
Sacred ibis
Shoebill
Snow bunting
Song sparrow
Southern red bishop
Spotted bowerbird
Striped honeyeater
Sunbittern
Sungrebe

Village weaver
Wood duck
Yellow-breasted chat
Yellow-fronted tinkerbird

SEASHORE
American cliff swallow
American white pelican
Arctic warbler
Australian magpie-lark
Barn swallow
Beach thick-knee
Belted kingfisher
Black tern
Black-faced sheathbill
Blue-footed booby
Brown pelican
Cactus wren
California condor
Collared pratincole
Common iora
Common murre
Crab plover
Crag martin
Cuban tody
Fiery minivet
Golden whistler
Gray wagtail
Great auk
Great blue heron
Great cormorant
Greater flamingo
Gyrfalcon
Hood mockingbird
Horned lark
Magnificent frigatebird
Northern gannet
Osprey
Peregrine falcon
Puffin
Roseate spoonbill
Ruddy turnstone
Sacred ibis
Saunder's gull
Snow bunting

Song sparrow
Splendid fairy-wren
Stonechat
Variable oystercatcher
Victoria's riflebird
White-tailed tropicbird

TUNDRA
American robin
Arctic skua
Arctic warbler
Canada goose
Common loon
Gyrfalcon
Horned lark
Northern raven
Peregrine falcon
Red-throated loon
Ruddy turnstone
Savanna sparrow
Snow bunting
Snowy owl
Willow ptarmigan

WETLAND
African jacana
African snipe
American anhinga
American avocet
American cliff swallow
American white pelican
Australasian lark
Australian magpie-lark
Baltimore oriole
Barn swallow
Black rail
Black tern
Black-faced sheathbill
Black-winged stilt
Canada goose
Cattle egret
Common bulbul
Common iora
Crag martin
Crested caracara

Eurasian bittern
European white stork
Gray wagtail
Gray-crowned crane
Great blue heron
Great cormorant
Greater flamingo
Greater painted snipe
Hairy hermit
Hammerhead
Harris's hawk
Horned screamer
House sparrow
Killdeer

King eider
Leaf-love
Limpkin
Long-billed curlew
Mallard
Mute swan
Northern lapwing
Osprey
Peregrine falcon
Pheasant-tailed jacana
Red-crowned crane
Red-winged blackbird
Roseate spoonbill
Rosy-breasted longclaw

Ruddy turnstone
Rufous-bellied seedsnipe
Sacred ibis
Sandhill crane
Saunder's gull
Shoebill
Sunbittern
Village weaver
Wood duck
Wood stork
Yellow-breasted chat
Zebra finch
Zitting cisticola

Species List by Geographic Range

AFGHANISTAN
Barn swallow
Chaffinch
Common myna
Crag martin
Egyptian vulture
Eurasian golden oriole
European bee-eater
European roller
European starling
Gray hypocolius
Great cormorant
Great crested grebe
Great tit
Greater hoopoe-lark
Hoopoe
House sparrow
Mute swan
Northern lapwing
Northern raven
Peregrine falcon
Rock pigeon
Snow finch
Spotted flycatcher
Spotted nutcracker
Winter wren

ALBANIA
Barn swallow
Chaffinch

Common cuckoo
Corncrake
Crag martin
Dunnock
Egyptian vulture
Eurasian dipper
Eurasian golden oriole
European bee-eater
European roller
European starling
Gray wagtail
Great cormorant
Great crested grebe
Great tit
Hoopoe
Horned lark
House sparrow
Mallard
Northern gannet
Northern lapwing
Northern raven
Northern wryneck
Nuthatch
Peregrine falcon
Red crossbill
Rock pigmeon
Snow bunting
Spotted flycatcher
Stonechat
Winter wren

Zitting cisticola

ALGERIA
Barn swallow
Black-winged stilt
Chaffinch
Common bulbul
Common cuckoo
Common murre
Corncrake
Crag martin
Dunnock
Egyptian vulture
Eurasian bittern
Eurasian golden oriole
European bee-eater
European roller
European starling
Gray wagtail
Great cormorant
Great crested grebe
Greater hoopoe-lark
Hoopoe
House sparrow
Mallard
Northern gannet
Northern lapwing
Northern raven
Northern wryneck
Peregrine falcon

Rock pigeon
Ruddy turnstone
Small buttonquail
Spotted flycatcher
Stonechat
Winter wren
Zitting cisticola

ANDORRA
Great cormorant
Peregrine falcon

ANGOLA
African jacana
African palm swift
African paradise-flycatcher
African snipe
Bar-breasted mousebird
Barn swallow
Black tern
Black-winged stilt
Buff-spotted flufftail
Cattle egret
Collared pratincole
Common bulbul
Common cuckoo
Common waxbill
Eurasian golden oriole
European bee-eater
European roller
European white stork
Gray go-away-bird
Great cormorant
Greater painted snipe
Green woodhoopoe
Hammerhead
Helmeted guineafowl
Hoopoe
House sparrow
Lyre-tailed honeyguide
Namaqua sandgrouse
Osprey
Ostrich
Peregrine falcon
Red-billed oxpecker

Rock pigeon
Rosy-breasted longclaw
Ruddy turnstone
Sacred ibis
Secretary bird
Small buttonquail
Southern ground-hornbill
Southern red bishop
Spotted flycatcher
Square-tailed drongo
Stonechat
Village weaver
White-helmet shrike
Wilson's storm-petrel
Yellow-fronted tinkerbird
Zitting cisticola

ANTARCTICA
Black-faced sheathbill
Emperor penguin
Macaroni penguin
Wilson's storm-petrel

ARGENTINA
American anhinga
American cliff swallow
Arctic skua
Barn owl
Barn swallow
Barred antshrike
Baywing
Black rail
Black-capped donacobius
Black-winged stilt
Blue-black grassquit
Cattle egret
Common diving-petrel
Crested caracara
Emperor penguin
Gray potoo
Great kiskadee
Greater thornbird
Harris's hawk
House sparrow
King vulture
Lesser rhea

Limpkin
Macaroni penguin
Magellanic penguin
Manx shearwater
Peregrine falcon
Red-billed scythebill
Red-legged seriema
Rock pigeon
Roseate spoonbill
Ruddy turnstone
Rufous hornero
Rufous-bellied seedsnipe
Rufous-browed peppershrike
Rufous-tailed jacamar
Sharpbill
Sparkling violet-ear
Sungrebe
Toco toucan
Wilson's storm-petrel
Wood stork

ARMENIA
Barn swallow
Chaffinch
Common cuckoo
Dunnock
Egyptian vulture
Eurasian dipper
Eurasian golden oriole
European bee-eater
European roller
European starling
Great cormorant
Great crested grebe
Great tit
Hoopoe
Horned lark
House sparrow
Northern lapwing
Northern raven
Nuthatch
Peregrine falcon
Red crossbill
Rock pigeon
Snow finch
Stonechat

Winter wren

ASCENSION
White-tailed tropicbird

AUSTRALIA
Albert's lyrebird
Arctic skua
Australasian figbird
Australasian lark
Australian magpie-lark
Australian pratincole
Beach thick-knee
Black-winged stilt
Cattle egret
Common diving-petrel
Crimson chat
Dollarbird
Dusky woodswallow
Eclectus parrot
Emu
European starling
Golden whistler
Gray butcherbird
Gray-crowned babbler
Great cormorant
Great crested grebe
Greater painted snipe
House sparrow
Jacky winter
Laughing kookaburra
Mallard
Malleefowl
Mute swan
Osprey
Painted buttonquail
Peregrine falcon
Rainbow lorikeet
Rock pigeon
Ruddy turnstone
Rufous scrub-bird
Rufous treecreeper
Satin bowerbird
Southern cassowary
Southern logrunner
Southern scrub robin

Splendid fairy-wren
Spotted bowerbird
Spotted quail-thrush
Striated grasswren
Striated pardalote
Striped honeyeater
Tawny frogmouth
Victoria's riflebird
Willie wagtail
Wilson's storm-petrel
Yellow-rumped thornbill
Zebra finch
Zitting cisticola

AUSTRIA
Barn swallow
Black tern
Chaffinch
Collared pratincole
Common cuckoo
Corncrake
Crag martin
Dunnock
Eurasian golden oriole
European bee-eater
European roller
European starling
European white stork
Gray wagtail
Great cormorant
Great crested grebe
Great tit
Hoopoe
House sparrow
Mallard
Mute swan
Northern lapwing
Northern raven
Northern wryneck
Nuthatch
Peregrine falcon
Red crossbill
Rock pigeon
Snow bunting
Snow finch
Spotted flycatcher

Spotted nutcracker
Stonechat
Winter wren

AZERBAIJAN
Barn swallow
Cattle egret
Chaffinch
Common cuckoo
Dunnock
Egyptian vulture
Eurasian dipper
Eurasian golden oriole
European bee-eater
European roller
European starling
European white stork
Great cormorant
Great crested grebe
Great tit
Hoopoe
Horned lark
House sparrow
Mallard
Northern lapwing
Northern raven
Nuthatch
Peregrine falcon
Red crossbill
Red-throated loon
Rock pigeon
Snow finch
Spotted flycatcher
Winter wren

BAHAMAS
American avocet
American mourning dove
American robin
Barn owl
Belted kingfisher
Black-and-white warbler
Black-winged stilt
Blue-gray gnatcatcher
Brown pelican
Cattle egret

Crested caracara
European starling
Gray catbird
House sparrow
Killdeer
Kirtland's warbler
Osprey
Peregrine falcon
Rock pigeon
Ruddy turnstone
White-tailed tropicbird
Wood stork
Yellow-bellied sapsucker

BANGLADESH
Barn swallow
Baya weaver
Black bulbul
Black-naped monarch
Black-winged stilt
Cattle egret
Common cuckoo
Common iora
Common myna
Coppersmith barbet
Crested tree swift
Dollarbird
Eurasian bittern
European white stork
Gray nightjar
Gray wagtail
Great cormorant
Great crested grebe
Great tit
Greater painted snipe
Greater racket-tailed drongo
Green magpie
Hooded pitta
Hoopoe
House sparrow
Mallard
Northern wryneck
Osprey
Peregrine falcon
Pheasant-tailed jacana
Purple sunbird

Rock pigeon
Rose-ringed parakeet
Ruby-cheeked sunbird
Ruddy turnstone
Small buttonquail
Spotted munia
Stonechat
White-throated fantail
Zitting cisticola

BELARUS
Barn swallow
Black tern
Chaffinch
Common cuckoo
Corncrake
Dunnock
Eurasian bittern
Eurasian golden oriole
European roller
European starling
European white stork
Great cormorant
Great crested grebe
Great tit
Hoopoe
House sparrow
Mallard
Northern lapwing
Northern raven
Northern wryneck
Nuthatch
Peregrine falcon
Red crossbill
Rock pigeon
Spotted flycatcher
Spotted nutcracker
Winter wren

BELGIUM
Barn swallow
Black tern
Chaffinch
Common cuckoo
Common murre
Corncrake

Dunnock
Eurasian golden oriole
European roller
European starling
European white stork
Gray wagtail
Great auk
Great cormorant
Great crested grebe
Great tit
Hoopoe
House sparrow
Mallard
Manx shearwater
Mute swan
Northern fulmar
Northern gannet
Northern lapwing
Northern wryneck
Nuthatch
Peregrine falcon
Puffin
Red-throated loon
Rock pigeon
Ruddy turnstone
Spotted flycatcher
Stonechat
Winter wren

BELIZE
American anhinga
American mourning dove
Baltimore oriole
Barn owl
Barred antshrike
Belted kingfisher
Black rail
Black-and-white warbler
Black-winged stilt
Blue-black grassquit
Blue-crowned motmot
Blue-gray gnatcatcher
Brown pelican
Cattle egret
Cedar waxwing
Crested caracara

Gray catbird
Great blue heron
Great kiskadee
Harris's hawk
House sparrow
Killdeer
King vulture
Limpkin
Magnificent frigatebird
Northern raven
Osprey
Peregrine falcon
Plain chachalaca
Rock pigeon
Rose-throated becard
Ruddy turnstone
Rufous-browed peppershrike
Rufous-tailed jacamar
Savanna sparrow
Scarlet macaw
Sungrebe
Whip-poor-will
White-necked puffbird
Wood stork
Yellow-bellied sapsucker
Yellow-breasted chat

BENIN
African jacana
African palm swift
African paradise-flycatcher
Barn swallow
Black tern
Black-winged stilt
Cattle egret
Collared pratincole
Common bulbul
Eurasian bittern
European bee-eater
European roller
Gray parrot
Gray woodpecker
Great blue turaco
Greater painted snipe
Green woodhoopoe
Hammerhead

Helmeted guineafowl
Hoopoe
Leaf-love
Northern wryneck
Osprey
Peregrine falcon
Rose-ringed parakeet
Ruddy turnstone
Sacred ibis
Secretary bird
Small buttonquail
Spotted flycatcher
Square-tailed drongo
Village weaver
White-helmet shrike
Wilson's storm-petrel
Yellow-fronted tinkerbird
Zitting cisticola

BERMUDA
European starling
Gray catbird
House sparrow
White-tailed tropicbird

BHUTAN
Asian fairy-bluebird
Barn swallow
Black-naped monarch
Cattle egret
Common cuckoo
Coppersmith barbet
Crested tree swift
Dollarbird
Eurasian bittern
European white stork
Fire-breasted flowerpecker
Gray nightjar
Great cormorant
Great crested grebe
Greater painted snipe
Hooded pitta
Hoopoe
House sparrow
Northern wryneck
Osprey

Pheasant-tailed jacana
Purple sunbird
Rock pigeon
Rose-ringed parakeet
Satyr tragopan
Small buttonquail
Snow finch
Spotted munia
Spotted nutcracker
Stonechat
White-throated fantail
Zitting cisticola

BOLIVIA
Amazonian umbrellabird
American anhinga
Barn owl
Barn swallow
Barred antshrike
Baywing
Black-capped donacobius
Black-winged stilt
Blue-black grassquit
Blue-crowned motmot
Cattle egret
Chimney swift
Crested caracara
Gray antbird
Gray potoo
Great kiskadee
Greater thornbird
Hairy hermit
Harris's hawk
Horned screamer
House sparrow
Killdeer
King vulture
Lesser rhea
Limpkin
Oilbird
Peregrine falcon
Red-billed scythebill
Red-legged seriema
Roseate spoonbill
Rufous hornero
Rufous-bellied seedsnipe

Rufous-browed peppershrike
Rufous-capped nunlet
Rufous-tailed jacamar
Scarlet macaw
Sharpbill
Spangled cotinga
Sparkling violet-ear
Sunbittern
Sungrebe
Toco toucan
Wattled curassow
White-necked puffbird
Wood stork

BOSNIA AND HERZEGOVINA
Barn swallow
Chaffinch
Common cuckoo
Corncrake
Dunnock
Eurasian dipper
Eurasian golden oriole
European bee-eater
European roller
European starling
European white stork
Gray wagtail
Great cormorant
Great crested grebe
Great tit
Hoopoe
House sparrow
Mallard
Northern lapwing
Northern raven
Northern wryneck
Nuthatch
Peregrine falcon
Red crossbill
Rock pigeon
Snow bunting
Snow finch
Spotted flycatcher
Stonechat
Winter wren

Zitting cisticola

BOTSWANA
African jacana
African palm swift
African paradise-flycatcher
African snipe
Bar-breasted mousebird
Barn swallow
Black-winged stilt
Cattle egret
Common bulbul
Common waxbill
Corncrake
Eurasian golden oriole
European roller
European white stork
Gray go-away-bird
Great cormorant
Greater painted snipe
Green woodhoopoe
Hammerhead
Helmeted guineafowl
Hoopoe
House sparrow
Namaqua sandgrouse
Osprey
Ostrich
Peregrine falcon
Red-billed oxpecker
Rock pigeon
Rosy-breasted longclaw
Sacred ibis
Secretary bird
Small buttonquail
Southern ground-hornbill
Southern red bishop
Spotted flycatcher
Stonechat
Village weaver
White-helmet shrike
Yellow-fronted tinkerbird
Zitting cisticola

BRAZIL
Amazonian umbrellabird

American anhinga
American cliff swallow
Barn owl
Barn swallow
Barred antshrike
Baywing
Black-capped donacobius
Black-winged stilt
Blue-black grassquit
Blue-crowned motmot
Brown pelican
Cattle egret
Chimney swift
Common trumpeter
Coppery-chested jacamar
Crested caracara
Gray antbird
Gray potoo
Great kiskadee
Greater thornbird
Guianan cock-of-the-rock
Hairy hermit
Harris's hawk
Hoatzin
Horned screamer
House sparrow
King vulture
Limpkin
Magellanic penguin
Magnificent frigatebird
Manx shearwater
Oilbird
Osprey
Peregrine falcon
Red-billed scythebill
Red-legged seriema
Rock pigeon
Roseate spoonbill
Ruddy turnstone
Rufous hornero
Rufous-browed peppershrike
Rufous-capped nunlet
Rufous-tailed jacamar
Rusty-belted tapaculo
Scarlet macaw

Sharpbill
Spangled cotinga
Sparkling violet-ear
Sunbittern
Sungrebe
Toco toucan
Wattled curassow
White-necked puffbird
Wilson's storm-petrel
Wire-tailed manakin
Wood stork

BULGARIA
Barn swallow
Black-winged stilt
Chaffinch
Common cuckoo
Corncrake
Dunnock
Egyptian vulture
Eurasian bittern
Eurasian golden oriole
European bee-eater
European roller
European starling
European white stork
Gray wagtail
Great cormorant
Great crested grebe
Great tit
Hoopoe
House sparrow
Mallard
Mute swan
Northern lapwing
Northern raven
Northern wryneck
Nuthatch
Peregrine falcon
Red crossbill
Red-throated loon
Rock pigeon
Snow bunting
Spotted flycatcher
Stonechat
Winter wren

Zitting cisticola

BURKINA FASO
African jacana
African palm swift
Barn swallow
Black-winged stilt
Cattle egret
Collared pratincole
Common bulbul
Egyptian vulture
Eurasian bittern
European bee-eater
European roller
European white stork
Gray woodpecker
Greater painted snipe
Green woodhoopoe
Hammerhead
Helmeted guineafowl
Hoopoe
Northern wryneck
Osprey
Peregrine falcon
Rose-ringed parakeet
Sacred ibis
Secretary bird
Small buttonquail
Village weaver
White-helmet shrike
Yellow-fronted tinkerbird

BURUNDI
African jacana
African palm swift
African paradise-flycatcher
African pitta
African snipe
Bar-breasted mousebird
Barn swallow
Black-winged stilt
Buff-spotted flufftail
Cattle egret
Collared pratincole
Common bulbul
Common cuckoo

Common waxbill
Corncrake
Eurasian golden oriole
European bee-eater
European roller
European white stork
Gray parrot
Gray-crowned crane
Great blue turaco
Great cormorant
Great crested grebe
Green woodhoopoe
Hammerhead
Helmeted guineafowl
Hoopoe
Osprey
Ostrich
Peregrine falcon
Red-billed oxpecker
Sacred ibis
Small buttonquail
Southern ground-hornbill
Southern red bishop
Spotted flycatcher
Stonechat
Village weaver
Yellow-fronted tinkerbird
Zitting cisticola

CAMBODIA
Arctic warbler
Asian fairy-bluebird
Australasian lark
Barn swallow
Baya weaver
Black-naped monarch
Black-winged stilt
Cattle egret
Common cuckoo
Common iora
Common myna
Coppersmith barbet
Crested tree swift
Dollarbird
Fire-breasted flowerpecker
Gray nightjar

Gray wagtail
Great cormorant
Great tit
Greater painted snipe
Greater racket-tailed drongo
Green magpie
Hoopoe
Northern wryneck
Orange-breasted trogon
Osprey
Peregrine falcon
Pheasant-tailed jacana
Purple sunbird
Rock pigeon
Ruby-cheeked sunbird
Ruddy turnstone
Small buttonquail
Spotted munia
Stonechat
White-throated fantail
Zitting cisticola

CAMEROON
African broadbill
African jacana
African palm swift
African paradise-flycatcher
African pitta
Bar-breasted mousebird
Barn swallow
Black tern
Black-winged stilt
Buff-spotted flufftail
Cattle egret
Collared pratincole
Common bulbul
Common waxbill
Eurasian bittern
Eurasian golden oriole
European roller
European white stork
Gray parrot
Gray woodpecker
Gray-necked picathartes
Great blue turaco
Great cormorant

Green woodhoopoe
Hammerhead
Helmeted guineafowl
Hoopoe
Leaf-love
Lyre-tailed honeyguide
Northern wryneck
Osprey
Peregrine falcon
Rose-ringed parakeet
Ruddy turnstone
Sacred ibis
Secretary bird
Small buttonquail
Spotted flycatcher
Square-tailed drongo
Stonechat
Village weaver
White-helmet shrike
Wilson's storm-petrel
Yellow-fronted tinkerbird
Zitting cisticola

CANADA
American cliff swallow
American dipper
American goldfinch
American mourning dove
American robin
American white pelican
Anna's hummingbird
Arctic skua
Baltimore oriole
Barn owl
Barn swallow
Belted kingfisher
Black tern
Black-and-white warbler
Black-capped chickadee
Blue jay
Brown creeper
Bushtit
Canada goose
Cattle egret
Cedar waxwing
Chimney swift

Common loon
Common murre
Eastern bluebird
Eastern phoebe
Eastern screech-owl
European starling
Gray catbird
Great auk
Great blue heron
Great cormorant
Gyrfalcon
Horned lark
House sparrow
House wren
Killdeer
King eider
Loggerhead shrike
Long-billed curlew
Mallard
Manx shearwater
Northern fulmar
Northern gannet
Northern raven
Osprey
Peregrine falcon
Puffin
Red crossbill
Red-breasted nuthatch
Red-throated loon
Red-winged blackbird
Rock pigeon
Ruddy turnstone
Sandhill crane
Savanna sparrow
Snow bunting
Snowy owl
Song sparrow
Sprague's pipit
Western grebe
Whip-poor-will
Willow ptarmigan
Wilson's storm-petrel
Winter wren
Wood duck
Yellow-bellied sapsucker
Yellow-breasted chat

CENTRAL AFRICAN REPUBLIC

African broadbill
African jacana
African palm swift
African paradise-flycatcher
Bar-breasted mousebird
Barn swallow
Black-winged stilt
Buff-spotted flufftail
Cattle egret
Collared pratincole
Common bulbul
Common waxbill
Eurasian bittern
Eurasian golden oriole
European white stork
Gray parrot
Gray woodpecker
Great blue turaco
Great cormorant
Green woodhoopoe
Hammerhead
Helmeted guineafowl
Hoopoe
Leaf-love
Lyre-tailed honeyguide
Northern wryneck
Osprey
Ostrich
Peregrine falcon
Red-billed oxpecker
Rose-ringed parakeet
Sacred ibis
Secretary bird
Shoebill
Small buttonquail
Spotted flycatcher
Square-tailed drongo
Village weaver
White-helmet shrike
Yellow-fronted tinkerbird

CHAD

African jacana
African palm swift
African paradise-flycatcher
Barn swallow
Black-winged stilt
Cattle egret
Collared pratincole
Common bulbul
Egyptian vulture
Eurasian bittern
European white stork
Gray woodpecker
Great cormorant
Green woodhoopoe
Hammerhead
Helmeted guineafowl
Hoopoe
Northern wryneck
Osprey
Ostrich
Peregrine falcon
Rock pigeon
Rose-ringed parakeet
Sacred ibis
Secretary bird
Small buttonquail
Square-tailed drongo
Village weaver
White-helmet shrike
Yellow-fronted tinkerbird

CHILE

Arctic skua
Barn owl
Barn swallow
Black rail
Black-winged stilt
Blue-black grassquit
Brown pelican
Cattle egret
Chimney swift
Common diving-petrel
Crested caracara
Emperor penguin
Harris's hawk
House sparrow
Killdeer

Lesser rhea
Macaroni penguin
Magellanic penguin
Osprey
Peregrine falcon
Rock pigeon
Ruddy turnstone
Rufous-bellied seedsnipe
Sparkling violet-ear
Wilson's storm-petrel

CHINA

Arctic warbler
Asian fairy-bluebird
Barn swallow
Baya weaver
Black bulbul
Black tern
Black-naped monarch
Black-winged stilt
Cattle egret
Chaffinch
Common cuckoo
Common iora
Common murre
Common myna
Coppersmith barbet
Crag martin
Crested tree swift
Dollarbird
Eurasian bittern
Eurasian dipper
Eurasian golden oriole
European roller
European starling
Fire-breasted flowerpecker
Gray nightjar
Gray wagtail
Great bustard
Great cormorant
Great crested grebe
Great tit
Greater painted snipe
Greater racket-tailed drongo
Green magpie

Hooded pitta
Hoopoe
Horned lark
House sparrow
Japanese white-eye
Mallard
Mute swan
Northern lapwing
Northern raven
Northern wryneck
Nuthatch
Orange-breasted trogon
Osprey
Pallas's sandgrouse
Peregrine falcon
Pheasant-tailed jacana
Purple sunbird
Red crossbill
Red-crowned crane
Red-throated loon
Rock pigeon
Rose-ringed parakeet
Ruby-cheeked sunbird
Ruddy turnstone
Satyr tragopan
Saunder's gull
Small buttonquail
Snow bunting
Snow finch
Spotted flycatcher
Spotted munia
Spotted nutcracker
Stonechat
White-throated fantail
Willow ptarmigan
Winter wren
Zitting cisticola

COLOMBIA
Amazonian umbrellabird
American anhinga
Baltimore oriole
Barn owl
Barn swallow
Barred antshrike

Belted kingfisher
Black tern
Black-and-white warbler
Black-capped donacobius
Black-winged stilt
Blue-black grassquit
Blue-crowned motmot
Blue-footed booby
Brown pelican
Cattle egret
Common trumpeter
Coppery-chested jacamar
Crested caracara
Gray antbird
Gray potoo
Gray-breasted mountain-
    toucan
Great blue heron
Great kiskadee
Greater flamingo
Guianan cock-of-the-rock
Hairy hermit
Harris's hawk
Highland tinamou
Hoatzin
Horned lark
Horned screamer
House sparrow
Killdeer
King vulture
Limpkin
Magnificent frigatebird
Oilbird
Osprey
Peregrine falcon
Red-billed scythebill
Roseate spoonbill
Ruddy turnstone
Rufous-browed peppershrike
Rufous-tailed jacamar
Rusty-belted tapaculo
Scarlet macaw
Spangled cotinga
Sparkling violet-ear
Sunbittern
Sungrebe

Toucan barbet
Wattled curassow
White-necked puffbird
Wilson's storm-petrel
Wire-tailed manakin
Wood stork

COMOROS
White-tailed tropicbird

CONGO
African jacana
African palm swift
African paradise-flycatcher
African pitta
Bar-breasted mousebird
Barn swallow
Black tern
Black-winged stilt
Buff-spotted flufftail
Cattle egret
Collared pratincole
Common bulbul
Common cuckoo
Common waxbill
Eurasian golden oriole
Gray parrot
Great blue turaco
Great cormorant
Greater painted snipe
Hammerhead
Helmeted guineafowl
Hoopoe
Leaf-love
Lyre-tailed honeyguide
Osprey
Peregrine falcon
Ruddy turnstone
Sacred ibis
Small buttonquail
Spotted flycatcher
Square-tailed drongo
Stonechat
Village weaver
Zitting cisticola

COSTA RICA

American anhinga
American dipper
American mourning dove
Baltimore oriole
Barn owl
Barn swallow
Barred antshrike
Belted kingfisher
Black guan
Black rail
Black tern
Black-and-white warbler
Black-winged stilt
Blue-black grassquit
Blue-crowned motmot
Blue-footed booby
Brown pelican
Cattle egret
Cedar waxwing
Crested caracara
Gray catbird
Gray potoo
Great blue heron
Great kiskadee
Harris's hawk
Highland tinamou
House sparrow
Killdeer
King vulture
Limpkin
Long-tailed manakin
Magnificent frigatebird
Oilbird
Osprey
Peregrine falcon
Plain chachalaca
Resplendent quetzal
Rock pigeon
Roseate spoonbill
Rose-throated becard
Ruddy turnstone
Rufous-browed peppershrike
Rufous-tailed jacamar
Scarlet macaw
Sharpbill

Sunbittern
Sungrebe
White-necked puffbird
Wood stork
Yellow-bellied sapsucker
Yellow-breasted chat

CROATIA

Barn swallow
Chaffinch
Collared pratincole
Common cuckoo
Corncrake
Dunnock
Eurasian bittern
Eurasian dipper
Eurasian golden oriole
European bee-eater
European roller
European starling
European white stork
Gray wagtail
Great cormorant
Great crested grebe
Great tit
Hoopoe
House sparrow
Mallard
Northern lapwing
Northern raven
Northern wryneck
Nuthatch
Peregrine falcon
Red crossbill
Red-throated loon
Rock pigeon
Snow bunting
Snow finch
Spotted flycatcher
Stonechat
Winter wren
Zitting cisticola

CUBA

American avocet
American mourning dove

Barn owl
Belted kingfisher
Black rail
Black-and-white warbler
Black-winged stilt
Blue-gray gnatcatcher
Brown pelican
Crested caracara
Cuban tody
Gray catbird
Greater flamingo
House sparrow
Ivory-billed woodpecker
Killdeer
Limpkin
Magnificent frigatebird
Northern bobwhite quail
Osprey
Peregrine falcon
Rock pigeon
Roseate spoonbill
Ruddy turnstone
Whip-poor-will
White-tailed tropicbird
Wood duck
Wood stork
Yellow-bellied sapsucker

CYPRUS

European roller
Great cormorant
Northern gannet
Peregrine falcon
Zitting cisticola

CZECH REPUBLIC

Barn swallow
Black tern
Chaffinch
Common cuckoo
Corncrake
Dunnock
Eurasian dipper
Eurasian golden oriole
European roller
European starling

European white stork
Gray wagtail
Great cormorant
Great crested grebe
Great tit
Hoopoe
House sparrow
Mallard
Mute swan
Northern lapwing
Northern raven
Northern wryneck
Nuthatch
Peregrine falcon
Red crossbill
Rock pigeon
Snow bunting
Spotted flycatcher
Spotted nutcracker
Stonechat
Winter wren

DEMOCRATIC REPUBLIC OF THE CONGO

African broadbill
African jacana
African palm swift
African paradise-flycatcher
African pitta
African snipe
Barn swallow
Black tern
Black-winged stilt
Buff-spotted flufftail
Cattle egret
Collared pratincole
Common bulbul
Common cuckoo
Common waxbill
Corncrake
Egyptian vulture
Eurasian bittern
Eurasian golden oriole
European bee-eater
European roller

European white stork
Golden-winged sunbird
Gray go-away-bird
Gray parrot
Gray woodpecker
Gray-crowned crane
Great blue turaco
Great cormorant
Great crested grebe
Greater painted snipe
Green woodhoopoe
Hammerhead
Helmeted guineafowl
Hoopoe
House sparrow
Leaf-love
Lyre-tailed honeyguide
Northern wryneck
Osprey
Peregrine falcon
Red-billed oxpecker
Ruddy turnstone
Sacred ibis
Secretary bird
Shoebill
Small buttonquail
Southern ground-hornbill
Southern red bishop
Spotted flycatcher
Square-tailed drongo
Stonechat
Village weaver
White-helmet shrike
Yellow-fronted tinkerbird
Zitting cisticola

DENMARK

Barn swallow
Canada goose
Chaffinch
Common cuckoo
Common murre
Corncrake
Dunnock
Eurasian bittern
European roller

European starling
Great auk
Great cormorant
Great crested grebe
Great tit
House sparrow
Mallard
Manx shearwater
Mute swan
Northern fulmar
Northern gannet
Northern lapwing
Northern wryneck
Nuthatch
Peregrine falcon
Puffin
Red crossbill
Red-throated loon
Rock pigeon
Snow bunting
Spotted flycatcher
Stonechat
Winter wren

DJIBOUTI

African paradise-flycatcher
African snipe
Bar-breasted mousebird
Cattle egret
Collared pratincole
Common bulbul
Corncrake
Crab plovers
Egyptian vulture
European roller
Great cormorant
Greater flamingo
Greater hoopoe-lark
Green woodhoopoe
Hammerhead
Hoopoe
Osprey
Ostrich
Peregrine falcon
Red-billed oxpecker
Ruddy turnstone

Sacred ibis
Secretary bird
Small buttonquail
Stonechat
Wilson's storm-petrel

DOMINICAN REPUBLIC
American mourning dove
Barn owl
Belted kingfisher
Black rail
Black-and-white warbler
Black-winged stilt
Brown pelican
Cattle egret
Crested caracara
Greater flamingo
House sparrow
Killdeer
Limpkin
Magnificent frigatebird
Osprey
Palmchat
Peregrine falcon
Rock pigeon
Roseate spoonbill
Ruddy turnstone
White-tailed tropicbird
Wilson's storm-petrel
Wood stork
Yellow-bellied sapsucker

ECUADOR
Amazonian umbrellabird
American anhinga
Barn owl
Barn swallow
Barred antshrike
Black tern
Black-winged stilt
Blue-black grassquit
Blue-crowned motmot
Blue-footed booby
Brown pelican
Cattle egret
Chimney swift

Common trumpeter
Coppery-chested jacamar
Crested caracara
Gray antbird
Gray potoo
Gray-breasted mountain-
  toucan
Great kiskadee
Greater flamingo
Harris's hawk
Highland tinamou
Hood mockingbird
Horned screamer
House sparrow
Killdeer
King vulture
Limpkin
Magnificent frigatebird
Oilbird
Osprey
Peregrine falcon
Red-billed scythebill
Roseate spoonbill
Ruddy turnstone
Rufous-bellied seedsnipe
Rufous-browed peppershrike
Rufous-tailed jacamar
Rusty-belted tapaculo
Scarlet macaw
Sharpbill
Spangled cotinga
Sparkling violet-ear
Sunbittern
Sungrebe
Toucan barbet
White-necked puffbird
Wilson's storm-petrel
Wire-tailed manakin

EGYPT
Barn swallow
Black tern
Black-winged stilt
Cattle egret
Common bulbul
Corncrake

Egyptian vulture
Eurasian bittern
European roller
Gray wagtail
Great cormorant
Great crested grebe
Greater flamingo
Greater hoopoe-lark
Greater painted snipe
Hoopoe
House sparrow
Mallard
Northern gannet
Northern lapwing
Northern raven
Osprey
Peregrine falcon
Rock pigeon
Ruddy turnstone
Stonechat
Zitting cisticola

EL SALVADOR
American anhinga
American mourning dove
Baltimore oriole
Barn owl
Barred antshrike
Belted kingfisher
Black rail
Black tern
Black-and-white warbler
Black-winged stilt
Blue-black grassquit
Blue-crowned motmot
Blue-footed booby
Blue-gray gnatcatcher
Brown creeper
Brown pelican
Cattle egret
Cedar waxwing
Crested caracara
Great blue heron
Great kiskadee
Harris's hawk
House sparrow

Killdeer
King vulture
Limpkin
Long-tailed manakin
Magnificent frigatebird
Northern raven
Osprey
Peregrine falcon
Rock pigeon
Roseate spoonbill
Rose-throated becard
Ruddy turnstone
Rufous-browed peppershrike
Rufous-tailed jacamar
Sunbittern
Sungrebe
Whip-poor-will
White-necked puffbird
Wood stork
Yellow-bellied sapsucker
Yellow-breasted chat

EQUATORIAL GUINEA
African jacana
African palm swift
African paradise-flycatcher
African pitta
Barn swallow
Black tern
Black-winged stilt
Cattle egret
Collared pratincole
Common bulbul
Common waxbill
Gray parrot
Gray-necked picathartes
Great blue turaco
Great cormorant
Great crested grebe
Hammerhead
Helmeted guineafowl
Leaf-love
Lyre-tailed honeyguide
Osprey
Peregrine falcon
Ruddy turnstone

Sacred ibis
Spotted flycatcher
Village weaver
Wilson's storm-petrel
Zitting cisticola

ERITREA
African paradise-flycatcher
African snipe
Bar-breasted mousebird
Cattle egret
Collared pratincole
Common bulbul
Corncrake
Crab plovers
Egyptian vulture
Eurasian bittern
European roller
European white stork
Gray woodpecker
Greater flamingo
Greater hoopoe-lark
Greater painted snipe
Green woodhoopoe
Hammerhead
Helmeted guineafowl
Hoopoe
Osprey
Ostrich
Peregrine falcon
Red-billed oxpecker
Rock pigeon
Rose-ringed parakeet
Ruddy turnstone
Sacred ibis
Secretary bird
Small buttonquail
Stonechat
White-helmet shrike
Wilson's storm-petrel
Zitting cisticola

ESTONIA
Barn swallow
Black tern
Chaffinch

Common cuckoo
Common murre
Corncrake
Dunnock
Eurasian bittern
Eurasian dipper
Eurasian golden oriole
European roller
European starling
European white stork
Great cormorant
Great crested grebe
Great tit
Hoopoe
House sparrow
Mallard
Northern fulmar
Northern gannet
Northern lapwing
Northern raven
Northern wryneck
Nuthatch
Osprey
Red crossbill
Rock pigeon
Spotted flycatcher
Willow ptarmigan
Winter wren

ETHIOPIA
African jacana
African palm swift
African paradise-flycatcher
African snipe
Bar-breasted mousebird
Barn swallow
Black-winged stilt
Buff-spotted flufftail
Cattle egret
Collared pratincole
Common bulbul
Common waxbill
Corncrake
Egyptian vulture
Eurasian bittern
European roller

European white stork
Gray wagtail
Gray woodpecker
Great cormorant
Great crested grebe
Greater painted snipe
Green woodhoopoe
Hammerhead
Helmeted guineafowl
Hoopoe
Northern wryneck
Osprey
Ostrich
Peregrine falcon
Red-billed oxpecker
Rose-ringed parakeet
Sacred ibis
Secretary bird
Small buttonquail
Stonechat
Village weaver
White-helmet shrike
Yellow-fronted tinkerbird
Zitting cisticola

FALKLAND ISLANDS
Arctic skua
Crested caracara
Emperor penguin
House sparrow
Macaroni penguin
Magellanic penguin
Peregrine falcon

FIJI
European starling
Golden whistler
White-tailed tropicbird

FINLAND
Arctic warbler
Barn swallow
Chaffinch
Common cuckoo
Common murre

Corncrake
Dunnock
Eurasian bittern
Eurasian dipper
European roller
European starling
Gray wagtail
Great cormorant
Great crested grebe
Great tit
Gyrfalcon
Horned lark
House sparrow
Mute swan
Northern fulmar
Northern gannet
Northern lapwing
Northern raven
Northern wryneck
Osprey
Peregrine falcon
Puffin
Red crossbill
Red-throated loon
Rock pigeon
Ruddy turnstone
Spotted flycatcher
Spotted nutcracker
Willow ptarmigan
Winter wren

FRANCE
Barn swallow
Black tern
Black-winged stilt
Cattle egret
Chaffinch
Common cuckoo
Common loon
Common murre
Corncrake
Dunnock
Eurasian bittern
Eurasian dipper
Eurasian golden oriole
European bee-eater

European roller
European starling
European white stork
Gray wagtail
Great auk
Great cormorant
Great crested grebe
Great tit
Greater flamingo
Hoopoe
House sparrow
Mallard
Manx shearwater
Mute swan
Northern fulmar
Northern gannet
Northern lapwing
Northern raven
Northern wryneck
Nuthatch
Osprey
Peregrine falcon
Puffin
Red crossbill
Red-throated loon
Rock pigeon
Ruddy turnstone
Snow finch
Spotted flycatcher
Stonechat
Wilson's storm-petrel
Winter wren
Zitting cisticola

FRENCH GUIANA
American anhinga
Barn owl
Barn swallow
Barred antshrike
Black tern
Black-capped donacobius
Black-winged stilt
Blue-black grassquit
Blue-crowned motmot
Brown pelican
Cattle egret

Common trumpeter
Crested caracara
Gray antbird
Gray potoo
Great kiskadee
Guianan cock-of-the-rock
Hairy hermit
Hoatzin
King vulture
Limpkin
Magnificent frigatebird
Osprey
Peregrine falcon
Roseate spoonbill
Ruddy turnstone
Rufous-browed peppershrike
Rufous-tailed jacamar
Scarlet macaw
Spangled cotinga
Sunbittern
Sungrebe
White-necked puffbird
Wilson's storm-petrel
Wood stork

GABON
African broadbill
African jacana
African palm swift
African paradise-flycatcher
African pitta
Bar-breasted mousebird
Barn swallow
Black tern
Black-winged stilt
Buff-spotted flufftail
Cattle egret
Collared pratincole
Common bulbul
Common cuckoo
Common waxbill
Eurasian golden oriole
Gray parrot
Gray-necked picathartes
Great blue turaco
Great cormorant

Greater painted snipe
Hammerhead
Helmeted guineafowl
Hoopoe
Leaf-love
Lyre-tailed honeyguide
Osprey
Peregrine falcon
Ruddy turnstone
Sacred ibis
Small buttonquail
Spotted flycatcher
Square-tailed drongo
Stonechat
Village weaver
Wilson's storm-petrel
Zitting cisticola

GAMBIA
African palm swift
African paradise-flycatcher
Black tern
Black-winged stilt
Cattle egret
Collared pratincole
Common bulbul
Egyptian vulture
Eurasian bittern
Gray woodpecker
Greater flamingo
Green woodhoopoe
Hammerhead
Helmeted guineafowl
Hoopoe
Leaf-love
Magnificent frigatebird
Northern wryneck
Osprey
Peregrine falcon
Rose-ringed parakeet
Ruddy turnstone
Sacred ibis
Secretary bird
Small buttonquail
Village weaver
White-helmet shrike

Wilson's storm-petrel
Yellow-fronted tinkerbird

GEORGIA
Barn swallow
Chaffinch
Common cuckoo
Corncrake
Dunnock
Egyptian vulture
Eurasian dipper
Eurasian golden oriole
European bee-eater
European roller
European starling
Gray wagtail
Great cormorant
Great crested grebe
Great tit
Hoopoe
Horned lark
House sparrow
Northern raven
Northern wryneck
Nuthatch
Peregrine falcon
Red crossbill
Rock pigeon
Snow finch
Spotted flycatcher
Stonechat
Winter wren

GERMANY
Barn swallow
Black tern
Canada goose
Chaffinch
Common cuckoo
Common murre
Corncrake
Dunnock
Eurasian bittern
Eurasian dipper
Eurasian golden oriole

European roller
European starling
European white stork
Gray wagtail
Great auk
Great bustard
Great cormorant
Great crested grebe
Great tit
Hoopoe
House sparrow
Mallard
Manx shearwater
Mute swan
Northern fulmar
Northern gannet
Northern lapwing
Northern raven
Northern wryneck
Nuthatch
Peregrine falcon
Puffin
Red crossbill
Red-throated loon
Rock pigeon
Ruddy turnstone
Snow bunting
Snow finch
Spotted flycatcher
Spotted nutcracker
Stonechat
Winter wren

GHANA
African broadbill
African jacana
African palm swift
African paradise-flycatcher
African pitta
Barn swallow
Black tern
Black-winged stilt
Cattle egret
Collared pratincole
Common bulbul
Eurasian bittern

European bee-eater
European roller
Gray parrot
Gray woodpecker
Great blue turaco
Greater painted snipe
Green woodhoopoe
Hammerhead
Helmeted guineafowl
Hoopoe
Leaf-love
Northern wryneck
Osprey
Peregrine falcon
Rose-ringed parakeet
Ruddy turnstone
Sacred ibis
Secretary bird
Small buttonquail
Spotted flycatcher
Square-tailed drongo
Village weaver
White-helmet shrike
Wilson's storm-petrel
Yellow-fronted tinkerbird
Zitting cisticola

GREECE
Barn swallow
Chaffinch
Common cuckoo
Corncrake
Crag martin
Dunnock
Egyptian vulture
Eurasian bittern
Eurasian dipper
Eurasian golden oriole
European bee-eater
European roller
European starling
Gray wagtail
Great cormorant
Great crested grebe
Great tit
Hoopoe

Horned lark
House sparrow
Mallard
Mute swan
Northern gannet
Northern lapwing
Northern raven
Northern wryneck
Peregrine falcon
Red crossbill
Rock pigeon
Spotted flycatcher
Stonechat
Winter wren
Zitting cisticola

GREENLAND
Arctic skua
Common loon
Common murre
Great auk
Great cormorant
Gyrfalcon
King eider
Mallard
Manx shearwater
Northern fulmar
Northern gannet
Northern raven
Peregrine falcon
Puffin
Red-throated loon
Ruddy turnstone
Snow bunting
Snowy owl

GUATEMALA
American anhinga
American dipper
American mourning dove
American robin
Baltimore oriole
Barn owl
Barred antshrike
Belted kingfisher
Black rail

Black tern
Black-and-white warbler
Black-capped vireo
Black-winged stilt
Blue-black grassquit
Blue-crowned motmot
Blue-footed booby
Blue-gray gnatcatcher
Brown creeper
Brown pelican
Cattle egret
Cedar waxwing
Crested caracara
Gray catbird
Great blue heron
Great kiskadee
Harris's hawk
House sparrow
Killdeer
King vulture
Limpkin
Long-tailed manakin
Magnificent frigatebird
Northern raven
Osprey
Peregrine falcon
Plain chachalaca
Resplendent quetzal
Rock pigeon
Roseate spoonbill
Rose-throated becard
Ruddy turnstone
Rufous-browed peppershrike
Rufous-tailed jacamar
Savanna sparrow
Scarlet macaw
Sunbittern
Sungrebe
Whip-poor-will
White-necked puffbird
Wood stork
Yellow-bellied sapsucker
Yellow-breasted chat

GUINEA
African palm swift

African paradise-flycatcher
Barn swallow
Black tern
Black-winged stilt
Buff-spotted flufftail
Cattle egret
Collared pratincole
Common bulbul
Common waxbill
Eurasian bittern
European bee-eater
European roller
Gray parrot
Gray woodpecker
Great blue turaco
Green woodhoopoe
Hammerhead
Helmeted guineafowl
Hoopoe
Leaf-love
Northern wryneck
Osprey
Peregrine falcon
Rock pigeon
Rose-ringed parakeet
Ruddy turnstone
Sacred ibis
Small buttonquail
Square-tailed drongo
Stonechat
Village weaver
White-helmet shrike
Wilson's storm-petrel
Yellow-fronted tinkerbird

GUINEA-BISSAU
African palm swift
African paradise-flycatcher
Barn swallow
Black tern
Black-winged stilt
Cattle egret
Collared pratincole
Common bulbul
Common waxbill
Egyptian vulture

Eurasian bittern
Gray parrot
Gray woodpecker
Green woodhoopoe
Hammerhead
Helmeted guineafowl
Hoopoe
Leaf-love
Magnificent frigatebird
Northern wryneck
Osprey
Peregrine falcon
Rose-ringed parakeet
Ruddy turnstone
Sacred ibis
Small buttonquail
Square-tailed drongo
Village weaver
Wilson's storm-petrel

GUYANA
American anhinga
Barn owl
Barn swallow
Barred antshrike
Belted kingfisher
Black tern
Black-capped donacobius
Black-winged stilt
Blue-black grassquit
Blue-crowned motmot
Brown pelican
Cattle egret
Common trumpeter
Crested caracara
Gray antbird
Gray potoo
Great kiskadee
Greater flamingo
Guianan cock-of-the-rock
Hairy hermit
Hoatzin
King vulture
Limpkin
Magnificent frigatebird
Oilbird

Osprey
Peregrine falcon
Roseate spoonbill
Ruddy turnstone
Rufous-browed peppershrike
Rufous-tailed jacamar
Scarlet macaw
Sharpbill
Spangled cotinga
Sparkling violet-ear
Sunbittern
Sungrebe
White-necked puffbird
Wilson's storm-petrel
Wood stork

HAITI

American mourning dove
Barn owl
Belted kingfisher
Black-and-white warbler
Black-winged stilt
Brown pelican
Cattle egret
Crested caracara
Greater flamingo
House sparrow
Killdeer
Limpkin
Magnificent frigatebird
Osprey
Palmchat
Peregrine falcon
Rock pigeon
Roseate spoonbill
Ruddy turnstone
White-tailed tropicbird
Wood stork
Yellow-bellied sapsucker

HONDURAS

American anhinga
American mourning dove
Baltimore oriole
Barn owl
Barred antshrike

Belted kingfisher
Black tern
Black-and-white warbler
Black-winged stilt
Blue-black grassquit
Blue-crowned motmot
Blue-footed booby
Blue-gray gnatcatcher
Brown creeper
Brown pelican
Cattle egret
Cedar waxwing
Crested caracara
Gray catbird
Great blue heron
Great kiskadee
Harris's hawk
House sparrow
Killdeer
King vulture
Limpkin
Long-tailed manakin
Magnificent frigatebird
Northern raven
Osprey
Peregrine falcon
Plain chachalaca
Resplendent quetzal
Rock pigeon
Roseate spoonbill
Rose-throated becard
Ruddy turnstone
Rufous-browed peppershrike
Rufous-tailed jacamar
Scarlet macaw
Sunbittern
Sungrebe
Whip-poor-will
White-necked puffbird
Wood stork
Yellow-bellied sapsucker
Yellow-breasted chat

HUNGARY

Barn swallow
Black tern

Chaffinch
Collared pratincole
Common cuckoo
Corncrake
Dunnock
Eurasian golden oriole
European bee-eater
European roller
European starling
European white stork
Gray wagtail
Great bustard
Great cormorant
Great crested grebe
Great tit
Hoopoe
House sparrow
Mallard
Northern lapwing
Northern raven
Northern wryneck
Nuthatch
Peregrine falcon
Red crossbill
Rock pigeon
Snow bunting
Spotted flycatcher
Stonechat
Winter wren

ICELAND

Arctic skua
Common loon
Common murre
European starling
Great auk
Great cormorant
Gyrfalcon
King eider
Mallard
Manx shearwater
Northern fulmar
Northern gannet
Northern raven
Puffin
Red-throated loon

Snow bunting

INDIA
Asian fairy-bluebird
Barn swallow
Baya weaver
Black bulbul
Black-naped monarch
Black-winged stilt
Cattle egret
Chaffinch
Collared pratincole
Common cuckoo
Common iora
Common myna
Coppersmith barbet
Crab plovers
Crag martin
Crested tree swift
Dollarbird
Egyptian vulture
Eurasian bittern
Eurasian golden oriole
European bee-eater
European roller
European starling
European white stork
Fire-breasted flowerpecker
Gray hypocolius
Gray nightjar
Gray wagtail
Great cormorant
Great crested grebe
Great tit
Greater flamingo
Greater painted snipe
Greater racket-tailed drongo
Green magpie
Hooded pitta
Hoopoe
House sparrow
Mallard
Northern lapwing
Northern raven
Northern wryneck
Osprey

Peregrine falcon
Pheasant-tailed jacana
Purple sunbird
Rock pigeon
Rose-ringed parakeet
Ruby-cheeked sunbird
Ruddy turnstone
Satyr tragopan
Small buttonquail
Spotted munia
Spotted nutcracker
Stonechat
White-throated fantail
Wilson's storm-petrel
Zitting cisticola

INDONESIA
Arctic warbler
Asian fairy-bluebird
Australasian figbird
Australasian lark
Australian magpie-lark
Australian pratincole
Barn swallow
Barred eagle-owl
Baya weaver
Beach thick-knee
Black-and-red broadbill
Black-naped monarch
Black-winged stilt
Bornean bristlehead
Cattle egret
Common iora
Coppersmith barbet
Dollarbird
Eclectus parrot
Fan-tailed berrypecker
Feline owlet-nightjar
Fiery minivet
Fire-breasted flowerpecker
Golden whistler
Gray nightjar
Gray wagtail
Gray-crowned babbler
Great cormorant
Great tit

Greater painted snipe
Greater racket-tailed drongo
Green magpie
Helmeted hornbill
Hooded pitta
King bird of paradise
Malaysian honeyguide
Maleo
Orange-breasted trogon
Osprey
Peregrine falcon
Pheasant-tailed jacana
Purple-bearded bee-eater
Rainbow lorikeet
Rock pigeon
Ruby-cheeked sunbird
Ruddy turnstone
Rufous-collared kingfisher
Small buttonquail
Southern cassowary
Spotted munia
Sulawesi red-knobbed
  hornbill
Variable pitohui
White-throated fantail
Willie wagtail
Wilson's storm-petrel
Zebra finch
Zitting cisticola

IRAN
Barn swallow
Black-winged stilt
Cattle egret
Chaffinch
Common cuckoo
Common myna
Corncrake
Crab plovers
Crag martin
Dunnock
Egyptian vulture
Eurasian dipper
Eurasian golden oriole
European bee-eater
European roller

European starling
European white stork
Gray hypocolius
Gray wagtail
Great bustard
Great cormorant
Great crested grebe
Great tit
Greater flamingo
Greater hoopoe-lark
Hoopoe
Horned lark
House sparrow
Mallard
Mute swan
Northern lapwing
Northern raven
Nuthatch
Osprey
Peregrine falcon
Purple sunbird
Red-throated loon
Rock pigeon
Ruddy turnstone
Snow finch
Spotted flycatcher
Stonechat
Wilson's storm-petrel
Winter wren

IRAQ
Black-winged stilt
Cattle egret
Chaffinch
Collared pratincole
Corncrake
Dunnock
Egyptian vulture
Eurasian bittern
European bee-eater
European roller
European starling
Gray hypocolius
Gray wagtail
Great cormorant
Great crested grebe

Greater hoopoe-lark
Hoopoe
House sparrow
Mallard
Northern lapwing
Nuthatch
Osprey
Peregrine falcon
Rock pigeon
Spotted flycatcher
Stonechat

IRELAND
Barn owl
Barn swallow
Canada goose
Chaffinch
Common cuckoo
Common loon
Common murre
Corncrake
Dunnock
Eurasian dipper
European starling
Gray wagtail
Great auk
Great cormorant
Great crested grebe
Great tit
House sparrow
Mallard
Manx shearwater
Mute swan
Northern gannet
Northern lapwing
Northern raven
Peregrine falcon
Puffin
Red-throated loon
Rock pigeon
Ruddy turnstone
Spotted flycatcher
Stonechat
Willow ptarmigan
Winter wren

ISRAEL
Black-winged stilt
Cattle egret
Collared pratincole
Common cuckoo
Egyptian vulture
European bee-eater
European roller
Great cormorant
Greater flamingo
Hoopoe
Horned lark
House sparrow
Mallard
Northern gannet
Northern lapwing
Peregrine falcon
Rock pigeon
Stonechat
Winter wren
Zitting cisticola

ITALY
Barn swallow
Black tern
Black-winged stilt
Cattle egret
Chaffinch
Common cuckoo
Corncrake
Crag martin
Dunnock
Egyptian vulture
Eurasian dipper
Eurasian golden oriole
European bee-eater
European roller
European starling
Gray wagtail
Great cormorant
Great crested grebe
Great tit
Greater flamingo
Hoopoe
House sparrow
Mallard

Mute swan
Northern gannet
Northern lapwing
Northern raven
Northern wryneck
Nuthatch
Peregrine falcon
Red crossbill
Rock pigeon
Snow finch
Spotted flycatcher
Stonechat
Winter wren
Zitting cisticola

IVORY COAST
African broadbill
African jacana
African palm swift
African paradise-flycatcher
African pitta
Barn swallow
Black tern
Black-winged stilt
Cattle egret
Collared pratincole
Common bulbul
Common waxbill
Eurasian bittern
European bee-eater
European roller
Gray parrot
Gray woodpecker
Great blue turaco
Green woodhoopoe
Hammerhead
Hoopoe
Leaf-love
Lyre-tailed honeyguide
Northern wryneck
Osprey
Peregrine falcon
Rose-ringed parakeet
Ruddy turnstone
Sacred ibis
Small buttonquail

Spotted flycatcher
Square-tailed drongo
Village weaver
White-helmet shrike
Wilson's storm-petrel
Yellow-fronted tinkerbird
Zitting cisticola

JAMAICA
American mourning dove
Barn owl
Belted kingfisher
Black rail
Black-and-white warbler
Brown pelican
Cattle egret
Crested caracara
European starling
Gray catbird
House sparrow
Killdeer
Magnificent frigatebird
Osprey
Peregrine falcon
Rock pigeon
Ruddy turnstone
White-tailed tropicbird
Wood stork

JAPAN
Arctic warbler
Barn swallow
Cattle egret
Common murre
Dollarbird
Eurasian bittern
Gray nightjar
Gray wagtail
Great cormorant
Great tit
Greater painted snipe
Hoopoe
Japanese white-eye
Laysan albatross
Mallard
Mute swan

Northern fulmar
Northern lapwing
Northern raven
Nuthatch
Osprey
Peregrine falcon
Red crossbill
Red-crowned crane
Red-throated loon
Rock pigeon
Saunder's gull
Spotted nutcracker
Stonechat
Willow ptarmigan
Winter wren

JORDAN
Black-winged stilt
Cattle egret
Collared pratincole
Common bulbul
Egyptian vulture
European bee-eater
European roller
Gray wagtail
Great cormorant
Hoopoe
House sparrow
Northern gannet
Northern lapwing
Peregrine falcon
Rock pigeon
Stonechat
Winter wren

KAZAKHSTAN
Barn swallow
Black tern
Black-winged stilt
Chaffinch
Collared pratincole
Common cuckoo
Common myna
Corncrake
Egyptian vulture
Eurasian bittern

Eurasian golden oriole
European bee-eater
European roller
European starling
European white stork
Great cormorant
Great crested grebe
Great tit
Greater flamingo
Hoopoe
Horned lark
House sparrow
Mallard
Mute swan
Northern raven
Pallas's sandgrouse
Peregrine falcon
Red crossbill
Red-throated loon
Rock pigeon
Snow bunting
Spotted flycatcher
Spotted nutcracker
Stonechat
Willow ptarmigan
Winter wren

KENYA
African broadbill
African jacana
African palm swift
African paradise-flycatcher
African snipe
Bar-breasted mousebird
Barn swallow
Black-winged stilt
Buff-spotted flufftail
Cattle egret
Collared pratincole
Common bulbul
Common cuckoo
Common waxbill
Corncrake
Crab plovers
Egyptian vulture
Eurasian golden oriole

European bee-eater
European roller
European white stork
Golden-winged sunbird
Gray parrot
Gray wagtail
Gray woodpecker
Gray-crowned crane
Great blue turaco
Great cormorant
Great crested grebe
Greater flamingo
Greater painted snipe
Green woodhoopoe
Hammerhead
Helmeted guineafowl
Hoopoe
Northern wryneck
Osprey
Ostrich
Peregrine falcon
Red-billed oxpecker
Rock pigeon
Rosy-breasted longclaw
Ruddy turnstone
Sacred ibis
Secretary bird
Shoebill
Small buttonquail
Southern ground-hornbill
Southern red bishop
Spotted flycatcher
Square-tailed drongo
Stonechat
Village weaver
White-helmet shrike
Wilson's storm-petrel
Zitting cisticola

KUWAIT
Black-winged stilt
Cattle egret
Chaffinch
Collared pratincole
Crab plovers
Eurasian bittern

European roller
Gray wagtail
Great cormorant
Great crested grebe
Greater hoopoe-lark
House sparrow
Mallard
Northern lapwing
Nuthatch
Osprey
Peregrine falcon
Rock pigeon
Ruddy turnstone
Spotted flycatcher
Wilson's storm-petrel
Zitting cisticola

KYRGYZSTAN
Barn swallow
Chaffinch
Common cuckoo
Crag martin
Egyptian vulture
Eurasian bittern
Eurasian golden oriole
European roller
European starling
Gray wagtail
Great cormorant
Great crested grebe
Great tit
Hoopoe
House sparrow
Mallard
Northern raven
Pallas's sandgrouse
Peregrine falcon
Rock pigeon
Snow finch
Spotted flycatcher
Stonechat
Winter wren

LAOS
Asian fairy-bluebird
Australasian lark

Barn swallow
Baya weaver
Black bulbul
Black-and-red broadbill
Black-crowned barwing
Black-naped monarch
Black-winged stilt
Cattle egret
Common cuckoo
Common iora
Common myna
Coppersmith barbet
Crested tree swift
Dollarbird
Eurasian bittern
Fire-breasted flowerpecker
Gray nightjar
Gray wagtail
Great cormorant
Greater painted snipe
Greater racket-tailed drongo
Green magpie
Hoopoe
Northern wryneck
Orange-breasted trogon
Peregrine falcon
Pheasant-tailed jacana
Purple sunbird
Rock pigeon
Ruby-cheeked sunbird
Small buttonquail
Spotted munia
Stonechat
White-throated fantail
Zitting cisticola

LATVIA
Barn swallow
Black tern
Chaffinch
Common cuckoo
Common murre
Corncrake
Dunnock
Eurasian bittern
Eurasian dipper

Eurasian golden oriole
European roller
European starling
European white stork
Great cormorant
Great crested grebe
Great tit
Hoopoe
House sparrow
Mallard
Northern fulmar
Northern gannet
Northern lapwing
Northern raven
Northern wryneck
Nuthatch
Red crossbill
Rock pigeon
Spotted flycatcher
Spotted nutcracker
Willow ptarmigan
Winter wren

LEBANON
Black-winged stilt
Cattle egret
Collared pratincole
Common bulbul
Common cuckoo
Dunnock
Egyptian vulture
European bee-eater
European roller
Great cormorant
Greater flamingo
Hoopoe
Horned lark
House sparrow
Mallard
Northern gannet
Northern lapwing
Nuthatch
Peregrine falcon
Rock pigeon
Spotted flycatcher
Stonechat

Winter wren

LESOTHO
African jacana
African snipe
Barn swallow
Black-winged stilt
Blue bustard
Cattle egret
Common cuckoo
Common waxbill
Corncrake
European roller
European white stork
Great cormorant
Great crested grebe
Greater painted snipe
Green woodhoopoe
Hammerhead
Helmeted guineafowl
Hoopoe
House sparrow
Osprey
Peregrine falcon
Sacred ibis
Secretary bird
Small buttonquail
Southern red bishop
Spotted flycatcher
Stonechat
Village weaver
Zitting cisticola

LESSER ANTILLES
Barn owl
Belted kingfisher
Brown pelican
Cattle egret
Crested caracara
Greater flamingo
House sparrow
Killdeer
Magnificent frigatebird
Osprey
Peregrine falcon
Rock pigeon

Ruddy turnstone
White-tailed tropicbird
Wood stork

LIBERIA
African broadbill
African palm swift
African paradise-flycatcher
African pitta
Barn swallow
Black tern
Black-winged stilt
Buff-spotted flufftail
Cattle egret
Collared pratincole
Common bulbul
Common waxbill
Eurasian bittern
Gray parrot
Gray woodpecker
Great blue turaco
Hammerhead
Leaf-love
Lyre-tailed honeyguide
Northern wryneck
Osprey
Peregrine falcon
Ruddy turnstone
Sacred ibis
Small buttonquail
Spotted flycatcher
Village weaver
Wilson's storm-petrel

LIBYA
Barn swallow
Black-winged stilt
Common bulbul
Crag martin
Egyptian vulture
Eurasian bittern
Gray wagtail
Greater hoopoe-lark
House sparrow
Mallard
Northern gannet

Northern lapwing
Northern raven
Peregrine falcon
Rock pigeon
Ruddy turnstone
Stonechat
Winter wren

LIECHTENSTEIN
Barn swallow
Black tern
Chaffinch
Common cuckoo
Corncrake
Dunnock
Eurasian golden oriole
European roller
European starling
Gray wagtail
Great cormorant
Great crested grebe
Great tit
Hoopoe
House sparrow
Mallard
Mute swan
Northern lapwing
Northern raven
Northern wryneck
Nuthatch
Peregrine falcon
Red crossbill
Rock pigeon
Snow finch
Spotted flycatcher
Stonechat
Winter wren

LITHUANIA
Barn swallow
Black tern
Chaffinch
Common cuckoo
Common murre
Corncrake
Dunnock

Eurasian bittern
Eurasian dipper
Eurasian golden oriole
European roller
European starling
European white stork
Great cormorant
Great crested grebe
Great tit
Hoopoe
House sparrow
Mallard
Northern fulmar
Northern gannet
Northern lapwing
Northern raven
Northern wryneck
Nuthatch
Red crossbill
Rock pigeon
Spotted flycatcher
Spotted nutcracker
Winter wren

LUXEMBOURG
Barn swallow
Black tern
Chaffinch
Common cuckoo
Corncrake
Dunnock
Eurasian golden oriole
European roller
European starling
European white stork
Gray wagtail
Great cormorant
Great crested grebe
Great tit
Hoopoe
House sparrow
Mallard
Mute swan
Northern lapwing
Northern raven
Northern wryneck

Nuthatch
Peregrine falcon
Red crossbill
Rock pigeon
Spotted flycatcher
Stonechat
Winter wren

MACEDONIA
Barn swallow
Chaffinch
Common cuckoo
Corncrake
Crag martin
Dunnock
Egyptian vulture
Eurasian dipper
Eurasian golden oriole
European bee-eater
European roller
European starling
European white stork
Gray wagtail
Great cormorant
Great crested grebe
Great tit
Hoopoe
Horned lark
House sparrow
Mallard
Northern lapwing
Northern raven
Northern wryneck
Nuthatch
Peregrine falcon
Red crossbill
Rock pigeon
Snow bunting
Spotted flycatcher
Stonechat
Winter wren

MADAGASCAR
African palm swift
Black-winged stilt
Cattle egret

Common sunbird-asity
Crab plovers
Greater flamingo
Greater painted snipe
Hammerhead
Hoopoe
Peregrine falcon
Ruddy turnstone
Rufous vanga
Sacred ibis
Stonechat
White-breasted mesite
Wilson's storm-petrel

MALAWI
African broadbill
African jacana
African palm swift
African paradise-flycatcher
African pitta
African snipe
Bar-breasted mousebird
Barn swallow
Black-winged stilt
Buff-spotted flufftail
Cape batis
Cattle egret
Collared pratincole
Common bulbul
Common cuckoo
Common waxbill
Corncrake
Eurasian golden oriole
European bee-eater
European roller
European white stork
Gray go-away-bird
Gray-crowned crane
Great cormorant
Greater painted snipe
Green woodhoopoe
Hammerhead
Helmeted guineafowl
Hoopoe
House sparrow
Osprey

Peregrine falcon
Red-billed oxpecker
Rock pigeon
Sacred ibis
Secretary bird
Small buttonquail
Southern ground-hornbill
Southern red bishop
Spotted flycatcher
Square-tailed drongo
Stonechat
Village weaver
White-helmet shrike
Yellow-fronted tinkerbird
Zitting cisticola

MALAYSIA
Arctic warbler
Asian fairy-bluebird
Barn swallow
Barred eagle-owl
Baya weaver
Black-and-red broadbill
Black-naped monarch
Black-winged stilt
Common iora
Common myna
Coppersmith barbet
Dollarbird
Fiery minivet
Fire-breasted flowerpecker
Gray nightjar
Gray wagtail
Great cormorant
Greater painted snipe
Greater racket-tailed drongo
Green magpie
Helmeted hornbill
Hooded pitta
Malaysian honeyguide
Orange-breasted trogon
Osprey
Peregrine falcon
Pheasant-tailed jacana
Rock pigeon
Ruby-cheeked sunbird

Ruddy turnstone
Rufous-collared kingfisher
Spotted munia
White-throated fantail
Zitting cisticola

MALI
African jacana
African palm swift
African paradise-flycatcher
Barn swallow
Black-winged stilt
Cattle egret
Collared pratincole
Common bulbul
Egyptian vulture
Eurasian bittern
European bee-eater
European roller
European white stork
Gray wagtail
Gray woodpecker
Greater hoopoe-lark
Greater painted snipe
Green woodhoopoe
Hammerhead
Helmeted guineafowl
Hoopoe
Leaf-love
Northern wryneck
Osprey
Ostrich
Peregrine falcon
Rock pigeon
Rose-ringed parakeet
Sacred ibis
Secretary bird
Small buttonquail
Stonechat
Village weaver
White-helmet shrike
Yellow-fronted tinkerbird
Zitting cisticola

MAURITANIA
Barn swallow

Black-winged stilt
Cattle egret
Collared pratincole
Common bulbul
Crag martin
Egyptian vulture
Eurasian bittern
European roller
European white stork
Gray woodpecker
Greater flamingo
Greater hoopoe-lark
Greater painted snipe
Green woodhoopoe
Hammerhead
Helmeted guineafowl
Hoopoe
Magnificent frigatebird
Manx shearwater
Northern gannet
Osprey
Ostrich
Peregrine falcon
Rock pigeon
Rose-ringed parakeet
Ruddy turnstone
Secretary bird
Small buttonquail
Wilson's storm-petrel
Zitting cisticola

MAURITIUS
Dodo
Mauritius cuckoo-shrike

MEXICO
American anhinga
American avocet
American cliff swallow
American dipper
American goldfinch
American mourning dove
American robin
American white pelican
Anna's hummingbird
Baltimore oriole

Barn owl
Barn swallow
Barred antshrike
Belted kingfisher
Black rail
Black tern
Black-and-white warbler
Black-capped vireo
Black-winged stilt
Blue jay
Blue-black grassquit
Blue-crowned motmot
Blue-footed booby
Blue-gray gnatcatcher
Brown creeper
Brown pelican
Bushtit
Cactus wren
Canada goose
Cattle egret
Cedar waxwing
Common loon
Crested caracara
Eastern bluebird
Eastern phoebe
Eastern screech-owl
European starling
Gray catbird
Great blue heron
Great kiskadee
Greater roadrunner
Harris's hawk
Horned lark
House sparrow
House wren
Killdeer
King vulture
Limpkin
Loggerhead shrike
Long-billed curlew
Long-tailed manakin
Magnificent frigatebird
Mallard
Northern bobwhite quail
Northern gannet
Northern raven

Osprey
Peregrine falcon
Plain chachalaca
Red-throated loon
Red-winged blackbird
Resplendent quetzal
Rock pigeon
Roseate spoonbill
Rose-throated becard
Ruddy turnstone
Rufous-browed peppershrike
Rufous-tailed jacamar
Sandhill crane
Savanna sparrow
Scarlet macaw
Song sparrow
Sprague's pipit
Sungrebe
Verdin
Western grebe
Western scrub-jay
Whip-poor-will
White-necked puffbird
Wild turkey
Wilson's storm-petrel
Winter wren
Wood duck
Wood stork
Wrentit
Yellow-bellied sapsucker
Yellow-breasted chat

MOLDOVA
Barn swallow
Black tern
Chaffinch
Collared pratincole
Common cuckoo
Corncrake
Dunnock
Eurasian bittern
Eurasian golden oriole
European bee-eater
European roller
European starling
European white stork

Great cormorant
Great crested grebe
Great tit
Hoopoe
House sparrow
Mallard
Northern lapwing
Northern raven
Northern wryneck
Nuthatch
Peregrine falcon
Rock pigeon
Snow bunting
Spotted flycatcher
Stonechat
Winter wren

MONACO
Greater flamingo
Northern gannet

MONGOLIA
Barn swallow
Black tern
Black-winged stilt
Common cuckoo
Crag martin
Eurasian bittern
Gray wagtail
Great bustard
Great cormorant
Great crested grebe
Hoopoe
Horned lark
House sparrow
Mallard
Mute swan
Northern raven
Northern wryneck
Nuthatch
Pallas's sandgrouse
Peregrine falcon
Red crossbill
Rock pigeon
Snow bunting
Snow finch

Spotted flycatcher
Spotted nutcracker
Stonechat

MOROCCO
Barn swallow
Black-winged stilt
Cattle egret
Chaffinch
Collared pratincole
Common bulbul
Common cuckoo
Common murre
Corncrake
Crag martin
Dunnock
Egyptian vulture
Eurasian dipper
Eurasian golden oriole
European bee-eater
European roller
European starling
Gray wagtail
Great bustard
Great cormorant
Great crested grebe
Greater flamingo
Greater hoopoe-lark
Hoopoe
Horned lark
House sparrow
Magnificent frigatebird
Mallard
Manx shearwater
Northern gannet
Northern raven
Ostrich
Peregrine falcon
Rock pigeon
Ruddy turnstone
Small buttonquail
Spotted flycatcher
Stonechat
Wilson's storm-petrel
Winter wren
Zitting cisticola

MOZAMBIQUE

African broadbill
African jacana
African palm swift
African paradise-flycatcher
African pitta
African snipe
Bar-breasted mousebird
Barn swallow
Black-winged stilt
Buff-spotted flufftail
Cape batis
Cattle egret
Collared pratincole
Common bulbul
Common cuckoo
Common waxbill
Corncrake
Crab plovers
Eurasian golden oriole
European bee-eater
European roller
European white stork
Gray go-away-bird
Gray-crowned crane
Great cormorant
Greater painted snipe
Green woodhoopoe
Hammerhead
Helmeted guineafowl
Hoopoe
House sparrow
Osprey
Ostrich
Peregrine falcon
Rock pigeon
Rosy-breasted longclaw
Ruddy turnstone
Sacred ibis
Secretary bird
Small buttonquail
Southern ground-hornbill
Southern red bishop
Spotted flycatcher
Square-tailed drongo
Stonechat
Village weaver
White-helmet shrike
Wilson's storm-petrel
Yellow-fronted tinkerbird
Zitting cisticola

MYANMAR

Asian fairy-bluebird
Australasian lark
Barn swallow
Barred eagle-owl
Baya weaver
Black bulbul
Black-and-red broadbill
Black-naped monarch
Black-winged stilt
Cattle egret
Common cuckoo
Common iora
Common myna
Coppersmith barbet
Crested tree swift
Dollarbird
Fiery minivet
Fire-breasted flowerpecker
Gray nightjar
Gray wagtail
Great cormorant
Great crested grebe
Great tit
Greater painted snipe
Greater racket-tailed drongo
Green magpie
Helmeted hornbill
Hooded pitta
Hoopoe
House sparrow
Mallard
Northern wryneck
Orange-breasted trogon
Osprey
Peregrine falcon
Pheasant-tailed jacana
Purple sunbird
Rock pigeon
Rose-ringed parakeet
Ruby-cheeked sunbird
Ruddy turnstone
Rufous-collared kingfisher
Small buttonquail
Spotted munia
Stonechat
White-throated fantail
Winter wren
Zitting cisticola

NAMIBIA

African jacana
African palm swift
African paradise-flycatcher
Arctic skua
Barn swallow
Black tern
Black-winged stilt
Cattle egret
Common cuckoo
Common waxbill
Egyptian vulture
Eurasian golden oriole
European roller
European white stork
Gray go-away-bird
Great cormorant
Great crested grebe
Greater painted snipe
Green woodhoopoe
Hammerhead
Helmeted guineafowl
Hoopoe
House sparrow
Namaqua sandgrouse
Osprey
Ostrich
Peregrine falcon
Rock pigeon
Ruddy turnstone
Sacred ibis
Secretary bird
Small buttonquail
Southern ground-hornbill
Southern red bishop

Spotted flycatcher
White-helmet shrike
Wilson's storm-petrel
Yellow-fronted tinkerbird
Zitting cisticola

NEPAL
Asian fairy-bluebird
Barn swallow
Black-naped monarch
Cattle egret
Common cuckoo
Coppersmith barbet
Crested tree swift
Dollarbird
Egyptian vulture
Eurasian bittern
Eurasian golden oriole
European roller
European white stork
Fire-breasted flowerpecker
Gray nightjar
Gray wagtail
Great cormorant
Great crested grebe
Greater painted snipe
Hooded pitta
Hoopoe
House sparrow
Northern wryneck
Osprey
Peregrine falcon
Pheasant-tailed jacana
Purple sunbird
Rock pigeon
Rose-ringed parakeet
Ruby-cheeked sunbird
Satyr tragopan
Small buttonquail
Snow finch
Spotted munia
Spotted nutcracker
Stonechat
White-throated fantail
Winter wren

Zitting cisticola

NETHERLANDS
Barn swallow
Black tern
Chaffinch
Common cuckoo
Common murre
Corncrake
Dunnock
Eurasian golden oriole
European roller
European starling
European white stork
Great auk
Great cormorant
Great crested grebe
Great tit
House sparrow
Mallard
Manx shearwater
Mute swan
Northern fulmar
Northern gannet
Northern lapwing
Northern wryneck
Nuthatch
Peregrine falcon
Puffin
Red-throated loon
Rock pigeon
Ruddy turnstone
Spotted flycatcher
Stonechat
Winter wren

NEW CALEDONIA
Beach thick-knee
Black-winged stilt
House sparrow
Kagu
Osprey
Painted buttonquail
Peregrine falcon
Rainbow lorikeet

White-tailed tropicbird

NEW ZEALAND
Arctic skua
Black-winged stilt
Brown kiwi
Canada goose
Cattle egret
Chatham mollymawk
Common diving-petrel
Emperor penguin
European starling
Great cormorant
Great crested grebe
House sparrow
Kokako
Laughing kookaburra
Mallard
Mute swan
Rifleman
Rock pigeon
Ruddy turnstone
Variable oystercatcher
Wilson's storm-petrel
Yellowhead

NICARAGUA
American anhinga
American dipper
American mourning dove
Baltimore oriole
Barn owl
Barred antshrike
Belted kingfisher
Black tern
Black-and-white warbler
Black-winged stilt
Blue-black grassquit
Blue-crowned motmot
Blue-footed booby
Brown creeper
Brown pelican
Cattle egret
Cedar waxwing
Crested caracara

Gray catbird
Gray potoo
Great blue heron
Great kiskadee
Harris's hawk
House sparrow
Killdeer
King vulture
Limpkin
Long-tailed manakin
Magnificent frigatebird
Northern raven
Osprey
Peregrine falcon
Plain chachalaca
Resplendent quetzal
Rock pigeon
Roseate spoonbill
Rose-throated becard
Ruddy turnstone
Rufous-browed peppershrike
Rufous-tailed jacamar
Scarlet macaw
Sunbittern
Sungrebe
White-necked puffbird
Wood stork
Yellow-bellied sapsucker
Yellow-breasted chat

NIGER
African jacana
African palm swift
African paradise-flycatcher
Barn swallow
Black-winged stilt
Cattle egret
Collared pratincole
Common bulbul
Egyptian vulture
Eurasian bittern
European white stork
Gray woodpecker
Greater hoopoe-lark
Greater painted snipe
Green woodhoopoe

Hammerhead
Helmeted guineafowl
Hoopoe
Northern wryneck
Osprey
Ostrich
Peregrine falcon
Rock pigeon
Rose-ringed parakeet
Sacred ibis
Secretary bird
Small buttonquail
Village weaver
Yellow-fronted tinkerbird
Zitting cisticola

NIGERIA
African jacana
African palm swift
African paradise-flycatcher
African pitta
Bar-breasted mousebird
Barn swallow
Black tern
Black-winged stilt
Buff-spotted flufftail
Cattle egret
Collared pratincole
Common bulbul
Common waxbill
Eurasian bittern
European roller
European white stork
Gray parrot
Gray woodpecker
Gray-necked picathartes
Great blue turaco
Greater painted snipe
Green woodhoopoe
Hammerhead
Helmeted guineafowl
Hoopoe
Leaf-love
Lyre-tailed honeyguide
Northern wryneck
Osprey

Peregrine falcon
Rose-ringed parakeet
Ruddy turnstone
Sacred ibis
Secretary bird
Small buttonquail
Spotted flycatcher
Square-tailed drongo
White-helmet shrike
Wilson's storm-petrel
Yellow-fronted tinkerbird
Zitting cisticola

NORTH KOREA
Arctic warbler
Barn swallow
Common cuckoo
Common murre
Dollarbird
Eurasian bittern
Gray nightjar
Gray wagtail
Great bustard
Great cormorant
Great tit
Greater painted snipe
Hoopoe
Mute swan
Nuthatch
Red crossbill
Red-crowned crane
Red-throated loon
Rock pigeon
Saunder's gull
Stonechat
Winter wren

NORWAY
Arctic skua
Arctic warbler
Barn swallow
Chaffinch
Common cuckoo
Common loon
Common murre

Corncrake
Dunnock
Eurasian dipper
European starling
Gray wagtail
Great auk
Great cormorant
Great crested grebe
Great tit
Gyrfalcon
Horned lark
House sparrow
King eider
Manx shearwater
Northern fulmar
Northern gannet
Northern lapwing
Northern raven
Northern wryneck
Nuthatch
Osprey
Peregrine falcon
Puffin
Red crossbill
Red-throated loon
Rock pigeon
Ruddy turnstone
Snow bunting
Snowy owl
Spotted flycatcher
Spotted nutcracker
Willow ptarmigan
Winter wren

OMAN
Crab plovers
Egyptian vulture
European roller
Gray wagtail
Greater hoopoe-lark
Hoopoe
House sparrow
Osprey
Peregrine falcon
Purple sunbird
Rock pigeon

Ruddy turnstone
Wilson's storm-petrel

PAKISTAN
Barn swallow
Baya weaver
Black bulbul
Black-winged stilt
Cattle egret
Chaffinch
Collared pratincole
Common cuckoo
Common myna
Coppersmith barbet
Crab plovers
Crag martin
Egyptian vulture
Eurasian bittern
Eurasian golden oriole
European bee-eater
European roller
European starling
European white stork
Gray hypocolius
Gray wagtail
Great cormorant
Great crested grebe
Great tit
Greater flamingo
Greater hoopoe-lark
Greater painted snipe
Hoopoe
House sparrow
Mallard
Mute swan
Northern lapwing
Northern raven
Osprey
Peregrine falcon
Pheasant-tailed jacana
Purple sunbird
Rock pigeon
Rose-ringed parakeet
Ruddy turnstone
Small buttonquail
Snow finch

Spotted flycatcher
Spotted nutcracker
Stonechat
White-throated fantail
Wilson's storm-petrel

PANAMA
American anhinga
American dipper
American mourning dove
Baltimore oriole
Barn owl
Barn swallow
Barred antshrike
Belted kingfisher
Black guan
Black rail
Black tern
Black-and-white warbler
Black-capped donacobius
Black-winged stilt
Blue-black grassquit
Blue-crowned motmot
Blue-footed booby
Brown pelican
Cattle egret
Crested caracara
Gray catbird
Gray potoo
Great blue heron
Great kiskadee
Hairy hermit
Harris's hawk
Highland tinamou
House sparrow
Killdeer
King vulture
Limpkin
Magnificent frigatebird
Oilbird
Osprey
Peregrine falcon
Red-billed scythebill
Resplendent quetzal
Rock pigeon
Roseate spoonbill

Rose-throated becard
Ruddy turnstone
Rufous-browed peppershrike
Rufous-tailed jacamar
Scarlet macaw
Sharpbill
Sunbittern
Sungrebe
White-necked puffbird
Wood stork
Yellow-bellied sapsucker

PAPUA NEW GUINEA
Australasian figbird
Australasian lark
Australian magpie-lark
Australian pratincole
Barn swallow
Beach thick-knee
Black-winged stilt
Cattle egret
Dollarbird
Eclectus parrot
Fan-tailed berrypecker
Feline owlet-nightjar
Golden whistler
Gray wagtail
Gray-crowned babbler
Hooded pitta
Jacky winter
King bird of paradise
Osprey
Peregrine falcon
Rainbow lorikeet
Ribbon-tailed astrapia
Ruddy turnstone
Southern cassowary
Variable pitohui
White-tailed tropicbird
Willie wagtail
Wilson's storm-petrel
Zitting cisticola

PARAGUAY
American anhinga
American cliff swallow

Barn owl
Barn swallow
Barred antshrike
Baywing
Black-capped donacobius
Black-winged stilt
Blue-black grassquit
Blue-crowned motmot
Cattle egret
Crested caracara
Gray potoo
Great kiskadee
Greater thornbird
Hairy hermit
Harris's hawk
House sparrow
King vulture
Limpkin
Peregrine falcon
Red-billed scythebill
Red-legged seriema
Roseate spoonbill
Rufous hornero
Rufous-browed peppershrike
Rufous-tailed jacamar
Sharpbill
Sungrebe
Toco toucan
Wood stork

PERU
Amazonian umbrellabird
American anhinga
Arctic skua
Barn owl
Barn swallow
Barred antshrike
Black rail
Black tern
Black-capped donacobius
Black-winged stilt
Blue-black grassquit
Blue-crowned motmot
Blue-footed booby
Brown pelican
Cattle egret

Chimney swift
Common trumpeter
Coppery-chested jacamar
Crested caracara
Gray antbird
Gray potoo
Gray-breasted mountain-
  toucan
Great kiskadee
Hairy hermit
Harris's hawk
Highland tinamou
Hoatzin
Horned screamer
House sparrow
Killdeer
King vulture
Lesser rhea
Limpkin
Magellanic penguin
Oilbird
Osprey
Peregrine falcon
Peruvian plantcutter
Red-billed scythebill
Rock pigeon
Roseate spoonbill
Ruddy turnstone
Rufous-bellied seedsnipe
Rufous-browed peppershrike
Rufous-capped nunlet
Rufous-tailed jacamar
Rusty-belted tapaculo
Scarlet macaw
Sharpbill
Spangled cotinga
Sparkling violet-ear
Sunbittern
Sungrebe
Wattled curassow
White-necked puffbird
Wilson's storm-petrel
Wire-tailed manakin
Wood stork

PHILIPPINES
Arctic warbler

Asian fairy-bluebird
Australasian lark
Barn swallow
Beach thick-knee
Black-naped monarch
Black-winged stilt
Cattle egret
Coppersmith barbet
Dollarbird
Fiery minivet
Fire-breasted flowerpecker
Gray nightjar
Gray wagtail
Greater painted snipe
Hooded pitta
Japanese white-eye
Little slaty flycatcher
Luzon bleeding heart
Osprey
Peregrine falcon
Pheasant-tailed jacana
Rock pigeon
Ruddy turnstone
Small buttonquail
Spotted munia
Stripe-headed rhabdornis
Zitting cisticola

POLAND
Barn swallow
Black tern
Chaffinch
Common cuckoo
Common murre
Corncrake
Dunnock
Eurasian bittern
Eurasian dipper
Eurasian golden oriole
European roller
European starling
European white stork
Gray wagtail
Great cormorant
Great crested grebe
Great tit

Hoopoe
House sparrow
Mallard
Northern fulmar
Northern gannet
Northern lapwing
Northern raven
Northern wryneck
Nuthatch
Osprey
Peregrine falcon
Puffin
Red crossbill
Rock pigeon
Snow bunting
Snow finch
Spotted flycatcher
Spotted nutcracker
Winter wren

PORTUGAL
Barn swallow
Black-winged stilt
Chaffinch
Collared pratincole
Common cuckoo
Common loon
Common murre
Crag martin
Dunnock
Egyptian vulture
Eurasian dipper
Eurasian golden oriole
European bee-eater
European roller
European white stork
Gray wagtail
Great bustard
Great cormorant
Great crested grebe
Great tit
Hoopoe
House sparrow
Mallard
Manx shearwater
Northern gannet

Northern lapwing
Northern raven
Northern wryneck
Nuthatch
Osprey
Peregrine falcon
Red crossbill
Red-throated loon
Rock pigeon
Ruddy turnstone
Spotted flycatcher
Stonechat
Wilson's storm-petrel
Winter wren
Zitting cisticola

PUERTO RICO
American mourning dove
Barn owl
Belted kingfisher
Brown pelican
Cattle egret
Crested caracara
European starling
Greater flamingo
House sparrow
Killdeer
Magnificent frigatebird
Osprey
Peregrine falcon
Rock pigeon
Ruddy turnstone
White-tailed tropicbird
Wood stork
Yellow-bellied sapsucker

QATAR
European roller
Greater hoopoe-lark
Hoopoe
House sparrow
Stonechat

ROMANIA
Barn swallow

Black tern
Black-winged stilt
Chaffinch
Collared pratincole
Common cuckoo
Corncrake
Dunnock
Egyptian vulture
Eurasian bittern
Eurasian dipper
Eurasian golden oriole
European bee-eater
European roller
European starling
European white stork
Gray wagtail
Great cormorant
Great crested grebe
Great tit
Hoopoe
House sparrow
Mallard
Northern lapwing
Northern raven
Northern wryneck
Nuthatch
Peregrine falcon
Red crossbill
Red-throated loon
Rock pigeon
Snow bunting
Spotted flycatcher
Stonechat
Winter wren

RUSSIA
Arctic skua
Arctic warbler
Barn swallow
Black tern
Black-winged stilt
Cattle egret
Chaffinch
Collared pratincole
Common cuckoo

Common murre
Corncrake
Crag martin
Dollarbird
Dunnock
Eurasian bittern
Eurasian dipper
Eurasian golden oriole
European bee-eater
European starling
European white stork
Gray nightjar
Gray wagtail
Great bustard
Great cormorant
Great crested grebe
Great tit
Greater painted snipe
Gyrfalcon
Hoopoe
Horned lark
House sparrow
King eider
Mallard
Mute swan
Northern fulmar
Northern gannet
Northern lapwing
Northern raven
Northern wryneck
Nuthatch
Osprey
Pallas's sandgrouse
Peregrine falcon
Puffin
Red crossbill
Red-crowned crane
Red-throated loon
Rock pigeon
Ruddy turnstone
Sandhill crane
Snow bunting
Snow finch
Snowy owl
Spotted flycatcher
Spotted nutcracker

Stonechat
Willow ptarmigan
Winter wren

RWANDA
African jacana
African palm swift
African paradise-flycatcher
African pitta
African snipe
Bar-breasted mousebird
Barn swallow
Black-winged stilt
Buff-spotted flufftail
Cattle egret
Collared pratincole
Common bulbul
Common cuckoo
Common waxbill
Corncrake
Eurasian golden oriole
European bee-eater
European roller
European white stork
Gray parrot
Gray woodpecker
Gray-crowned crane
Great blue turaco
Great cormorant
Great crested grebe
Green woodhoopoe
Hammerhead
Helmeted guineafowl
Hoopoe
Osprey
Ostrich
Peregrine falcon
Red-billed oxpecker
Sacred ibis
Shoebill
Small buttonquail
Southern red bishop
Spotted flycatcher
Stonechat
Village weaver

Yellow-fronted tinkerbird
Zitting cisticola

SÃO TOMÉ AND PRÍNCIPE
White-tailed tropicbird

SAUDI ARABIA
African palm swift
Black-winged stilt
Cattle egret
Crab plovers
Crag martin
Egyptian vulture
European roller
Gray hypocolius
Gray wagtail
Great cormorant
Greater hoopoe-lark
Hammerhead
Hoopoe
House sparrow
Mallard
Northern lapwing
Osprey
Peregrine falcon
Rock pigeon
Ruddy turnstone
Stonechat
Wilson's storm-petrel

SENEGAL
African palm swift
African paradise-flycatcher
Black tern
Black-winged stilt
Cattle egret
Collared pratincole
Common bulbul
Common waxbill
Egyptian vulture
Eurasian bittern
European roller
European white stork
Gray wagtail

Gray woodpecker
Greater flamingo
Greater hoopoe-lark
Greater painted snipe
Green woodhoopoe
Hammerhead
Helmeted guineafowl
Hoopoe
Leaf-love
Magnificent frigatebird
Northern wryneck
Osprey
Peregrine falcon
Rose-ringed parakeet
Ruddy turnstone
Sacred ibis
Secretary bird
Small buttonquail
Village weaver
White-helmet shrike
Wilson's storm-petrel
Yellow-fronted tinkerbird
Zitting cisticola

SEYCHELLES
White-tailed tropicbird

SIERRA LEONE
African broadbill
African palm swift
African paradise-flycatcher
African pitta
Barn swallow
Black tern
Black-winged stilt
Buff-spotted flufftail
Cattle egret
Collared pratincole
Common bulbul
Common waxbill
Eurasian bittern
Gray parrot
Gray woodpecker
Great blue turaco
Hammerhead
Leaf-love

Lyre-tailed honeyguide
Northern wryneck
Osprey
Peregrine falcon
Rose-ringed parakeet
Ruddy turnstone
Sacred ibis
Small buttonquail
Spotted flycatcher
Square-tailed drongo
Village weaver
Wilson's storm-petrel

SINGAPORE
Baya weaver

SLOVAKIA
Barn swallow
Black tern
Chaffinch
Collared pratincole
Common cuckoo
Corncrake
Dunnock
Eurasian golden oriole
European bee-eater
European roller
European starling
European white stork
Gray wagtail
Great cormorant
Great crested grebe
Great tit
Hoopoe
House sparrow
Mallard
Northern lapwing
Northern raven
Northern wryneck
Nuthatch
Peregrine falcon
Red crossbill
Rock pigeon
Snow bunting
Snow finch
Spotted flycatcher

Stonechat
Winter wren

SLOVENIA
Barn swallow
Black tern
Chaffinch
Collared pratincole
Common cuckoo
Corncrake
Dunnock
Eurasian dipper
Eurasian golden oriole
European bee-eater
European roller
European starling
Gray wagtail
Great cormorant
Great crested grebe
Great tit
Hoopoe
House sparrow
Mallard
Northern lapwing
Northern raven
Northern wryneck
Nuthatch
Peregrine falcon
Rock pigeon
Snow bunting
Snow finch
Spotted flycatcher
Stonechat
Winter wren
Zitting cisticola

SOMALIA
African jacana
African palm swift
African paradise-flycatcher
Bar-breasted mousebird
Barn swallow
Black-winged stilt
Cattle egret
Collared pratincole
Common bulbul

Corncrake
Crab plovers
Egyptian vulture
European roller
European white stork
Gray wagtail
Great cormorant
Greater hoopoe-lark
Green woodhoopoe
Hammerhead
Hoopoe
Ostrich
Peregrine falcon
Red-billed oxpecker
Rose-ringed parakeet
Ruddy turnstone
Sacred ibis
Small buttonquail
Spotted flycatcher
Square-tailed drongo
Stonechat
White-helmet shrike
Wilson's storm-petrel

SOUTH AFRICA
African jacana
African palm swift
African paradise-flycatcher
African snipe
Arctic skua
Bar-breasted mousebird
Barn swallow
Black tern
Black-winged stilt
Blue bustard
Buff-spotted flufftail
Cape batis
Cape sugarbird
Cattle egret
Collared pratincole
Common bulbul
Common cuckoo
Common waxbill
Corncrake
Crab plovers
Eurasian golden oriole

European bee-eater
European roller
European starling
European white stork
Gray-crowned crane
Great cormorant
Great crested grebe
Greater flamingo
Greater painted snipe
Green woodhoopoe
Hammerhead
Helmeted guineafowl
Hoopoe
House sparrow
Manx shearwater
Mute swan
Namaqua sandgrouse
Osprey
Ostrich
Peregrine falcon
Red-billed oxpecker
Rock pigeon
Rosy-breasted longclaw
Ruddy turnstone
Sacred ibis
Secretary bird
Small buttonquail
Southern ground-hornbill
Southern red bishop
Spotted flycatcher
Square-tailed drongo
Stonechat
Village weaver
White-helmet shrike
Wilson's storm-petrel
Yellow-fronted tinkerbird
Zitting cisticola

SOUTH KOREA
Arctic warbler
Barn swallow
Cattle egret
Common cuckoo
Common murre
Dollarbird
Eurasian bittern

Gray nightjar
Gray wagtail
Great cormorant
Great tit
Greater painted snipe
Japanese white-eye
Mallard
Mute swan
Northern lapwing
Nuthatch
Red crossbill
Red-throated loon
Rock pigeon
Saunder's gull
Stonechat
Winter wren

SPAIN
Barn swallow
Black-winged stilt
Chaffinch
Collared pratincole
Common cuckoo
Common loon
Common murre
Corncrake
Crag martin
Dunnock
Egyptian vulture
Eurasian bittern
Eurasian dipper
Eurasian golden oriole
European bee-eater
European roller
European white stork
Gray wagtail
Great auk
Great bustard
Great cormorant
Great crested grebe
Great tit
Greater flamingo
Hoopoe
House sparrow
Mallard
Manx shearwater

Northern fulmar
Northern gannet
Northern lapwing
Northern raven
Northern wryneck
Nuthatch
Peregrine falcon
Red crossbill
Red-throated loon
Rock pigeon
Ruddy turnstone
Small buttonquail
Snow finch
Spotted flycatcher
Stonechat
Wilson's storm-petrel
Winter wren
Zitting cisticola

SRI LANKA
Baya weaver
Black bulbul
Common iora
Common myna
Coppersmith barbet
Crested tree swift
Dollarbird
Eurasian golden oriole
Gray nightjar
Great tit
Greater racket-tailed drongo
House sparrow
Pheasant-tailed jacana
Purple sunbird
Rose-ringed parakeet
Spotted munia
White-throated fantail
Wilson's storm-petrel

SUDAN
African jacana
African palm swift
African paradise-flycatcher
Bar-breasted mousebird
Barn swallow

Black tern
Black-winged stilt
Buff-spotted flufftail
Cattle egret
Collared pratincole
Common bulbul
Common waxbill
Corncrake
Crab plovers
Crag martin
Egyptian vulture
Eurasian bittern
European roller
European white stork
Gray wagtail
Gray woodpecker
Great blue turaco
Great cormorant
Greater flamingo
Greater hoopoe-lark
Greater painted snipe
Green woodhoopoe
Hammerhead
Helmeted guineafowl
Hoopoe
Leaf-love
Northern wryneck
Osprey
Ostrich
Peregrine falcon
Red-billed oxpecker
Rock pigeon
Rose-ringed parakeet
Ruddy turnstone
Sacred ibis
Secretary bird
Shoebill
Small buttonquail
Spotted flycatcher
Square-tailed drongo
Stonechat
Village weaver
White-helmet shrike
Wilson's storm-petrel
Yellow-fronted tinkerbird
Zitting cisticola

SURINAME

American anhinga
Barn owl
Barn swallow
Barred antshrike
Black tern
Black-capped donacobius
Black-winged stilt
Blue-black grassquit
Blue-crowned motmot
Brown pelican
Cattle egret
Common trumpeter
Crested caracara
Gray antbird
Gray potoo
Great kiskadee
Guianan cock-of-the-rock
Hairy hermit
Hoatzin
King vulture
Limpkin
Magnificent frigatebird
Osprey
Peregrine falcon
Roseate spoonbill
Ruddy turnstone
Rufous-browed peppershrike
Scarlet macaw
Sharpbill
Spangled cotinga
Sunbittern
Sungrebe
White-necked puffbird
Wilson's storm-petrel
Wood stork

SWAZILAND

African jacana
African palm swift
African paradise-flycatcher
African snipe
Barn swallow
Black-winged stilt
Buff-spotted flufftail
Cape batis

Cattle egret
Collared pratincole
Common bulbul
Common cuckoo
Common waxbill
Corncrake
European bee-eater
European roller
European white stork
Great cormorant
Greater painted snipe
Green woodhoopoe
Hammerhead
Helmeted guineafowl
Hoopoe
House sparrow
Osprey
Peregrine falcon
Sacred ibis
Secretary bird
Small buttonquail
Southern ground-hornbill
Southern red bishop
Spotted flycatcher
Stonechat
Village weaver
White-helmet shrike
Zitting cisticola

SWEDEN

Barn swallow
Chaffinch
Common cuckoo
Common murre
Corncrake
Dunnock
Eurasian bittern
Eurasian dipper
European roller
European starling
Gray wagtail
Great auk
Great cormorant
Great crested grebe
Great tit
Gyrfalcon

Hoopoe
Horned lark
House sparrow
Mute swan
Northern fulmar
Northern gannet
Northern lapwing
Northern raven
Northern wryneck
Nuthatch
Osprey
Peregrine falcon
Puffin
Red crossbill
Red-throated loon
Rock pigeon
Ruddy turnstone
Snow bunting
Spotted flycatcher
Spotted nutcracker
Willow ptarmigan
Winter wren

SWITZERLAND

Barn swallow
Black tern
Chaffinch
Common cuckoo
Corncrake
Dunnock
Eurasian dipper
Eurasian golden oriole
European roller
European starling
European white stork
Gray wagtail
Great cormorant
Great crested grebe
Great tit
Hoopoe
House sparrow
Mallard
Mute swan
Northern lapwing
Northern raven
Northern wryneck

Nuthatch
Peregrine falcon
Red crossbill
Rock pigeon
Snow finch
Spotted flycatcher
Spotted nutcracker
Stonechat
Winter wren

SYRIA
Black-winged stilt
Cattle egret
Chaffinch
Collared pratincole
Common bulbul
Common cuckoo
Corncrake
Crag martin
Dunnock
Egyptian vulture
European bee-eater
European roller
European starling
Great bustard
Great cormorant
Greater flamingo
Hoopoe
House sparrow
Mallard
Northern gannet
Northern lapwing
Nuthatch
Peregrine falcon
Red crossbill
Rock pigeon
Spotted flycatcher
Stonechat
Winter wren

TAJIKISTAN
Barn swallow
Chaffinch
Common cuckoo
Crag martin
Egyptian vulture

Eurasian golden oriole
European roller
European starling
Great bustard
Great cormorant
Great crested grebe
Great tit
Hoopoe
House sparrow
Mallard
Northern raven
Peregrine falcon
Rock pigeon
Snow finch
Spotted flycatcher
Stonechat
Winter wren

TANZANIA
African broadbill
African jacana
African palm swift
African paradise-flycatcher
African pitta
African snipe
Bar-breasted mousebird
Barn swallow
Black-winged stilt
Buff-spotted flufftail
Cattle egret
Collared pratincole
Common bulbul
Common waxbill
Corncrake
Crab plovers
Eurasian golden oriole
European bee-eater
European roller
European white stork
Golden-winged sunbird
Gray go-away-bird
Gray wagtail
Gray woodpecker
Great cormorant
Great crested grebe
Greater flamingo

Greater painted snipe
Green woodhoopoe
Hammerhead
Helmeted guineafowl
Hoopoe
House sparrow
Leaf-love
Osprey
Ostrich
Peregrine falcon
Red-billed oxpecker
Rock pigeon
Rosy-breasted longclaw
Ruddy turnstone
Sacred ibis
Secretary bird
Shoebill
Small buttonquail
Southern ground-hornbill
Southern red bishop
Spotted flycatcher
Square-tailed drongo
Stonechat
Village weaver
White-helmet shrike
Wilson's storm-petrel
Yellow-fronted tinkerbird
Zitting cisticola

THAILAND
Arctic warbler
Asian fairy-bluebird
Australasian lark
Barn swallow
Barred eagle-owl
Baya weaver
Black bulbul
Black-and-red broadbill
Black-naped monarch
Black-winged stilt
Cattle egret
Common cuckoo
Common iora
Common myna
Coppersmith barbet
Crested tree swift

Dollarbird
Fiery minivet
Fire-breasted flowerpecker
Gray nightjar
Gray wagtail
Great cormorant
Greater painted snipe
Greater racket-tailed drongo
Green magpie
Helmeted hornbill
Hooded pitta
Hoopoe
Malaysian honeyguide
Northern lapwing
Northern wryneck
Orange-breasted trogon
Osprey
Peregrine falcon
Pheasant-tailed jacana
Purple sunbird
Rock pigeon
Ruby-cheeked sunbird
Ruddy turnstone
Rufous-collared kingfisher
Small buttonquail
Spotted munia
Stonechat
White-throated fantail
Zitting cisticola

TOGO
African jacana
African palm swift
African paradise-flycatcher
Barn swallow
Black tern
Black-winged stilt
Cattle egret
Collared pratincole
Common bulbul
Eurasian bittern
European bee-eater
European roller
Gray parrot
Gray woodpecker
Great blue turaco

Greater painted snipe
Green woodhoopoe
Hammerhead
Helmeted guineafowl
Hoopoe
Leaf-love
Northern wryneck
Osprey
Peregrine falcon
Rose-ringed parakeet
Ruddy turnstone
Sacred ibis
Secretary bird
Small buttonquail
Spotted flycatcher
Square-tailed drongo
Village weaver
White-helmet shrike
Wilson's storm-petrel
Yellow-fronted tinkerbird
Zitting cisticola

TRINIDAD AND TOBAGO
Blue-crowned motmot
Gray potoo
Hairy hermit
Oilbird
Rufous-tailed jacamar

TUNISIA
Barn swallow
Black-winged stilt
Collared pratincole
Common bulbul
Corncrake
Crag martin
Dunnock
Egyptian vulture
Eurasian bittern
European bee-eater
European roller
European starling
Gray wagtail
Great cormorant
Great crested grebe

Greater flamingo
Greater hoopoe-lark
Hoopoe
House sparrow
Northern gannet
Northern lapwing
Northern raven
Northern wryneck
Peregrine falcon
Rock pigeon
Ruddy turnstone
Small buttonquail
Spotted flycatcher
Stonechat
Winter wren
Zitting cisticola

TURKEY
Barn swallow
Black tern
Cattle egret
Chaffinch
Collared pratincole
Common bulbul
Common cuckoo
Corncrake
Crag martin
Dunnock
Egyptian vulture
Eurasian bittern
Eurasian dipper
Eurasian golden oriole
European bee-eater
European roller
European starling
Gray wagtail
Great bustard
Great cormorant
Great crested grebe
Great tit
Greater flamingo
Hoopoe
Horned lark
House sparrow
Mallard
Mute swan

Northern gannet
Northern lapwing
Northern raven
Northern wryneck
Nuthatch
Peregrine falcon
Red crossbill
Red-throated loon
Rock pigeon
Snow finch
Spotted flycatcher
Stonechat
Winter wren
Zitting cisticola

TURKMENISTAN
Barn swallow
Black-winged stilt
Cattle egret
Chaffinch
Collared pratincole
Common cuckoo
Common myna
Crag martin
Egyptian vulture
Eurasian bittern
Eurasian golden oriole
European bee-eater
European roller
European starling
Gray hypocolius
Great cormorant
Great crested grebe
Great tit
Hoopoe
Horned lark
House sparrow
Mallard
Northern lapwing
Northern raven
Nuthatch
Peregrine falcon
Red-throated loon
Rock pigeon
Spotted flycatcher

Winter wren

UGANDA
African broadbill
African jacana
African palm swift
African paradise-flycatcher
African pitta
African snipe
Bar-breasted mousebird
Barn swallow
Black-winged stilt
Buff-spotted flufftail
Cattle egret
Collared pratincole
Common bulbul
Common cuckoo
Common waxbill
Corncrake
Egyptian vulture
Eurasian golden oriole
European roller
European white stork
Golden-winged sunbird
Gray parrot
Gray woodpecker
Gray-crowned crane
Great blue turaco
Great cormorant
Great crested grebe
Greater painted snipe
Green woodhoopoe
Hammerhead
Helmeted guineafowl
Hoopoe
Leaf-love
Northern wryneck
Osprey
Ostrich
Peregrine falcon
Red-billed oxpecker
Rose-ringed parakeet
Sacred ibis
Secretary bird
Shoebill

Small buttonquail
Southern red bishop
Spotted flycatcher
Village weaver
White-helmet shrike
Yellow-fronted tinkerbird
Zitting cisticola

UKRAINE
Barn swallow
Black tern
Black-winged stilt
Chaffinch
Collared pratincole
Common cuckoo
Corncrake
Dunnock
Eurasian bittern
Eurasian golden oriole
European bee-eater
European roller
European starling
European white stork
Gray wagtail
Great bustard
Great cormorant
Great crested grebe
Great tit
Hoopoe
Horned lark
House sparrow
Mallard
Mute swan
Northern lapwing
Northern raven
Northern wryneck
Nuthatch
Osprey
Peregrine falcon
Red crossbill
Red-throated loon
Rock pigeon
Snow bunting
Spotted flycatcher
Spotted nutcracker

Stonechat
Winter wren

UNITED ARAB EMIRATES

Crab plovers
Egyptian vulture
European roller
Greater hoopoe-lark
Hoopoe
House sparrow
Northern lapwing
Osprey
Purple sunbird
Rock pigeon
Ruddy turnstone
Stonechat
Wilson's storm-petrel

UNITED KINGDOM

Barn owl
Barn swallow
Canada goose
Chaffinch
Common cuckoo
Common loon
Common murre
Corncrake
Dunnock
Eurasian bittern
Eurasian dipper
Eurasian golden oriole
European roller
European starling
Gray wagtail
Great auk
Great cormorant
Great crested grebe
Great tit
House sparrow
Mallard
Manx shearwater
Mute swan
Northern gannet
Northern lapwing

Northern raven
Northern wryneck
Nuthatch
Osprey
Peregrine falcon
Puffin
Red crossbill
Red-throated loon
Rock pigeon
Ruddy turnstone
Snow bunting
Spotted flycatcher
Stonechat
Willow ptarmigan
Winter wren

UNITED STATES

American anhinga
American avocet
American cliff swallow
American dipper
American goldfinch
American mourning dove
American robin
American white pelican
Anna's hummingbird
Apapane
Arctic skua
Arctic warbler
Baltimore oriole
Barn owl
Barn swallow
Belted kingfisher
Bishop's oo
Black rail
Black tern
Black-and-white warbler
Black-capped chickadee
Black-capped vireo
Black-winged stilt
Blue jay
Blue-gray gnatcatcher
Brown creeper
Brown pelican
Bushtit

Cactus wren
California condor
Canada goose
Cattle egret
Cedar waxwing
Chimney swift
Common loon
Common murre
Crested caracara
Eastern bluebird
Eastern phoebe
Eastern screech-owl
European starling
Gray catbird
Great auk
Great blue heron
Great cormorant
Great kiskadee
Greater roadrunner
Gyrfalcon
Harris's hawk
Hawaiian honeycreepers
Horned lark
House sparrow
House wren
Ivory-billed woodpecker
Killdeer
King eider
Kirtland's warbler
Laysan albatross
Laysan finch
Limpkin
Loggerhead shrike
Long-billed curlew
Magnificent frigatebird
Mallard
Manx shearwater
Mute swan
Northern bobwhite quail
Northern fulmar
Northern gannet
Northern raven
Osprey
Peregrine falcon
Plain chachalaca
Puffin

Red crossbill
Red-breasted nuthatch
Red-cockaded woodpecker
Red-throated loon
Red-winged blackbird
Rock pigeon
Roseate spoonbill
Rose-throated becard
Ruddy turnstone
Sandhill crane
Savanna sparrow
Snow bunting
Song sparrow
Sprague's pipit
Verdin
Western grebe
Western scrub-jay
Whip-poor-will
White-tailed tropicbird
Wild turkey
Willow ptarmigan
Wilson's storm-petrel
Winter wren
Wood duck
Wood stork
Wrentit
Yellow-bellied sapsucker
Yellow-breasted chat

URUGUAY
American anhinga
American cliff swallow
Barn owl
Baywing
Black-winged stilt
Cattle egret
Crested caracara
Gray potoo
Great kiskadee
Greater thornbird
Harris's hawk
House sparrow
King vulture
Limpkin
Magellanic penguin
Manx shearwater

Peregrine falcon
Red-legged seriema
Rock pigeon
Roseate spoonbill
Ruddy turnstone
Rufous hornero
Wilson's storm-petrel
Wood stork

UZBEKISTAN
Barn swallow
Black-winged stilt
Chaffinch
Collared pratincole
Common cuckoo
Common myna
Crag martin
Egyptian vulture
Eurasian bittern
Eurasian dipper
Eurasian golden oriole
European bee-eater
European roller
European starling
Great bustard
Great cormorant
Great crested grebe
Great tit
Hoopoe
Horned lark
House sparrow
Mallard
Northern raven
Pallas's sandgrouse
Peregrine falcon
Rock pigeon

VENEZUELA
Amazonian umbrellabird
American anhinga
Baltimore oriole
Barn owl
Barn swallow
Barred antshrike
Belted kingfisher
Black tern

Black-and-white warbler
Black-capped donacobius
Black-winged stilt
Blue-black grassquit
Blue-crowned motmot
Brown pelican
Cattle egret
Common trumpeter
Crested caracara
Gray antbird
Gray potoo
Great kiskadee
Greater flamingo
Guianan cock-of-the-rock
Hairy hermit
Harris's hawk
Highland tinamou
Hoatzin
Horned screamer
King vulture
Limpkin
Magnificent frigatebird
Oilbird
Osprey
Peregrine falcon
Red-billed scythebill
Roseate spoonbill
Ruddy turnstone
Rufous-browed peppershrike
Rufous-tailed jacamar
Scarlet macaw
Sharpbill
Spangled cotinga
Sparkling violet-ear
Sunbittern
Sungrebe
White-necked puffbird
Wilson's storm-petrel
Wire-tailed manakin
Wood stork

VIETNAM
Arctic warbler
Asian fairy-bluebird
Australasian lark
Barn swallow

Baya weaver
Black bulbul
Black-and-red broadbill
Black-crowned barwing
Black-naped monarch
Black-winged stilt
Cattle egret
Common cuckoo
Common iora
Common myna
Coppersmith barbet
Crag martin
Crested tree swift
Dollarbird
Eurasian bittern
Fire-breasted flowerpecker
Gray nightjar
Gray wagtail
Great cormorant
Great tit
Greater painted snipe
Greater racket-tailed drongo
Green magpie
Hoopoe
Northern wryneck
Orange-breasted trogon
Osprey
Peregrine falcon
Pheasant-tailed jacana
Purple sunbird
Rock pigeon
Ruby-cheeked sunbird
Ruddy turnstone
Saunder's gull
Small buttonquail
Spotted munia
Stonechat
White-throated fantail
Zitting cisticola

YEMEN
African palm swift
Cattle egret
Crab plovers
Crag martin
Egyptian vulture

European roller
Gray wagtail
Greater hoopoe-lark
Hammerhead
Hoopoe
House sparrow
Osprey
Peregrine falcon
Rock pigeon
Ruddy turnstone
Stonechat
Wilson's storm-petrel

YUGOSLAVIA
Common cuckoo
Corncrake
Crag martin
Egyptian vulture
Eurasian dipper
European bee-eater
European roller
European white stork
Gray wagtail
Great cormorant
Great crested grebe
Hoopoe
Horned lark
Mallard
Northern lapwing
Peregrine falcon
Rock pigeon
Snow bunting
Zitting cisticola

ZAMBIA
African broadbill
African jacana
African palm swift
African paradise-flycatcher
African pitta
African snipe
Bar-breasted mousebird
Barn swallow
Black-winged stilt
Buff-spotted flufftail

Cattle egret
Collared pratincole
Common bulbul
Common cuckoo
Common waxbill
Corncrake
Eurasian golden oriole
European bee-eater
European roller
European white stork
Gray go-away-bird
Gray-crowned crane
Great cormorant
Greater flamingo
Greater painted snipe
Green woodhoopoe
Hammerhead
Helmeted guineafowl
Hoopoe
House sparrow
Osprey
Ostrich
Peregrine falcon
Red-billed oxpecker
Rosy-breasted longclaw
Sacred ibis
Secretary bird
Shoebill
Small buttonquail
Southern ground-hornbill
Southern red bishop
Spotted flycatcher
Square-tailed drongo
Stonechat
Village weaver
White-helmet shrike
Yellow-fronted tinkerbird
Zitting cisticola

ZIMBABWE
African broadbill
African palm swift
African paradise-flycatcher
African pitta
African snipe
Bar-breasted mousebird

Barn swallow
Black-winged stilt
Buff-spotted flufftail
Cape batis
Cattle egret
Collared pratincole
Common bulbul
Common cuckoo
Common waxbill
Corncrake
Eurasian golden oriole
European bee-eater
European roller
European white stork

Gray go-away-bird
Gray-crowned crane
Great cormorant
Greater painted snipe
Green woodhoopoe
Hammerhead
Helmeted guineafowl
Hoopoe
House sparrow
Osprey
Ostrich
Peregrine falcon
Red-billed oxpecker
Rock pigeon

Rosy-breasted longclaw
Sacred ibis
Secretary bird
Shoebill
Small buttonquail
Southern ground-hornbill
Southern red bishop
Spotted flycatcher
Stonechat
Village weaver
White-helmet shrike
Yellow-fronted tinkerbird
Zitting cisticola

Index

Italic type indicates volume number; **boldface** type indicates entries and their pages; (ill.) indicates illustrations.

American black rails, *2:* 315

American cliff swallows, *4:* 919–21, 919 (ill.), 920 (ill.)

American dippers, *4:* 1005, 1007–9, 1007 (ill.), 1008 (ill.)

American goldfinches, *5:* 1282–84, 1282 (ill.), 1283 (ill.)

American mourning doves, *3:* 513–14, 513 (ill.), 514 (ill.)

American pearl kites, *1:* 212

American redstarts, *4:* 792

American robins, *4:* 1014, 1015, 1022–23, 1022 (ill.), 1023 (ill.)

American white pelicans, *1:* 139–41, 139 (ill.), 140 (ill.)

Amytornis striatus. See Striated grasswrens

Anas platyrhynchos. See Mallards

Anatidae. *See* Ducks; Geese; Swans

Andean condors, *1:* 177

Andean flamingos, *1:* 201, 202

Andean stilts, *2:* 423

Andigena hypoglauca. See Gray-breasted mountain-toucans

Anhima cornuta. See Horned screamers

Anhimidae. *See* Screamers

Anhinga anhinga. See American anhingas

Anhingas, *1:* 98, 99, **116–24**

Anis, *3:* **545–51**

Anna's hummingbirds, *3:* 636–38, 636 (ill.), 637 (ill.)

Anseriformes, *2:* **241–45**

Ant thrushes, *4:* **836–44**

Antbirds. *See* Ant thrushes

Antcatchers. *See* Ant thrushes

Anthreptes species, *5:* 1209

Anthus spragueii. See Sprague's pipits

Anting behavior, *4:* 1005

Antiphonal duets, *5:* 1361

Antpittas. *See* Ant thrushes

Antshrikes. *See* Ant thrushes

Antwrens. *See* Ant thrushes

Apapanes, *5:* 1289, 1291–92, 1291 (ill.), 1292 (ill.)

Aphelocoma californica. See Western scrub-jays

Apodidae. *See* Swifts

Apodiformes, *3:* **610–14**

Apolinar's wrens, *4:* 1039

Apostlebirds, *5:* 1360

Aptenodytes forsteri. See Emperor penguins

Apterygidae. *See* Kiwis

Apteryx australis. See Brown kiwis

Ara macao. See Scarlet macaws

Arabian babblers, *4:* 1026

Arabian ostriches, *1:* 39

Arachnothera, 5: 1209

Aramidae. *See* Limpkins

Aramus guarauna. See Limpkins

Araripe manakins, *4:* 866

Archer's larks, *4:* 905

Arctic skuas, *2:* 479–80, 479 (ill.), 480 (ill.)

Arctic terns, *2:* 396

Arctic warblers, *4:* 1058–59, 1058 (ill.), 1059 (ill.)

Ardea herodias. See Great blue herons

Ardeidae. *See* Bitterns; Herons

Arenaria interpres. See Ruddy turnstones

Artamidae. *See* Woodswallows

Artamus cyanopterus. See Dusky woodswallows

Ascension frigatebirds, *1:* 110

Ash's larks, *4:* 905

Asian dowitchers, *2:* 454

Asian fairy bluebirds, *4:* 960–61, 960 (ill.), 961 (ill.)

Asian frogmouths, *3:* 586, 587

Asities, *4:* **801–6;** *5:* 1209

Astley's leiothrix, *4:* 1027

Astrapia mayeri. See Ribbon-tailed astrapias

Astrapias, ribbon-tailed, *5:* 1391–92, 1391 (ill.), 1392 (ill.)

Asynchronous hatching, *2:* 476

Atoll fruit doves, *3:* 505, 509

Atrichornis rufescens. See Rufous scrub-birds

Atrichornithidae. *See* Scrub-birds

Attagis gayi. See Rufous-bellied seedsnipes

Auckland Island teals, *2:* 241

Audubon, John James, *4:* 852, 933

Auklets, *2:* 486

Auks, *2:* 397, **486–95**

Auriparus flaviceps. See Verdins

Australasian figbirds, *5:* 1340–41, 1340 (ill.), 1341 (ill.)

Australasian larks, *4:* 906–7, 906 (ill.), 907 (ill.)

Australian brush-turkeys, *2:* 270

Australian chats, *4:* **1087–92**

Australian chestnut-backed buttonquails, *2:* 328

Australian creepers, *5:* **1145–50**

Australian diamond doves, *3:* 504

Australian fairy-wrens, *4:* **1070–78**

Australian frogmouths, *3:* 585–86, 587

Australian greater painted snipes, *2:* 408, 409, 410, 412

Australian honeyeaters, *4:* 1087; *5:* 1124, **1225–34**

Australian magpie-larks, *5:* 1360, 1361, 1362–64, 1362 (ill.), 1363 (ill.)

Australian magpies, *5:* 1372–74

Australian masked owls, *3:* 557

Australian owlet-nightjars, *3:* 592, 593

Black pillows. *See* Black-naped monarchs

Black rails, *2*: 356, 362 (ill.), 363, 363 (ill.)

Black sicklebills, *5*: 1390

Black stilts, *2*: 424, 425

Black storks, *1*: 166

Black-tailed native-hens, *2*: 358

Black-tailed treecreepers, *5*: 1147

Black terns, *2*: 483–84, 483 (ill.), 484 (ill.)

Black tinamous, *1*: 7

Black vultures, *1*: 175

Black-winged stilts, *2*: 424, 425, 426–27, 426 (ill.), 427 (ill.)

Black woodpeckers, *3*: 728

Blackbirds, New World, *4*: 1013; *5*: **1268–77**

Blue birds of paradise, *5*: 1390

Blue-black grassquits, *5*: 1253–54, 1253 (ill.), 1254 (ill.)

Blue bustards, *2*: 392–94, 392 (ill.), 393 (ill.)

Blue cranes, *2*: 319

Blue-crowned motmots, *3*: 679–81, 679 (ill.), 680 (ill.)

Blue fairies of the forest. *See* Black-naped monarchs

Blue-footed boobies, *1*: 130–31, 130 (ill.), 131 (ill.)

Blue-gray gnatcatchers, *4*: 1051, 1055–57, 1055 (ill.), 1056 (ill.)

Blue-headed picathartes. *See* Gray-necked picathartes

Blue jays, *5*: 1398, 1401–2, 1401 (ill.), 1402 (ill.)

Blue-naped mousebirds, *3*: 639

Blue swallows, *4*: 915

Blue-throated motmots, *3*: 677

Blue toucans, *3*: 728, 759

Blue vangas, *4*: 972, 973

Blue wattled crows. *See* Kokakos

Bluebirds
 eastern, *4*: 1017–19, 1017 (ill.), 1018 (ill.)
 fairy, *4*: **955–61**

Boat-billed herons, *1*: 149

Bobwhites, *2*: 303, 304
 masked, *2*: 308
 northern, *2*: 306–8, 306 (ill.), 307 (ill.)

Bombycilla cedrorum. See Cedar waxwings

Bombycillidae. *See* Silky flycatchers; Waxwings

Bonaparte's nightjars, *3*: 577, 604

Boobies, *1*: 99, 100, **125–33**

Boreal owls, *3*: 565

Bornean bristleheads, *5*: 1374, 1375–76, 1375 (ill.), 1376 (ill.)

Bornean frogmouths, *3*: 587

Botaurus stellaris. See Eurasian bitterns

Botha's larks, *4*: 905

Boubous, *4*: 963

Bowerbirds, *5*: 1146, **1380–88**

Branta canadensis. See Canada geese

Breeding, communal, *5*: 1140
 See also specific species

Bristle-thighed curlews, *2*: 456

Bristlebirds, *4*: 1080

Bristlefronts, Streseman's, *4*: 847

Bristleheads, *5*: 1372–74

Bristles, whisker-like, *3*: 603

Broad-billed rollers, *3*: 655

Broad-billed todies, *3*: 669

Broadbills, *4*: **793–800**

Bronze-cuckoos, *4*: 1071, 1080, 1089

Brood parasitism, *5*: 1259
 See also specific species

Brown creepers, *5*: 1184–86, 1184 (ill.), 1185 (ill.)

Brown-eared bulbuls, *4*: 945

Brown flycatchers. *See* Jacky winters

Brown-headed cowbirds, *5*: 1249, 1259

Brown kiwis, *1*: 30, 32–34, 32 (ill.), 33 (ill.)

Brown mesites, *2*: 320–21, 322

Brown pelicans, *1*: 101, 134, 135, 136–38, 136 (ill.), 137 (ill.)

Brown roatelos. *See* Brown mesites

Brown treecreepers, *5*: 1145, 1146, 1147

Bubo sumatranus. See Barred eagle-owls

Bucconidae. *See* Puffbirds

Bucerotidae. *See* Hornbills

Bucorvus leadbeateri. See Southern ground-hornbills

Buff-breasted buttonquails, *2*: 328

Buff-breasted sandpipers, *2*: 455

Buff-spotted flufftails, *2*: 360–61, 360 (ill.), 361 (ill.)

Buff-throated purpletufts, *4*: 874

Buffalo-weavers, red-billed, *5*: 1307, 1308–9

Bulbuls, *4*: **943–54**

Buphagus erythrorhynchus. See Red-billed oxpeckers

Burhinidae. *See* Thick-knees

Burrowing owls, *3*: 554, 565

Burrows, nest, *2*: 414
 See also specific species

Bush-shrikes, *4*: 962, 963, 964

Bush thick-knees, *2*: 433

Bushbirds, Rondonia, *4*: 838

Bushlarks, Sidamo, *4*: 905

Bushtits, *5*: 1151–53, 1154–56, 1154 (ill.), 1155 (ill.)

Bustards, *2*: 315, 316, 318–19, **387–94**

Butcherbirds, *5*: 1372–74, 1377–79, 1377 (ill.), 1378 (ill.)
 See also Loggerhead shrikes; Shrikes

Chlidonias niger. See Black terns

Choco tinamous, 1: 7

Choughs, white-winged, 5: 1360

Chowchillas, 4: 1093–98

Christmas frigatebirds, 1: 110

Cicinnurus regius. See King birds of paradise

Ciconia ciconia. See European white storks

Ciconiidae. See Storks

Ciconiiformes, 1: 143–48

Cinclidae. See Dippers

Cinclosoma punctatum. See Spotted quail-thrushes

Cinclus cinclus. See Eurasian dippers

Cinclus mexicanus. See American dippers

Cinerous wattled birds. See Kokakos

Cinnamon-tailed fantails, 4: 1109

Cinnyris asiaticus. See Purple sunbirds

Cissa chinensis. See Green magpies

Cisticola juncidis. See Zitting cisticolas

Cisticolas, zitting, 4: 1053–54, 1053 (ill.), 1054 (ill.)

CITES (Convention on International Trade in Endangered Species)
    on eclectus parrots, 3: 528
    on helmeted hornbills, 3: 721

Clarion wrens, 4: 1039

Cliff swallows, 4: 913, 919–21, 919 (ill.), 920 (ill.)

Climacteridae. See Australian creepers

Climacteris rufa. See Rufous treecreepers

Cobb's wrens, 4: 1039

Cobeldick, William, 5: 1355

Cocks-of-the-rock, Guianan, 4: 879–80, 879 (ill.), 880 (ill.)

Cockerell's fantails, 4: 1109

Coleridge, Samuel Taylor, 1: 46

Colibri coruscans. See Sparkling violet-ears

Colies. See Mousebirds

Coliidae. See Mousebirds

Coliiformes. See Mousebirds

Colinus virginianus. See Northern bobwhite quails

Colius striatus. See Bar-breasted mousebirds

Collared pratincoles, 2: 437, 439–41, 439 (ill.), 440 (ill.)

Collared sunbirds, 5: 1209

Collocalia species, 3: 613

Colombian grebes, 1: 92

Colombian tinamous, 1: 7

Colonial nesters, 2: 396
    See also specific species

Columba livia. See Rock pigeons

Columbidae. See Doves; Pigeons

Columbiformes, 3: 504–7

Common barn owls, 3: 557, 560–62, 560 (ill.), 561 (ill.)

Common bulbuls, 4: 938 (ill.), 943, 944, 947–49, 947 (ill.)

Common buttonquails, 2: 328

Common cuckoos, 3: 545, 547–48, 547 (ill.), 548 (ill.); 4: 1061

Common diving-petrels, 1: 67, 68, 69–70, 69 (ill.), 70 (ill.)

Common ioras, 4: 956, 958–59, 958 (ill.), 959 (ill.)

Common loons, 1: 87–89, 87 (ill.), 88 (ill.)

Common murres, 2: 489–91, 489 (ill.), 490 (ill.)

Common mynas, 5: 1329–30, 1329 (ill.), 1330 (ill.)

Common potoos. See Gray potoos

Common redshanks, 2: 454

Common sunbird-asities, 4: 801, 802, 803, 804–5, 804 (ill.), 805 (ill.)

Common trumpeters, 2: 379–81, 379 (ill.), 380 (ill.)

Common waxbills, 5: 1299–1300, 1299 (ill.), 1300 (ill.)

Communal breeding, 5: 1140
    See also specific species

Condors, 1: 143, 146, 175, 176
    Andean, 1: 177
    California, 1: 147, 177, 181–82, 181 (ill.), 182 (ill.)

Congo bay owls, 3: 565

Congo swifts, 3: 617

Convention on International Trade in Endangered Species. See CITES

Cooling mechanisms, 1: 187

Coorong gerygones, 4: 1081

Coots, 2: 316, 356–65

Coppersmith barbets, 3: 750–51, 750 (ill.), 751 (ill.)

Coppery-chested jacamars, 3: 732, 735–36, 735 (ill.), 736 (ill.)

Coracias garrulus. See European rollers

Coraciidae. See Rollers

Coraciiformes, 3: 653–57

Coracina typica. See Mauritius cuckoo-shrikes

Cormorants, 1: 99, 100, 101, 116–24

Corncrakes, 2: 364–65, 364 (ill.), 365 (ill.)

Cortaplantas. See Plantcutters

Corvidae. See Crows; Jays

Corvus corax. See Northern ravens

Corvus species, 5: 1398

Corythaeola cristata. See Great blue turacos

Corythaixoides concolor. See Gray go-away-birds

Cotarramas. See Plantcutters

Cotinga cayana. See Spangled cotingas

European white storks, *1:* 171–73, 171 (ill.), 172 (ill.)

Eurylaimidae. *See* Broadbills

Eurypyga helias. See Sunbitterns

Eurypygidae. *See* Sunbitterns

Eurystomus orientalis. See Dollarbirds

Evaporation, *1:* 187

Exxon Valdez, 1: 91

F

Fairy bluebirds, *4:* **955–61**

Fairy-wrens, Australian, *4:* **1070–78**

Falco peregrinus. See Peregrine falcons

Falco rusticolis. See Gyrfalcons

Falconets, *1:* 207, 229

Falconidae. *See* Caracaras; Falcons

Falconiformes. *See* Diurnal birds of prey

Falconry, *1:* 209, 230

Falcons, *1:* 207, 208–10, **229–39;** *2:* 318

False sunbirds, *4:* **801–6**

Families (Taxonomy), *4:* 861
  See also specific family names

Fan-tailed berrypeckers, *5:* 1199–1201, 1199 (ill.), 1200 (ill.)

Fantailed cisticolas. *See* Zitting cisticolas

Fantailed warblers. *See* Zitting cisticolas

Fantails, *4:* **1105–14;** *5:* 1354

Feathers, grooming, *1:* 126
  See also specific species

Feline owlet-nightjars, *3:* 594–95, 594 (ill.), 595 (ill.)

Ferruginous pygmy-owls, *3:* 555

Ficedula basilanica. See Little slaty flycatchers

Fieldfares, *4:* 1015

Fiery minivets, *4:* 936, 940–41, 940 (ill.), 941 (ill.)

Figbirds, *5:* **1337–44**

Finches, *4:* 789; *5:* **1278–87,** 1288
  cardueline, *5:* 1289
  cuckoo, *5:* 1308
  Gouldian, *5:* 1298
  grassfinches, *5:* **1296–1305**
  Hawaiian, *5:* 1288
  Laysan, *5:* 1293–94, 1293 (ill.), 1294 (ill.)
  New World, *5:* **1244–57**
  snow, *5:* 1323–24, 1323 (ill.), 1324 (ill.)
  See also Weavers

Fire-breasted flowerpeckers, *5:* 1197–98, 1197 (ill.), 1198 (ill.)

Fire-eyes, fringe-backed, *4:* 838

Fish and Wildlife Service (U.S.), *2:* 243
  on black-capped vireos, *5:* 1240
  on cranes, *2:* 340
  on Kirtland's warblers, *5:* 1266
  on Laysan finches, *5:* 1294
  on murrelets, *2:* 488
  on New World warblers, *5:* 1260

Fish hawks. *See* Osprey

Fishing owls, *3:* 553, 565

Fishing with birds, *1:* 117

Flamingos, *1:* **200–206**

Flapped larks, *4:* 902, 903

Flightless birds, *2:* 318, 358; *3:* 518

Flood, Bob, *1:* 62

Flowerpeckers, *5:* **1194–1201**

Flufftails, *2:* 356, 360–61, 360 (ill.), 361 (ill.)

Flycatchers, *4:* 789
  monarch, *5:* **1115–22**
  Old World, *4:* **1060–69**

silky, *4:* **979–87**

tyrant, *4:* **850–59,** 861, 872, 882

See also Fantails; Gray hypocolius; Great kiskadees; Jacky winters

Flying jewels. *See* Hummingbirds

Fodies, *5:* 1306

Food and Drug Administration (FDA), on emu oil, *1:* 27

Forests, sclerophyll, *4:* 1095

Forktailed drongos, *5:* 1346

Formicariidae. *See* Ant thrushes

Forty-spotted pardalotes, *5:* 1204

Fowl, *2:* **294–302**

Fratercula arctica. See Puffins

Fregata magnificens. See Magnificent frigatebirds

Fregatidae. *See* Frigatebirds

Frigatebirds, *1:* 98, 99, 100, **109–15**

Fringe-backed fire-eyes, *4:* 838

Fringilla coelebs. See Chaffinches

Fringillidae. *See* Finches

Frogmouths, *3:* 575, 576, **585–90,** 591

Fruit doves, *3:* 505, 509

Fulmars, *1:* **53–60**

Fulmarus glacialis. See Northern fulmars

Furnariidae. *See* Ovenbirds

Furnarius rufus. See Rufous horneros

G

Galápagos cormorants, *1:* 116

Galápagos doves, *3:* 509

Galápagos penguins, *1:* 71, 73

Galbula pastazae. See Coppery-chested jacamars

Galbula ruficauda. See Rufous-tailed jacamars

Galbulidae. *See* Jacamars

Great kiskadees, 4: 850, 856–57, 856 (ill.), 857 (ill.)

Great snipes, 2: 455

Great spotted cuckoos, 3: 545

Great spotted kiwis, 1: 29, 30

Great-tailed grackles, 5: 1268

Great tits, 5: 1170–72, 1170 (ill.), 1171 (ill.)

Greater adjutant storks, 1: 166

Greater anis, 3: 545, 546

Greater flamingos, 1: 203–5, 203 (ill.), 204 (ill.)

Greater hoopoe-larks, 4: 908–9, 908 (ill.), 909 (ill.)

Greater melampittas, 4: 1100

Greater painted snipes, 2: 407, 408–9, 410–12, 410 (ill.), 411 (ill.)

Greater racket-tailed drongos, 5: 1350–51, 1350 (ill.), 1351 (ill.)

Greater rhabdornis, 5: 1188, 1190

Greater rheas, 1: 13

Greater roadrunners, 3: 545, 549–50, 549 (ill.), 550 (ill.)

Greater scythebills, 4: 832

Greater thornbirds, 4: 827–29, 827 (ill.), 828 (ill.)

Grebes, 1: 90–97

Green ioras, 4: 957

Green magpies, 5: 1398, 1405–6, 1405 (ill.), 1406 (ill.)

Green peafowl, 2: 266

Green woodhoopoes, 3: 710–12, 710 (ill.), 711 (ill.)

Greenbuls, 4: 944, 945–46

Grenadier weavers. See Southern red bishops

Griffon vultures, 1: 207

Grooming feathers, 1: 126

Grosbeak weavers, 5: 1306

Ground antbirds, 4: 836

Ground cuckoo-shrikes, 4: 935, 936

Ground-hornbills
Abyssinian, 3: 653–54

southern, 3: 717–19, 717 (ill.), 718 (ill.)

Ground jays, Hume's, 5: 1398

Ground-rollers, 3: 691, 692, 693

Grouse, 2: 298

Gruidae. See Cranes

Gruiformes, 2: 315–19

Grus canadensis. See Sandhill cranes

Grus japonensis. See Red-crowned cranes

Guácharos. See Oilbirds

Guadalupe storm-petrels, 1: 43

Guam boatbills. See Guam flycatchers

Guam flycatchers, 5: 1116

Guam rails, 2: 318, 359

Guam swiftlets, 3: 617

Guans, 2: 279–87

Guianan cocks-of-the-rock, 4: 879–80, 879 (ill.), 880 (ill.)

Guillemots, 2: 486, 487

Guineafowl, 2: 268–69, 288–93

Gulls, 2: 395–98, 475–85

Gymnogyps californianus. See California condors

Gyrfalcons, 1: 229, 234–35, 234 (ill.), 235 (ill.)

H

Haast brown kiwis. See Haast tokoeka kiwis

Haast tokoeka kiwis, 1: 29, 32, 33

Haematopodidae. See Oystercatchers

Haematopus unicolor. See Variable oystercatchers

Hairy hermits, 3: 632–33, 632 (ill.), 633 (ill.)

Hamerkops. See Hammerheads

Hammerheads, 1: 143, 146, 160–65, 162 (ill.), 163 (ill.)

Happy family. See Gray-crowned babblers

Harpactes oreskios. See Orange-breasted trogons

Harris's hawks, 1: 213, 217–18, 217 (ill.), 218 (ill.)

Hatching, asynchronous, 2: 476
See also specific species

Hawaiian creepers, 5: 1288

Hawaiian crows, 5: 1400

Hawaiian finches, 5: 1288

Hawaiian honeycreepers, 5: 1209, 1288–95

Hawks, 1: 207, 208, 209, 212–22, 230

Hedge sparrows, 4: 991–96

Heliornis fulica. See Sungrebes

Heliornithidae. See Sungrebes

Helmet shrikes, 4: 962, 964

Helmet vangas, 4: 972, 973, 975

Helmeted guineafowl, 2: 291–92, 291 (ill.), 292 (ill.)

Helmeted hornbills, 3: 720–21, 720 (ill.), 721 (ill.)

Hemiprocne coronata. See Crested tree swifts

Hemiprocnidae. See Tree swifts

Hermits, hairy, 3: 632–33, 632 (ill.), 633 (ill.)

Herons, 1: 143, 144, 145, 146, 149–59, 186

Highland tinamous, 1: 8–10, 8 (ill.), 9 (ill.)

Himalayan accentors, 4: 992

Himalayan vultures, 1: 212

Himantopus himantopus. See Black-winged stilts

Himatione sanguinea. See Apapanes

Hirundinidae. See Swallows

Hirundo pyrrhonota. See American cliff swallows

Hirundo rustica. See Barn swallows

Hoatzins, 2: 310–14, 312 (ill.), 313 (ill.)

Hobbies, 1: 229

Malaysian honeyguides, 3: 768, 769–70, 769 (ill.), 770 (ill.)

Malaysian plovers, 2: 446

Maleos, 2: 276–77, 276 (ill.), 277 (ill.)

Malimbes, 5: 1306

Mallards, 2: 247, 254–55, 254 (ill.), 255 (ill.)

Malleefowl, 2: 270, 273–75, 273 (ill.), 274 (ill.)

Maluridae. See Australian fairy-wrens

Malurus splendens. See Splendid fairy-wrens

Mamos, 5: 1288

Manakins, 4: 864–71

Mangrove fantails, 4: 1106

Manucodes, glossy-mantled, 5: 1389

Manus fantails, 4: 1109

Manx shearwaters, 1: 54, 56–57, 56 (ill.), 57 (ill.)

Marabou storks, 1: 166

Marbled murrelets, 2: 488

Marching eagles. See Secretary birds

Marsh tchagra, 4: 963

Marsh warblers, 4: 1052

Marshall's ioras, 4: 956

Martineta tinamous. See Crested tinamous

Martins
  crag, 4: 922 (ill.), 923 (ill.), 2128–923
  purple, 4: 914
  white-eyed river, 4: 914–15

Masai ostriches, 1: 35

Masked bobwhites, 2: 308

Masked finfoot, 2: 366–68

Matthias fantails, 4: 1106, 1109

Mauritius cuckoo-shrikes, 4: 935, 937, 938–39, 938 (ill.), 939 (ill.)

Meadowlarks, 5: 1268

Meat, rotten, 1: 176

Megaceryle alcyon. See Belted kingfishers

Megalaima haemacephala. See Coppersmith barbets

Megapodes, 2: 267–68

Megapodiidae. See Moundbuilders

Megapodius layardi. See Vanuatu megapodes

Melampittas, 4: 1099, 1100

Melanocharis versteri. See Fan-tailed berrypeckers

Meleagris gallopavo. See Wild turkeys

Melichneutes robustus. See Lyre-tailed honeyguides

Meliphagidae. See Australian honeyeaters

Melodious larks, 4: 903, 905

Melospiza melodia. See Song sparrows

Menura alberti. See Albert's lyrebirds

Menuridae. See Lyrebirds

Merlins, 1: 229

Meropidae. See Bee-eaters

Meropogon forsteni. See Purple-bearded bee-eaters

Merops apiaster. See European bee-eaters

Mesites, 2: 316, 317, 320–25

Mesitornis variegata. See White-breasted mesites

Mesitornithidae. See Mesites; Roatelos

Mexican dippers. See American dippers

Microeca fascinans. See Jacky winters

Migrant shrikes. See Loggerhead shrikes

Migration, 1: 54, 145; 3: 613
  See also specific species

Milk, crop, 3: 506, 509

Milky storks, 1: 166

Mimidae. See Mockingbirds; Thrashers

Minahass masked owls, 3: 559

Minas Gerais tyrannulets, 4: 853

Minivets, fiery, 4: 936, 940–41, 940 (ill.), 941 (ill.)

Mirafra javanica. See Australasian larks

Mississippi cranes, 2: 340

Mistletoebirds, 5: 1195

Mitchell's plovers, 2: 445, 446

Mniotilta varia. See Black-and-white warblers

Mockingbirds, 4: 997–1003

Moho bishopi. See Bishop's oos

Mohua ochrocephala. See Yellowheads

Moluccan woodcocks, 2: 456

Momotidae. See Motmots

Momotus momota. See Blue-crowned motmots

Monarch flycatchers, 5: 1115–22

Monarchidae. See Monarch flycatchers

Mongolian larks, 4: 903

Monkey-faced owls. See Common barn owls

Monogamy, 2: 327, 367
  See also specific species

Montifringilla nivalis. See Snow finches

Moorhens, 2: 356–65

Morus bassanus. See Northern gannets

Motacilla cinerea. See Gray wagtails

Motacillidae. See Pipits; Wagtails

Motmots, 3: 653, 654, 655–56, 676–81

Moundbuilders, 2: 270–78

Mountain owlet-nightjars, 3: 592

Mountain plovers, 2: 446

Mountain-toucans, gray-breasted, 3: 759, 761–62, 761 (ill.), 762 (ill.)

Mourning doves, American, 3: 513–14, 513 (ill.), 514 (ill.)

Podiceps cristatus. See Great crested grebes
Podicipedidae. *See* Grebes
Podicipediformes. *See* Grebes
Poecile atricapilla. See Black-capped chickadees
Pogoniulus chrysoconus. See Yellow-fronted tinkerbirds
Poisonous birds, 5: 1132
        See also specific species
Poisons, 1: 135
Polioptila caerulea. See Blue-gray gnatcatchers
Pollen's vangas, 4: 972, 973
Polyandry, sequential, 2: 327
Polyborus plancus. See Crested caracaras
Polygamy, 2: 327
        See also specific species
Polynesian swifts, 3: 617
Pomatostomidae. *See* Pseudo babblers
Pomatostomus temporalis. See Gray-crowned babblers
Ponapé fantails, 4: 1106
Poor-me-ones. *See* Gray potoos
Potoos, 3: 575, 576, **596–601**
Poughbills, 5: 1131
Powder downs, 1: 143, 149
Pratincoles, 2: **436–43**
Precocial chicks, 2: 321
Prince Albert's lyrebirds. *See* Albert's lyrebirds
Prionops plumatus. See White helmet-shrikes
ProAvesPeru, 4: 885–86
Procellaridae. *See* Fulmars; Petrels; Shearwaters
Procellariiformes. *See* Tubenosed seabirds
Promerops cafer. See Cape sugarbirds
Prunella modularis. See Dunnocks
Prunellidae. *See* Hedge sparrows
Psaltriparus minimus. See Bushtits

Pseudo babblers, 5: **1139–44**
Psittacidae. *See* Parrots
Psittaciformes. *See* Parrots
Psittacula krameri. See Rose-ringed parakeets
Psittacus erithacus. See Gray parrots
Psittirostra cantans. See Laysan finches
Psophia crepitans. See Common trumpeters
Psophiidae. *See* Trumpeters
Pterocles namaqua. See Namaqua sandgrouse
Pteroclididae. *See* Sandgrouse
Pterocliformes. *See* Sandgrouse
Pterocnemia pennata. See Lesser rheas
Ptilonorhynchidae. *See* Bowerbirds
Ptilonorhynchus violaceus. See Satin bowerbirds
Ptiloris victoriae. See Victoria's riflebirds
Ptyonoprogne rupestris. See Crag martins
Puerto Rican nightjars, 3: 577, 604
Puerto Rican todies, 3: 653, 669
Puffbacks, 4: 963
Puffbirds, 3: 725, 726, 727, **738–46**
Puffins, 2: **486–95**, 492 (ill.), 493 (ill.)
Puffinus puffinus. See Manx shearwaters
Puna rheas, 1: 13, 16
Purple-bearded bee-eaters, 3: 685–87, 685 (ill.), 686 (ill.)
Purple-crowned fairy-wrens, 4: 1071
Purple gallinules, 2: 401
Purple martins, 4: 914
Purple sunbirds, 5: 1213–14, 1213 (ill.), 1214 (ill.)
Purple swamphens, 2: 358
Purpletufts, buff-throated, 4: 874

Pycnonotidae. *See* Bulbuls
Pycnonotus barbatus. See Common bulbuls
Pygmy-geese, 2: 241
Pygmy-owls, 3: 555, 565
Pygmy tits, 5: 1151, 1152, 1153

Q

Quail thrushes, 4: **1099–1104**
Quails, 2: 266
        See also New World quails
Queleas, 5: 1306, 1309
Quetzals, resplendent, 3: 649–51, 649 (ill.), 650 (ill.)

R

Radiation, Great Australasian, 5: 1146
Rail-babblers, 4: 1099, 1100, 1101
Rails, 2: 315–19, 345, **356–65**
Rainbow lorikeets, 3: 535–36, 535 (ill.), 536 (ill.)
Rainforests, 2: 280
        See also specific species
Rallidae. *See* Coots; Moorhens; Rails
Ramphastidae. *See* Toucans
Ramphastos toco. See Toco toucans
Raphidae. *See* Dodos; Solitaires
Raphus cucullatus. See Dodos
Raptors. *See* Birds of prey
Raras. *See* Plantcutters
Raso larks, 4: 905
Ratites, 1: **1–4**, 7, 12, 18, 24, 29
Ravens, 5: 1398, 1400, 1409–10, 1409 (ill.), 1410 (ill.)
Razorbills, 2: 487
Recurvirostra americana. See American avocets
Recurvirostridae. *See* Avocets; Stilts

Red-backed shrikes, *4:* 962

Red-billed buffalo-weavers, *5:* 1307, 1308–9

Red-billed oxpeckers, *5:* 1334–36, 1334 (ill.), 1335 (ill.)

Red-billed queleas, *5:* 1309

Red-billed scythebills, *4:* 833–35, 833 (ill.), 834 (ill.)

Red-billed tropicbirds, *1:* 103

Red birds of paradise, *5:* 1390

Red bishops, *5:* 1309

Red-breasted cacklers. *See* Gray-crowned babblers

Red-breasted nuthatches, *5:* 1176–78, 1176 (ill.), 1177 (ill.)

Red-breasted plantcutters, *4:* 881–82, 883

Red-breasted pygmy parrots, *3:* 522

Red-browed treecreepers, *5:* 1145

Red-cockaded woodpeckers, *3:* 781–83, 781 (ill.), 782 (ill.)

Red-collared widowbirds, *5:* 1306–7

Red crossbills, *5:* 1285–87, 1285 (ill.), 1286 (ill.)

Red-crowned cranes, *2:* 319, 341–42, 341 (ill.), 342 (ill.)

Red-eyed bulbuls, *4:* 944

Red-eyed vireos, *4:* 792

Red-faced mousebirds, *3:* 639

Red-headed rockfowl. *See* Gray-necked picathartes

Red-headed weavers, *5:* 1308

Red-kneed dotterels, *2:* 445

Red larks, *4:* 905

Red-legged seriemas, *2:* 384–86, 384 (ill.), 385 (ill.)

Red List of Threatened Species. *See* World Conservation Union (IUCN) Red List of Threatened Species

Red-lored whistlers, *5:* 1132

Red-shouldered vangas, *4:* 974–75

Red-tailed newtonias, *4:* 1062

Red-tailed vangas, *4:* 972

Red-throated loons, *1:* 85–86, 85 (ill.), 86 (ill.)

Red-vented bulbuls, *4:* 944

Red-whiskered bulbuls, *4:* 944

Red-winged blackbirds, *5:* 1269, 1272–74, 1272 (ill.), 1273 (ill.)

Reed warblers, *4:* 1051

Reedlings, bearded, *4:* 1026, 1027

Regent bowerbirds, *5:* 1380

Remizidae. *See* Penduline titmice

Resplendent quetzals, *3:* 649–51, 649 (ill.), 650 (ill.)

Réunion cuckoo-shrikes, *4:* 937

Réunion flightless ibises, *1:* 193

Réunion solitaires, *3:* 517

Rhabdornis, *5:* 1188–93

Rhabdornis mysticalis. See Stripe-headed rhabdornis

Rhabdornithidae. *See* Philippine creepers

Rheas, *1:* 2, 3, **11–17**

Rheidae. *See* Rheas

Rhinocryptidae. *See* Tapaculos

Rhinoplax vigil. See Helmeted hornbills

Rhipidura albicollis. See White-throated fantails

Rhipidura leucophrys. See Willie wagtails

Rhipiduridae. *See* Fantails

Rhynochetidae. *See* Kagus

Rhynochetos jubatus. See Kagus

Ribbon-tailed astrapias, *5:* 1391–92, 1391 (ill.), 1392 (ill.)

Ribbon-tailed birds of paradise, *5:* 1390

Riflebirds, Victoria's, *5:* 1393–94, 1393 (ill.), 1394 (ill.)

Riflemen, *4:* 816, 817–19, 817 (ill.), 818 (ill.)

The Rime of the Ancient Mariner, 1: 46

Ring ouzels, *4:* 1015

Rio de Janeiro antwrens, *4:* 838

River-martins, white-eyed, *4:* 914–15

Roadrunners, *3:* 545–51

Roatelos, *2:* 320–25

Robin accentors, *4:* 992

Robins, *4:* 1038; *5:* 1124
American, *4:* 1014, 1015, 1022–23, 1022 (ill.), 1023 (ill.)
Australian, *5:* 1123–29

Rock pigeons, *3:* 511–12, 511 (ill.), 512 (ill.)

Rock thrushes, *4:* 1014, 1015

Rockfowl, *4:* 1025
See also Gray-necked picathartes

Rockwarblers, *4:* 1079

Rodrigues solitaires, *3:* 517–18

Rollers, *3:* 653, 654, 655, 691–99

Rondonia bushbirds, *4:* 838

Rooks, *5:* 1398

Rose-ringed parakeets, *3:* 524–25, 524 (ill.), 525 (ill.)

Rose-throated becards, *4:* 854–55, 854 (ill.), 855 (ill.)

Roseate spoonbills, *1:* 196–97, 196 (ill.), 197 (ill.)

Rostratula benghalensis. See Greater painted snipes

Rostratulidae. *See* Painted snipes

Rosy-breasted longclaws, *4:* 930–31, 930 (ill.), 931 (ill.)

Rotten meat, *1:* 176

Ruby-cheeked sunbirds, *5:* 1211–12, 1211 (ill.), 1212 (ill.)

Rudd's larks, *4:* 905

Ruddy turnstones, *2:* 461–62, 461 (ill.), 462 (ill.)

Ruffs, 2: 455

Rufous babblers, 5: 1139, 1140

Rufous-bellied seedsnipes, 2: 466–67, 466 (ill.), 467 (ill.)

Rufous-breasted hermits. *See* Hairy hermits

Rufous-browed peppershrikes, 5: 1241–43, 1241 (ill.), 1242 (ill.)

Rufous-capped nunlets, 3: 744–45, 744 (ill.), 745 (ill.)

Rufous-collared kingfishers, 3: 664–65, 664 (ill.), 665 (ill.)

Rufous fantails, 4: 1106, 1107, 1108

Rufous horneros, 4: 822, 823, 824–26, 824 (ill.), 825 (ill.)

Rufous-necked wood-rails, 2: 357

Rufous potoos, 3: 596

Rufous scrub-birds, 4: 895–900, 898 (ill.), 899 (ill.)

Rufous-tailed jacamars, 3: 732, 733–34, 733 (ill.), 734 (ill.)

Rufous-tailed plantcutters, 4: 881–82, 883

Rufous treecreepers, 5: 1146, 1147, 1148–50, 1148 (ill.), 1149 (ill.)

Rufous vangas, 4: 976–77, 976 (ill.), 977 (ill.)

Rupicola rupicola. See Guianan cocks-of-the-rock

Rusty-belted tapaculos, 4: 848–49, 848 (ill.), 849 (ill.)

S

Sacred ibises, 1: 193, 194–95, 194 (ill.), 195 (ill.)

Saddlebacks, 5: 1353, 1354, 1355

Saffron toucanets, 3: 759

Sagittariidae. *See* Secretary birds

Sagittarius serpentarius. See Secretary birds

St. Helena plovers, 2: 446

San Clemente loggerhead

shrikes, 4: 970

Sandgrouse, 3: 497–503

Sandhill cranes, 2: 334, 339–40, 339 (ill.), 340 (ill.)

Sandpipers, 2: 397, 453–63

Sandstone shrike-thrushes, 5: 1132

Sangihe shrike-thrushes, 5: 1132

São Tomé sunbirds, 5: 1208

Sarcoramphus papa. See King vultures

Sarothrura elegans. See Buff-spotted flufftails

Sarus cranes, 2: 315

Satanic-eared nightjars, 3: 577, 604

Satin bowerbirds, 5: 1383–85, 1383 (ill.), 1384 (ill.)

Satyr tragopans, 2: 300–301, 300 (ill.), 301 (ill.)

Saunder's gulls, 2: 481–82, 481 (ill.), 482 (ill.)

Savanna sparrows, 5: 1255–57, 1255 (ill.), 1256 (ill.)

Saw-whet owls, northern, 3: 565

Saxicola torquata. See Stonechats

Sayornis phoebe. See Eastern phoebes

Scarlet-collared berrypeckers, 5: 1196

Scarlet macaws, 3: 532 (ill.), 533–34, 533 (ill.)

Schetba rufa. See Rufous vangas

Schlegel's asities, 4: 801, 802, 803

Scimitar babblers, 4: 1025

Scissor-tailed flycatchers, 4: 850

Sclater's larks, 4: 905

Sclerophyll forests, 4: 1095

Scolopacidae. *See* Sandpipers

Scopidae. *See* Hammerheads

Scopus umbretta. See Hammerheads

Screamers, 2: 241–45, **261–65**

Screaming cowbirds, 5: 1276

Screaming pihas, 4: 872

Screech-owls, 3: 553, 567–69, 567 (ill.), 568 (ill.)

Scrub-birds, 4: **895–900**; 5: 1146

Scrub-jays, western, 5: 1403–4, 1403 (ill.), 1404 (ill.)

Scrub robins, 5: 1123, 1127–28 (ill.), 1127 (ill.), 1128 (ill.)

Scythebills

greater, 4: 832

red-billed, 4: 833–35, 833 (ill.), 834 (ill.)

Sea eagles, 1: 212

Seabirds, 1: 101

Secretary birds, 1: 207, **223–28**, 225 (ill.), 226 (ill.)

Seed-eaters, 5: 1288

See also specific species

Seedsnipes, 2: 396, **464–68**

Semnornis ramphastinus. See Toucan barbets

Semper's warblers, 5: 1260

Senegal thick-knees, 2: 431

Sequential polyandry, 2: 327

Seriemas, 2: 316, 317, 318, **382–86**

Seychelles sunbirds, 5: 1208

Seychelles swiftlets, 3: 617

Shakespeare, William, 3: 555; 5: 1327

Shanks, 2: 454

Sharp-tailed sandpipers, 2: 455

Sharpbills, 4: **860–63**, 862 (ill.), 863 (ill.)

Shearwaters, 1: 43, **53–60**

Sheathbills, 2: 396, **469–74**

Shoebills, 1: 143, 145, **186–91**, 188 (ill.), 189 (ill.)

Shore plovers, 2: 445, 446

Shorebirds. *See* Charadriiformes

Short-eared owls, 3: 554

Shovel-billed kingfishers, 3: 655